overweight sensation

BRANDEIS SERIES IN AMERICAN JEWISH HISTORY, CULTURE, AND LIFE
Jonathan D. Sarna, Editor | Sylvia Barack Fishman, Associate Editor

For a complete list of books that are available in the series, visit www.upne.com

Mark Cohen
Overweight Sensation: The Life and Comedy of Allan Sherman

David E. Kaufman
Jewhooing the Sixties: American Celebrity and Jewish Identity— Sandy Koufax, Lenny Bruce, Bob Dylan, and Barbra Streisand

Jack Wertheimer, editor
The New Jewish Leaders: Reshaping the American Jewish Landscape

Eitan P. Fishbane and
Jonathan D. Sarna, editors
Jewish Renaissance and Revival in America

Jonathan B. Krasner
The Benderly Boys and American Jewish Education

Derek Rubin, editor
Promised Lands: New Jewish American Fiction on Longing and Belonging

Susan G. Solomon
Louis I. Kahn's Jewish Architecture: Mikveh Israel and the Midcentury American Synagogue

Amy Neustein, editor
Tempest in the Temple: Jewish Communities and Child Sex Scandals

Jack Wertheimer, editor
Learning and Community: Jewish Supplementary Schools in the Twenty-first Century

Carole S. Kessner
Marie Syrkin: Values Beyond the Self

Leonard Saxe and Barry Chazan
Ten Days of Birthright Israel: A Journey in Young Adult Identity

Jack Wertheimer, editor
Imagining the American Jewish Community

Murray Zimiles
Gilded Lions and Jeweled Horses: The Synagogue to the Carousel

Marianne R. Sanua
Be of Good Courage: The American Jewish Committee, 1945–2006

Hollace Ava Weiner and
Kenneth D. Roseman, editors
Lone Stars of David: The Jews of Texas

Jack Wertheimer, editor
Jewish Education in an Age of Choice

Edward S. Shapiro
Crown Heights: Blacks, Jews, and the 1991 Brooklyn Riot

Mark Cohen

OVERWEIGHT SENSATION

THE LIFE AND COMEDY OF

ALLAN SHERMAN

Brandeis University Press / Waltham, Massachusetts

Brandeis University Press
An imprint of University Press of New England
www.upne.com
© 2013 Mark Cohen
Manufactured in the United States of America
Designed by Mindy Basinger Hill
Typeset in Garamond Premier Pro

University Press of New England is a member of the
Green Press Initiative. The paper used in this book meets
their minimum requirement for recycled paper.

For permission to reproduce any of the material in this book,
contact Permissions, University Press of New England,
One Court Street, Suite 250, Lebanon NH 03766;
or visit www.upne.com

Library of Congress Cataloging-in-Publication Data

Cohen, Mark.
Overweight sensation : the life and comedy
of Allan Sherman / Mark Cohen.
p.   cm. — (Brandeis series in American Jewish
history, culture, and life)
Includes bibliographical references and index.
ISBN 978-1-61168-256-4 (cloth : alk. paper) —
ISBN 978-1-61168-427-8 (ebook)
1. Sherman, Allan, 1924–1973. 2. Singers—United States—
Biography. 3. Jewish comedians—United States—Biography.
4. Humorous songs—United States—20th century—
History and criticism. I. Title.

ML420.S5373C65 2013
782'.42164092—dc23

[B]
2012038565

5   4   3   2   1

FOR DANIELLE

CONTENTS

PROLOGUE / Overweight Sensation / xi

INTRODUCTION / Humpty Dumpty / 1

ONE / Witz-Krieg! / 8

TWO / College in Sex Acts (Printer's Error) / 33

THREE / I've Got a Secret / 58

FOUR / There Is Nothing Like a Lox / 83

FIVE / Ollavood! / 103

SIX / My Son, the Folk Singer / 121

SEVEN / My Son, the Celebrity / 145

EIGHT / My Son, the Nut / 170

NINE / Allan in Wonderland / 188

TEN / Peyton Place, U.S.A. / 207

ELEVEN / Oddball / 222

TWELVE / Hallowed Be Thy Game / 236

THIRTEEN / Hail to Thee, Fat Person / 251

Acknowledgments / 261

APPENDIX / "Goldeneh Moments from Broadway"
and Other Parody Song Lyrics / 265

Notes / 284

Bibliography / 324

Index / 340

Illustrations follow page 144.

Prologue
OVERWEIGHT SENSATION

On October 26, 1962, it still wasn't clear everything would be okay and the Cuban Missile Crisis would not lead to nuclear war. There were two days to go in the thirteen-day showdown between the United States and the Soviet Union. Missile construction in Cuba charged ahead, and Fidel Castro urged the Soviets to bomb America if the U.S. invaded Cuba. It was a good day to count your blessings, especially if you were a top government official in Washington. So Newton N. Minow, chairman of the Federal Communications Commission, wrote a note of thanks to Allan Sherman.

"Dear Allan Sherman: MY SON, THE FOLK SINGER has brought brightness into our lives in some difficult hours here. It's very, very funny."

Minow was not the only Washington official to put Sherman's new million-selling album on the turntable when things got crazy. In the Camelot years, President John F. Kennedy and his wife Jackie swung open the doors of the White House to welcome America's greatest artists, musicians, actors, and writers. But in addition to the energy of Leonard Bernstein, the sober gravity of Pablo Casals, the sturdiness of Carl Sandburg and the elegance of George

Balanchine there was a record album by a fat man with a coarse voice singing about seltzer, the garment industry, and why being a knight wasn't really so great (aluminum pants). President Kennedy had trouble sitting through a cello concert. He grew fidgety during chamber music pieces. But he loved the Jewish song parodies of Allan Sherman.

"I can't say how much we have enjoyed the record," wrote the president's special assistant, Arthur Schlesinger Jr., in a November 6, 1962, note to Sherman about his first album, *My Son, the Folk Singer*.

That record lifted Sherman from obscurity to the heights of American celebrity and kicked off one of the most sensational winning streaks in American comedy. Between October 1962 and August 1963, Sherman released *My Son, The Folk Singer*, *My Son, The Celebrity*, and *My Son, The Nut*. All three albums went gold, sold a total of 3 million copies, sparked a fifteen-city concert tour and landed Sherman dozens of national television appearances that brought his comedy to tens of millions. Audiences across the country laughed and applauded as he thumbed his nose at classic American songs. "The Streets of Laredo" became "The Streets of Miami," where Jewish businessmen gunned it out and the loser "crumbled / Just like a piece halvah." "The Ballad of Harry Lewis" replaced "The Battle Hymn of the Republic," and in Sherman's version the warehouse stored "the drapes of Roth," not grapes of wrath (difficult to mark down).

He played Carnegie Hall; befriended Harpo Marx; discovered Bill Cosby; met President Kennedy; sang for the National Press Club, the U.S. Department of Labor, and Lyndon Johnson's presidential campaign; and very incongruously participated in a New York orgy frequented by luminaries including George Plimpton. The country's greatest songwriters and composers and comedians recognized his talent. Richard Rodgers had worked with Lorenz Hart and Oscar Hammerstein II, two of Broadway's best lyricists, and he explored partnering with Sherman to create an original musical. Johnny Mercer and the great Irving Berlin sent congratulations through mutual friends, and Harpo Marx showed him off to Jack Benny and George Burns. They loved him, and so did much of the country. His fame hit its peak in the summer of 1963 with the extraordinary international success of "Hello Muddah, Hello Fadduh! (A Letter from Camp)," which won Sherman a Grammy Award and was turned into a children's book and even a board game. As an account of the record industry noted, in the early 1960s Sherman personified The Moment.

Sherman's completely unexpected and extraordinary success changed American comedy and popular culture. For the first time since the end of vaudeville more than a half-century earlier, Jewish dialect humor spread to mainstream culture and led to fame and fortune. Ethnicity was back.

The ethnic identity business has long been a very Jewish occupation. From the time of Israel Zangwill's 1908 play, *The Melting Pot*, American Jews have struggled to balance "the competing impulses of assimilation and ethnic self-affirmation." In the first decades of the twentieth century, with the encouragement of a country in an inhospitable mood, many Jews sacrificed ethnicity. To ensure it would die out, Congress in 1924 dramatically reduced immigration. Sherman was born in Chicago that year to parents who, as Saul Bellow described the phenomenon, "brought so much enthusiasm, verve, love to this American life" they surrendered almost their entire selves to it to become totally American.

His parents' lives did not work out so well, and Sherman rejected their approach. Instead, he took inspiration from his maternal grandparents, the Yiddish-speaking immigrants Esther and Leon Sherman. He owed them a great debt of love, and in return he was determined to find a way to make America accept, celebrate, and enjoy their accented and ungrammatical Jewish voices and stories. He found the way in a comedy that hijacked the country's songs and dubbed them with his grandparents' quirky brand of English. Strange new words came out of old tunes. The characters were not saying what they were supposed to be saying. Tradition was both preserved and made new.

Sherman crafted the perfect comic model for a country that continues to transform immigrants into Americans. Nobody has ever done it better.

overweight sensation

INTRODUCTION

HUMPTY DUMPTY

By September 1936, Allan Segal was an eighth grader who had been around.
Just shy of turning twelve, he was already on his second last name, third father,
and fourth school, and he still had one more name and four high schools ahead
of him. But for now the years spent rambling between Chicago, Los Angeles,
and New York were over and he was settled in Los Angeles, a city he first saw
in 1930, when the twenties boom had burst but had done its work. Los Angeles
had become a great city, a great port, a major industrial center and the capital
of show business, which was his business. He'd put on some weight, but that
could be funny, and he was a funnyman.

Within a year of his return to Los Angeles he had made his mark. In November 1937, his name appeared in his junior high school's gossipy "Guess
Who" newspaper column, which noted that Segal was "roly-poly" and also
"very witty." In February 1938, he contributed a letter to the *Los Angeles Herald*'s "Listen, World," column that won him a cash prize, and in June he spoke
on "The Passing Parade of Invention" at his ninth-grade graduation. Segal's
funny and sometimes coyly risqué school newspaper articles, exuberant wit,

and performance as a comic character named Roundy Robins in a school theatrical called *Laundry Mark* made him a celebrity among his fellow students. They were an elite group from tony Hancock Park, where stringent zoning ensured the houses were large enough and the lawns deep enough to attract Howard Hughes and Mae West. Segal blossomed there, and in the spring of 1938 he cracked the code of his comic gift and discovered his life's work while knocking out some copy at 300 McCadden Place, probably in room 100-M, where Mrs. Munscher held homeroom at John Burroughs Junior High School. That is where Allan Segal first got in touch with his future as Allan Sherman.

> Humpty Dumpty sat on a train
> Happily singing "Bei Mir Bist Du Schoen";
> All the conductors and all the porters,
> Couldn't get Humpty out of his quarters!

In four lines the parody nails the themes of Sherman's childhood world as well as his future life and career. At thirteen he knew who he was and what he liked. Not all the news was good. Humpty Dumpty was and would remain the perfect metaphor for the rotund, damaged Sherman. The ill-fated egg man suggests the fatal cracks in Sherman's personality that in this little ditty, and in his later life, he papered over with charm, brains, and wit. (Eventually he ran out of material.) Crucially, the parody links Jewishness and singing to happiness. It combines a Jewish work — the originally Yiddish song "Bei Mir Bistu Shein" that in 1937 was an English-language hit for the Andrews Sisters — with the Humpty Dumpty nursery rhyme, making it just a step and twenty-five years removed from "Sarah Jackman," Sherman's fame-making 1962 parody of "Frère Jacques."

Just as important as Humpty Dumpty is the fact that he is on the move.

The Union Pacific rail link between Los Angeles and Chicago was one of the most important elements of Sherman's unsettled childhood. The rhyme doesn't say where Humpty is traveling, but Allan often headed to Chicago to live with his Yiddish-speaking maternal grandparents, Esther and Leon Sherman, whom he came to love deeply. Other relatives felt differently. "My grandmother would not look at Leon and Esther Sherman," said Evelyn Raden, one of Allan's cousins. "She said Leon was a *shikker* and Esther a whore.

She would not be on the same side of the room as them." Whatever drinking and fooling around took place paled next to what young Allan learned about another Chicago relative. His paternal uncle, Abraham Coplon, was a dentist, nudist, raw foodist, and author of *Man Alive! An Analysis of the Human Struggle*, which condemned as evil medicine, bread, cooking, and clothing. "He screwed every woman in Chicago who was standing," said Lee Cooper, a relation. "If they were standing he made them lie down." Allan was friendly with his cousin Morris, Coplon's son, who as a boy in the 1930s decided that Allan's mother, Rose, was crazy. "It didn't take me long to see that she was a congenital liar. Rose couldn't tell the truth if her life depended on it. Clinically she could be labeled schizophrenic. She lived in a fantasy world, literally."

Allan faced a family life at the same level of headlong eccentricity when he traveled in the opposite direction, from Chicago to Los Angeles. That is where his mother met and married, in a church, her last husband and Allan's third father. Dave Segal was a Jewish con man and gangster whose name became a byword in the family for illegal or merely crazy shenanigans. "Anything that was remotely shady was a Dave Segal thing," recalled celebrity defense attorney Mickey Sherman, one of Allan's first cousins. "One day the doorbell rang and he was trying to hide in our basement in Connecticut. He just sold the Fontainebleau Hotel in Miami to Cuban gangsters, but he didn't own it. My father wouldn't let him in."

So it is irrelevant which way Allan Segal's Humpty was heading. Either destination had its travails. What is vital is that Humpty was on the train and *did not want to get off*. "All the conductors and all the porters / Couldn't get Humpty out of his quarters!" He was happy in the physical space between departures and arrivals, and happy also in the identity he created between those places, an identity that was mid-point between his old world Yiddish grandparents and fiercely Americanizing mother. Sherman's contribution to American popular culture was this hybrid midpoint comedy that preserved ethnic identity without pretending he was not also steeped in American culture.

He invented this hybrid comedy to preserve his sanity. The riot of family energy, sexuality, *Yiddishkeit*, Americanism, recrimination, enmity, and criminality that greeted Allan on all sides had by 1938 become his own. Those forces fueled and necessitated his wit. He was helpless against the power of his erratic mother, who shipped him back and forth across the country like a forwarded letter, but with his words he could move others and become a power himself. He was angry, eager to be sexually adventurous, hungry for fame, and pleased to be Jewish. The adolescent Sherman was also excited by his own talents, confidence, and daring, the scope of his comic invention, his facility with language, the riches of English and the pungency of Yiddish, and how valuable all these comic gifts could be, how much he could get away with and how much money he might one day make from humor. His Yiddish-inflected Mother Goose rhyme appeared in the 1938 John Burroughs Junior High *Burr*, the yearbook for and by graduating ninth graders, and in it is another Sherman article called "Humor for Sale." The piece zeroes in on the size of the humor market and imagines a comedy department store that "would be the busiest store in the world. That is because people love to laugh." At the lunch counter customers order the "fried Jack Benny Special," and on "the Humorous Poetry Floor one can spy customers asking for 'A parody on "Hiawatha" to wear with baby blue.'" Best of all is the joke department. "Floors upon floors containing drawers upon drawers of jokes." Sherman did not need a career counselor. He knew what he wanted to do.

That optimistic vision of comic commerce presents Sherman as a wide-eyed, spirited ingénue, but he also mocked claims to innocence. In "Catastrophe," Sherman displays a shrewd sexual flirtatiousness that seems unlikely for a boy not yet thirteen. But maybe it was adult insistence on childhood innocence that permitted the poem to appear in the October 7, 1937, *Far and Near*, his junior high school's student newspaper. Surely Sherman did not know what he was saying. But the poem indicates the opposite is true.

> What teacher, walking down the street
> With a fast and very steady beat,
> Came upon a safety lad,
> Said, "Hello," and was very glad
> To see what a fine committee we had.
> The safety boy was not too slow,
> In turning round to say hello,
> And then with his terrible black and white stick,

He gave Miss _____ a terrible nick.
To think that one who's cracked up to be our savior
Could be guilty of such behavior.
He turned, bowed, said, "I'm sorry.
I'll be a better boy tomorry."

The sexual imagery is inescapable. The stick/nick rhyme evokes a host of unmentioned but unavoidable four-letter words. But even more attention grabbing is the comic pretense of shock. The cynicism here, complete with an insincere apology that winks at the reader with the cutesy "tomorry" is breathtaking. Before he was thirteen the student journalist possessed the world-weariness of a hardened hack reporter from Ben Hecht's *Front Page*. And the slangy expression, "cracked up," that explodes in the middle of the key line signals emerging writing talent as well as the wisenheimer attitude that's coming our way. "To think that one who's cracked up to be our savior / Could be guilty of such behavior." Captain Renault in *Casablanca* was similarly shocked to discover that Rick's Café allowed gambling.

Sherman clearly knew plenty about what the world was cracked up to be and what it really was, about so-called saviors who neglected to guard those under their care because they were off satisfying powerful urges. His jaundiced view of human nature was reflected in his report cards, which monitored his level of Social Concern. Sherman's teachers were concerned about his lack of it. On his January 29, 1937, report card, four of his six teachers agreed he "needs to improve." Six months later on June 25 it was a landslide. Six out of seven teachers gave him a thumbs-down in the category. His bad attitude was a side effect of the lessons he learned from his mother's and grandmother's and uncle's loose ways, lessons "Catastrophe" proves were not lost on him. An ungovernable desire for that most problem-causing human need ran in the family, and Sherman early discovered his own way to satisfy it. Humor was how to get, and get away with, the act suggested in the poem, and also the poem itself. About that social concern he was expert and canny and needed no improvement. The sexual rewards of wit were as valuable as humor for sale. When Sherman's comedy later won him fame it paid off big in sexual currency. Money wasn't everything.

Comedy greased the wheels of sexual expression and it did the same for anger. Beneath the photograph of Segal's homeroom class in the 1938 *Burr* the forty-four ninth-graders were given a chance to express their individuality. The results were underwhelming. Each student stated his Undertaking, Saying, and Ambition, which accounts for the patriotic "USA" that appears in a vertical row under every name. Nearly all of Segal's classmates offered predictable drivel. Bob Rothman's undertaking, saying, and ambition were "Fool around," "Howdy partner," and "bartender." George Schweitzer's undertaking was also "Fool around," but his saying was "Oh, yeah." Dolores Rubin's saying was, "My oh my." Philip Simon's was, "Nuts to you and I do mean foo." The preponderance of Jewish names was not unique to homeroom 100-M. On September 24, 1936, the *Far and Near* reported, "30% of J.B. Pupils Observe Jewish Holidays." The previous week, on the first day of Rosh Hashanah, 650 students were absent from school. But this population largely defied laudatory ethnic stereotypes. There is little evidence that John Burroughs was a hotbed of witty invention. Many dared to be dull.

Allan Segal stood out. His undertaking was "Miraculous gustatorial feats." The dictionary disagrees with Segal about the existence of "gustatorial," but it seems necessary as a step beyond mere gustatory, suggesting an act requiring the death-defying instincts of someone gladiatorial. Sherman had such instincts, and for the rest of his life miraculous gustatorial feats remained part of his repertoire of self-destruction. His aim was "Editor in chief, New York Times." This was also grand, but it certainly pointed in the right direction. During his senior year at John Burroughs he took a journalism class and served as city editor of the *Far and Near*. But the truest measure of his ambition revealed itself in his saying, which at eleven words was five times the length of most, and three times greater than all but a few. When measured by the syllable, however, and also comic sensibility and exultant literacy, Sherman's saying dwarfed the others like a Gulliver. He wrote, "I shall reward your impertinence by striking you upon the cranium." The saying presents a cynical view of the "reward" that awaits the one who speaks inappropriately. Being impertinent is one way of speaking your mind and rebuking authority, but being funny is smarter.

A cliché in the telling of a humorist's life is a trauma, sadness, or despair that comedy never assuages, and there is no escaping that cliché here. Of the five articles that Sherman wrote or cowrote for the *Burr*, four are about homelessness and migration. His childhood was practically nomadic, and he was powerfully drawn to people on the move, people in train stations, trailer camps, and tourists. In a brief article called, "There's No Place Like Home — On Wheels!" he visited Pepper Grove, where "children, pets, relatives, and large families live in trailers." Walking around, "license plates of every color, size, and shape, greet the eye." Then he noticed something else. "Those people are happy! They eat from crude dishes, cook on crude stoves. Nevertheless, they have the feeling of roughing it and everybody is happy."

Everybody wasn't happy in the Segal household. Daddy number one disappeared after the divorce from Mommy. Daddy number two died blaming Mommy for the fact that his wife was trapped in wartime Europe. Daddy number three was cheating his ex-wife out of her alimony and child support. Mommy pretended to be younger, more American, and less frequently married than she was. Allan had no Social Concern. Superficially, his family was like the ones at Pepper Grove. He moved around the country a lot and then settled in Los Angeles. But there was something different about his migration, his family, his people, and that difference would fascinate Sherman and form the basis of his comedy.

one
WITZ-KRIEG!

Among the two million Jews who left Europe for America at the turn of the twentieth century was a passel of Lustigs. Between 1906 and 1920, siblings Anna, Abraham, Fanny, and Saul Lustig arrived in Chicago as single adults in their late teens and early twenties. Their sister Esther joined the family exodus in 1909, but she left Stashev, in Russian-ruled Poland, as the twenty-six-year-old wife of Leon Sherman and the mother of two daughters, Rose, four, and Kate, three. More than any of her siblings, Esther carried the greatest weight of the old world with her when she arrived in America, and that weight burdened her daughter, Rose, who struggled mightily to shrug it off. It was a gift to Rose's son, Allan Sherman, who saw in it something to anchor his rootless life.

"To Grandma and Grandpa, Jewishness was a basic condition of life," Sherman wrote. "Everybody was meant to be Jewish; the fact that some people weren't was some kind of clerical error on God's part."

The patriarch of the Lustig clan followed his five children to Chicago in 1921, and he imparted another key legacy. Most Stashev Jews worked as craftsmen, as merchants dealing in cloth, wheat, lumber, and leather, or as home-based laborers doing piecework for garment makers or shoemakers. But Esther's father did none of the above. Instead, he practiced a risky trade that will forever instill fear in prospective in-laws. Leib Lustig was a musician.

The Lustig family's search for a better life began in 1883, when Leib, twenty-two, left his birthplace in the tiny Polish shtetl of Ozarow for the neighboring but larger Stashev. Sometimes even a musician must be practical. Leib's daughter Esther was a baby, there were more on the way, and in Ozarow the Jews were so poor four children sometimes shared one bed on a mattress made of straw. Three slept side by side and the fourth lay across the bottom at the feet of the others. An even more practical move would have been for Leib not to be a musician, but that decision was out of his hands. He had to play the violin. By the time he was born it was an established family calling. Jews in the Ozarow region adopted European-style family names beginning in 1805, and many took the name of their occupation. One name for the musicians who played at weddings and festive holidays was merry makers, or *lustik-makhers*.

So the best Leib could do was find a larger and richer town than Ozarow, which might also have been too strict and monolithic in its religious observance for the Lustigs. Leib was a rule-breaker and he encouraged family members to follow in his footsteps. "He called my mother old-fashioned because she did not smoke cigarettes," said Syril Gilbert, one of Leib's great-grandchildren. That outlook made Ozarow a poor fit. In the mid-nineteenth century, it held fewer than eighteen hundred people, with two-thirds or about twelve hundred being Jews. That number was small enough for a powerful Hasidic dynasty to exert a large influence, and Ozarow became home to such a dynasty in 1812, when Rabbi Yehuda Arie Leib ha-Levi Epstein, a disciple of the Seer of Lublin, became a rabbi there. The Seer taught that certain holy men had "divine authority to lead a community," and in Ozarow Epstein's descendants led the town's Hasidim for over a century, until the last Epstein immigrated to America in 1927. Religious practice was pervasive. Among the orthodox, even letters to family began "by citing the Torah portion of the week." In Ozarow, "taking the right road meant going straight from *cheder* [Jewish primary school] to yeshiva."

For Leib Lustig the right road led to Stashev. It was not a great town, but with eight thousand people, including more than five thousand Jews, it was quadruple the size of Ozarow, and that meant four times as many weddings. Stashev also was home to a military garrison of eight hundred soldiers, which was great news for Jewish tavern owners and brewers, who also had children to marry off. In short, it was a town amenable to musicians, and when Leib arrived there the Jewish community was grooming several that in the early twentieth century were recognized more widely, such as the pianist and conductor Israel Schwoger, violinist Moses Rotenberg, and violinist and violin craftsman Jakub Cymerman.

Leib's move paid off for his son Abraham, who was born in Stashev in 1883 and became a violinist like his father, and it appears that Esther also liked the world of her father's *lustik-makhers*. Her marriage to Leibush Sherman was almost certainly arranged by a matchmaker. Marriages in Ozarow, for example, were still being arranged as late as 1938, and Esther married no later than 1903, when she was about twenty-one. But any good matchmaker must look for promising signs that a deal will close, and the match between Esther and Leibush had many.

First, Esther's father and the proposed groom were both from Ozarow, and they shared almost the same name. Leibush meant Little Leib. Plus, the Leibush name was a good sign. Ozarow's revered early nineteenth-century Hasidic rabbi, Yehuda Arie Leib ha-Levi Epstein, was known as The Great Leibush. But the clincher must have been that Leibush Sherman was also a *lustik-makher*. Allan Sherman wrote that in the old country his grandpa Leibush was a *grom*. The word is Yiddish for rhyme, and is close to a term that describes a *lustik-makher* skill. In addition to musicians, there were poets at weddings who recited rhyming songs, known as *gramen zogn*. As Sherman wrote, it was a case of "My Grandfather, The Folk Singer."

After the assassination of Russia's czar in 1881, the terrible pogrom against the Russian Jews of Kishinev in 1903, and the suppressed Russian Revolution of 1905 and subsequent pogroms, great masses of Jews left Eastern Europe for America. That is where everything changed.

Leibush Sherman landed alone at Ellis Island on October 30, 1907, and headed for Chicago, where his sister-in-law Anna Lustig had arrived the year before. The not unusual plan was for Leibush to work and save money and then send for his wife and children, which is what he did. Leibush worked as a presser in Chicago's garment industry and after eighteen months of separation his wife Esther landed in New York on March 18, 1909, with her daughters, then called Rivke and Kreindel. Nine months later on December 19 Esther gave birth to a son, Morris.

But the match that looked promising in Stashev did not work in America. The new country exposed the differences between husband and wife. Leibush, now Leon, developed a longing for the old country and his orthodox little hometown of Ozarow. He was one of seven men to ask members of Chicago's Stashev *landsmanshaft*, an immigrant mutual-aid society, to change its name and accept members from nearby towns. Despite his residence in Stashev, Leon remained an Ozarower, never mind a Chicagoan. In response to this plea, on June 7, 1909, the Stashev organization became the American Progressive Society, a name precisely wrong but part of the comedy of immigrant life, an unintentional parody. Leon was anything but an American progressive. As one of the founders of this newly chartered *landsmanshaft*, he was, like other such founders, "steeped in Eastern-European Yiddishkeit, the age-old traditions and ideals of the Yiddish-speaking diaspora."

It was not the best résumé for success in America.

"Leon was a smart and frustrated person," remembered granddaughter Gilbert. "He became an alcoholic."

Esther remained true to her roots, as a Lustig.

"Esther screwed around," said Carol Selsberg, another granddaughter. "They took in boarders and Esther was in bed with the boarders."

Allan Sherman's ex-wife, Dee Golden, corroborated the account. "Esther necked with all the men that came to the door. More than that, is what I hear."

She also liked to play poker, and Sherman wrote she was what pros call "a mechanic," a dealer who could cheat undetected. She certainly did like to cheat. "She was ruthless," Golden said. "She never paid for anything." Esther sneaked into theaters, made phone calls and then demanded that operators return the money, saying the call never went through. She was a classic example of the *kurtn shpiler*, the card playing and gambling Jewish women that smoked cigarettes, used rough language and humor, and "understood that [life] included *good times*." There were many in Chicago like her, and Saul Bellow celebrated the type in Grandma Lausch. Like that character in *The Adventures of Augie March*, Grandma Esther was a cutthroat, loving, and thoroughly unsentimental immigrant woman who always had her eye out for an advantage and a useful lie. Esther's husband, Leon, detested this behavior, and it is likely Esther considered him a fool. "They fought a lot and gave each other dirty looks," said Gilbert. Selsberg said, "They hated each other." Selsberg's brother, Mickey Sherman, summed it up with comic understatement. "It was several miles from the Cleaver family." As their marriage deteriorated, Leon took to drink. "He walked around with a flask in his pocket," remembered Helen Stricker, a relation. Leon managed to keep his job by staying sober during the day. "He started drinking when he came home," said relation Vivian Mailand, and then kept drinking until he passed out for the night.

Meanwhile, daughters Rivka and Kreindel, now Rose and Kate, and son Morris grew up in a freedom bordering on chaos. "Morris had burns from trying to cook for himself as a child," said his daughter Carol Selsberg. "There was no parenting." When Esther did cook, dinner was a free-for-all. "Everybody reached in to grab," recalled Golden. "I didn't have any. I wasn't used to grabbing." The rush might have stemmed from her reputation in the kitchen. "Esther was a wonderful Jewish cook," Gilbert said. "Best matzo balls I ever tasted." Rose and Kate soon entered dancing contests and won prizes, and all of this whirling activity and sexuality and aggression and misery were common in 1920 among Chicago's two hundred twenty-five thousand Jews, and especially so in the immigrant quarters such as the Humboldt Park area, where the Sherman family lived at 1226 North Wood Street, and also around the corner at 1800 West Division Street, amid more than sixty thousand newcomers to the area. Moralists cautioned young Jewish women to "stay clear of the dance hall's charms," but the appeal of these sexually charged environments was irresistible. Young people were unfettered by the constraints and stability their parents knew in the *shtetl*, where tradition, religion, and parental and rabbinical authority ruled. In America, they experienced a "wild sense of freedom" that was as "disorienting as it was intoxicating." The early twentieth century Jewish sociologist Louis Wirth was not amused by what he saw happening in Chicago. Immigration "constitutes a crisis in the immigrant's life," he wrote. And when the bond between the individual and the Jewish community weakens, these newly liberated people suffer "personal disorganization."

A disrupted and disorganized life applied to immigrants generally, but conditions were exacerbated among Jews. America filled them with an extraordinary sense of gratitude and hope as an escape from poverty and persecution, and they fervently embraced their new country. Newspapers serving other immigrant groups admonished female readers to preserve ethnic or religious traditions. The *Jewish Daily Forward*'s women's page urged Americanization. Jewish immigrants were also on average younger than those of other groups because Jews more commonly arrived as families, with far fewer single men seeking to make their fortune and return home. Neighborhoods bursting with recently arrived teenagers and young adults filled the dance halls frequented by Rose and Kate, and dancing created a readership for Yiddish sex guides. Margaret Sanger's guide to birth control, *What Every Girl Should Know*, appeared in Yiddish in 1916 and 1921. Ben Zion Liber's *Dos geshlekhts lebn*, or *Sex Life*, saw four editions from 1914 to 1927.

Chicago itself turned up the heat that brought young Jews to a boil. It was not New York, where Jews were a multitude that changed the character of the city. In 1920, Chicago's Jews were just 8 percent of the population, and Jews Americanized more quickly there and were less comfortable asserting visible signs of ethnicity. They took the lead in a national campaign to stamp out the vaudeville performances and "low comedy songs" that poked fun at Yiddish accents and Jewish life, behavior, and appearance. In 1913, the city's Anti-Stage Ridicule Committee and the new Anti-Defamation League of the B'nai B'rith protested such entertainments. Young Jewish immigrants everywhere were driven to master proper English. In the immigrant novel *The Rise of David Levinsky*, the hero undertakes a "long excruciating struggle to shake off his accent," and in the immigrant memoir *The Promised Land*, "Americanization is measured by [the author's] conquest of the 'dreadful English th.'" But Chicago's Jews were especially keen to achieve these goals. In the Midwest, Jews "were bound to be aware of 'America' as a more compelling geographic and cultural reality," and this encouraged assimilation. Saul Bellow hammered this point home. His Augie March announces, "I am an American, Chicago-born." As one writer slyly noted, "I am an American, New York-born" would have "lacked the same power of conviction."

Esther escaped the worst repercussions of this unbridled freedom, pressure to become an American, and embarrassment about how she spoke and who she was. She and her husband were girded by their upbringing in a traditional Jewish world. They "kissed a Mazuzah [*sic*] as they walked through their front door, and were shamelessly unselfconscious about being Jewish," Sherman wrote. This comfort and pleasure in being Jewish impressed him greatly and was crucial to his later fame. In the 1950s, when he began singing Jewish parodies of Broadway musicals for his friends, that ease was something American Jews realized they had lost and wanted to regain. "This is the great thing about the Jews described by Sholom Aleichem," Alfred Kazin wrote with amazement in 1956. "They enjoy being Jews, they enjoy the idea of belonging to the people who are called Jews." Sherman became a star with comedy that communicated that same pleasure.

It was not a pleasure for Sherman's mother, Rose. Though born in a *shtetl* she arrived in America at the age of four and completely lacked her mother Esther's unselfconscious Jewishness. She grew up without tradition in a world of anarchic freedom that was "a sort of moral void," and she was surrounded by an atmosphere that objected to depictions of people who spoke and behaved like her parents. Rose got the message and did what she could to leave Jewish life. Louis Wirth predicted her case in an ominous warning. "The immigrant is braced by certain Old World loyalties, but his child may grow up loyal to nothing whatsoever, a rank egoist and an incorrigible who will give us vast trouble before we are done with him."

Or her.

Hello Muddah

Sherman wrote that his mother was a "beautiful-looking little thing with brunette hair and mischief in the eyes, and she believed life to be a bowl of cherries." It is a description more suited to a child than a parent, but some think that is what makes it accurate. "She had the mentality of an eight-year-old kid," said Morris Coplon. "How she dressed, how she put on her makeup, a different hairstyle every month, forever buying new clothes. Rose was a very sick woman." Other relations paint a similar picture, but with less condemnation. "Rose liked to live dramatically and big. She loved nice clothes," said Gilbert.

"She had a dynamic personality." Rose also was the one family members went to for advice. "She was half kidding, half serious when she said about husbands, 'Don't be a dummy. He's gonna walk off with the money and you're going to be left with the kids.' Shrewd about real life," Gilbert said. Mincing words was not her style. "Rose was like Roseanne Barr, very much like her," Mailand remembered. "Rose had a faculty of saying — she said what she felt like."

A 1925 photograph of Rose and her sister, Kate, is a study in contrasts and suggests that Morris Coplon's less charitable assessment is closer to the truth. Kate is dressed conventionally and looks intelligent and amused. Rose is dressed exotically in a flowing robe over an embroidered dress, with one ring on her right hand and two on her left. But it is her expression that sets off alarms. Her fixed gaze expresses an angry misunderstanding with the world.

Rose Sherman was born in Ozarow on May 16, 1904, according to the citizenship papers completed by her father, who had a greater allegiance to the truth than his wife. But when on January 17, 1920, the U.S. government census-taker stopped by the Sherman household, Esther told him Rose was fourteen and born in 1906. Esther manipulated her daughters' ages for convenience. Making Rose younger narrowed the gap between Rose and her sister, Kate, who was born on August 20, 1906. "Esther entered Kate and Rose as twins in school," Gilbert said. Both Rose and Kate attended Chicago's Tuley high school in the early 1920s, but neither graduated.

An early photograph agrees with family assurances that when Rose was young she was slim, attractive, and stylish, with painted lips and a hairstyle familiar today from silent film images. But she was also tiny, and in the photograph her left arm that faces the camera looks so soft, weak, and childish that it is startling to see it end in a hand sporting an engagement ring.

On July 17, 1922, Rose, eighteen, married Jacob Carp, a twenty-three-year-old shipping clerk in a clothing factory. Rose needed to escape her parents' unhappy marriage, and Carp was a good catch because he had something going for him Rose would always find attractive. He was not obviously Jewish. Though of Russian Jewish heritage like herself, he was born in Manchester, England, lived there until he was sixteen, and undoubtedly spoke with an English accent. This made him a rare bird. Some Russian Jews immigrated to America via England to save money (it was cheaper than embarking directly from the continent), but they were relatively few. Even fewer grew up there, so English-accented Russian Jews were in short supply. That Rose found one is the first sign of many that she was on the lookout for ways to distance herself from her origins.

There is no record of Rose's divorce from Carp, but on October 18, 1923, she married her second husband and Allan Sherman's father, Percy Coplon, aka Perry Coplon, aka Percy Copelon, aka Perry Copelon. Rose never quit changing his name and finally gave up trying to perfect him and just divorced him. But Coplon's outsized personality, adventurous exploits true and imagined, long absence, reemergence, pledges made and apparently broken, and bizarre and widely publicized death hammered many cracks into the shell of his Humpty Dumpty son.

Hello, Fadduh

In 1901 the city of Birmingham, Alabama, was only thirty years old and did not have much tradition or history to interfere with its energetic pursuit of the new. But as if to ensure that Peretz Kaplan would never be encumbered by any idea that had some dust on it, on March 25, 1901, fate sent Birmingham a "wild wind and conscienceless storm" to destroy anything old, dilapidated, or past its prime. Three months later, on June 21, 1901, Peretz, five, and his mother, Keile; brother, Benjamin; and sister, Chane, landed at Ellis Island. Their destination was the so-called Magic City that seemed to spring fully-formed as a center of iron and steel manufacturing from the ground beneath it, rich in iron ore, coal, and limestone. In 1880 Birmingham's population was 3,086. In 1893 it was 50,000. Miners dynamited into the hillsides, steel mill furnaces pumped black smoke, nine railroad lines connected the city to the rest of the nation, and with the arrival of Peretz and his mother and siblings Moses Kaplan had reunited his family for the first time since he immigrated to Birmingham in 1898. Two additional children, Abraham and daughter Sime, had arrived from Europe on June 8, 1900. It was time to begin anew.

For Moses, that meant continuing with the old. He joined Birmingham's only Orthodox synagogue, K'hilah K'nesseth Israel, which was founded in 1889 to serve the city's small but growing population of traditional East European

Jews. K'nesseth Israel catered to "gentlemen whose devotion to Judaism has never permitted them to diverge from its most orthodox aspects," and for the rest of their lives Moses and his wife Keile, now Kate, ate kosher food, observed the Sabbath, spoke Yiddish within the family, and in general lived as they had in Lizensk, a shtetl in Austro-Hungarian Galicia. Some few concessions were made. Kaplan became Coplon, a spelling pioneered by Moses's brother Dave, who was the first in the family to settle in Birmingham. Peretz became Percy and sisters Chane and Sima turned into Annie and Celia. But the truly great changes took place without Moses' permission.

"Percy was strictly a southerner," recalled Joe Resnick, a family friend. "He wasn't so much ingrained with Judaism. He was an American boy."

In the South, the school day commenced with prayer and readings from the New Testament, including "the most offensive tirades against the Jews in the Book of John." Though prejudice against Catholics and blacks took precedence over discrimination against Jews, "assimilation was highly desirable."

This was not a problem for the young. In June 1911, Birmingham High School published a literary journal called the *Mirror*, and in it a contemporary of Percy's, high school senior Sara S. Sewelovitz, published "The Call to the Open." It recounts an early morning spent watching laborers march to work. "One I remember had a remarkably pleasing countenance that held a suggestion of great power behind it. I've seen him often since, coming from work, his face grimed with toil, yet still having that expression of latent power."

Power was catnip to Percy, and so was its deployment to experience risk, speed, and danger. He was a man of high spirits. "Percy was one of the most convivial men you ever met," said nephew Morris Coplon. "He had that earthy humor of the South. Southern blue collar."

Percy inherited his exuberance from his father. "You want to write about a character? Mose Coplon was a character. He could sell shoes to a billy goat and get him to wear 'em and like 'em," said Resnick. Percy channeled that spirit into diagnosing, fixing, and racing automobiles, a symbol of progress in the mostly poor and rural South, and America's greatest surrogate for male power. Birmingham's machine- and engine-dominated world seeped into Percy's bones and nerves. Morris Coplon remembered that Percy "could take a metal bar, listen to one end, put the other end to the engine" and figure out what was wrong. Another nephew, Daniel Isenberg, said, "In my mind he could do anything. He was my god."

Percy's affinity for machinery displayed itself early. By the time he was seventeen he appeared in the 1913 Birmingham City Directory as a machinist, and on October 29, 1913, Percy served as the "mechanician" for a racecar driver competing in a hundred-mile contest at Birmingham's State Fair grounds. The *Age-Herald* reported that Percy rode in car 14 with driver W. R. Lawson and was with him when it "left the track at the southwest turn and crashed through the inner fence, injuring both occupants seriously." As it turned out, Percy was not badly hurt. But the incident gave him the chance to issue the jaunty boast to a reporter from the *Birmingham News* that, "he didn't reckon you could kill a tough nut like him." After that, publicity joined machines as something Percy loved.

He remained in Birmingham until June 1918, when the First World War took him to the University of Alabama in Tuscaloosa, where he worked as an instructor, probably in automobile repair. Percy wasn't satisfied with this story and invented a more daring and romantic one that had him flying bi-planes in Europe, a story Sherman loved and apparently believed even as it distorted his sense of reality. "Percy said he wanted to go to Europe as a flyer but never did," Morris Coplon said. His 1918 draft registration card hints that his breezy attitude toward the truth was causing family trouble. He named his mother as his nearest relative, not his father. The traditional Moses and Percy the southerner lived in different worlds, and even their bodies seemed to reflect their opposition. Percy's registration card noted that at age twenty-one he was already "stout." His father remained "a well-built old man," Isenberg said.

After the war Percy returned to Birmingham and in January 1919 founded the Coplon Auto Company. A year later he started the Minute Change Lever Co., a manufacturing concern, and on September 6, 1920, he drove a Chevrolet 490 and won a ten-mile automobile race that was part of Birmingham's Labor Day weekend celebrations. The race was for amateurs, and Percy's win was partly due to luck. According to a newspaper account, another driver "led the race until his engine developed ignition trouble in the fourth mile." This tarnished victory was followed by failures. The local paper reported Percy would race again in the State Fair in October, but he did not, and his two businesses apparently closed, because in 1922 he was no longer his own boss but worked for the Alabama Auto Service Company. His ventures likely were victims of the now forgotten 1920–21 financial depression. Percy was twenty-six, estranged from his father, and a failed businessman. It was time to move on.

The place to go was Chicago, where Percy's older brother, Abraham, moved in 1918 to practice dentistry and become a well-known eccentric. Notoriety was inevitable. There were not many dentists who were also raw foodists, nudists, free-love advocates, and public philanderers. Abe dedicated his 1928 book, *Man Alive! An Analysis of the Human Struggle*, to his mistress. "My dad was marvelous, unique, strange and complex and probably manic depressive," said Dorothy Macarus. Lee Cooper said that when George Gershwin died, Abe announced, "'I could have saved him.' He was convinced he was a healer." That belief could be dangerous. Cooper's father went on one of Abe's "crazy diets of just water for thirty days, wasting away into virtually nothing to cure ulcers. My dad never recovered from this absolutely stupid regimen."

Percy later followed a more extreme version of the diet. It cost him his life. But in June 1923, things were looking up. Percy had a new business in Chicago, the Roco Motor & Garage Company at 2342 West Division Street. "Roco" was a composite, named for Rose Coplon. In June 1923, however, there was no Rose Coplon. She did not acquire that name until her marriage to Percy on October 18. But if the Roco Motor name had no basis in fact, it was a true sign of the young lovers' unwary exuberance.

Percy's love of fast cars found a counterpart in Rose's love of a fast life, of dance halls and showy clothes, and they were both child immigrants who grew up divorced from their Jewish heritage and in love with their very American hometowns and their very American selves. Rose's first husband may have spoken like an Englishman, but Percy topped that with his Southern drawl. It was just as un-Jewish, and American to boot. Acting like a southerner was then a shortcut to Americanization, and Jewish songwriters capitalized on this trend with tunes such as Irving Berlin's "Alexander's Ragtime Band," and George Gershwin's "Swanee." The composers and fans of such tunes became "facsimile southerners," real Americans, and by marrying Percy, Rose did the same.

The two were married in Chicago by Judge H. Sterling Pomeroy. There was no Jewish ceremony for these natives of the East European shtetl, and their marriage certificate records the first improvement Rose made to her new husband. He married as Perry Coplon. Percy did not take this change very seriously. On legal papers for Roco Motor he continued to use Percy. But the change was a warning of the confusion that would become their life and the life of their son.

Shake Hands with Your Uncle Max

Allan Sherman was born in Chicago on November 30, 1924, as Allan Coplon. Better make that Copelon. A close look at the handwritten birth certificate reveals that Allan's last name was first spelled Coplon, and that a small awkward upper case E was later wedged between the p and l. This was not the end of the awkwardness. Percy himself was unsure of the new family name. Unused to writing Copelon in a cursive hand he wrote "Coprlon." "Rose started spelling Coplon with an *e* because people were mispronouncing it," said Coplon relation Jackie Sheinberg. That is, people pronounced it as it was written, almost identically to the more common Kaplan. But Rose wanted it pronounced with a long o, something the addition of the e would indicate. The only explanation for Rose's irritation is that without the e, Coplon was too Jewish.

If Rose had not made the retroactive change to her son's family name, the Jewish sounding Coplon might have undermined her choice of hospital. She gave birth at Norwegian Deaconess at a time when Chicago Jews flocked either to Mount Sinai or the larger Michael Reese, a Jewish-founded and funded institution that was a leader in pediatrics. In 1922, it inaugurated the first nursery in the world dedicated to the care of premature babies. But taken together Norwegian Deaconess and the new Copelon name was meant to rescue Allan from a Jewish identity Rose found intolerable. Many facts about her life were intolerable. Where Allan's birth certificate asks for Rose's place of birth, she wrote Chicago, not Poland or Russia. The form also requests Rose's age. In 1923 she stated, accurately, that she married Percy at age nineteen. Now, a year later, Rose said she was eighteen.

She may have been crazy, but she was not lonely, and neither was her son. Allan was surrounded by a throng of family members that left its mark on many of his parodies, from "Sarah Jackman" with its motley collection of relatives to "Shake Hands with Your Uncle Max," about a traveling salesman who returns home and is greeted, in fact mobbed, by family. The young Allan experienced this overflow of Jewish family connections with their curious accents and curious names sometimes curiously spelled. They were his first audience and his first fans. "As a child he was a celebrity," said Golden. "He stood in the middle of the room and entertained."

He probably played to a full house. On the Lustig side there was Great-grandpa Leib; Grandma Esther and Grandpa Leon; their children Rose, Kate, and Morris; and at least fifteen of Rose's aunts, uncles, and cousins. Uncle Abraham Lustig, the violinist, was married to Blanche. They gave their two daughters the rhyming and unusual names of Vera and Irma. Aunt Anna Lustig married a jeweler named Samuel Strowiss, an odd spelling of the common Strauss. Their children were Rose, Jeanette, and Aaron. Uncle Sol Lustig was a barber married to Dora, and they had two boys, Nathan and Theodore. Finally there was Aunt Fanny (Lustig) Friedman, and her son, Charlie. The Coplon side was short on uncles and aunts, contributing only Percy's brother, Abraham, and his wife, Emma, but they made up for it with their six children Helen, Julian, Herman, Milton, Morris, and Dorothy.

It was a paradise for a born performer, and Allan inherited the performing gene from all sides: Great-grandpa Leib, the musician; Grandpa Leon, the wedding singer; Grandpa Moses Coplon, who could sell shoes to a billy goat; his father, Percy, an exhibitionist that loved press coverage; and his mother, Rose, a natural actress that played a life role from her own script. With relatives like that, Allan had to compete for the limelight. He managed it. "Allan mentioned that his folks were proud of him. He made them laugh as a kid," said friend Leonid Hambro. "Even as a kid, he already exhibited a gift with words."

It was a kooky Jewish paradise rich in family attention and love that Sherman never forgot and always longed for. It did not last long.

Paradise Lost

On April 23, 1925, with the economy booming, Percy and a partner each contributed $4,000 to expand and incorporate Roco Motor, but as in Alabama, his business soon foundered. May 15, 1928, brought the first sign of trouble, when Roco Motor was late in filing its annual report and paying the required $10 fee. On November 10, Illinois asked the Cook County sheriff to collect the still unpaid amount. By then the Copelon family had left its home at 1158 Christiana Street and was living with Leon and Esther Sherman at 2909 West Division. Roco Motor officially died on June 14, 1929, and the Copelon family went into reverse. Percy, Rose, and Allan alternated between living with Rose's parents and Percy's brother Abraham, his wife, then five children, father-in-law, and a boarder. With perfect timing, the August 23, 1929, Chicago Jewish *Sentinel* reported that, "Mrs. M. Coplon of Birmingham, Alabama, has left for Chicago, where she will make her home with her sons, Dr. A. G. Coplon and Percy Coplon and their families at 1550 North Hoyne avenue." Her visit, without her husband, was another sign of Moses's estrangement from his sons, but it was a blessing in disguise. There was no room for an additional visitor. With their mother's arrival, the crowded Coplon apartment rivaled the ship's cabin in *A Night at the Opera*, and if Groucho Marx had been there he might have told Mrs. Coplon, "You know I had a premonition you were going to show up." The stock market soon crashed, the Depression began, and by the time Allan turned five on November 30, 1929, he was well into his chaotic childhood.

After Chicago did not work out, the place to go was Los Angeles, where Rose's uncle, Abe Lustig, had moved in 1928. He provided Rose a bit of family security without the overwhelming family, and Los Angeles offered Percy business opportunities. In 1930, the Los Angeles metropolitan area of 2.3 million people was the national symbol of the "triumph of motor transport." Best of all, Los Angeles was America's "gigantic improvisation." The city lacked traditions, and that went double for the Jewish community. Jewish life in Los Angeles was "post-Judaic, post-secular, and remote even from an earlier subculture of Jewishness." It was a city made for people like Rose Coplon/ Copelon and her husband Percy/Perry. In Los Angeles, they would be free to be anything they wanted. The city attracted many midwesterners with a utopian vision of a suburban life that was "spacious, affluent, clean, decent, permanent, predictable and homogenous." In other words, everything that Rose and Percy were not, and everything their son Allan would mock and parody.

In less than two years, Rose and Percy's California dream was over. They were in Los Angeles with Allan when the census taker canvassed their building at 2825 West Boulevard on April 16, 1930; on February 2, 1932, they separated. Their divorce records show why Humpty Dumpty did not want to get off the train.

Rose claimed Percy beat her, accused her of robbing him, called her "a God-Damned-Liar" and a "Son-of-a-Bitch," drew a gun "and threatened to kill her and stated 'I will end it all for you,'" and was regularly drunk. Percy denied everything and said Rose threatened to kill him "in his sleep," often left home without explanation and did not return until 3 AM, and that on February 2, 1932, she took off for Chicago and sent him a letter from the train saying "she had taken all the money in the bank" and was not coming back.

This ugliness culminated in a wrenching moment when Rose told Allan that she and Percy were going to separate, and he had to make a decision. "'Allan,' she said, 'you have to choose. Which one of us do you want to live with?'"

Sherman never recovered from that moment. He referred to it often in newspaper interviews and gave it great prominence in his autobiography, *A Gift of Laughter*. It left him with a permanent aversion to adulthood. Grown-ups "walk around looking serious and acting very somber," he wrote in *Gift*. The ideal existence was childhood, a life of "more laughter and simpler music, and funny games to play." In reaction to his parents' madness he took refuge in a character finely tuned to a child's world and its wish for family love that resulted in some of his greatest creations, including the "Hello Muddah, Hello Fadduh" song that made enduring comedy out of a child's fear of parental abandonment.

Sherman also had less innocent reasons to prefer childlike innocence as an adult. It allowed him to indulge in unfettered and guilt-free adult sexuality under the banner of being free and natural. He associated childhood with a supposed lost historical moment "when there were no hang-ups and people were still childlike, when strangers could meet in a clearing and touch and play with each other wordlessly and lie down together joyously." The flip side of Sherman's romantic and self-serving depiction of childhood's innocence was his childish self-pity and "indecision and disorganization" that all but guaranteed he would die young.

Food and Love

Sherman wrote he chose to live with Rose because he could not look her in the face and refuse her. The divorce settlement allowed Percy to see him whenever reasonable, but by the time the divorce was finalized on June 30, 1933, such conditions were beside the point. Neither parent demonstrated an extraordinary interest in their child. Percy returned to Birmingham in late 1933 in time to be included in the 1934 Birmingham City Directory. Allan's whereabouts are harder to pin down. In June 1932 he attended a day camp, probably in New York, where his Grandma Esther had a cousin, Max Lustig, in Manhattan's Washington Heights neighborhood at 540 Audubon Avenue. School records confirm Allan was a fourth grader in New York City in May 1933. On May 10 he moved to Chicago to live with his grandparents, Esther and Leon, at 1305 North Spaulding Avenue and attend school at Lowell Elementary. Four months later on September 18, 1933, he left Chicago and returned to Los Angeles, which means that in little more than a year Allan crossed the country twice and lived in three states. He was eight.

Two years of relative stability followed. From September 1933 to September 1935, Sherman lived in Los Angeles with his mother and her new husband or boyfriend, an upholsterer known only as Dave. "He was the love of Rose's life," said Syril Gilbert. That may be, but things were not so simple. Dave was a Jewish refugee from Europe who was supposed to bring his wife and children to America but instead became involved with Rose. Before he died of diabetes in 1935 he regretted his negligence, which left his family trapped in Europe, and he blamed Rose, Golden said.

In response, Rose went through an uncharacteristic moment of seriousness. After Dave died she again sent Allan to her parents in Chicago, and on his 1935 Lowell Elementary registration card she entered his father's name as Dave, occupation, upholsterer, though Allan still bore the family name Copelon. More interesting is how Rose answered the question of her and Dave's nationality. When she first registered Allan at Lowell in May 1933, Rose and Percy's nationality was "U.S." In September 1935, Rose identified herself and Dave as Jewish.

Rose's Jewish identification did not last long, but Allan was about to begin the most Jewish year of his life. He spent his entire seventh grade year, from September 16, 1935, until June 14, 1936, in Chicago with his grandparents Leon and Esther Sherman at 3219 W. Division Street, a street that was the neighborhood's Jewish commercial center, home to the restaurants Moishe Pippic, Brown and Koppel, and Itzkovitz; the Deborah Boys' Club; and Ceshinsky's Book Store, and just a block from the 207-acre Humboldt Park, where Jewish family and immigrant clubs and other organizations gathered alongside the swimmers and ballplayers, and where Jews symbolically tossed away their sins on Rosh Hashanah. This whole Jewish world that Sherman's mother rejected was now his to discover and enjoy, and he did. It was the year he became familiar with the typical experiences, language, and behavior of American Jews. He basked in the attention of his grandparents, learned to speak some Yiddish and understand more, enjoyed regular meals of traditional Jewish cooking, and rediscovered his many relations on both the Sherman and Coplon sides of the family. As he wrote in his autobiography,

At Grandma's big Friday-night family dinners she would prepare a roast duck or a roast chicken, and there was chopped liver and soup with kasha or kreplach, and vegetables and honey cake and tea. It's unbelievable how my family could eat. Right up to dinnertime, we'd be in the parlor hollering and arguing and insulting each other, my mother, her sister Katie, her brother Maury, various aunts and uncles and great-aunts and great-uncles; but as soon as Grandma said, "Come, eat!" the arguments ceased.

Sherman's school year in Chicago was even better than this raucous dinner scene. In 1935–36, his mother was in Los Angeles meeting and nabbing her third or perhaps fourth but definitely last husband, and Allan had his grandparents and his mother's aunts and uncles and cousins to himself. Sherman thrived in this environment. His grandparents had been difficult people who put their own children through the wringer. Their son Morris became alcoholic. But in 1935 Leon was fifty-five, Esther was fifty-two, and the battles of an earlier time were long ago won or lost. Grandma's poker playing and grandpa's drinking now made them charming, colorful characters, at least in the eyes of their American grandson. Best of all, they loved him, and he formed an especially strong attachment to his grandmother. Esther supplied Allan with food and love, and the two were not easily distinguishable. "My grandma's love for her family was expressed in the magnificent foods she cooked for us," Sherman wrote. This is certainly how Sherman's gluttony began, from a time when food meant love. Things were different at home with his mother. "I never knew Rose to cook," Golden said. No wonder Sherman said of his Grandma Esther, "I loved her very much and I would have done anything for her." If his 1930 departure from Chicago was a Jewish family paradise lost, his 1935 return was paradise regained.

Grandpa Leon took his grandson to the Division Street Baths where naked Jews had sweated and soaked since 1906, and also to the Yiddish theater, where Allan saw the overwrought melodramas that are best forgotten by those who want to brag about the cultural tastes of immigrant Jews. As Sherman recalled, "the Yiddish theater doesn't bother with subtleties or psychological nuances. It concerns itself with the big things of life: birth and death and marriage and incurable illness and infidelity and illegitimate babies. And the point is that every Yiddish play includes all these things — otherwise the audience would walk out in the middle, because they didn't come there to see a lot of trivialities." This is not much of an exaggeration. The standard fare included "stories of abandoned wives, estranged American children, neglected parents." These were the popular *shund*, or trash, plays that Jewish intellectuals attacked but many enjoyed, and in his future entertainments Sherman sided with the many.

School at Lowell was also a success. His conduct, scholarship, and interest were all rated satisfactory, and hints emerged of his future songwriting career. Teachers recognized his special aptitude in poetry. Math was a problem, though Sherman later exhibited a talent for it. He might not have been developmentally ready for the seventh-grade curriculum. When he started the year he was only ten years old and would not have been out of place in the fifth grade. Rose changed his age, Golden said, just as Esther had done to her, and Sherman would always be young for his grade.

One of the most important outcomes of the year was that Sherman discovered a way to distance himself from his mother and, in his own mind, dominate her. He developed the classic earmarks of the "grandfather complex," which through identification with the grandparents allows a child to view his parents as his children. Sherman wrote this way about Rose when he called her a "beautiful little thing," and this superior position allows a child to "act out its hostilities toward its own parents." Few children have a shortage of that commodity, and few had more reason to have more of it than Sherman. When he returned to Los Angeles in June 1936, his mother gave him one more.

Rose Meets Her Match

"Dave Segal was a small-time con artist," said Syril Gilbert. "Some people thought he was nice looking." Vivian Mailand was one of them. "Dave Segal was quite good looking, in a bootleggery kind of way. To me he looked like a bootlegger." Golden agreed with that description. "Dave Segal was just like you imagine, like George Raft in the movies. He looked like a gangster, the way he dressed, conducted himself." When Dee was told that Segal sounded like a tough guy she did not hesitate. "He *was* a tough guy."

He was also a charmer. "People liked him. He was charismatic, friendly, helpful to people," said Rose and Segal's daughter, Sherry Segal. "He had a charisma that could easily draw people in, that allowed him to do some of the crooked things he did."

Dave Segal, aka Sam Bass, aka Ben Bass, was perhaps not so small time. After his death, Miami banker Lou Poller, who was said to have laundered money for Jimmy Hoffa and the Teamsters, told the newspapers, "Segal has hooked more friends on phony deals than anyone I know. He'd take your eye teeth. As far as I am concerned, he was the foremost con man in the United States."

Rose Sherman married Segal in Los Angeles on May 10, 1936. Chester Napier Redmond, a Christian clergyman, performed the ceremony, but that was the least of it. Segal was not yet divorced from his first wife and Rose was pregnant. So when Allan left Chicago and moved back to Los Angeles, the eleven-year-old found his mother part of a family unit that was complete without him. He had left a Jewish family that loved him for a nominally non-Jewish one that apparently did not. Here was one more reason to identify with the Jewish world of his grandparents that Rose rejected. There was no better revenge than to become what his mother tried to put behind her, a Sherman. But for the time being he had no choice but to become Allan Segal.

His new stepfather fit the pattern of Rose's earlier husbands. Like Jacob Carp, Segal was born in London, and at five feet eleven inches and 190 pounds he was a powerful man, like Percy, whom even during their divorce Rose described admiringly as "a strong and healthy man." Segal was born on December 4, 1905, to Russian Jewish parents, Isaac and Sarah Segalowitz, and the family immigrated to Chicago in 1906. By 1908 the family name was Segal, and in 1912 Dave was the fourth of seven children. The family lived in the Humboldt Park area at 2004 West Division Street, not far from Rose Sherman's family. The Segals remained in that Chicago neighborhood for the next twenty years, and it seems impossible that they and the extended Sherman-Lustig family did not know or know of each other. When Segal was eight, his mother, Sarah, died in childbirth on March 30, 1914. It is not clear whether the child survived. Dave never forgot his mother and, because of her, retained one traditional Jewish practice. He named his daughter Sherry for her.

In 1930, the twenty-four-year-old Segal was arrested three times, once for larceny and twice for unspecified confidence games. He was single, living with his father and stepmother, and working in the family's shoe store while obviously looking to cut corners and make some easy money. He found it in the marriage game. It took advantage of his charm and good looks and was even legal. He made it part of his con man career. Segal married five times. His first marriage shows how it worked.

Helen Toppel, née Mandel, was married to Louis Toppel, and in 1930 they lived with their two daughters, Phyllis, seven, and Bertha, three, and Louis's brother Morris at 3074 Palmer Square, directly across from Chicago's seven-acre Palmer Park, a tranquil neighborhood green designed in 1905 by the great architects of American parks, the Olmsted Brothers. It was an upscale neighborhood, and the Toppel family's neighbors included doctors and others that owned their homes, worth on average about $20,000. The Toppels rented for $95 a month. Louis worked in a malt store. But they were still able to afford a live-in German maid named Johanne Oltmanns.

Helen divorced her husband and on October 3, 1932, married Segal. On August 16, 1933, she gave birth to their son, Fred. Helen had walked away from her marriage with $30,000, a fortune of money during the Depression, and Segal used some of it to make good on checks he had forged and invested the rest without telling his wife how or where. He also beat her. By September 22, 1935, when the couple separated and Helen sued for divorce, they were living in Los Angeles. She was left to her own devices to support herself and her three children. Segal claimed his net worth was zero.

When Segal married Rose on May 10, 1936, it was not clear who was conning whom. Rose had no money, and Segal had his ex-wife's money squirreled away somewhere. But no matchmaker could have found two people better suited to each other. Their marriage certificate is a kind of deception contest. It is not easy to determine who is the greater liar. Dave was thirty. He claimed to be thirty-six. Rose was thirty-two but said she was twenty-nine. Dave's divorce would not come through until February 1937, so he said he was single and his marriage to Rose was his first. This was, at a minimum, Rose's third wedding, but she listed it as her second. Rose stuck to her story that she was born in Chicago. Dave was happy to tell the truth about his birth in London.

Less than eight months later on January 1, 1937, Rose gave birth to Sheldon Harvey Segal. Sheldon was born in Cedars of Lebanon Hospital. It was popular with the Los Angeles Jewish community. Almost every week the local *B'nai B'rith Messenger* announced the births of Jewish children there, but it never announced Sheldon. As with Allan, Rose's philosophy seemed to be that her having a Jewish background was one thing, but having Jewish children was something else again.

Witz-Krieg!

After graduating ninth grade from John Burroughs Junior High, Sherman entered Fairfax High in Los Angeles as a sophomore in September 1938, when the school's twenty-eight acres of buildings and grounds were a glorious tribute to the California version of the American dream. The school opened in 1924. It was named for Lord Fairfax of colonial Virginia, and its first principal desired to make the school "American and Democratic." The students were aligned with this sentiment and christened the student body the Colonials. A 1,400-seat auditorium was added in 1926, and 1927 saw sunken gardens and a fountain, a fine arts building and a gymnasium. Groves of trees shaded the walks and benches around the school, and archways framed views of the nearby hills. The Segals lived only 1.4 miles away at 160 North Alta Vista, just down the street from 451, where Rose's aunt, Anna Strowiss, lived with her husband and two children. The Strowiss family moved to Los Angeles in 1937 to join Rose and also Anna's brother, Abe Lustig, and his family.

It was a moment that combined an ideal situation, location, and education, and Sherman blossomed. In the fall of 1938 his Fairfax transcript's Merit Record was a 93, and in the spring of 1939 it was 100. But this stability lasted only one year. Shortly after Allan began his junior year, chaos erupted. On November 22, 1939, the day before Thanksgiving, Dave Segal was arrested in Beverly Hills for passing bad checks. Three months later, in February 1940, the Segals disappeared.

Fairfax High records reveal that the administration could not cope with the Segals. Notes contradict each other. According to one entry, on March 1, 1940, Allan attended school in Ohio. No city or school is mentioned, but a high school photograph of Sherman was taken at an Olan Mills Studio in Springfield, Ohio. On March 19, Fairfax records have Sherman at Chicago's Tuley High School. In June, he was spotted in Florida at Miami Senior High School. A Miami High permanent record card confirms this, but Miami believed the last high school Allan attended was Chicago's Amundsen, not Tuley. Allan started at Miami High on May 2, 1940, and was there until the school year ended on June 14. During those six weeks he did well, scoring in the high 80s and low 90s in English, Civics, and Latin.

After this whirlwind of activity and confusion that saw Allan Segal attend four high schools in Los Angeles, Ohio, Chicago, and Miami in just five months, he was back at Fairfax in September 1940 for the start of his senior year. But something had changed. His months on the road with his mother and Segal were transformative. He returned as someone new named Allan Sherman.

The new name announced that Allan was against everything that surrounded him and for everything that his mother threw away. It meant down with down with Fairfax's colonial Americanism, perfect English, Dave Segal, and especially his mother Rose. It meant up with Jewishness, mangled English, Grandpa Leon and especially Grandma Esther. It announced Allan's independence from his mother and her various husbands and signaled that his true parents were the parents she rejected. The Sherman name was a declaration of war, and that is the way Allan seems to have understood it. When he got back to Fairfax he launched a humor column under his new name in the school's weekly *Colonial Gazette* newspaper. It was called "Witz-Krieg."

The title betrays an interest in puns and threatens a comic bombardment. Sherman poured himself into it and experimented with humor and wordplay, throwing into this juvenile grab bag everything from Ogden Nash's nonsense poetry to inside jokes and insults and comic complaints. In one bit of poetry that delivered on the promise and threat of the *Witz-Krieg* name, Sherman playfully lambasted an anonymous moviegoer who ruined his enjoyment.

> The curse of Achmed be upon
> the headgear-maker's son
> Who made the hat that sat ahead
> and spoiled the evening's fun.
> And for the wearer of the thing
> (I wish I knew her name)
> May all her sons be daughters,
> is the curse that I proclaim.

He also composed rhymes with a sexual theme, but now without the innocent act he donned in junior high. *The Physics Student's Valentine* joins childish wit to language that is sophisticated and surprisingly fresh. It also successfully gets across the writer's unabashed fascination with the female figure.

> I love you for your sweet inertia,
> For it I'd follow you to Pertia;
> And for your great acceleration,
> And for your radius of gyration!

The only thing keeping it from perfection is the exclamation point.

"Witz-Krieg" features only a few Jewish references, and the rare Jewish themes are dealt with obliquely. On the eve of the Second World War, Americanism muted ethnicity. In one piece of doggerel Sherman complains about the state of American humor, but doesn't make his complaint plain. He wrote that reading the works of Samuel Clemens brings on "something similar to delirium tremens." O. Henry and Ogden Nash bring on afflictions.

> I also imagine that at a party
> All present would be bored with these members of the literarty,
> As it is probably true that Charles Chaplin
> Has never read "The Education of Hyman Kaplan."
> And other such facts too numerous to mention
> Should be brought to the public's attention.
> And so, whether you are a nobody or a somebody,
> You ought to be as disgusted as I am with American humor,
>   including the musical comebody.

This is an early cry for cultural diversity. The problem with American humor is that it is not Jewish enough. Chaplin's crime is not reading *The Education of Hyman Kaplan*, Leo Rosten's 1937 novel about a Jewish immigrant's comic determination to resist the tyranny of proper English. The book celebrates Kaplan's broken English, which he delivers in a heavy Yiddish accent.

Sherman demands that this American humor problem "be brought to the public's attention." He was talking to himself. He had found his calling.

TWO
COLLEGE IN SEX ACTS (PRINTER'S ERROR)

In the fall of 1941, Sherman wrote a letter to the editor of his college newspaper decrying the lack of a student humor magazine. The University of Illinois had one once, but it had folded four years before. Sherman heard it was considered too risqué. That was more than he could bear. He was just one month into his freshman year and not yet seventeen years old when he opened fire in the October 8 *Daily Illini* with, "And had the judges of the *Siren* read the *Harvard Lampoon*, or the *Yale Record*, or the *California Pelican*? And had the judges of the *Siren* read *The New Yorker*, or *Esquire* magazines?"

This was quite a how-do-you-do. He defended his demand for the return of the *Siren* with the obligatory, "obscenity, as such, has no business on a campus," but a careful reader might have wondered what the vague qualifier, "as such," would allow Sherman to get away with, especially as it was followed by a plea for the college to embrace "broadmindedness." Over the next several years, the school found out. Sherman wrote an *Illini* column and packed it with satire, parody, wisecracks, fictional football games and apropos-of-nothing references to the Moscow Art Theater. He dreamed up student stunt shows that featured a song parody about the murder of Leon Trotsky, an obscene version of an English folktale, and salutes to the 4Fs unqualified for military service. Sherman ripped apart the custom of "pin hanging" that saw a coed wearing a college man's fraternity pin as a sign of intention to marry, instead of a license to have sex, and his "Don't Take My Pin" parody of "Don't Fence Me In" became an official song of the local Sigma Alpha Mu (SAM) chapter of the national Jewish fraternity. Sherman became a campus celebrity and, based on his dean's disciplinary file, a marked man. He never graduated from the University of Illinois.

"Sherman was so bright, he was ahead of all of us," said Arte Johnson, the comic actor best known for his roles on the 1960s *Rowan & Martin's Laugh-In* television show. "We were children compared to him. He was my hero."

His inventive wit and charm won him friends and fans, but Sherman's condescending letter to the editor also announced the arrival of a troublemaker, and in a movie version the dean would look up from the *Daily Illini* and give his assistant the nod that means, yes, watch him. The University of Illinois was founded in 1867 as one of the original public land-grant colleges made possible by the 1862 Morrill Act, signed into law by President Lincoln, and its location in Urbana-Champaign put it roughly equidistant from Chicago, St. Louis, and Indianapolis. But despite being born in Chicago, Sherman was no Midwesterner. "Allan was different," said Bruce Clorfene, a college friend. "He was very honest, outspoken. Most of the fellas did not like him."

That was because he emerged from his chaotic childhood and adolescence as a jesting, sexual, cynical, literate, Jewish kid on the make eager to enter show business or journalism. In the Midwest, those traits made him a virtual New Yorker. All of Rose's attempts to assimilate had backfired. Her son was not just Jewish, but a Jewish *type*.

Starting in the 1930s, New York Jews fanned out across the country to attend college where tuitions were cheaper and the competition from other Jewish students less intense. Midwest Jews came to know their New York counterparts, and familiarity bred contempt. New York Jews "look down on the mid-westerner," wrote a Hillel director at the University of Wisconsin. They are "obnoxious," chimed in a Hillel official at Illinois. The descriptions fit Sherman when he did not bother to turn on the charm. "He was aloof from the guys in the SAM fraternity house," said fraternity brother Sherman Wolf. It could be worse than that. "If he didn't respect you, you were nothing. Nothing," Clorfene said.

The University of Illinois was not his first choice. Sherman applied to the University of Chicago with the help of a recommendation letter from one of his Fairfax High School teachers, and according to the farewell-to-seniors edition of his high school newspaper he was headed to Columbia University's Pulitzer School of Journalism. This may have been boasting or keeping up appearances. His crucial junior year of high school was spent on the run. Besides, Chicago and Columbia were expensive, and both schools curtailed Jewish enrollment. Chicago limited Jews to their proportion in the Chicago area, which prevented it from becoming a "Semitic school," which the university thought would repel ambitious Jews and non-Jews alike. At Columbia, a study of the Jewish quota found that its limit on Jewish enrollment made even "Harvard's restrictions moderate in comparison."

Sherman had aimed higher, but Illinois allowed him to be a bigger fish than he might have been at Chicago and Columbia. His letter to the editor sniffed at Illinois as a backwater, but in that sniff he seems to have caught a whiff of opportunity. The campus was his for the taking. "His brightness and energy are what I remember," said Dr. Henry Swain, who worked with Sherman on the *Daily Illini*. "He was popular almost as a phenomenon. He was so good people were proud to know him." In the fall of 1941, Illinois admitted 2,911 freshmen, and Sherman placed in the top 2.5 percent by becoming one of only 74 students to test out of taking Rhetoric 1. By the end of October he was on the Operating Committee of the Illini Union building and a member of the men's debating team, and by the spring of 1942 his debating activity won him entry to the honorary Tomahawk society. He also began accumulating press clippings. On February 19, 1942, the *Daily Illini* reported that "Al Sherman, natural born comedian, will be master of ceremonies" at the Freshman Frolic. The comedy revue was the first floor show to open at the new Illini Union, which together with the *Daily Illini* newsroom became Sherman's college haunts, his platforms, his stages, and his bullhorns.

The *Daily Illini*'s "Campus Scout" column was a roundup of student gossip and news about the dating and sports scenes. Names were named, and to help ensure a loyal following, the first two readers to present the column at the local Rialto movie theater box office entered gratis. Sherman became a regular Scout columnist in March 1942 and made some changes. "First 29 readers to present this item to the backstage door of the Moscow Art theater will be given two front row seats." News of pin hangings continued to be a Scout staple, but now a smirk replaced the gee-whiz earnestness. "Since there are few, if any, pin hangings this weekend, we will continue the policy of mentioning as many names as possible in the Scout by listing the names of all those who have sent their laundry home this semester."

Before his freshman year was over Sherman befriended and collaborated with fellow comic and future Emmy Award–winning television writer Sheldon Keller, who in the 1950s worked on Sid Caesar's "Caesar's Hour." On May 15, 1942, they presented what the *Daily Illini* called "a refreshing five minutes of jokes and gags" to a crowd of approximately four thousand at the Huff Gymnasium, where the graduating seniors had their send-off. The same month Sherman appeared on the "Ten Top Men" list in the *Hillel Post*. His winning attribute was humorist, but he was at least attractive enough to appear on the same page linked romantically — perhaps only tenuously — to an Audrey Offenberg. Sherman's celebrity star was rising, though his freshman grades were average. He was not included on the published list of freshman honor roll students. "An Introduction to Literature" was his only A for the year.

But it was a nonacademic weakness that would catch up with him later. Since junior high Sherman had marshaled his wit and verbal facility to overcome the social handicap of being overweight, but the Second World War made fitness a matter of patriotism. In the fall of 1942, the university library mounted an exhibit on exercise "in keeping with the present day trend toward nation-wide physical fitness." That was not a trend that caught Sherman's interest. He got a D in wrestling.

If not his physique, his writing and jokes were winning him fame and women. The only tin note Sherman struck in his column freshman year came when he was forced to acknowledge the arrival of Mother's Day. The prospect defeated his wit. He closed his April 26, 1942, Scout column with the desultory, "the most important thing about Mothers day weekend, May 1, 2, and 3, will be the appearance on campus of some really swell people . . . our mothers."

Return of Copelon

At the start of Sherman's freshman year, Rose Segal, her husband Dave and their four-year-old son, Sheldon, lived in Chicago at 511 Aldine Avenue on the city's so-called Gold Coast, just a half-block from Lake Michigan. Crucially, their apartment building was east of Broadway, on the posh side of that dividing line. This suited Rose's pretensions. It was also within walking distance of two prominent Chicago synagogues that Rose would later claim to have patronized, though Golden does not believe it. "Nobody [in the family] belonged to a synagogue," she said. But despite deep ambivalence about her Jewish identity, Rose chose to live in one of Chicago's upscale Jewish neighborhoods. Three blocks to the north, facing the lake, was Temple Sholom, a Reform community housed in a 1928 Moorish-Byzantine temple that could accommodate more than two thousand worshippers during the High Holidays. Anshe Emet, aligned with the more traditional Conservative movement, was about the same distance away on North Broadway. Rose must have perceived that Allan was fond of her parents' Jewishness, and his own, and calculated that synagogue affiliation — whether real or invented — might pay off. She was right. In 1945, Sherman would marry at Anshe Emet. That the Segals resided near these synagogues and also had a son at the University of Illinois completed a picture of upper-middle-class Jewish respectability.

It was a great cover. The Segals left California to evade Dave Segal's ex-wife, Helen, and her attempts to collect the $40 a month in child support that Segal had never paid since their 1936 divorce. By October 5, 1941, Segal owed her $2,720. Helen tried to collect the money through the courts, but according to her sworn statement, "immediately after rendition of the decree [Segal] fled to Chicago and engaged in the liquor business."

Chicago was a good place for Dave and Rose to regroup. They both had family there, and Segal probably had criminal connections in the city. But whatever advantages it offered were offset by their constitutionally unbalanced lives. By the end of Allan's freshman year, Dave and Rose were off the Gold Coast and back in their old Humboldt Park neighborhood at 1542 North Kedzie Avenue. Segal's liquor business also brought problems. On December 14, 1943, the *Chicago Daily Tribune* reported that the previous night Segal was at Royale Liquors when it was robbed. Two armed men took $458 and then forced Segal into the storage refrigerator, which they barred with beer cases so he couldn't get out. A customer later freed him. That was the official story, anyway. Bruce Clorfene knew Segal during these years. "He opened a tavern. What else he did was not known," Clorfene said. "He was a rough guy, rough guy. Tough Jewish hoodlum."

Rose and Segal were only half of Sherman's parent problem. In August 1942, Rose sent Sherman to Birmingham, Alabama, to visit and get money from the other half, his father, Percy Copelon.

Rose's return to Chicago put her back in touch with her ex-husband Percy's family. His brother Abraham still practiced dentistry in the city, and when Sherman spent the 1935–36 school year in Chicago with his grandparents he had become friendly with his cousin Morris, Abraham's youngest son. These connections brought Rose interesting news. "Allan's mother found out, from a visiting relative, that Percy had become a successful businessman," said Percy's niece, Louise Goldstein Cole.

Percy put his talent for cars and machines back to work in 1937 when he founded, with partner Dwight M. Sandlin, the Magic City Armature Works. It was one of three companies in the Birmingham area to specialize in the rewinding of armatures, the spindles in motors and generators that are tightly wrapped in copper wire to carry an electric current. The business prospered, and in 1938 the Birmingham City Directory listed the Magic City name in boldface type, a more expensive option. The operation was at a new and larger address, too, and it had a telephone number, then a luxury service. Percy also had a new partner. Sandlin was out, replaced by Flora Mae Mulkin, Percy's new non-Jewish common-law wife. Alabama recognizes common-law marriage, and it was a convenient way for the two to marry without a ceremony, civil or otherwise, that was sure to involve and upset family. Percy's mother died on December 6, 1933, but his religiously observant father, Moses, lived until October 21, 1939, and so was still alive when Percy took up with Flora.

By the time Allan arrived in Birmingham in August 1942, there was one more change in his father's life. Percy and Flora were parents to Hilda, an eight-month-old girl they adopted. Just like his mother, his father had formed a new family with a new spouse and child, and both of his parents chose partners divorced from Jewish life.

"My mother said that all of the relatives welcomed Allan with open arms," wrote Jackie Sheinberg of Sherman's Birmingham visit. "They could not do enough for him. Uncle Percy and Aunt Flo bought him clothes, a tuxedo (he needed for something), and a car." Sherman's new clothes were ordered from Loveman's, one of Birmingham's finest department stores.

The visit was fine, but its aftermath was ugly. Sherman wrote that Percy promised to help him with college expenses if he carried the Copelon name. The demand was ironic, since Copelon was Rose's invention, but Sherman agreed and on September 24, 1942, his "Campus Scout" byline read "By Allan Copelon (Formerly Allan Sherman)." The change was widely enforced. Every mention of Sherman in the *Daily Illini*, *Hillel Post*, and the *Satyr*, a new satiric weekly (Sherman's call for its existence paid off), called him Allan Copelon. Sherman claimed he sent his father the clippings but never received any money, or even a reply. Soon he had the depressing opportunity to observe more typical father-son relationships. October 24 was the university's Dad Day, when more than nine hundred fathers arrived on campus to visit their students. In his Dad Day column Sherman vented his emotions with bitter humor. "As Glaugus Bleevitch, prominent BMOC on campus (redundant, but it takes up space) said to his pater on the old boy's arrival, 'I'll be glad when you're Dad you rascal you.'"

A week later there was trouble. Sherman did not write his October 31 column because, a replacement wrote, he had "dashed to Chicago." Then on November 12, Allan Copelon used his Scout column to reclaim the name he gave himself as a senior in high school. It was his final break with his father. Allan's last name was Sherman, but it was not what is commonly called a family name. He was the only one. The name changing episode amounted to just about the worst college student moment since *Hamlet*, and it had many of the same elements: no father, loose mother, criminal stepfather, and a bright, wordy, and immature son at the center of it all apparently ready to throw in the towel. "My God, my own father doesn't care whether I live or die," Sherman wrote of Percy's broken promise to help him pay for college. A few months later Sherman joined the army.

Don't Burn Down Bidwell's

If his enlistment was Sherman's wartime flirtation with a death wish, it ended in farce, not tragedy, but the self-destructive streak was real. It first became prominent in college and contributed mightily to his death shortly before he turned forty-nine. "He was his own worst enemy," said Bill Hamer, a SAM brother. "Heavy smoker, asthma, overweight." And Sherman did not forget about alcohol. "He drank the popular drink of the day, Southern Comfort," said Clorfene. "He drank a lot of it." Many of his problems originated with his mother and the disordered life she thrust on him. "It disturbed him a lot that his mother married often," recalled college buddy Larry Stewart. "College was a respite for him. He could settle down without the family problems. He almost found a new family there." But he could not find a new self that he liked better than the original. "He didn't like the way he looked. He didn't like that he was short and fat, yet he couldn't do anything about it," said Clorfene. "He was self-hating but he covered it up with a huge ego act."

The weight issue may have been partly genetic. "Everybody in his family was fat," Golden said. "Rose, his aunts, uncles, everybody." Sherman's father also became obese. Still, Sherman abetted any natural tendency to heaviness with a gluttonous appetite. Clorfene and Sherman and mutual friend Howard Weinstein sometimes went to a local restaurant where they could order T-bone steaks after midnight. "We would cut the fat off our steaks and he would eat the fat from ours, and his own," Clorfene said. Overeating was the most obvious symptom of Sherman's self-destructiveness, and it worked its way into several of his songs, including "Hail to Thee, Fat Person," "Little Butterball," and "Overweight People," a parody of "Over the Rainbow."

The Birmingham visit, subsequent name change, and his father's betrayal put Sherman's academic career on a downhill trajectory, but before he hit bottom he did some of his best comedy work. The Percy incident seems to have released him from any restraints, and Sherman gave in to himself fully. It was a trick he would reprise twenty years later when in 1962 he wrote his chart-topping *My Son, the Folk Singer* album material in a matter of weeks after being fired from the Steve Allen television show. In the fall of 1942, he wrote his twice-weekly "Campus Scout" column for the *Daily Illini*, a weekly column for the new *Satyr*, penned and performed a song parody that made him a campus celebrity, wrote an original student musical, and pinned one of the most desirable Jewish coeds on campus. He chuckled at the pinning custom's pretense as a step toward marriage, but he was not about to abstain from a practice that sanctioned sexual activity. The only problem was he was still enrolled in classes, which in all the excitement seems to have slipped his mind. Sherman could never restrict himself to one activity. At the end of his first sophomore semester he earned a B in English and Cs in everything else, including classes he should have found interesting and easy, such as journalism, psychology, and rhetoric.

But even more interesting and easy was the world of song. On September 5, 1942, in the first Scout column of his sophomore year, he was excited to recommend the new Bing Crosby film *Holiday Inn* and its Irving Berlin songs, especially "Be Careful, It's My Heart," an instant standard recorded by Frank Sinatra, Tony Bennett, and Rosemary Clooney. Sherman's first Jewish song parodies would be send-ups of Broadway musicals, and they grew out of his deep knowledge and admiration for the great works of the American song-book. During college he sometimes took his future wife to record stores to listen to songs "over and over again," Golden said. It was not fun and games. Sherman was studying, and at Illinois he would soon write his first parodies of popular songs and musicals. His devotion to the great songwriters never abated. "He played records again and again and again" until he knew the lyrics, the rhyme pattern, the style of diction, everything, recalled his son, Robert Sherman. "He had an enormous background."

Berlin's delicate brand of wooing impressed Sherman with its craft, but it did not reflect his approach to life or love. His style was earthier, and in his September 10 column he shared ideas gleaned from his Birmingham visit, which included a side trip to the University of Alabama. These included rent-a-car places on campus "to facilitate dating... drinks served in two glasses, one full of cracked ice, so that by filling the ice with the beverage every now and then, the drinks last quite some time," and Southern fried chicken.

Seduction, drinking, and eating make a pretty fair checklist of Sherman's Dionysian obsessions, but seduction was the first among equals. He knew what pin hanging was said to be for, and what it was for. "There are, if one is broad

minded enough to realize the fact, several reasons for the hanging of fraternity pins. One of these is engagement. The others this columnist is extremely
eager to discuss thoroughly with any inquisitive reader." The reappearance of
"broad minded" confirms it as a codeword for sex, but Sherman's real subject is
honesty, reality. His enemies were falseness and pretense, and Sherman battled
them with laughter. Pin hanging adhered to a clichéd formula he was happy to
do in. "Required: one moon, beaming joyfully down upon the snow-covered
(or leaf ridden, or dew-saturated, or corpse littered) campus." The moon had
another job, too. "The moon must be shining through something. Through
the clouds, maybe, or through the branches of a tree, or through the wash of
the old lady who lives next door."

Jewish dialect humor was another way to deflate pretension, and while
Sherman did not make prominent use of it during his college years it was on
a low simmer, not extinguished. On October 17, he used his "Scout" column
to publish a comic murder mystery called, "'The Off-tackle Murder,' or 'Dead
End,' a play in two gasps." The football hero is a character named Shtilenkowitz,
who plays for Notre Dame. "Shore 'an I thot that last play was bein' a touch-
down," Shtilenkowitz says to his Notre Dame coach. Then in an aside to the
reader the athlete continues in a very different brogue. "Two Notre Dame plays
I'm prektissing and hallreddy I'm gatting a Hirish heksent." Sherman loved the
comic possibilities of his grandparents' Yiddish-accented English. "He would
call up frat houses and say he was someone's grandfather," Hamer said. "In a
Jewish accent he would say, 'Is bubeleh there? This is his grandfather. I'm at
the station. Can someone come pick up bubeleh's grandfather?'"

None of his witticisms, however, won him the celebrity that followed his
first Illinois song parody. On Saturday evening, October 10, 1942, Sherman,
still in the midst of his Copelon period, was a featured performer in the university stunt show, one of the headline events of Homecoming weekend. He
won first prize in the single acts category and grabbed the lead the next day in
the *Daily Illini*'s front-page recap. "It was laugh, laugh at the Stunt show last
night with Al Copelon '45," who performed "his incomparable imitations and
his rendition of his latest lyric, 'Don't Burn Down Bidwell's!'" The *Hillel Post*
named Sherman its man of the year for the song and noted the fat head he was
getting from all the attention when it referred to him as "Al (Just Call Me a

Genius) Copelon." Bidwell's was a popular student watering hole renowned for its dimly lit backroom, popular with couples. Sherman's song about it parodied the Dixieland classic, "Won't You Come Home Bill Bailey," a tune he would borrow again in 1962 for his Jewish, "Won't You Come Home Disraeli?"

> Burn down that Union Building,
> Burn Lincoln Hall,
> But, please, boys, don't burn down Bidwell's!
> Burn down the football stadium
> Huff Gym as well,
> But, please, boys, don't burn down Bidwell's!
> We know you love this campus, we think it's swell,
> You can burn it till it flames like hell!
> But if that backroom's found in flames,
> We're gonna call you dirty names,
> So don't burn Bidwell's down!

The parody displays the talent that later impressed New York Philharmonic pianist Leonid Hambro, who befriended Sherman in New York in the 1950s. "Sherman was an extraordinary talent. He was unequalled in working with words, their meaning and rhythm. One of the most difficult things is to write words to music." Sherman's "Bidwell's" lyric was a triumph and proved his gift, but it also slyly expressed Sherman's rage. The 1940s were not the 1960s. It was not an era of campus and inner-city anger, of burn, baby, burn, but it was such an era for Sherman. He wrote this at the height of his anger toward his father, and surely toward his mother, as well, who sent him down to Alabama. Rather than risk a blow to the cranium for his impertinence, Sherman found a funny way to send the world the grim message he wanted to see it burn.

The Lover Type

An exception was the Jewish friendships Sherman found at precisely the moment his parents were driving him crazy. Before the 1942 summertime break, Sheldon Keller brought Sherman into the Jewish fraternity house Sigma Alpha

Mu, or SAM, whose members are known as Sammies. Sherman somehow spent freshman year living in Newman Hall, the Catholic dormitory residence. It did not suit him. "On the other hand, I felt very much at home in the SAM house."

The fraternity's undistinguished social status also helped put him at ease. Exclusive ones screened out Jews "from the wrong part of Europe," or those whose fathers had a "humble occupation, such as butchering or tailoring." The Sammies got caught up in such snobbery during the 1930s, but social condescension was never its core value. Founded in 1909 at the City College of New York, the original members flirted with the idea of founding SAM as a parody organization. The idea was to name it the Cosmic Fraternal Order, and use Hindu instead of Greek letters. A comic perspective, as Sherman realized young, aids seduction. Not surprisingly, SAM men developed a "characteristic smooth confidence in their ultimate appeal to women." Sherman caught on and founded the "Tau Lambda Tau (or TLT, The Lover Type)" society. It was a gag the *Hillel Post* viewed as one of Sherman's unattractive New York traits. "The organization is dedicated to the proposition that all women who love men like 'brothers' are 'nogoods,' as they say in Noo Yawk." But his boldness, his willingness to treat sex with sophistication and sly amusement won followers. TLT was "sweeping male circles on campus," the *Post* reported, including "the cream of the campus BMOCs, and what have you."

Sherman was just getting started, and what he did next was not fit to print in the *Hillel Post*. "Allan would stay on the phone till two or three in the morning calling the gentile sororities," said Hamer. "He would say, 'I'm doing a paper on sex on campus. Don't tell me your name.' They would tell their whole life story and he would figure out who they were. And if they were promiscuous he'd call them for a date." Sherman's calls were probably driven more by a desire to understand than to know (in the biblical sense). Gentile sororities were off limits to Jewish men. "The campus was loaded with these cute blond shiksas and we couldn't touch them," Clorfene said. "It would kill us." The phone calls must have confirmed for Sherman that what he knew about his motley band of randy Jewish relations, and himself, pertained also among the non-Jewish part of humanity. Their attractive masks and refined manners concealed the same comical human animal. He had to have known this to have the guts to go for the sexual jugular, the way Clorfene remembers he did. "'Do you want to fuck?' was what he asked when he phoned a sorority. Sometimes he had interesting conversations."

Sex is a typical college obsession, but Sherman had the presence of mind to take a step back and observe the topic with the remove required for wit. After a couple was caught fooling around in the backseat of car, Sherman wrote a fraternity stunt show about it called, "The Girl with the Golden Arm," said classmate Ed Dessen. The lyric is lost, but can be imagined. The title comes from a traditional folktale that Mark Twain wrote about in *How to Tell a Story and Other Essays*. Sherman may have read it as a freshman in his "Principles of Effective Speaking" class.

The sex theme appeared in his Scout column again on November 29 with the playlet, "Aha!" described as "A Drama in Sex Acts (Printer's Error)." By this time, Sherman was in sure possession of the knowledge that separates the sexually savvy young man from the naïf. Women like sex, too. Early in the play, Prudence, the heroine, protests too much when her would-be lover approaches. "Will no one protect me in my hour of need?" But later, in an aside, she speaks her mind. "I wonder if he will threaten my honor? Would that he would! O would!"

By this time, word had gotten out as to how Sherman knew what he knew. In the November 20 issue of the *Hillel Post*, the gossip column "The Looking Glass" reported that "Al Sherman Copelon (choose your own name) has astonished his fellow Sammies by being seen more frequently with lovely blonde Seena Minkus" than any of her other suitors. Minkus was a well-known heart-throb who in the spring of 1943 was named Hillel carnival queen, and people were astonished because Sherman was not the slim athletic handsome type. But Sherman proved that the power of Cyrano was still potent. He wooed Minkus with words. "He was very gregarious," she recalled. "He wasn't physically attractive, but I thought he was very, very bright and clever." She even accepted his fraternity pin, an act that Sherman had already jokingly defined in his column as sanctioning sexual relations. It was a clever move that reveals how Sherman connected comedy to seduction. After that column, no girl who accepted his pin could defend her honor with claims of innocence.

The relationship with Minkus ended when Sherman joined the army in March 1943, but at eighteen it was his first sustained adult relationship. His lifelong sexual compulsion began earlier, with passing sexual encounters in junior high and high school that he wrote about in his autobiography. But in college others noticed that his hunger was unusually powerful. "He was an erotic person," Clorfene said. "We talked a lot about sex. We would compare notes." Sherman and Minkus corresponded while he was in the army, and he later gave the letters to frat brother Hamer. "These letters were something to behold," Hamer said. "They were unbelievable. So poetic. So erotic. He was a very erotic man, very sensual. He was really into sensuality." Hamer's wife advised him to burn the letters.

Sherman's sexual Scout columns, Golden Arm stunt show act, and TLT society meant there was not very much broadminded material left over for the *Satyr*, the suggestively titled independent student weekly that debuted on September 8, 1942, eleven months after Sherman's letter to the editor demanded a publication like it. On the masthead of the first four issues, Sherman appeared as one of nine casual contributors, but by the fifth week he was humor editor. Eventually he was holding up the paper nearly single-handedly. In the October 5 issue, in addition to his own front-page byline for the "Sideshow" column, it is a sure bet he was also I.Q. Verylow. Two weeks later, he was B.P. Glutzfishbein and I. Feltastein, which name appeared above another Sherman playlet. "The Zeta House Murder" delivered at least one good joke. The criminal speaks first.

"It was I," she screamed, "My father was a werewolf and my mother a banshee."
"I told you girls to look up the pledges' families," chided the President.

Sherman surely felt lucky the SAM chapter did not look up his own family. In Dave and Rose Segal it would have discovered characters only slightly less monstrous.

Sherman's relationship with the *Satyr* was over by November 19. The paper, and not just his column, was a sideshow. His *Daily Illini* Scout column and his parody performances at the Illini Union were where the action was. But Sherman's time at the satiric sheet also may have been cut short because it touched a sensitive Jewish nerve. The *Satyr* featured caricatures of its columnists, and the profile sketch of Sherman made him look almost as stereotypically Jewish as the hateful Nazi propaganda of the era, with long hooked nose, thick lips, jowls, and a weak chin. Photographs show he could appear attractive or homely. In a high school portrait Sherman is slim, his face more angular than round, and he looks confident and almost dashing. But in a *Daily Illini* front-page photograph on February 19, 1943, he could pass for the heavy in a 1930s gangster movie. His nose is thick and his face communicates intelligence and power but also sadness and stewing anger. The *Satyr* emphasized his least attractive features, and it was the worst possible time for such an unflattering depiction. The most coveted compliment among Jews at that time was, "you don't look Jewish," and with the advent of Hitler and the war, college Jews avoided those "who were too stereotypically 'Jewish' in manner or appearance." Sherman braved the embarrassment by calling himself Glutzfishbein and Feltastein, but during the summer of 1944 he got his nose fixed.

He dropped the grotesque Jewish pseudonyms when he left the *Satyr*, but he held on to a Jewish viewpoint and some Jewish pain that erupted in anger in a November 26, 1942, "Scout" column that tore into Irving Berlin's now classic "White Christmas." In the fall of 1942, the song was a new hit, but it transformed Sherman into a gleefully nasty Scrooge after he felt bombarded by the song at a university sing. "It seemed as if every time there was a lull in the program (and there were many) someone got up and saved the day by singing 'White Christmas' until he was blue in the face." Sherman lost his cool in the column and became blue in the face himself. He declared he would write a protest song that would begin, "I'm dreaming of a _____ _____," and fill in the blank spaces with crazy and obscene language. "I am going to sing them loud and disrupt everyone else's fun," he wrote. "And when all the performers are sufficiently embarrassed and everyone sitting around me is looking for the word O'Sullivan printed on my face because they think I'm such a heel, I'll sit back and be satisfied." Freud wrote that comedy is disguised hostility. In this case, the hostility was so great the comedy got scared and ran away.

In the last months before Sherman enlisted in the army he emphasized his misfit nature. To support the government's Good Neighbor policy, which sought to build alliances with the nations of South America, Illinois students planned an entertainment gala with a Latin theme, called "Alice in Rhumbal-and." Sherman contributed a parody of the Andrews Sisters' 1941 hit song, "The Boogie Woogie Bugle Boy of Company B." The original tells the story of a gifted bugler who finds a place in the army "blowin' reveille," and its message is that everyone can make a contribution to the army, and the army can find a place for everyone. Sherman had his doubts. There was no way the army could make a soldier out of him. Wartime meant that every semester he took classes in Infantry Theory and Infantry Drill. He got straight Cs. So he tested the "Boogie Woogie Bugle Boy" thesis by imagining a musical soldier like himself. His parody, "The Conscientious Objector of Company Z," is about a soldier that likes to dance the rumba and the conga and is thrown into the mythical misfit group of Company Z. Sherman's hero is not a conscientious objector on moral grounds. He is a conscientious objector in that he conscientiously objects to everything about the army. In the second verse, he even flops at KP duty.

> He taught the second lieutenant to swing and to sway
> And when he started to conga they took him away
> He didn't let them have peace
> While in the kitchen police
> So they put him in Company Z.

We Are Civilians '43

On February 19, 1943, Sherman graduated from writing individual song parodies to creating an original musical. *Nothing Ventured* delivered sentimentality and patriotism within a farcical situation and triumphed. The *Daily Illini* reported that the opening night audience demanded "six curtain calls of the cast, author, and composer." If that crowd encouraged Sherman to dream of one day writing a sentimental musical comedy, it bears some responsibility for *The Fig Leaves Are Falling*, Sherman's 1969 Broadway flop. *Nothing Ventured* lampooned Hitler, Mussolini, and Hirohito as the unholy trinity who mistake Urbana for Havana and wind up at the University of Illinois. It was a twist on a common notion. The Three Stooges had already mocked Hitler in *You Nazty Spy!* and *I'll Never Heil Again*. Charlie Chaplin's 1940 film, *The Great Dictator*, is the greatest example of the genre. In *Nothing Ventured* the three dictators, with Sherman playing Hitler, introduce themselves in "The Road to Urbana," a song written to original music by Sherman's buddy, Bill Pilkenton.

This is the road to Urbana, it isn't Havana
It isn't the gay Argentine
There's no Crosby or Dottie, [Dorothy Lamour]
The show isn't naughty
But it's not the worst that you've seen.

As long as Sherman sticks to comedy, *Nothing Ventured* is fine, but he strays further off course than his dictators with three songs that offer the audience heartfelt and witless sincerity. They amount to a recantation of all his previous barbed comedy. "Once Upon a Serenade" treats tenderly the campus wooing that Sherman once roasted. "Then amid the stars on high / The moon looked down and winked his eye." The old lady's wash must have been inside. "Lovely as a Lullaby" takes a shot at Irving Berlin's romantic style. It misses. "Lovely as a lullaby / A whispered tune, a sleepy sigh." Finally, the musical's title song booms out dull patriotism. "From the plains to the sea / Our America is free."

Army life cured his sentimentality. "I hated the Army," he wrote in *Gift*. "It was too damned organized." He joined up on March 12, 1943, and spent most of his time in the Army hospital at Camp Wolters, Texas. His asthma put him out of commission, and it was aggravated by allergies to nearly everything, but he was proud to be a natural Company Z man. "I was allergic to thirty-one different things: sheep dander, horse dander, palm fronds, corned beef and Brazil nuts," and more, he boasted in his autobiography. After he was honorably discharged on May 26 with a Certificate of Disability, he returned to college and spread the allergy story around so hard that by September 30, 1943, a *Daily Illini* columnist could take it for granted that everyone knew about it. Sergeant Jack Adams wrote in the "Illini War Chant" that a new soldier signs his name so many times it even tops the number of "of Al Sherman's allergies." His asthma and ailments were crutches he leaned on, and he needed them. "When we got married his asthma went away, and then we got divorced and his asthma came back," Golden said. "It was psychological." The same might be said of his need to be overweight. He could slim down. Clorfene remembered that after his three months in the Army, Sherman was trim. But he was soon heavy again.

Because of his few months in the Army, Sherman completed only three semesters of academic work in two years, but when he started college as a junior in September 1943 he showed no interest in making up for lost time. Sherman registered for six classes, completed only four, and in three of those he received two Cs and a D. He earned his one B in expository writing. His C in "Introduction to Shakespeare" was also earned, because he must have strenuously avoided doing well. He displayed a literature lover's engagement with Shakespeare by finding comical ways to work the Bard into his Scout column. "Tomorrow, and tomorrow, and tomorrow, creeps on this petty pace from day to day. Is that a dagger that you see before you, its handle toward your hand? If so, use it to clip out this coupon." But engagement or no, Sherman would devote no more time to his coursework. "He lost interest in school," Golden said. "He'd sign up for class and not show up." He might have gotten away with it if his new policy made an exception for a one-credit course in Adapted Sports. The war made such classes a top priority, and on February 4, 1944, the Sub-Committee on Student Discipline expelled Sherman for cutting gym.

He was readmitted for the spring 1944 semester, on probation, after he petitioned the dean, but the administration did not like him and Sherman's behavior made it easy for the college to eventually bust him. All the mismatches between him and the university that Sherman so helpfully outlined in his freshman letter to the editor began to yield the predictable result.

The trouble started on September 4, 1943, when Sherman was master of ceremonies for an evening of entertainment in the Illini Union's Pine Lounge. The Dean of Students, Fred H. Turner, was in the audience and did not like something Sherman said. Or maybe it was everything. The records do not specify. But Turner had Sherman come to his office to discuss it and he wrote to social director Irene Pierson about it. She replied, "we had the same difficulty last year, and I had to request that he not be invited to return or be on another program." Sherman defended himself in a letter to Turner that addressed the recent incident and also the still festering issue from the previous year. No one wanted to repeat the offending statements, so Sherman is vague, but he did admit making "a bad mistake: I made wisecracks against the ASTP." The Army Specialized Training Program was an officer-training program for select college men.

He dutifully apologized and claimed to be "completely sincere" and "sincerely sorry," but he was not chastened. Sherman was ebullient, and he closed his letter on an eager note as he anticipated performing the new comic creations he had in mind. "It is still my hope to appear again on Club Commons, and to write another Union show, or maybe two. I have even applied for a position on the Union show committee." College had become for Sherman what New Haven was to Broadway. It was a place to try out new material, and during his last two years at Illinois he tried out plenty.

Comically reenergized by his brief experience with Army life and his own misfit nature, Sherman's first song parody of the 1943–44 school year picked up where his conga-dancing conscientious objector left off. In the fall of 1943, Sherman defended the guys who could not even cut it in Company Z. Those were the men in Sherman's outfit, the civilians, who had a lowly status in a nation at war. The best way to strike a blow for his brothers without arms was to go after the biggest target of them all, Irving Berlin's 1942 smash stage show and, by the summer of 1943, Warner Brothers film release, *This Is the Army*, and its title song, "This Is the Army, Mr. Jones." It was a chancy project. First Lady Eleanor Roosevelt loved the show, saw it on Broadway three times, encouraged its national tour, and had Irving Berlin bring it to the National Theater in Washington, D.C., on October 8, 1942, so President Roosevelt could see it. The following day, the president had the entire cast to the White House and stayed up until 1:30 in the morning to shake the hands of all 359 men in the company.

Sherman went for broke in his October 30, 1943, parody performance on Homecoming weekend, an occasion that included a night of stunt shows in the nearly two-thousand-seat auditorium put on by at least four fraternities and sororities, the navy signal school, and the local WAVES (women's reserve division of the U.S. Navy) recruiting team. Sherman appeared "draped as the 'Blue Fairy,'" an outrageous idea that, like when he dubbed himself Glutzfishbein to preempt any barbs about his Jewish looks, disarmed any potential criticism that civilians are not real men by being the first to deliver the blow. Dressed as a fairy, Sherman "sang the poetical praises of 'The Civilians of 1943' in the Sigma Alpha Mu stunt honoring four-effers on campus." The only fragment that survives is the verse Bill Hamer remembered more than sixty years later.

We are civilians '43
Poor samples of humanity
We are either blind or deaf
We're either 2B or 4F

It is a tribute to Sherman's comic intuition as much as to his skill as a parodist that the song was a hit. In the midst of a culture celebrating everything he was not, he saw an opportunity to mock that celebration and make a comic case for him and his people, the outcasts. "Sherman was a brilliant guy," said Sheldon Keller. "He could do parodies like no one else." "The Civilians of 1943" won the SAM fraternity first-place honors in what the chapter newsletter described as "one of the big events of the year." It also won the Sammies first place in the Hillel stunt show.

Sherman continued picking on great cultural monuments instead of opponents his own size with a parody of the hit musical, *Oklahoma!* The show opened on Broadway on March 31, 1943, as a joyous cornucopia of Americanism — the action culminates in Oklahoma becoming a state — that offered audiences a respite from the war while giving them a victory over evil with the death of the sinister Jud. Sherman and friend Clorfene parodied at least two numbers from the musical, including the title song, "Oklahoma!" and "Everything's Up to Date in Kansas City." The new lyrics brought the war front and center. *"Yoooooookohama, where the planes come sweeping through the wind!"* is all that remains of the title song parody, and the only thing known about the other is its outrageous title, "Everything's Up to Date in Berchtesgaden."

The send-up gave the university another reason to dislike Sherman even as it unintentionally connected the young parodist to one of the giants he enjoyed slaying. An Illinois faculty member, Olive Goldman, would not let the *Oklahoma!* parody go forward as a stunt show without permission from the composers. "Allan called New York and somehow, somehow, actually got Richard Rodgers on the phone and he said he had no problem," Clorfene said. "And Rodgers spoke to Goldman and said to her, 'Don't be an idiot.' She was absolutely floored. She was so snotty about it."

Take My Pin

The writing ambitions Sherman shared with Dean Turner were not pipe dreams, and in the spring of 1944 he wrote twelve songs for his second original musical comedy, *Mirth of a Nation*. It made him a campus star. The *Daily Illini* ran five stories about Sherman's musical before it even opened on March 11, 1944, and on March 12 the paper's front page raved, "Audience Wowed by Song Hits, Al Sherman's Second Musical Is Success." More applause came from an otherwise crabby contributor to the *University of Illinois Alumni News*, who informed readers that *Mirth* "contained real wit, good humor," and that its "gags were better than most we've heard on the professional stage this year."

Its comic premise once again has Sherman taking on the most revered icons of his day. The central character is President Roosevelt, played by Sherman, who in 1976 is considering a run for his twelfth term. Sherman's comedy songs were hits and even his love songs showed wit. In "This Is Where I Came In," the moon makes an appearance, but it is unwanted.

> Remove the sentimental music
> Don't let the sweet beguine begin
> Turn off the moon on high, the starlit sky —
> This is where I came in!

Sherman always liked to rework nursery rhymes into adult entertainment, and in "Eleanor, Eleanor," he did it to "Pussycat, pussycat, where have you been? / I've been to London to visit the Queen." The parody lampoons the First Lady's active travel schedule.

> Eleanor, Eleanor, where have you been?
> I've been to London to visit the queen
> I've been to Manchuria,
> And I can assuria
> I've been to more places than you've ever seen!

Sherman's celebrity hit its peak during this season of mirth. In April 1944 he won the Hillel "Sing," and he landed on the *Daily Illini*'s front page on June 21, 23, and 24 as emcee of the university "Sing." He did not do well academically, but at least in the spring of 1944 he got an A in Contemporary Poetry. Still, the university was intent upon getting rid of him. On May 1, the Student Discipline Committee questioned whether he was honoring his probation by showing up for gym. Professor Stafford claimed Sherman had unexcused absences. Sherman denied it. A follow-up hearing May 10 found Sherman was right. Similar charges were considered again on May 31, and on June 1 he was barred from registering for summer classes until he made up the missed gym classes. But the registrar's office goofed and Sherman was allowed to sign up for "Development of Modern Drama."

Then on July 23, 1944, at 1:35 AM, Sherman gave the discipline committee a gift. He and his then pinned girlfriend and future wife, Dolores "Dee" Chackes, together with Clorfene and his girlfriend, broke into the girls' Sigma Delta Tau sorority house to fool around. A neighbor heard the noise as Sherman and Clorfene entered through a window and called the police. Everyone was arrested, and on July 26 the discipline committee threw Sherman off campus. Rose Segal attended the hearing and pleaded for leniency, without result.

Clorfene helped Sherman land a summer job at Camp Ojibwa, a sports camp in Eagle River, Wisconsin, popular since 1928 with Jewish boys from the Chicago area. Sherman was in charge of the camp's entertainment program, and he had problems meeting deadlines even then. "Don't come back until you've written a show," is what the camp director told Sherman as he set him adrift in a canoe, remembered one former camper. Ojibwa was an odd fit for the overweight Sherman. Its manly spirit is exemplified by its yearbook, called *The Warrior*, and that culture made a lasting impression he naturally turned into comedy. In "Hello Muddah, Hello Fadduh" he sings, "And the head coach, wants no sissies / So he reads to us from something called Ulysses."

Dee was allowed to return to college in the fall of 1944. Sherman applied for readmission and was denied. He applied again and was refused again on October 3, 1944. Finally, on January 23, 1945, he was allowed to register for the spring 1945 semester.

While awaiting readmission he worked at the Chicago advertising agency of Schwimmer & Scott and wrote more parodies. One defies classification, except that it clarifies Sherman's delight in absurdities. His parody of the Irish drinking song, "The Night That Paddy Murphy Died," is about the murder of the Russian-Jewish socialist leader and revolutionary, Leon Trotsky. "We all dressed up as Russians and came up through the audience," said Arte Johnson. "People screamed because we were so wacky." Sherman took liberties with the historical record to produce a gem, and surely the only humor on the subject.

On the night that Leon Trotsky died
I never shall forget
The Russians got so stinking drunk
That some aren't sober yet.
There are some things they did that night
That gave me quite a jar.
They took the buckshot from the corpse
And called it caviar.

The Trotsky bit did not get press in the *Daily Illini* or *Hillel Post*. In the fall of 1944, Sherman was not enrolled and had no newspaper column. He was, as the Amish say, shunned, a policy that still had momentum when he came back to school, on parole, in the spring of 1945. His "Don't Take My Pin" parody of "Don't Fence Me In" received just one parenthetical mention that semester, in the March 1945 *Hillel Post*, but official neglect had no effect on the song's popularity. For the next twenty years it won fans among college men across the country. "Don't Take My Pin" was included in a collection of Alpha Sigma Phi fraternity party songs at Rutgers, New Jersey, in 1956, and it was still a favorite among Theta Chi men at Illinois Wesleyan as late as 1966.

If I should drink and you think that I'm thinking of romance
Don't take my pin
Although you're swell, what the hell, give the other girls a chance
Don't take my pin.
I know I'm the guy and there is no other, I know you'd like to take me
    home to mother
But can't you get a pin from my fraternity brother? Don't take my pin.

It was Sherman's parting shot at the custom that he lambasted but also adopted. He had pinned Seena Minkus, and in February 1944 he pinned his future wife, Dee. Sherman was attracted to her by her slim figure and dark good looks, and also because like his mother he was drawn to Jews with roots in England. "They didn't come to America with babushkas on their heads," Golden said of her family.

Her father, Emanuel Chackes, was born in Russia but arrived in London as a baby in 1885. In 1906, at age twenty-one he immigrated to America with his mother, sister, and two brothers to join his father, Alexander. The family had been in the clothing business in London and they pursued the same line of work in East St. Louis, where in 1918 the thirty-three-year-old Emanuel met twenty-year-old Theresa Silberstein, who was on a family visit from her little hometown of DeSoto, Missouri, about 45 miles away. "My mother was a beautiful, beautiful woman," said Golden. "Universally known as the prettiest woman in town." The two married, settled in DeSoto, and lived on North Main Street over the Silberstein family's general store, which became the Chackes Department Store. Dolores "Dee" Chackes was born in DeSoto on February 27, 1925, joined the girl scouts, and enjoyed a small-town American childhood foreign to most American Jews, but it was also a childhood foreign to non-Jews in DeSoto. "I lived two lives: DeSoto and St. Louis."

Dolores and her older brother, Alex, went to Jewish religious school in St. Louis every Sunday. "We caught the train at 7 AM, the Sunshine Special, that came from Texas," she said. The trip included some adventure. Dolores and her brother paid the children's half-fare rate, and as they were the only passengers waiting in DeSoto at 7 AM on Sunday morning, it did not pay for the train to come to a full stop. "The conductor and a porter leaned out and pulled us on." Alex attended B'nai Emunah and Dee went to United Hebrew Temple until her confirmation at fifteen. She developed a parallel life in St. Louis, spending weekends there with her paternal aunt and uncle. That was not the only difference between her life and that of her DeSoto friends. At home, her parents switched traditional gender roles. After a stroke, her father quit work and sat in the front yard being sociable. "He was known as a wonderful storyteller," Golden said. Her mother ran the store, and by the time Dee was sixteen she was attracted to garrulous men destined for show business. A high school boyfriend was Hugh Shannon, who went on to have a successful career as a high-end saloon singer. From the 1950s until his death in 1982, he performed in cafés and cabarets that attracted the jet set in Capri, the Virgin Islands, the

Hamptons, and New York City. In 1941, remembered Golden, "We'd neck in the car and I'd say, oh, what time is it? I've got to go to girl scouts."

Chackes entered Illinois in September 1942 and met Sherman in the fall of 1943 during Rosh Hashanah services at the university Hillel. In December 1943 the SAM chapter newsletter reported that she and Sherman were "having an on-again-off-again affair." Affair is not too strong a word. The *Hillel Post* noted that the coeds at Chackes's Sigma Delta Tau sorority had "learned many secrets about the SAM's, namely Al 'Scimitar' Sherman," and also "Corkscrew" Scher and "Left Hook" Bergman. It was not the newspaper's style to engage in sexual innuendo, so perhaps the editor did not know that the nicknames referred to the fraternity members' members.

After Sherman's summer of 1944 expulsion from college he and Dee broke up, and when he was allowed on campus for the spring 1945 semester he was back to his old sexual bravado, taking bets on "who his next pin-up girl will be." Sherman backed up his bluff with "Don't Take My Pin," a parody that transfers the original song's theme of freedom from the geographical to the matrimonial sphere.

In April 1945, Sherman and Chackes were once again pinned. It probably happened before April 11, when Sherman was kicked out of college for the last time. In May, he left for New York. He had an idea for another musical.

Three

I'VE GOT A SECRET

After getting everything he wants Sam Noodleman is miserable, and that is the moral of *The Golden Touch*. Better known as Cheesecake Sam and owner of a New York delicatessen of the same name, Noodleman curses the day he was tempted by riches and glamour to go upscale and French. He made a lot of money, yes, but is he happy serving paté? The question answers itself because, after all, what is paté? "Chopped liver! But without the chicken fat!!"

When Sherman told his college dean he wanted to write another musical, maybe two, the first was *Mirth of a Nation*. The second was *The Golden Touch*, a comic fable about the evils of Jewish assimilation that is a retelling of the Greek myth of King Midas. The musical's fumbling hero is Joe Midasovich, a Cheesecake Sam's busboy too poor to marry the girl he loves and so is easily conned into signing away his soul to the devilish Benny. He is the one who shortens Joe's last name to Midas and seduces him with visions of joining the "horsey set." In his new life, Benny tells Joe, "You're out on an open field, surrounded by your guests in formal riding regalia. Suddenly you hear the call of the hunting horn and off you gallop on your trusty steed, with the baying hounds at your side." Joe falls for it and his new power transforms everything it touches. This leads to Midas-type success and unhappiness. Cheesecake Sam's becomes Chez Kaique Sam, where instead of serving sandwiches named after the great Jewish comedians — the Milton Berle on rye, the Joe E. Lewis triple-decker — dishes are named for unhappy heiresses, such as "Sauté of Mutton a la Barbara Hutton" and "Filet of Fluke a la Doris Duke." Sam regrets that he turned his back on his background. Life was good. "Then we had to get fancy. High class!" Others that Joe made rich have the same problem. They no longer recognize themselves, they do not know who they have become, and together they sing, "Down with success."

> Success! Success!
> He wanted to be a success but it made him a mess! A mess!
> A woe is meable, Simon Lagreeable [*sic*] mess!

Joe comes to the same conclusion. He gained the money he needs to marry, but in the process lost his girl. She misses the old Joe. At the close of the play, he goes back to being Joe Midasovich and working at Cheesecake Sam's, but now as a waiter, a job that earns him just enough to marry.

Sherman cowrote *The Golden Touch* in 1947 in New York with Bud Burtson, a comedy songwriter who commanded as much as $1,500 for the three-minute songs he sold to clients such as jokester Jerry Lester. Sherman could not write music and would always need a composer partner for original tunes, but he was fluent in the argumentative, rapid, and emphatic speech that makes the distinctive New York delivery a Jewish language. His *Golden Touch* characters shout and argue like natives. The style probably "represents the influence of conversational norms of East European immigrants," and Sherman picked that up from his immigrant grandparents. He made it part of his persona, and the Illinois *Hillel Post* correctly associated it with "Noo Yawk." It was the only place in America where the Jewish population was great enough to nurture such speech into a regional dialect. From 1920 until 1960, the city's two million Jews accounted for 40 percent of the group's national population and formed New York's largest "ethnic-religious" group.

Sherman was part of that dominant New York group from 1945 to 1960, and during those years he got his graduate education in Jewish life. That life was not always very Jewish. Such paradoxes are what made New York "the Jewish Camelot." Wonderful and contradictory things were possible. As a community, the Jews built institutions that made New York the national Jewish cultural center, but as individuals they reveled in the city as a "cosmopolitan paradise" and took "Jewishness quite for granted."

Sherman also lived it up, but when it came to Jewishness he had the fervor of the convert. It was not an inheritance he received at birth but a decision, a strategy for survival, and his self-made identity required expression. Many New York Jews disagreed. Between 1945 and 1955, a period of Jewish American life sometimes called the Golden Decade, Jews "deepened and intensified their identity as Americans." They joined synagogues, but Jewishness went underground. It became a secret. Sherman searched for a way to tell that secret.

It was a disposition he brought with him when he arrived in New York. *Golden Touch* stemmed from Sherman's days at the University of Illinois. He mentions it in a June 24, 1945, letter to his college composer friend Bill Pilkenton. "There will be a series of shocks in this letter, so brace yourself tightly against that nurse whose bosoms you are now feeling, and read on, Mac Duff." In December 1944, Pilkenton was with a tank battalion in Belgium when he was wounded by bazooka fire that paralyzed his right arm and hand. Sherman did not realize his friend was no longer in the company of nurses at Camp Lockett, California, but back home in Farmer City, Illinois. Still, Sherman's effort to cheer him with ribald humor reveals his decency, and also that sex was never far from his mind. That would serve him well in 1950s New York. Then came one of the shocks. "Mike Todd interested in the GOLDEN TOUCH IDEA. No shit. Honest. Straight from the shoulder. On the level." The letter offers no details about *Golden Touch*, and apparently none were needed. Pilkenton must have been familiar with it from their college days. As for theatrical producer Mike Todd, his interest in the *Golden Touch* idea was only natural. Todd was born Avrom Hirsch Goldbogen. But his interest must have fizzled because his name did not come up again.

The letter's biggest shock was that Sherman was married to Dee. "Allan was in New York and his mother called to say that his grandmother had a heart attack," Golden said. Sherman had been in New York one month when he returned to Chicago in early June 1945 to find his grandmother was fine. The move cost him a job he landed writing for radio, but Rose knew what she was doing. "She said to Allan, now that you are here, why don't you get married?" recalled Golden. "We got married on the spur of the moment."

They had planned on getting married at some point. Sherman gave Dee an engagement ring before he left for New York. He hid it in her dessert. It was either romantic, or expressed an unconscious desire to get rid of her. But Dee had another year at the University of Illinois ahead of her, and their on-again off-again relationship might not have survived the long-distance separation. Rose Segal was taking no chances. She had her eye on Dee for more than two years, ever since Rose and her mother visited the University of Illinois to see Sherman's *Nothing Ventured*. The women stayed in the SDT sorority house and there met Dee. "I see people, I ask who they are," Golden explained. "I'm gracious." This behavior appealed to Rose, whose antennae must have picked up the Anglo signals that Dee emanated, signals that Rose tried to attain by furnishing herself with two husbands born in England. "Rose took to me right away. This was before I was going with Allan, but she remembered me later."

She not only remembered, she planned ahead. Rose was determined to see Allan married. She was shrewd enough to realize that her son — bright but also overweight, afflicted by maladies, and as the army and college proved, allergic to organizations and rules — was a handful and no bargain, though she could not recognize the part she played in his maladjustment. "She worried about him," said Syril Gilbert. "She said to Allan, you know what, you're crazy. He said, all right. If I'm crazy, I'll go to a psychiatrist."

Dr. Ben Lichtenstein, a Chicago neurologist, was distantly related to the family through marriage, and he told Rose that her son was a genius. Sherman agreed. His boasting about this verdict may account for the *Hillel Post* dubbing him, "Al (Just Call Me a Genius) Copelon." But Rose's ability to arrange his marriage to Dee, to manipulate him, to manage things so that he felt he could do nothing but what she wanted him to do underscored a character weakness that dogged Sherman throughout his life. When he became famous, business managers, lawyers, and agents found it easy to demand unreasonable conditions and fees. Acquaintances borrowed money, and women who told absurd sob stories won his sympathy, financial help, and love.

Sherman married Dolores Chackes on June 15, 1945, at Chicago's Anshe

Emet synagogue, in the rabbi's study, a small-scale venue common during the war years. Despite the last minute planning, Sherman may have been the one to pick the synagogue, because Anshe Emet's musically gifted and celebrated cantor, Moses J. Silverman, performed the ceremony. Silverman was Sherman's kind of cantor. He had a weakness for show business and attracted the attention of stars such as Jan Peerce, Victor Borge and Harry Belafonte. After the ceremony the couple and about two-dozen guests enjoyed a high-end dinner at Chicago's fashionable Pump Room restaurant, and then the newlyweds took the night train to New York.

Rose and Dave Segal headed in the opposite direction. Segal's ex-wife was after him in Chicago, so on August 1 he and Rose moved back to Los Angeles, and on August 15 they bought a three-bedroom, two-bath house in Beverly Hills at 300 South LaPeer Drive for $36,000. When Segal's ex-wife, who was owed years of alimony and child support brought this to the court's attention, Segal claimed it was not his house. His mother-in-law Esther Sherman bought it. The immigrant two-bit poker player and Leon, her retired clothes presser husband, were on a bit of a spending spree, because Segal said that on April 12, 1946, Leon bought a Plymouth Club Coupe automobile that was mistakenly identified as his own. There were plenty of Shermans, and Segal found a way to use nearly all of them. He used Rose's brother, Maury Sherman, to hide the purchase of another Los Angeles property. Rose and Dave Segal's underhanded and just plain crazy existence played in the background of Sherman's life for years to come.

Producers, Not Angels

His mother's comfort with lies drove Sherman toward the truth, and for Sherman the fundamental truths were the twin forces of his life, Jewishness and sex. In *The Golden Touch*, he took on Jewishness. That bucked the trend. Jewishness was then at the height of a "decades-long popular-culture disappearing act." With the exception of a "no-goodnik" and a "nu?" in *Guys and Dolls* and similar scattered clues elsewhere, Jewish ethnicity was kept offstage. Only with ingenious detective work did scholars decades later uncover Broadway's disguised Jewish themes, such as love overcoming "ancient rivalries and prejudices" in *South Pacific*, *West Side Story*, and *The King and I*, a story line alluring to Jewish playwrights eager for the "possibility of the Jews' absorption into the larger society."

The Golden Touch offered a much franker embrace of Jewishness than the works of Sherman's more successful (and talented) contemporaries. In fact, it overturns an idea essential to many of their musicals. Absorption into the larger society is rejected. Love does not conquer all when the desired woman is finally able to overcome her prejudices to focus on the person under the surface that is just like her. It is just the opposite. Joe's apparently non-Jewish fiancé, Sally, is in love with Joe's ethnic difference. She rejects him when he changes his name, leaves the delicatessen, and loses his Jewish flavor. "Failure, smailure — he'd better get rid of that Benny!" is how she summarizes — in an only partly successful attempt at Jewish English — what has to happen before she and Joe can get back together. He has to become Jewish again.

This put *The Golden Touch* out of touch. In 1947, entertainment about Jews avoided being too Jewish. The Oscar for best picture that year went to *Gentleman's Agreement*, a movie about a non-Jewish New Yorker who pretends to be Jewish but avoids anything recognizable as New York Jewish behavior. For that the studio didn't need Gregory Peck. Jewishness was off the table.

Sherman wanted it brought back, and he was in good company that he would not have found — were he to actually be in their presence — good company. Jewish intellectuals were so far beyond his ken he could not even parody them, but they were on his side and helped nudge the culture in his direction. Elliot Cohen, editor of the new Jewish monthly, *Commentary*, founded in 1945, brought to his job instincts about Jewish life akin to Sherman's. Cohen had once cofounded a "pseudo-formal society" dedicated to evenings of "Jewish, that is, high (and loud) conversation." That is a good translation of what thinker Mordechai Kaplan meant when he defended maintaining the Jews' "customs and standards of conduct," and it is what philosopher Horace Kallen had in mind when he stressed the need for a Jewish life shaped by "the ethnic character of the people that live it."

Sherman did not know these people existed, but he felt as they did. "I'm Jewish oriented," Sherman later told the *Washington Post*. "I can't help it, that's the way I was born." That may have overstated the case, but his early childhood world in Chicago, cemented by his return to his grandparents' home as a schoolboy, bound Sherman to the Jews through what Kallen called "a moral obligation created in childhood." Sherman's *Golden Touch* was propelled by an agreement with Kallen's proposition that "a person could not reject his ancestry without serious emotional trauma." That was his mother Rose's trauma and Sherman was not having any. In *Golden Touch*, being Jewish is attractive and desirable, chopped liver is better than paté, Midasovich is a better name than Midas, and being poor but true to yourself is better than being a rich phony.

Like many of Broadway's assertions, this was not always true beyond the stage lights. Mike Todd was not about to change his name back to Goldbogen. But unreality is no obstacle to Broadway success and the musical attracted attention. It looked like it might get produced. On August 28, 1947, the *New York Times* briefly noted that *The Golden Touch* was making the rounds among producers, and on May 18, 1948, it reported the musical was acquired by the "new producing team of Ned Warren and W. B. Steuer," and that producer Jack Wildberg, who from 1944 to 1946 had a Broadway hit with an African-American cast production of the gritty *Anna Lucasta*, might also come on board. In June, *Billboard* wrote that Wildberg had signed on and Dean Martin and Jerry Lewis were being considered for lead roles. The same month the *Times* contributed news that film director John Berry, a favorite of theater innovator John Houseman, might direct.

This was heady stuff. Sherman and his wife were twenty-three years old and lived in a $50-a-month Manhattan studio apartment at 340 East 66th Street that faced the courtyard. Their view was of the back of nearby buildings. "A woman across the air shaft was anti-Semitic and threw garbage at us," Golden remembered. There was just as much chaos in the apartment. Sherman was writing bits for comedians and singers, but not on schedule. "Genius that he was, they'd ring the doorbell and he said he'd think of something," Golden said. "He worked best under pressure." His clients obliged. "Hey fats, waiting with open mailbox for insurance bit," wrote comic Jerry Lester from Miami. "Hurry!! You fat fool!"

Other lifelong bad habits soon surfaced. Sherman was a night owl prone to sleeping all day, and Dee had to make sure that her job as a clothes model for aspiring designers at Parsons and Pratt allowed her to be home midday to make sure her husband stayed awake. She also urged him to stop smoking and told him about a class that helped people quit. He asked the cost. The answer was fifty dollars. For Sherman, that was a straight line. "Think of how many cigarettes you could buy for that money!" It was one of the few times he measured the value of a dollar. In the 1950s their finances improved, but never enough to match his uncontrolled spending habits, which matched his eating habits. "He loved food," said Golden. When he had the money, one of his favorite restaurants was the expensive Danny's Hide-a-Way on East 45th Street's "steak row," where he ate big steaks, oysters, "everything. He never skipped a meal." And most infuriatingly, he had to be right. "He always blamed the other fellow." This guaranteed marital disputes, and when Allan and Dee argued she stewed in the bathtub, the only refuge in the one-room apartment. That was when Sherman turned on the charm and humor, his saving graces. "He'd always make me laugh."

Sherman first made a living in New York writing for *Leave It to Mike*, a situation comedy radio show about one Mike McNally, a young Irish-American with a charming brogue who works in a sporting goods store. Howard Merrill, a writer whose mother put him on stage when he was three, got Sherman the job. The jokes on the show are redolent of Sherman's college newspaper column. "I played the part of the bulb in *The Light That Failed*," quips Mike in an episode called "Broad as a Barn Door." *Mike* went off the air in February 1946, and the Shermans survived on small loans from their parents, Dee's modeling, and what Sherman made selling jokes and sketches to Jerry Lester and nightspot singers such as Frances Faye, Sylvia Froos, Estelle Loring, Georgia Kaye, Rosalind Courtright, and Wally Griffin, described by *Billboard* in 1949 as "a piano lad with some smart lyrics" working the Chanticleer, a "top-drawer" lounge in Baltimore. Sherman wrote "witty ditties," said Griffin. "He was very quick to come up with ideas. Very talented."

A Broadway musical promised to catapult Sherman from scribbler to lyricist, to playwright, and put him in the same arena as the songwriters he studied, admired, and also parodied, such as the great Irving Berlin. "That was his ambition, to write a musical," Golden said. But all the excitement and news stories about *Golden Touch* obscured an elaborate charade. In producers Warren and Steuer, Sherman had unwittingly fallen in with a couple of Jewish con men that belonged in his show, not behind it. Warren, born Nathan Jacques Waxman and later known as "the godfather of Arizona land fraud" was at the beginning of his criminal career when he agreed to produce Sherman's musical. He and partner Steuer were not angels, as producers are sometimes called, but producers of the kind made famous by Mel Brooks. They raised money in order to steal it. When they got involved with *Golden Touch* they had already raised $39,000 to produce *The Happiest Days*, a play lacking elements usually considered essential, such as an author and script. Warren and Steuer ran off with the *Happiest Days* money, and their sudden disappearance hurt *Golden Touch*. Wildberg, a legitimate producer, was still involved, but on July 16, 1948, he told the *Times* that money problems caused by production costs and taxes made him rethink a fall opening in New York in favor of a tryout on London's West End. That never happened. Warren and Steuer were caught, confessed, and served two years in Sing Sing prison, and on July 20, 1950, a *Times* round-up article included news that Eunice Healy, a dancer and actress engaged to a millionaire shirt manufacturer had optioned *Golden* and planned a November opening on Broadway. That also never happened, and the musical's last public sighting was May 2, 1951, when *Variety* reviewed a performance of it at Chicago's Loyola University. "Storywise the play is weak," but the songs "are good fare," *Variety* wrote. In 1969, his *The Fig Leaves Are Falling* would have the same problem. Sherman was desperate to see *Golden Touch* produced and at one point went to California to raise money. "Its failure broke his heart," Golden said.

"Well, It's Dirty"

With perfect timing, just as *Golden Touch* was going under, each of Sherman's parents made decisions to engage in bizarre self-destructive acts. Their actions shook him. It was late 1949, Dee was pregnant, and Sherman worried that his parents' antics might indicate a hereditary predisposition to madness.

Percy's path was the splashiest. Sometime during the summer of 1949, he visited his brother Abe in Chicago to get advice on how to lose weight. "I remember Percy coming to the house and he was wheeled in," said Abe's daughter, Dorothy Macarus. "He could not walk." Percy weighed 357 pounds. His brother the dentist, nudist, and naturopath gave Percy predictably eccentric advice, which was to engage in a long-term fast.

Percy added a twist to the prescription that called for widespread publicity, and when he returned home to Tarrant City, Alabama, he arranged for the construction of a six-by-six foot house, complete with roof, walls, and awnings. The house was welded to a twenty-foot steel pole, set upright and attached to the ground. At that point, Percy contacted the newspapers and announced a 100-day fast from August 27 to December 4 that would not only result in him losing 150 pounds, it would "prove that anything can be cured simply by fasting and drinking pure water," he said. "I'm not doing this as a publicity stunt. It's in the interest of science."

This is the kind of story newspapers love, and Percy's photograph and story appeared throughout Alabama, on the front page of the Army newspaper, *The Stars and Stripes*, and in newspapers across the country. He had to climb a fire engine ladder to reach his elevated roost, and on the day of the ascent, September 3, 1949, he capitalized on the publicity by charging gawkers ten cents and cars fifty cents to watch him from within a roped-off area close to the action. People showed up, but most stayed outside the rope. "It took Coplon five minutes to get up the 20 rung ladder," reported the *Dothan Eagle*. "Each rung called for a separate effort. Sometimes he had to lift a leg twice to get it up to the next step." Just as sad was Percy's bloated retelling of his moment of glory, back in 1913, when as a teenage mechanic he was thrown from the racecar. The minor incident was now a saga. "Newspapers carried my death front page," he falsely told a reporter. Sherman may have been right to worry about heritable flaws. He shared his father's weakness for the limelight.

On November 25, 1949, the front page of the *Birmingham Post's* late edition announced, "Percy (Fatty) Coplon Dies on 93rd Day of Long Fast." He had come down from his little house a few days earlier because he felt dizzy, and in his bathroom at home fell, hit his head, and died. Percy was fifty-three years old.

In New York, a pregnant Dee was sitting on a bench overlooking the East River and reading a local newspaper when she saw the news about Percy's death. She ran home and Allan called his mother. "Rose said, 'I thought you knew. It was in the newsreels,'" remembered Golden. Rose saw no reason to talk to her son about it, perhaps because she was distracted planning her own stunt.

Rose and Dave Segal and son Sheldon left Los Angeles in 1947 after two years there that included legal bouts with Segal's ex-wife, and in 1949 they were back on Chicago's Gold Coast at 625 W. Stratford Place, a modest four-story brick apartment building east of Broadway. Rose was forty-five years old. She had a husband who was a con man, and two sons from different marriages who barely knew one another. She decided to have another child. In late 1949, she and Dave adopted a two-year-old girl they named Sharon, in remembrance of Segal's mother, Sarah. This last addition completed the patchwork nature of Rose's family. She now had three children, including Allan, age twenty-five, Sheldon, twelve, and Sherry, two, all estranged from one another by age and their unique parentage. "It was a total surprise to the family when Rose and Dave adopted Sherry," Gilbert said. Rose may have done it because her daughter-in-law, Dee, was expecting. It was a way of keeping up with the young woman. "She couldn't stand to get older," said Golden. Age was a reality she could not tolerate, like being Jewish, born in Europe, or the pronunciation of Coplon. Golden remembered other odd behavior. Newspapers ran public notices of pending divorces, and Rose called people on the phone to talk them out of it.

All of this parental eccentricity and the disappointment of *Golden Touch* lent a touch of desperation and forced giddiness to Sherman's "special material," the songs and comedy bits he wrote on spec for a variety of entertainers. Sexual themes further revved up this mood of insistent happiness, joy, pleasure, and life itself. Practical considerations could wait. Indulge now, was his motto. "The Time of Your Life" begins,

My sermon for today
Can't be found in a book on a shelf
Today I shall speak on the subject of "Enjoy Yourself!"
Enjoy . . . Enjoy . . . Enjoy yourself!

Enjoyment was sexual, as song titles such as "History Was Made at Night" make clear. "Have Yourself a Wonderful Time" advises women to "Worry about the sin / After you begin," and in another song a husband gives gossip columnists Hedda Hopper, Louella Parsons, and Elsa Maxwell the scoop on an impending story, "Cause Harvey Stone is gonna be a father / Nine months from tomorrow night!!" For the cabaret singer Frances Faye, whose suggestive lyrics sometimes hinted at her bisexual adventures, Sherman wrote "Live! Be Happy! Enjoy!"

> Don't be jealous of those wealthy fellas with a chauffeur and a Cadillac!
> When you're out, with a gal you're nuts about . . .
> Who needs a chauffeur in the front to watch the action in the back!

Sherman had always written about sex, but in postwar New York he was in tune with a more permissive mood. The Latin Quarter nightclub in Times Square, opened in 1942, featured chorus girls who "did their best to show you their breasts." That was almost what passed for a drama review from New York *Post* gossip columnist Earl Wilson. He often featured breast jokes, and in late 1945 Sherman sent Wilson some material. Wilson thanked him in a note postmarked January 29, 1946. "Best wishes as you walk down Mammary Lane!" Wilson did not write literature. But the new permissiveness allowed those who did to do wonderful things. As Sherman wrote in a song for Faye, her audience was great because "you came to see Frances stead of *Kiss Me, Kate*," and terrific "cause you came to see me instead of *South Pacific*." Both musicals were new hits in 1949, and both gloried in a healthy and un-neurotic American sexuality. In "Too Darn Hot," Paul of *Kiss Me, Kate* laments, "I'd like to fool with my baby tonight," except the weather is not right, and the sailors in *South Pacific* explain what is unique about a dame. "Nothin' else is built the same."

This more liberal sexual moment played to one of Sherman's strengths and compensated for the hush-hush atmosphere that still surrounded Jewishness. The same 1949 theater season that gave audiences Cole Porter's sexually suggestive "Too Darn Hot" also offered Arthur Miller's Jewishly mum *Death of a Salesman*. Despite its greatness, the critic Mary McCarthy astutely complained that Willy Loman was "a capitalized Human Being without being anyone." Sherman wanted to battle this Jewish disappearance but first he had to make a living. This was crucial, because in late 1949 a very pregnant Dee could no longer work as a clothes model. The couple left their tiny Manhattan apartment for a two-bedroom rental at 81–05 35th Avenue in Jackson Heights, in the borough of Queens, just weeks before their son Robert was born on January 9, 1950. He was named after the character Robert Shannon in the 1946 film, *The Green Years*, a story that had obvious appeal for Sherman. In the film, Robert is an orphan protected and nurtured by his great-grandfather, just as Sherman was a virtual orphan nurtured by his grandmother. Yet despite his attachment to his childhood wounds it was now Sherman's job to raise a child, and the still nascent but booming television industry came to the rescue.

In 1950, only 8 percent of American households owned a television, but that was quadruple the 2 percent that owned a set the year before, and the dramatic growth kept on coming. By 1955, the percentage of homes with a television increased eightfold from the 1950 level to 64 percent, and television stations across the country mushroomed from 104 in 1950 to 458 in 1955. This exploding new industry practically fell in Sherman's lap. In the early 1950s, New York, not Los Angeles, was the capital of television production, and the industry needed writers. In early 1950, Sherman wrote his first television bits for Jerry Lester, who headlined *Cavalcade of Stars*, and Sherman soon followed him to the short-lived *Broadway Open House*. But these vaudeville shows for the video screen, dubbed Vaudeo by *Variety*, missed the boat. It was Sid Caesar's 1950 *Your Show of Shows* that pointed the way forward for television comedy. It "aspired to be smart, sophisticated, and topical," and its parodies and social satire would later be recognized as brilliant examples of Jewish humor.

Sherman's television career took another direction. With his friend Howard Merrill he created the game show *I've Got a Secret*, a frank reworking of the existing show, *What's My Line?* In the latter, a panel of four stars asks contestants questions to figure out their occupations. On *Secret*, a panel of four stars asks contestants questions to figure out their personal secrets. But Sherman understood that the true appeal of *What's My Line?* lay elsewhere. "Well — it's dirty," he tells Merrill when asked the reason for the show's success. As Sherman recounted in his autobiography, a typical scenario involved a contestant who is a mattress salesman. After it is established that he sells a product, a panelist asks, "Is it used by both sexes?" The audience knows the contestant's job and screams with laughter. Sherman and Merrill's show allowed for the same naughty fun, and in August 1951 they sold *I've Got a Secret* for one dollar to Mark Goodson-Bill Todman Productions, the owner of *What's My Line?* That ended Sherman and Merrill's hopes to own *Secret*. Sherman did not shine in business negotiations. Besides, he was desperate and Goodson-Todman was not. In addition to the dollar, Goodson, "The Gameshow King," and his partner, super-salesman Todman, offered Sherman and Merrill a $125 weekly royalty each if the show aired. And one of them would be named associate producer at a $125 a week salary.

I've Got a Secret premiered on June 19, 1952, and after a rocky start became "the most popular of all prime-time panel shows." It stayed on the air until 1967, and was revived twice thereafter. Sherman became the producer. Merrill had already found another job. It was a life-changing lucky break. With a weekly salary and royalty payment that totaled $250 a week, Sherman's $13,000 annual income catapulted him into the elite. The median income for nonfarm families in 1952 was $4,100. Only 2 percent of American families earned Sherman's salary. And he was now *in*. He was at the swirling center of the latest action. Sherman was in New York, in television, producing a panel show for Goodson-Todman when New York was the television capital, television was booming, the *Times* called panel quiz shows "the hardy perennials of television," and Goodson was the king of panel shows.

Still, *I've Got a Secret* was nonsensical. *Variety* criticized its "artifice" a week after it launched, and even after a substantial tune-up it suffered from the same flaw. When *Secret* celebrated five years on the air, *Variety* slammed it for having a premise "so frail that when the panelists are not being especially funny" it falls flat. The show never intended to "divulge one [secret] of even moderate interest." Nevertheless, the show was a hit. As Sherman realized from the start, sexual suggestiveness was *Secret*'s trump card, and it was his job as producer to find contestants with secrets that allowed the sparks to fly. It was not too difficult. A good example was the fourth anniversary show that featured a man from Nebraska whose secret was, "I have the world's largest chest expansion." Host Garry Moore's hint to the panelists was, "It's something he can do with what he has." Panelist Jayne Meadows responded, "Could I assume a woman would be better at it?" There was often a can-you-top-this aspect to the repartee, with each panelist daring the other to take the insinuations to the legal limit. Moore measured the chests of male panelists Bill Cullen and Henry Morgan. He did not dare do the same to Meadows and Faye Emerson but, as *Variety* reported, "it was intimated that Mlles. Meadows and Emerson could have trimmed all comers in that respect but Moore didn't press the point."

The show's sexual atmosphere was inseparable from New York's emergence in the 1950s as the "capital of love and romance," when even its subway gratings aided seduction by lifting Marilyn Monroe's skirt in the 1955 movie *The Seven Year Itch*. Writer Calvin Trillin said that what made New York a sexual hothouse was the masses of men and women who were young, adult, and single. In the Midwest, people in their mid-twenties were married. Sherman married at twenty. In New York, single women were everywhere and, more to the point, on the twenty-ninth floor of 375 Park Avenue, at Goodson-Todman, where sexual innuendo paid the bills.

I've Got a Secret needed everyday people and also famous guests with secrets, real or fabricated, and Sherman's job was to find them, book them, prep them and make them feel welcome. He got to kid around with stars and act out fantasy scenarios. Photographs show him in the arms of Lucille Ball while her husband Desi Arnaz throttles him, and staring into the camera with suave nonchalance as bombshell actress Gina Lollobrigida beseeches his love. Alcohol flowed at Goodson-Todman Christmas parties, and it emboldened men and women to flirt, steal kisses, and pursue sexual opportunities. Sherman noticed, and in 1957 he wrote the definitive mock office memo on the subject that poked fun at his own fantasy of himself as a Don Juan. It outlined the rules women desperate for his attention at the office Christmas party must observe, "Due to the unprecedented demand for my services this year, and the limitations imposed on me by nature and time." The memo warns that "GIRLS WITH NO PREVIOUS SEXUAL EXPERIENCE" must report early for "pre-party instructions." But its comedy assures readers that Sherman is in on the joke. "ALL GIRLS WILL TAKE WHATEVER SPECIAL PRECAUTIONS ARE INDICATED. DON'T DEPEND ON ME FOR PRECAUTIONS — YOU KNOW WHAT A MAD, IMPETUOUS FOOL I AM." There is no hint he would later enact such a scenario. Perhaps even Sherman did not understand that some part of his psyche was in earnest.

Our Way of Life

This freewheeling environment made Goodson-Todman perfect for Sherman. It was where the overweight joke writer, procrastinating genius, wit, parodist, singer, performer, lyricist, Army wash-out, sex-obsessed college ejectee, and would-be Jewish playwright could impersonate — with the birth of daughter Nancy on November 13, 1952 — a respectable breadwinner and father of two. He appeared to undergo a fairy tale transformation from disorganized freelancer into stable family man. In 1953, the Shermans left Jackson Heights for a rented home in Yonkers, entry point to the suburban paradise of Westchester, and on February 17, 1954, the family bought a three-bedroom brick home with a fireplace for $26,500 at 53 Parkview Drive in Bronxville. "Not Bronxville, *goyishe*," Golden clarified. "Across from New Rochelle." It was the area where Jews lived.

That made sense, but little else did. Allan and Dee bought the house after they realized they could not afford presents for the Christmas holiday they celebrated. Like many Jews from California, Sherman grew up with a Christmas tree and bought one every year. But in 1953, instead of buying presents they visited a real estate office. To raise the $1,500 down payment, Allan and Dee scrounged where they could for every cent, even returning Coke bottles to collect the deposit. "I'm not exaggerating," Golden said. Part of the reason things were so tight was that Sherman was helping to support his grandparents, Leon and Esther Sherman. "It was not being generous; we had to," said Golden. "It was the inheritance Rose left us." Rose died of breast cancer on May 20, 1953, at age forty-nine.

"Allan took her death very hard, very hard," Gilbert said. "He went to a therapist to talk about it." There was a lot to talk about. Even the prospect of eternity could not reconcile Rose to the true facts of her life. Her death certificate stood by the falsehoods that she was only forty-four years old and born in Illinois. But at the end of her life she apparently decided that being a modern and affluent Jewish American woman could be a social asset. Her obituary made her sound like any respectable member of the community. The twice-divorced woman married to her criminal husband by a Christian minister "was an active member of Temple Sholem, Anshe Emmet of Chicago, and the Chicago Hadassah," and the swindler Dave Segal was "president of the American Plastics corporation," a maker of plastic dishes in business only from 1953 to 1954. Despite Rose's flaws, she had a gift, inherited by her son Allan, to make herself likable. "She could be very ingratiating," Golden said. "Charming, warm."

Rose's other legacy was the influence she wielded over her son, which did not end with her death. Her last home was at 1400 Jackson Avenue in the Chicago suburb of River Forest, a leafy village popular with area gangsters. The 3,100-square-foot house had a dining room that Sherry Segal remembers was outfitted with "a foot-operated buzzer to call the maid." Allan's mother always employed a maid, Golden said. Sherman seems to have purchased his house in Bronxville because he was driven to match his mother's luxurious life and the shrewd practices that supposedly made it possible. He tried to apply her advice to buy a distressed property in order to get a deal. Sherman did not get a deal. But neither had Rose. She did not owe her luxury home to shrewd dealings but to Dave Segal's fraud and crime. They lived off the money Segal stole from his ex-wife, and other exploits, including arson. "Allan and I were in Chicago" visiting Rose, Golden said, when Dave Segal "got a phone call that the business was burning and Dave was not surprised and Rose was not surprised. They planned it." It is not clear what business that might have been, but another example occurred a year after Rose's death. On October 17, 1954, a fire destroyed Shelly Furniture, a store at 4760 Lincoln Avenue in Chicago that Segal named for his son. The fire marshal told the *Daily Tribune* the damages ran to $100,000. Segal corrected him. It was $125,000. The FBI's record of Segal's many arrests for confidence games, embezzlement, grand theft, and the like suggests he got away with arson.

The trail of wreckage that followed Rose's death included the disrupted lives of Sherman's half- and stepsiblings, Sheldon and Sherry. They wandered the country with their father, Dave, living in Chicago, Coral Gables, Florida, and then at Miami's Fontainebleau Hotel. "One amusing story from those years," Sherry Segal said. "We went into the back of a closet and found stacks of money." Sheldon eventually joined the army, and his existence was unhappy and brief. Sheldon had "a lousy life," said Gilbert. He died in 1989 at age fifty-two. Dave could not care for his daughter, so Sherry lived with

Sherman's cousin Syril, and then Syril's brother Kenneth and his wife. "I like all my mothers," is how the girl described her life to Dee.

Rose's example might have induced caution, but in Sherman it bred a to-hell-with-it heedlessness, hedonism, and financial recklessness. He moved into 53 Parkview Drive, bought Dee a mink jacket, and hired a maid. The family joined the Reform movement's Free Synagogue of Westchester and the Vernon Hills Country Club, where Sherman took up golf, and he and Dee gave and attended house parties and entered a social scene that overlapped with and complemented Sherman's work life by fostering friendships he cherished and connections crucial to his later fame. On the surface, it was a suburban life that deserved the Good Housekeeping seal of approval. But Sherman's top priorities were still sex and comedy and drinking and eating and smoking and talking and laughing. His friends found it an irresistible combination. New York was crowded with Jewish family men — and non-Jews with a Jewish style — just a step removed from their rough, energetic, talk-happy immigrant backgrounds. They were giddy about their sudden affluence and their opportunities to fool around, and they loved Sherman.

"Allan was a joy to be with," said Leonid Hambro. "He would always come up with these funny lines." One example was the time Sherman uncharacteristically carried a copy of the *Daily Worker*, the Communist paper. Someone asked why. "I want to see how the Giants *really* made out," was his answer, said Hambro. "It's a political comment and a sociological comment, and it was quick. It's a great line."

Hambro was a classical pianist with the New York Philharmonic, an "improvising genius," according to the *New York Times*, but he was also a Chicago boy, the son of musical Russian immigrant Jews, a skirt chaser, cut-up, and in 1961, musical sidekick to Victor Borge, the Danish Jew who mocked the classical music world he and Hambro both loved. Sherman and Hambro met in New York through an alcoholic named Dave Vern, famed for his wit and talent for self-destruction. "Vern gave Sherman dozens of ideas," said Hambro. "His ability to be funny was unique, not like anybody else. Spontaneous, off the top of his head." Vern's bits do not survive, but he seems to have been one of those Jewish neighborhood wild men like Joe Ancis, inspiration to Lenny Bruce, who perfected the "Spritz," a runaway train of verbal comedy packed with "timing, mugging, dialects and sound effects." Sherman's wife did not like him. "Dave Vern was a very bad person," Golden said. "I think Allan thought, there but for the grace of God goes I."

In the 1940s, Vern kibitzed with folksy Jewish nostalgia writer Sam Levenson about what Levenson daintily called "our folk heritage." In the fifties he wrote comic books. Sherman produced a television game show. Hambro was a "sensitive and skilled chamber musician." The unlikely connection among them was typical of New York's fluid Jewish social world that valued personality, brightness, being a character. With the exception of the Jewish intellectuals who kept themselves corralled off from the rest of humanity, it was a world that arranged odd bedfellows. Hambro specialized in odd bedfellows. He became Sherman's connection for available women and more exotic sexual possibilities. "I was an orgy man for years," Hambro said. "I knew lots of girls . . . Allan knew I would come up with terrific girls. He was always up for that."

Sherman's need for buddies he could journey with high and low, talk books and writing, drink, laugh, and hunt for women bonded him also to journalist and Marilyn Monroe biographer Maurice Zolotow. He showed up at Goodson-Todman one day to write a story when Sherman interrupted him mid-interview to say, "I'd like to be your friend. That amused Morris," said Golden. Zolotow was eleven years older than Sherman, but he was also a child of Jewish immigrants ambitious to write, drink, pal around with stars, and get familiar with the female gender, so he and Sherman shared certain fundamentals. There was "a lot of drinking and a lot of screwing around," said Zolotow's daughter, Crescent Dragonwagon, who during the 1960s gave herself a new, and new-age name. Zolotow started out in the 1930s as press agent for Minsky's striptease artist Margie Hart. She got arrested for appearing without her G-string and turned her notoriety into renown and then marriage to a congressman.

Zolotow went on to become what the *Times* called "the Boswell of Broadway." He covered show business for *Billboard*, *Life*, *Variety*, the *Saturday Evening Post*, and other publications, and in 1944 published a novel, *Never Whistle in a Dressing Room; or, Breakfast in Bedlam*. "My father was more intellectual than Sherman, but he was interested in off-the-wall people," Dragonwagon said. Sherman did not meet Zolotow's literary companion, the poet Delmore Schwartz, but he did meet an off-the-wall type named Dick Gehman, legendary king of the freelance magazine writers who jotted liner notes for Sherman's first two albums. "Zolotow and Sherman were joined at the hip," remembered Betsey Gehman, one of Dick's five wives. "They smoked, drank, had affairs, and their families be damned. It was almost like a cult of booze and broads." She said Sherman and Zolotow were Marx Brothers fans and borrowed from *Horse Feathers* the password, "Swordfish," to discuss their sexual escapades.

Gehman was one of the non-Jews favored by Sherman and other New York Jews, for obvious reasons. "Gehman was always a maniac, writing many things at once," said Dragonwagon. He had the stereotypically Jewish energy. In New York in the fifties, interesting people were often assumed to be Jewish. Writer Dan Wakefield, a non-Jew, mistakenly thought his first New York girlfriend was Jewish because "she had dark hair and was highly intelligent." The same mistake was made about show business personal manager George "Bullets" Durgom, and it does not seem that Bullets, from Lebanese Christian stock, sought to correct anybody. His nickname was inspired by his bald head that sat atop a compact five-foot-three-inch frame, always in motion at high speed, and his job, as he described it in a profile article written by Gehman, was hard to pin down. "People call me. They know I'm around. They know I know what's happenin'!" For this he got 10 percent. Bullets met Sherman while getting his clients on *Secret*, and he handled Sherman's first contract with Warner Bros. Records.

Television talk show pioneer Steve Allen occupied a different category of Jewish non-Jew. Everyone knew he was not Jewish, but Jews treated him as a member in good standing. Allen came to New York from California in 1953 to host *What's My Line?* The following year he married *I've Got a Secret* panelist Jayne Meadows, and Sherman and Dee befriended them both. It was not a cultural stretch. When Allen later got his own show, Sherman and Mel Brooks appeared as guests on the same night, with Brooks appearing as the 2000-Year-Old Man. In his adorable version of the Jewish immigrant's accented English he told Allen, "We like you, too, even though you're not *in*. But you're okay. You're cute. You wear glasses and that's nearly Jewish."

The *Secret* show led to more friendships. At a party thrown by panelist Faye Emerson and her husband, the musical conductor Skitch Henderson, Sherman and Dee met NBC house drummer Bobby Rosengarden. "By coincidence,

Allan and I knew Bobby's wife," said Golden. She was the former Dorothy Kline, whom Sherman had briefly dated at the University of Illinois. This connection led to a close friendship between Sherman and Rosengarden, and then to connections with some of the gang that gathered at Rosengarden's house in Great Neck, Long Island, for summer Sunday pool parties. Regulars included Sid Caesar, the stand-up comic Professor Irwin Corey, pianist Dick Hyman, the film score composer Elmer Bernstein, and Rosengarden's brother-in-law Ray Charles, born Charles Raymond Offenberg. (He took the name Ray Charles when the soul singer Ray Charles was still an unknown.) Sherman and Rosengarden shared a taste for Jewish dialect humor. "My father and him sounded like two old rabbis," remembered Bobby's son, Neil Rosengarden. They also "loved to drink, those guys. Both of them." Sometimes that was a problem. "Sherman would come out every weekend and get drunk and get dirty and we had to sit on him because kids were around," said Ray Charles. But those summer gatherings epitomized what everyone there was after. "It was fun and it was our way of life, actually," Charles said. "Sherman was talented. We knew people like that. There was show people and there were civilians."

Civilians could be forgiven for wondering if what show people did counted as work. Sherman's schedule would have added to their confusion. On *Secret*'s fifth anniversary show in 1957, the entire seventy-three-person crew appeared on-stage during the closing credits and Sherman was there looking young, unshaven, round but healthy, casual in a white dress shirt open at the collar and his crew-cut hair so short it emerged from his scalp in bristles. He beamed as the blonde Faye Emerson pinched both his cheeks. He had to be there for that. He was going to be on the air. But if matters were less urgent he sometimes did not show up. "If I come in at show time, that's all I need," is how Golden remembers her husband explaining that he was headed for the golf course, or to art galleries — he had signed up for an art class and was painting — instead of to Goodson-Todman. "He was obsessed, obsessed with golf," said Golden. "As a short fat man, it was a game he could play. He played golf for months. Mark [Goodson] put up with him." And, as Sherman admitted in his autobiography, he was disorganized. "I was a Disorganization Man, playing a lonesome off-key melody in the Goodson-Todman Symphony of Organization."

Goodson-Todman's careful planning was part of the company's success, but it undermined the ad hoc nature of television's early days that accommodated Sherman. The first years were a time of amateurs, opportunists, fakers, losers, dreamers, and canny sharpies, who saw in television a new shot at making it or another chance to survive. In 1952, Sherman and Eugene O'Sullivan, a Jackson Heights neighbor and director of live television dramas, captured that moment in *The Happy Medium*. The three-act play is a comedy about the behind-the-scenes workings of the thoroughly commercial, fast-paced, amateurish, philistine, and lucrative new television industry. It took its story idea from the 1948 Moss Hart play, *Light Up the Sky*, that sends up the backstage world of Broadway. In April 1952, *Variety* reviewed *Happy Medium*'s one-night run in Albany, New York. "Sometimes it is quite funny: in spots it is biting and disturbing." In September 1954, it played for two weeks at the East Eden theater in Lincolnwood, outside Chicago, and garnered mildly positive reviews. It is valuable mainly as a window into Sherman's ambivalence about his television career, revealed in this exchange between the characters David Nichols, a writer, and Kathy Arnauld, a television executive.

NICHOLS: Then you must agree with me that Palmer and Blankenchip [the director and producer] are madmen?

ARNAULD: I do.

NICHOLS: And you know that Palmer would cut his grandmother's throat to get another Ike Award? And Blankenchip would parade naked through Times Square if [sponsor] G.K. Sheridan Junior told him to?

ARNAULD: Yes.

NICHOLS: And you're aware that Sheridan is interested only in selling shampoo, and he doesn't give a damn about the show?

ARNAULD: Completely.

NICHOLS: And you realize that the whole darn bunch of them won't do as much in a lifetime to entertain people as an organ grinder's monkey does in five minutes?

ARNAULD: Yes, I know.

NICHOLS: And you still believe that some kind of magic is going to happen in television?

ARNAULD: Yes, I do believe.

Goodson-Todman put up with Sherman because on the days he believed in the magic of television he was good, and others in the business agreed, though there were misses. In 1954, Goodson-Todman named Sherman producer for the premiere episode of its new game show, *What's Going On?* The show's complex structure — three panelists in the studio and another three in various New York locations — presented "a challenge in ingenuity to producer Allan Sherman, which he didn't quite meet," wrote *Variety*. In April 1956, he produced a variety show for humorist Herb Shriner. It bombed and Sherman was replaced. But in early 1958, Sherman produced and wrote for a Victor Borge television special that CBS aired February 19, and the *Times* loved the hour of "delightful entertainment." In March he was in conversations with Phil Silvers to produce and write his special. Sherman landed the job, and *Phil Silvers on Broadway* aired on May 13.

Sherman took on all these projects while also producing *Secret*, but the Borge and Silvers jobs during the winter and spring of 1958 pushed his penchant for multitasking to the limit and contributed to his June exit from *I've Got a Secret*. Stresses had long been building at the show. Some of them grew out of Sherman's sentimental weakness for alleged childhood innocence. For the 1956 Easter holiday show he invited 100 Boys' Club members onstage to receive their own Easter bunnies. The show's executive producer, Gil Fates, wrote that Sherman imagined "100 choir-boy types and 100 pink and white bunnies." It was the childish fantasy of someone who had a lousy childhood. The terrified bunnies did not cooperate, and the roughhousing boys stuffed as many as seven into their shirts. Sherman's standard refusal to admit mistakes or revise his thinking made things worse. "Allan would defend to the absolute death any idea that appealed to him," Fates wrote. To dismiss dissent he trotted out Ralph Waldo Emerson's line that "a foolish consistency is the hobgoblin of little minds." Fates heard this once too often and threatened to punch Sherman in the nose.

On June 11, 1958, Sherman's infatuation with lost childhood joys surfaced again. *Secret*'s guest star was Tony Curtis, and Sherman insisted he should demonstrate the New York City street games Curtis played as a boy. Curtis did not know such games, so Sherman improvised, and on the live show a "handkerchief parachute" did not open and Curtis tried and failed to "mash tin cans onto his feet and clomp around." But the show did not run out of material seven minutes before it ended, as Sherman recounted in his autobiography, and guest host Henry Morgan did not castigate him on the air as the empty seconds ticked by. In fact, there was too much material, not too little. Curtis had fun demonstrating Chinese handball and the *Secret* panel did not have enough time to guess at Curtis's secret, which was that he was going to be a father. But these minor flubs made the show the proverbial straw that broke the camel's back, and Sherman was fired.

Grandma Esther's Boy

Sherman did not hunker down after losing his job, he doubled down. He made reckless financial decisions that were in effect bets that all would be well or hell. He seemed determined either to create a crisis for himself, to tempt fate to let him have it, or to experience magical financial and professional salvation.

After Goodson-Todman he worked for a year producing the television game show *Masquerade Party*, and then during the summer of 1959 was head writer on *Perry Presents*, a thirteen-week Perry Como summer series. The Bobby Rosengarden pool parties had come through for him; Ray Charles, Rosengarden's brother-in-law, got him the position. But at the same moment Sherman was on this temporary new job he purchased a new house. On June 12, 1959, exactly a year after he was fired from *Secret*, he bought what Golden remembered as a "gorgeous Dutch Colonial home" at 61 Rye Road in Rye, New York. The three-thousand-square-foot, five-bedroom, four-bath house sat on more than a third of an acre and cost $50,000. A month later, on July 20, Sherman sold his Bronxville home for $13,000 to a buyer who assumed the $16,280 mortgage. The gap between the two transactions was considerable, especially for a man without a steady job. But the purchase was not a practical decision. It was comparable to a poor nation that bankrupts itself building a nuclear arsenal. It was a diplomatic act, a gesture intended for public consumption. Sherman's former boss Bill Todman had a brother who lived in Rye and "he wanted to show he was just as good," Golden said. The new house had access to a private beach on Long Island Sound, and at home the cook prepared dinner and served the Shermans their food as they sat around the dining room table.

It was an incongruous setting for a man preoccupied with his Jewish immigrant grandparents, but Sherman had always lived in two worlds: Chicago and Los Angeles, with his grandmother and with his mother, Jewish and non-Jewish. This moment was no different. Shortly before he bought the Rye house he was revisiting his childhood world. Grandpa Leon died on January 28, 1956, but Grandma Esther lived on, and in May 1959 Sherman still cherished her kindness to him as a child. That month *Kiwanis* magazine published his story "A Football for Grandma," which told how he once presented Esther with the football that she seemed to say, in her Yiddish accented English, she wanted. What she really wanted was a fruit bowl. In the story, Rose mocks her son's misunderstanding, but Esther puts the football in the fruit bowl and asks guests, "'It's beautiful, no?' Before Uncle Sol could answer Grandma continued. 'It's beautiful, yes — because from a child is beautiful, anything.'" She died on November 30, 1959.

The story's public embrace of his Jewish immigrant background was part of Sherman's lifelong goal to bridge the Jewish gap that divided his mother from her childhood world, and from him. That division was a common Jewish condition. Since the mid-19th century, the formula for Jewish life in Christian society was, "Be a Jew at home and a man on the street." That approach made nearly every modern Jew a potential contestant for *I've Got a Secret*. During the 1950s, Sherman himself would have been a good guest star on his show. He had a Jewish secret. When he was not at work he wrote and sang Jewish song parodies.

FOUR
THERE IS NOTHING LIKE A LOX

On the evenings of September 21 and September 28, 1957, two consecutive Saturdays that conveniently fell just before and after the Jewish New Year holiday, Vernon Hills Country Club in Eastchester, New York, presented an amateur variety show starring Allan Sherman and other members called "Handicaps of 1957." The event was held in the club's theater, which the "Handicaps" program called, "The Vernon Hills Little Theater (Very Little)." The self-deprecating humor was a good sign. Vernon Hills had claims to self-importance, but declined to exercise them.

Respected golf course architects Alfred H. Tull and Devereux Emmet designed its eighteen holes in 1926, and after World War II, Jews flocked to the club to live the good life in the New York suburbs. Brooklyn-born Milton Farber, president of the Farberware pots and pans company, was club president in 1947, and in 1953 Vernon Hills held a nine-hole benefit that guaranteed member attendance with guest celebrity golfers Dean Martin, Jerry Lewis, Perry Como, and Sid Caesar. Their high jinks and wisecracks were in tune with the club's genial mood, which could be disturbed by a major infraction: There was a "Cadillac Row" in the parking lot, said former member John Sturner. "If you had a Buick, you didn't park there."

The number Sherman prepared for the "Handicaps" show broke another club rule. "When you are Golfing at the Club, even though everybody around you is Jewish, you act gentile, and nobody in the foursome brings up his Uncle, the Junk Dealer." Those words were not written over the clubhouse door, but Sherman got the unspoken message and translated it into those words in his autobiography. The "Handicaps" program did not let on what Sherman had in mind. His performance, "Bewitched," was described as, "Music by Richard Rodgers — Words by Allan Sherman." This was true, but "Trampled by Allan Sherman" would have been truer.

I'm wild again
Beguiled again
A whimpering tsimpering tsild again
Tzimished, fachottered, and tzebulbet am I.
Can't sleep a wink
I lay and think
She's wearing my mink while she's out with Fink
Tzimished, fatroshket and tziboorjet am I.

Tzimished (confused), fachottered (screwed-up), and tzebulbet is not a bad translation of bewitched, bothered, and bewildered, except that tzebulbet does not seem to be a word in Yiddish or any other language, and it completely undermines, obliterates, laughs at and deflates the original. The parody is a comic assault. It is the kind of treatment that made Rodgers later call Sherman "a destroyer." Rodgers wrote "Bewitched, Bothered and Bewildered" with lyricist and friend Lorenz Hart for the 1940 musical *Pal Joey*. In the early twentieth century, Rodgers and Hart were both campers at the same Catskills resort for German Jews, and surely the last thing Rodgers expected to happen to "Bewitched" was that someone would turn the subtly racy confession of love into a song about a marital spat between two Jews from the old country. *Pal Joey*'s Vera Simpson, a San Francisco socialite, is amused at the fact that she, a sexually experienced woman, is so besotted with Joey that she "couldn't sleep." But Jews that sprinkle their speech with Yiddish are not known for their sophisticated habit of inspecting their troubles for their own bemusement. When they cannot get a good night's sleep it is because they are good and worried, like the jilted husband in Sherman's parody.

Goldeneh Moments from Broadway

Throughout the 1950s, Sherman wrote, rewrote and informally performed for friends and family more than twenty Jewish parodies of songs from the great Broadway musicals. This was a departure. In his musicals *Nothing Ventured*, *Mirth of a Nation*, and *The Golden Touch*, as well as his special material for various performers he honed his skills as a lyricist. Parodies, such as his college hits, "Don't Burn Down Bidwell's," "We Are Civilians '43," and "Yokohama" were also of longstanding interest. But with the exception of his early Humpty Dumpty rhyme, he rarely combined his love of song parody with his eagerness to express himself Jewishly.

In the 1950s, Sherman seized this neglected opportunity. The country was changing. Sherman's generation of Jews were now adults, and the "fine balancing act" of being a Jew and an American was tipping away from the early twentieth-century ideal of the Melting Pot toward a new hybrid formula that allowed for Jewishness. Sherman was on the right track with his Jewish "Golden Touch," except he was a little early. Within a few years, Jewish writers and comedians, including some that wrote song parodies, produced works that were frank about their Jewish material and depended less on code words such as "chopped liver." In the 1950s, Jewishness turned out to be just what everyone wanted. Marilyn Monroe got some in 1956 when she married playwright Arthur Miller and converted to Judaism. Elizabeth Taylor married two Jewish husbands, Mike Todd in 1957 and Eddie Fisher in 1959, the year she converted. The country did not have enough Jewish celebrities to go around, but the demand for Jewishness grew. Americans may have been reacting to the "fatal and monotonous similarity and mediocrity" Louis Wirth warned the Melting Pot would produce. For fast relief, he prescribed Jewishness. In the 1950s, many found it cured what ailed them.

In 1950, Carl Reiner and Mel Brooks wrote for the Sid Caesar television comedy, *Your Show of Shows*, and on the day they met, Brooks did an off-the-cuff bit about a Jewish pirate frustrated by the price of sails for his pirate ship. "You know what it cost for a sail cloth?" Inspired by Brooks, Reiner approached him the next day and said, "Here's a man who was actually at the scene of the Crucifixion." That was the start of their famous "2000 Year Old Man" routine, which they performed at house parties for the next ten years.

In September 1951, two Catskills-style comedy shows, *Bagels and Yox* and Mickey Katz's *Borscht Capades* opened on Broadway. Critics from the mainstream press hated them, and even sympathetic viewers from the Jewish community had to admit that the shows' substantial use of Yiddish was often silly, "a playing with sound effects regardless of meaning: for example, "She's a doll." "Yeah, *yisgadal*" (the first word in the prayer for the dead). That was Katz's fault, but in the 1950s his parodies of popular songs, such as Tennessee Ernie Ford's "Sixteen Tons," allowed Jews to make fun of American popular culture and their own with a song about a delicatessen worker, not a coal miner, who gets a hernia loading smoked fishes, blintzes, and knishes. Sherman's earliest Jewish song parodies imitated Katz's use of Yiddish and klezmer music interludes, but the strictly Jewish market for such songs could only support the original. When Sherman switched to Jewish-flavored English he became the first to prove ethnic material could go mainstream, and English offered another benefit. It allowed his parodies to mimic as closely as possible the sound of the original songs while subverting their meaning.

My Fair Lady opened on Broadway on March 15, 1956, and by July 24 the *Los Angeles Times* was able to report on a Jewish parody called *My Fairfax Lady* at Billy Gray's Bandbox: "Audiences have been packing the night club since the show went on." In *Fairfax*, a Jewish professor "struggles to correct the perfect English diction" of a young Englishwoman until she learns to turn "Britishisms into Yiddishisms." The professor promises her that, "When I'm through with you, my dear, you're going to get a life membership in the Hadassah!"

These works targeted Jewish audiences, but others succeeded with the general public. Herman Wouk's 1955 novel, *Marjorie Morningstar*, about a young Jewish woman with artistic aspirations became a national bestseller. Leon Uris's 1958 *Exodus*, about the birth of Israel, was another hit. These sentimental, earnest, and sincere books about Jews were not very Jewish. Wouk's novel tracks the movement of the heroine from the city to the suburb, and presents the Jewish success story as the "happy citizen at home in Mamaroneck." *Exodus* replaced the stereotype of the weak Eastern European Jew with the stereotype of the tough Israeli Jew, "swapping one simplification for the other," noted Philip Roth. Harry Golden's 1958 collection of tales about the Jewish Lower East Side, *Only in America*, peddled the same blend of "'vividness, energy, aspiration, discipline, and finally the warmth of life'" that yielded sales in the millions. What these works lacked was the double-edged humor of a Mel Brooks or Mickey Katz that viewed the majority culture through a Jewish lens at the expense of both. But America's taste for things Jewish was in its infancy, and it liked pablum. Brooks and Reiner cooked up richer dishes, but they did not think the public was ready. "No, this is for Jews," was Reiner's response when friends first urged he and Brooks to record the "2000 Year Old Man" routine.

Nobody suggested Sherman record his underground Jewish comedy. Sometimes they wished he would stop. "I've known Allan Sherman since 1954, and I've attended dozens of parties at which Sherman has either been guest or host, and invariably he would get up and sing his parodies of popular songs," wrote Maurice Zolotow. Choral director Ray Charles confirms Sherman was irrepressible. "He was just dazzling, he was exhausting. There was so much coming out of him, just to be with him was fun and exciting and exhausting."

What came out of him was *South Passaic*, a Jewish parody of *South Pacific*, and to the tune of "There Is Nothin' Like a Dame," he spelled out what Jewish men had on their minds.

> We got herring, sweet and sour,
> We got pickles, old and young,
> We got corned beef and salami and a lot of tasty tongue
> We got Philadelphia Cream Cheese in a little wooden box,
> What ain't we got?
> We ain't got lox!

Rodgers and Hammerstein's song celebrated the appeal of women in wartime, when they were scarce. But in the domestic life of Jews women were rarely scarce, and more typically stood for marriage, home, and responsibility than sexual excitement. In a Sholom Aleichem story the narrator's ironic tone assumes that his male listener shares his view. "*I* have a wife, *you* have a wife, we all have wives, we've had a taste of Paradise, we know what it means to be married." This attitude survived the *shtetl*. It surfaced in Henny Youngman's one-liner, "Take my wife — please!" In such a world, male fantasies turn to other pleasures, so Sherman transformed the original song's red-blooded celebration of woman into a hearty appreciation of food, which for reasons of survival and dietary law has long been a Jewish obsession.

> We got cole slaw, freshly made,
> And chopped liver, also fresh,
> And a lot of things to please a man
> Whose name is Moish or Hesh.
> We got plenty pumpernickel,
> We got bagels hard as rocks,
> What ain't we got?
> We ain't got lox!

Sherman originally came to New York for the theater, to continue his college successes, and land a musical on Broadway. *The Golden Touch* failed, but its suspicion of success, encouragement to remain true to oneself, and proud assurance that chopped liver and other homely hallmarks of Jewish life were worth keeping and nothing to be ashamed of remained the themes of Sherman's life. Once he had a steady income in television he could afford to think about them again. He did not have much else to think about. *I've Got a Secret* did not require much thought. "Allan frequently got depressed about television producing," wrote Zolotow. Dick Gehman explained that was because while he worked in television "the True Sherman was dormant, waking only occasionally to entertain friends at parties with song parodies he called 'Goldena Moments in Music.'"

The exact phrase was "Goldeneh Moments from Broadway," and they celebrated the Jewish moments that never appeared on Broadway. There was no shortage of those nonexistent moments. They were everywhere. That's because there were virtually no Jews on stage. They were all backstage, writing themselves out of the script. So Sherman turned Broadway inside out to discover the Jewish version of the smash hit. That is how Sherman found *Solly and Shirl*. It was hiding behind George and Ira Gershwin's *Porgy and Bess*.

Summertime
Everybody is shvitzing.
Schmaltz is melting
And the Catskills is high.
Oh, Your Daddy's sad
He'll come up for the veekend.
So hush little Bubbie,
Please don't cry.
Next Monday morning
He's going back to the garment
He'll be selling
Every sample and svatch
Your momma also
Gonna give out a few samples.
So sleep little Bubbie
For God's sake don't vy [cry].

Sherman knew what he was doing, and he wanted his listeners to know it, too. "What you are about to hear is entitled, 'Goldeneh Moments from Broadway,'" is how Sherman introduces a 1962 recording of his Jewish parody of *My Fair Lady*. "I said to myself, what would have happened, how would it have been, if all of the great Broadway hits of the great Broadway shows had been written by Jewish people — which they were." It was not a new line. He had been using it since the mid-1950s, and it represented Sherman's new strategy to take on Broadway. In 1948, he tried to get Jewish material on the stage. That did not work out. So in the 1950s, he took a path that did not require producers. Instead of writing original musicals, he turned already existing musicals into stories about Jews.

But Sherman's introductory patter is more significant than that, and as mind jarring as it is to contemplate any similarity between Sherman and that holy man of comic Jewish cool, Lenny Bruce, Sherman's paradox is as much a hipster riddle, as much a conundrum for insiders to get and outsiders to "huh?" over as Bruce's assertion that certain non-Jews are Jews and vice versa, that "Count Basie's Jewish . . . Eddie Cantor is *goyish*." Sherman's line said, "Dig, I'm Jewish. Lerner and Loewe are *goyish*." It points out that Broadway musicals are Jewish works without Jewish content. The Gershwins, Rodgers and Hart, Rodgers and Hammerstein, Lerner and Loewe, Frank Loesser, Stephen Sondheim, Irving Berlin, E. H. "Yip" Harburg, and other Jews created the bulk of Broadway's musical theater, but no one would ever guess it from what they wrote. The takeaway lesson was that success depended upon leaving Jewish ethnicity behind. That was a message Sherman had been fighting all his life, and his Broadway parodies were his battle plan. They peeled off the Christian camouflage worn by Broadway's Jewish creators, expelled them from the Eden of being assimilated Americans, and led them back into the exile of Jewishness, which for Sherman was a place of refuge and comfort.

Answering the Geshray

It took a while for Sherman to find his own approach to Jewish parody. In 1951, he wrote four Jewish song parodies for New York's Jubilee Records, three of which were false starts. Only one pointed the way forward. In 1951, he also cocreated the *I've Got A Secret* show. As a new father without a steady income, Sherman tried his hand at everything, and since he was already writing "witty ditties" for various singers, it was easy to branch out into the Jewish material he had always loved. It was especially easy with songwriting client Sylvia Froos, the former child vaudevillian known in the 1920s as Baby Sylvia Froos and later the Little Princess of Song. Sherman's material for her had a certain wised-up Jewish flavor, as in "Eh!"

> Oh, he comes from such a very lovely family
> They are symbols of respectability . . .
> Both his parents are the kind
> Who are genteel and refined.
> Eh — so his mother's a bookie . . .
> But he promised he would marry me!!!

The spur for Sherman's 1951 parodies was Mickey Katz, who had just proved that Jewish parodies of pop chart hits could make money. In November and December 1950, Capitol Records advertised in *Billboard* magazine to alert record dealers, juke box operators, and radio disc jockeys that Katz's parody of the 1950 hit, "Cry of the Wild Goose," translated literally as "Geshray of DeVilde Kotchke," was on the "Coming Up Fast!" and "Hot Sellers!" lists. It deserved to be. Katz here did not resort to "'She's a doll.' 'Yeah, yisgadal'" silliness but came up with a true parody. The melodramatic original salutes the wild goose as a symbol of the rugged American man, a loner and a wanderer. Katz turns the goose back into a bird he likes for dinner. "The butcher said that we have *kotchke* today / The *kotchke* heard him and he gave a *geshray*."

Sherman and Froos's duet on "A Satchel and a Seck," a parody of "A Bushel and a Peck," did not offer equivalent laughs. The vampy original from the *Guys and Dolls* musical that opened in New York on November 24, 1950, was by December 2 number four on *Billboard*'s list of "Records Most Played by Disk Jockeys." Sherman's "Satchel and a Seck" enters the ring against this champion and takes a dive. It surrenders to the original and accepts the stereotype that Yiddish has nothing to offer in the sex department but cutesy endearments. "I love you, a knadle and knish / A knadle and knish and a cnipple and a kish." The song is more novelty than parody, and it signals that Yiddish, ironically, hobbled Sherman's ability to express himself Jewishly. Despite his affinity and love for immigrant Yiddish speakers, he needed to create a new Jewish comedy in his native English.

"Jake's Song" parodies Bing Crosby's summer of 1950 "Sam's Song," a jaunty lyric that advertises its own cheerful appeal ("Here's a happy tune"). However, Sherman's version is mournful. He laments, "Isn't it a shame / He changed his name." That is, Bing Crosby's Sam is the assimilated Jake, and the "Jake's Song" parody is the original version of the original version. The name-changing theme harkens back to Joe Midas/Midasovich of *The Golden Touch*, and hints at Sherman's later Broadway parodies that unmask Jewish songwriters.

"Tennessee Frelich" is a parody of "Tennessee Waltz," and it mocks the original's earnestness with plainspoken Jewish comedy. Singer Patti Page made "Waltz" a big hit on the national charts in December 1950 with a sweetly heartbroken delivery that tells how she introduced her love to a friend, who then stole the boy away while they danced to the waltz. "Frelich," however, means happy, and Sherman's song turns the spurned woman's defeat into a victory. Yes, Naomi stole Froos's Mendel, but ten years later he turned up again and looked, "Not so bad."

The last of Sherman's 1951 parodies is "Tzimished," the original version of his 1957 "Bewitched" parody. "Bewitched" languished for ten years after its 1940 debut in *Pal Joey*. It was too suggestive for radio play. But in 1950 artists from Mel Tormé to Doris Day issued nine takes on the song, and all made it onto the *Billboard* singles chart, making it a good time for a parody.

> I should tell her I'm leaving
> But I can't — I'm afraid
> If I'll tell her, she'll tell me
> To "Gay genzintehaid." [go in good health]
> I say "Dot's all"
> Walk down the hall
> Then I turn around and say, noch a moll [again]
> Tzimished, fachottered and fablongett am I.

"Tzimished" heralded the future arrival of Sherman's "Goldeneh Moments from Broadway," which led to his first album, *My Son, the Folk Singer*. It was the first time since his 1938 "Humpty Dumpty" rhyme that Sherman took an English standard and with parody, dialect, and a bit of Yiddish transformed its meaning and transported its setting so completely that the new song takes on a life of its own and threatens to overshadow the original.

My Fair Sadie

This kind of songwriting ended soon after it began. In 1952, Sherman had to take care of more practical matters. His mother was dying of cancer, and the prospect of supporting his grandparents loomed. He had his hands full and does not seem to have written any more songs until his 1953, "How Are Things with Uncle Morris," a Jewish parody of E. H. "Yip" Harburg's "How Are Things in Glocca Morra," from the 1947 musical *Finian's Rainbow*.

"Glocca Morra" is an elegy to a lost childhood world but not, of course, a Jewish one. It pines for a childhood in Ireland. Finian wonders whether a certain brook there still runs "Through Killybegs, Kilkerry and Kildare?" But songwriter Harburg was born Isidore Hochberg on New York's Lower East Side to Yiddish-speaking Russian Jews, and that puts "Glocca Morra" at the heart of Sherman's paradox about Jews and the Broadway musical. *Finian's Rainbow*, formed in Harburg's Jewish imagination, was delivered to the world baptized into an ethnic vernacular acceptable to the Broadway audience of 1947. Sherman's "Uncle Morris" parody returns the song to the world of its father and allows it to speak its own accented English. Sherman probably wrote the parody after his mother died in May 1953. It is a comic valentine to the childhood world she ran from and he ran toward.

> How are things with Uncle Morris?
> Does he still work in the candy store?
> Does he still run like he always did
> To get some kid
> Fa nickel halavah?
> Is Aunt Bea with Uncle Morris?
> Do they still live on the second floor?
> Do they still live in the same old flat?
> Is he still fat?
> And does he walk around in his gatkes [long underwear] there
> Eating latkes there?
> Since I moved away to Scarsdale,
> And I joined a country club
> I lost touch with them and they lost touch with me
> How are things with Uncle Morris and Aunt Bea?

By turning Finian's old country into the Jews' old neighborhood Sherman was able to address the large-scale Jewish move from the city to suburbia, which represented "a transformational moment in American Judaism and Jewish life." During the 1950s, the American Jewish suburban population doubled, while the overall suburban population increase was only 29 percent. In *Marjorie Morningstar*, novelist Herman Wouk depicted upwardly mobile suburban Jews as a "new, more self-assured breed." Others were less sanguine. In 1953, the same year as Sherman's "Uncle Morris" parody, a synagogue director wrote an article called "Country Club Judaism." In it he complained that "Jewish suburban living seems diluted and pallid," partly because suburban Jews feel compelled to "modify their folkways and curb their personalities in an effort not to offend." Sherman's country club Jew feels the same way. He wonders if his relatives in the city still do things that he, in Scarsdale, presumably does not and perhaps cannot, such as eating Jewish foods that have Jewish names (latkes) and informally keeping warm by walking around in long winter underwear. Sherman's suburban Jew pines for a connection to that life even more than he wishes to live it, but the suburbs do not offer such a compromise. Only in the city, Sherman's parody seems to say, can a contemporary Jew dip into old-fashioned life for a quick pick-me-up. The suburbs offer only the new.

This ambivalence about the nature of Jewish life in the suburbs was a new subject. Philip Roth's novella about the Jewish city-suburb divide, *Goodbye, Columbus*, would not be published until 1959. But "Uncle Morris" proves Sherman had the presence of mind to make comedy from the enormous changes taking place right under his fixed nose, and so was ahead of Mel Brooks, Mickey Katz, and others in the 1950s who created only immigrant Jewish humor.

Sherman moved beyond immigrant humor also in his parody of *My Fair Lady*.

His version was inspired by a 1957 recording of *My Fairfax Lady*, the Los Angeles show written by Sid Kuller, who once wrote for the Marx Brothers. *Fairfax* was a brilliant idea. Its parody plot had immigrant Jews teach a non-Jewish young woman who speaks perfect English how to talk in Jewish dialect so she can fit into the Jewish Los Angeles neighborhood whose sights and smells charm her. However, everything she learns reflects the childhood world of Sid Kuller, born in 1910, not the 1950s world that existed outside the stage doors. Her Jewish language teacher trains her to pronounce the guttural *ch* sound in the Yiddish word *chrain* (horseradish), tells her about the two warring factions of East European Jews (Litvaks and Galitzianers), and in "Wouldn't That Be Milchadik" educates her about the Jewish food categories of *milchadik* (dairy), *fleichadik* (meat), and *pesachdik* (foods fit for Passover). She learns little about the Jewish world of 1950s Los Angeles, but the audience is treated to an evening of nostalgia.

Sherman's language teacher is also an immigrant, and he repeats the *Fairfax* bit about *chrain*, clinching that Sherman's parody originated in the earlier one. But Sherman's immigrant is aware of the 1950s New York Jewish world of suburbs, affluence, fur coats and jewelry. In Sherman's parody, the language student gets the inside scoop on contemporary Jewish American life, and the audience is treated to a funny but not very flattering look at the way they live now. In Sherman's version of "Wouldn't It Be Lovely," a song title he retains, *milchadik* is not on the menu.

All you need is a coat with minks
Cocktail watches and cocktail *rinks*
And other Jewish *thinks*
And wouldn't that be lovely
All you need is a matzah ball
Lots of carpet from wall-to-wall
A sleep-in maid, that's all
And wouldn't it be lovely
You'll start learning to play canasta like the girls all do
And by next December you'll
Wind up in the Fontainebleau.

A few years later, Woody Allen delivered his one-liner about the values of his old-world parents, which were "God and carpeting." Sherman was on this story early. He recognized what social critics realized a generation later, that consumer behavior can "be seen as a set of social and cultural practices, which establish differences between groups." Consumers "become distinct through their consumption," and Jewish American consumerism was a distinguishing feature of the group since immigrant days because shopping was the easiest and fastest way to become an American. Jews had a "hunger for splendor." Fur coats, especially, were a "deeply cherished" wish that stood for having arrived, being a success. When Sherman parodied *My Fair Lady*'s "On the Street Where You Live" in his "On the Streets Where We Live" there was little comedy about this social striving and how it was changing Jewish residential patterns. He had a field day with it.

We've got Scarsdale men
We've got Great Neck men
And just lately we've been sneaking into Darien.
Strange new noses there
Friends of Moses there
Near the goys on the streets where they live.

This is far removed from his Yiddish and dialect song parodies of 1951, and also from the endearing images offered by writers Wouk and Golden. As in his "Uncle Morris" parody, Sherman's Jews are not comfortably at home in the suburbs but realize the awkwardness of their new situation. "On the Streets Where We Live" continued,

Sports cars streaking there
Girls antiquing there
And you'll even find a little status seeking there
Lanes are curving there
Names are Irving there
Also Max on the streets where we live.

Sherman's shift from immigrant scene to the suburb better suited the cultural moment. Jews were Americanized and Yiddish was reserved for Jewish ceremonies, punch lines, and attitudes not meant for public consumption. But the switch to English, ironically, made it more difficult to imagine an audience for Sherman's creations. Songs with a substantial Yiddish vocabulary, like those by Katz, had a small but easy to identify public. Katz's customers were Jews raised or steeped in Yiddish-speaking culture. Jewish parodies in English seemed too Jewish for the general public and not Jewish enough for the Yiddish speakers, and in fact, Sherman's "Goldeneh Moments" repertoire was heard by very few. In the late 1950s, he sang these songs at house parties hosted by friends such as Maurice Zolotow and Bobby Rosengarden, and in one undated recording by Rosengarden, who was an audiophile with a high-quality reel-to-reel tape recorder, the audience appears to number no more than five or six people.

One of the songs they heard was "You're a Nudnick, Sondra Goldfein,"

Sherman's parody of the unsentimental courtship song, "You're a Queer One, Julie Jordan," from Rodgers and Hammerstein's *Carousel*. Julie Jordan's appeal is that she is not conventionally appealing. Neither is Sondra Goldfein, with her "nagging" and "kvetching."

> But I love you, Sondra Goldfein
> And some day up to the chuppeh we'll be led
> Till that day comes, Sondra Goldfein
> Let's get up and let the shvartze make the bed.

The casual Jewish racism here is not just Sherman's, but the community's. In fact, this kind of language was so common that anyone could have suggested it, and did. On one of Rosengarden's home recordings, the last line elicits howls of laughter, and as it dies down Sherman reminds Rosengarden's brother-in-law, choral director Ray Charles, that he suggested the line. Charles says, "I forgot." Sherman says, "Well, you did and it's beautiful." The beauty is in the casual treatment of premarital sex, and also in the comedy that comes at the expense of Jewish uneasiness with servants. They must be accommodated. The Jews must get up.

There is no Yiddish at all in "When You Walk through the Bronx," Sherman's parody of *Carousel*'s melodramatic tearjerker, "You'll Never Walk Alone." The original advises that we "walk on," but those instructions are vague. Sherman reworks the airy directions and makes them easy to follow, and as he does he follows a Jewish set of instructions laid down by the insistence on *tachlis*, down-to-earth details. The parody was a favorite of the group that gathered at Rosengarden's house. On a home recording someone repeatedly asks, "Allan, Allan, sing, 'You'll Never Walk Alone.'"

> When you walk through the Bronx
> Hold your head up high
> And look for a sign, "Fordham Road"
> Soon you'll come to a store that sells pizza pie
> Then you'll know that you're near my abode.
> Turn right, walk two blocks
> Turn left, cross the street

And no matter where you roam
Walk on
Walk on
Walk on through the Bronx
'Cause you'll find I won't be home.
Tonight I won't be home.

Heartfelt, chaste, and stirring lyrics were in mortal danger around Sherman. Irving Berlin's song, "Change Partners," first appeared in the 1938 film *Carefree*, but Sherman probably targeted it in 1958 when Ella Fitzgerald recorded it as part of her Grammy Award–nominated double album, *Ella Fitzgerald Sings the Irving Berlin Songbook*. Its lyric pleads with the desired love object to change partners and dance with the singer. Sherman's parody goes backstage, where Jewish writers knock out these *schmaltzy* songs and stories. It's a living.

Must you write
Every script
With the same fortunate man?
You've already got twenty-six in the can.
Won't you change partners and write with me?
You and me
Heaven knows
What we could become.
If you just get rid of that no talent bum
Then you'll change partners
And write with me.
I'll buy the paper and do all the typing, Max,
We'll work at your place
So you can deduct if from your income tax.

Sherman pulls the same trick with *West Side Story*'s "Maria." Frank Cooper was one of Sherman's agents.

Frank Cooper
I just met a man named Frank Cooper
He looked at me with eyes

So wonderful and wise to see
Frank Cooper
What god can I thank for Frank Cooper?
And how could I have known
He'd throw in Joel Cohen for free?
Frank Cooper
Say it loud and there's music playing
Say it soft and it's almost like praying
Frank Cooper
I'll never stop paying Frank Cooper.

The switch in that last line from the original song's "saying" to the parody's "paying" is exactly the kind of writing triumph Sherman delighted in, remembered his son, Robert. It was a personal challenge to Sherman to discover a song parody hiding within the original, and especially a parody that could be brought to life with the absolute minimum of alterations, so that the original lyrics are transformed into straight-lines for his punch line. At the height of his fame a *Los Angeles Times* reporter recognized that the similarities of Sherman's parodies to the originals were part of what made them great. "Sherman's new lyrics are phonetically close enough to the original ones to deceive the ear for that fraction of a second it takes to realize a comical change has taken place."

The last stop for Jewish life in the Fifties, after Yiddish, Jewish dialect, and the Bronx was left behind was the suburban country club, and that is where Sherman's Broadway parodies end up, too. *The Music Man* opened on Broadway on December 19, 1957, and Sherman borrowed its most famous song, "Seventy-Six Trombones," for a comic tribute to Jewish suburban and country club life. Parodying Meredith Wilson's work was at odds with his quip about Jews writing all the Broadway hits. Wilson was not Jewish. But Sherman evidently saw all musical theater as a Jewish realm. In any case, the opportunity was too good to pass up.

Seventy-six Sol Cohens in the country club!
And a hundred and ten nice men named Levine
And there's more than a thousand Finks
Who parade around the links

It's a sight that really must be seen.
Seventy-six Sol Cohens lead the big parade
With a hundred and nine Irv Kleins right behind
But the loveliest men I've known
Are the men they call Sol Cohen
At that good old country club of mine.

The booming, triumphant, oompah music is the perfect disorienting accompaniment to this absurd and wonderful folk song about Jewish life. But Sherman does not let his listeners or his community off easy. As much as the Jews changed the once gentlemanly and exclusive game of golf, the game also changed the Jews. The last verse delivers the punch line.

Seventy-six Sol Cohens in the country club
Seventy-six Sol Cohens playing gin
But they're hard to identify
'Cause as time goes passing by
One by one, they change their name to Quinn!

The "Sick" Comics

By the end of the 1950s, the performers that pointed Sherman toward a new ethnic comedy in America were on the wane. *My Fairfax Lady* and Mickey Katz were never popular beyond the older generation of American Jews who knew Yiddish and the traditional Jewish practices required to get the references and gags, but by the end of the decade even this market had had its fill. *My Fairfax Lady* ran for fourteen months and closed in the fall of 1957, was revived in July 1960, and closed by the end of September. Mickey Katz's popularity also declined after the mid-1950s. Comedy was headed in a new direction and Jews were taking it there, but they were not doing it as Jews.

Mort Sahl, Shelly Berman, Lenny Bruce, Tom Lehrer, and the comedy team of Mike Nichols and Elaine May made comedy out of material so unusual it was not only exciting and funny to hear it was also fascinating to think and argue about. "They joked about father and Freud, about mother and masochism, about sister and sadism," wrote *Time* magazine in a 1959 article about the so-called sick comics, and the topics raised predictable comparisons to the fall of Rome. But it was pretention, dishonesty, idiocy and the new bureaucracy of American life that got taken down, not empires. The 1959 album, *Inside Shelly Berman,* became what an ad in *Billboard* called the "all time best selling spoken word album." It sold more than a 150,000 copies and won a Grammy Award with bits like "The Department Store" that has Berman trying to notify a store that a woman is outside one of its windows hanging from a ledge. "Hello, uh, Nickels Department Store. See, I, uh. All right," Berman says as he undergoes his first hold that signals the lack of communication to come. The 1960 *An Evening with Nichols and May* won a Grammy for comedy sketches like the one about an adulterous couple that complains of their paralyzing guilt. Nichols tells May he feels so terribly that, "If I hadn't rented that room already I'd say forget it."

Time was especially fascinated and repulsed by Lenny Bruce and his mockery of religious leaders in the bit "Religions, Inc.," that imagines "Evangelist Oral Roberts putting in a long-distance call to the Vatican: 'Hello, John, what's shaking, baby? Say, that puff of white smoke was genius.'" Mort Sahl was the unofficial king of this new comedy, and on August 15, 1960, he landed on the cover of *Time*. His comedy had the college graduate's vocabulary and made fun of it, along with the pitfalls of a higher education. In his famous bit about the bank robber, the bank teller is told to act normal. "First you must define your terms," replies the teller. "After all, what is normal?"

All of this was a double-edged sword for Sherman. The new comics made humor a topic of interest for the media, and helped the comedy album category become a serious business. On the other hand, it seemed to signal the end of Jewish ethnic comedy. The "Mother and Son" sketch by Nichols and May is a classic depiction of the guilt-inducing, infantilizing mother, but the 1960 conversation between Mrs. White and her rocket scientist son Arthur did not tip its ethnic hat. It could be read as Jewish, or not. And despite profound underlying similarities with Lenny Bruce — who like Sherman also traveled from relation to relation as a virtual orphan after his parents divorced, and who also worked hard to get to the cemetery early — the way Bruce worked Jews into his material was too much his own to represent a path to follow.

Only Shelly Berman's 1959 "Father and Son" piece, on his *Outside Shelly*

Berman album, suggested that Jewish dialect humor could have widespread comic appeal. Berman plays his own father, an immigrant delicatessen owner on Chicago's West Side. He speaks English with a Yiddish accent and a gruff manner as he responds to his son's request for $100 for acting school. "A hundret dollas!"

That was little consolation as Sherman pondered the fix his Jewish parodies left him in. On Bobby Rosengarden's recording of Sherman's first performance of "Goldeneh Moments from Broadway" he is alternately proud and sheepish about his infatuation with such Jewish material. "From this whole thing that I do, you can't make a nickel," Sherman tells his audience. One of his listeners replied, "Just think how happy you're making us."

That was not enough. Sherman was tired of performing only at his and his friends' homes. He was a Jew at home, but he wanted to be a Jew in the street, too. When *Billboard* on June 23, 1958, announced his departure from *Secret*, it reported that Sherman was "eyeing his own music package." It was the first hint that Sherman dreamed of recording an album of his Jewish song parodies.

Five
OLLAVOOD!

In the summer of 1961, Allan Sherman met Harpo Marx, the meeting blossomed into a friendship, and the friendship produced one of the moments that helped Sherman launch his comedy career. "My dad just thought he was a genius" said Harpo's son, Bill Marx.

Harpo lived with his wife and children at El Rancho Harpo, his home in Rancho Mirage, California. But because summer in the California desert was so hot, in 1961 he rented a summerhouse at 301 North Saltair Avenue, in the exclusive Los Angeles neighborhood of Brentwood, which is near enough to the ocean to benefit from its cooling breezes. That same summer, Sherman and his family moved into a 3,400-square-foot rented house with a pool at 307 North Saltair Avenue. Sherman wrote that he heard harp music from the house next door, and one day returned a badminton birdie that had sailed into his rented garden and met Harpo. Harpo's son remembers that he had already met Sherman in New York. Bill Marx was a music student at Julliard in the mid-1950s when he appeared on an *I've Got a Secret* episode that featured relatives of famous people. That connection allowed Sherman to meet Harpo.

However the initial meeting took place, Harpo soon arranged for Sherman what Marx understatedly called a "fairly big" night. He threw a party to introduce Sherman to the greatest comedians in show business. Harpo had already attended a party at Sherman's house and heard the "Goldeneh Moments from Broadway" song parodies, and he wanted his friends to hear them, too. "Dad was so profoundly enamored with Allan's talent that he would arrange for people to come over now and then." Jack Benny, George Burns, Milton Berle, other Marx brothers, and "all the great vaudeville comedians from Hillcrest" came to the house, Marx said. Hillcrest Country Club, in Beverly Hills, was founded in 1920 as a Jewish golf and country club, and it attracted the sizable Jewish contingent in Hollywood, from studio heads Louis B. Mayer and the Warner brothers to performers Al Jolson, Milton Berle, and Groucho Marx.

Harpo may have been especially bowled over by Sherman's songs because he was old enough to remember their ancestors. He was born in 1888, and so was among the few in show business who grew up during the early twentieth-century "Jew-song craze," when the hit songs included Irving Berlin's 1909 "Yiddle on Your Fiddle" and "Sadie Salome, Go Home," about a sexually provocative, dance-loving young Jewish woman, much like Sherman's mother. Sadie's sweetheart, Mose, yells out during her performance, "Where is your clothes?" Other songs made comedy from "the incongruity of Jews in various situations," such as "I'm a Yiddish Cowboy," "Moshe from Nova Scotia," "Abie the Sporty Kid," about a sharp dresser, and Jews as ladies men in "Yiddisha Nightingale" and "Under the Matzos Tree."

Objections to these entertainments became organized with the founding of the Anti-Defamation League in 1913. The Jewish community won its battle against "the grotesque stage Jew, burdened with heavy beard and butchered dialect," but the fight went on until anything distinctly Jewish raised concerns and "in its place came invisibility." Jews were responding to stressful times. The 1908 play, *The Melting Pot*, by English-Jewish writer Israel Zangwill, urged Americanization, and President Theodore Roosevelt attended the premiere and applauded its message. This bias was strengthened by America's entry into World War I ten years later, which created a movement for "100 percent Americanism." All immigrant groups were advised to keep their heads down and wave the flag, but Jews most of all. The overarching "image of the Jew as a peculiarly and supremely international force" allowed Jews to be hated as representatives of the Russian communist threat, and also as greedy bankers. This antipathy continued for decades. In 1944, a poll found that one-quarter of Americans viewed Jews as a threat to the country.

But with the end of World War II came awareness of the Holocaust and a growing aversion to all bigotry. In 1947, President Truman supported the goals of equality outlined by his Committee on Civil Rights, and during his administration the American military was desegregated. In addition, as the nation became less agrarian, "the old suspicion of the city as a place of alien intrigue" declined. Jews, as the country's most urban community, benefitted from this change. Earlier immigration restrictions also had their intended effect. By the 1950s, the American Jewish population was overwhelmingly native born and Americanized, not immigrants with foreign ways. In 1962, only 1 percent of Americans named Jews as a threat. Sherman revived the "Jew song" tradition at the most receptive moment in more than fifty years, and at Harpo's house he performed his new songs for a generation familiar with the originals.

They got it.

"Jack Benny went positively ape over these ditties," Sherman wrote. "He gave a scream, lunged toward the floor and began wildly pounding on the carpet and laughing hysterically." This was a classic Benny reaction, but it was not a sham. "Jack had a great time. Everyone had a great time," Marx said. "Allan had talent. These guys who had worked up through the years, they knew a guy had to have talent to do what he did. They all knew."

It was a thrilling moment, and it signified that after a long hiatus, ethnicity was back. The decades-long silence enforced by Jewish embarrassment, on the one hand, and the general culture's insistence that minorities Americanize, on the other, was over. But there was no hint it would lead to anything substantial for Sherman himself. It was pivotal only in hindsight. At the time, it was a cherished moment of vindication sandwiched between times of unhappiness and family unrest. Sherman's 1961 move from New York to California threatened to split his family apart and re-create for his children the paternal abandonment of Sherman's own childhood.

Headaches

Sherman's last eighteen months in New York before his move to Los Angeles wore down himself and his family. After his writing gig for the summer television series *Perry Presents* ended in September 1959, he worked as a script doctor for troubled shows, including the short-lived *Charley Weaver Show*, and another disaster that gave rise to the barely true story that Sherman worked as a writer for Jackie Gleason. *Time* magazine described *You're in the Picture* as a "Jackie Gleason show, in which guest panelists, their heads protruding from backdrops of art reproductions or historical incidents, guess the picture they're in." In January 1961, the show's executive producer hired Sherman to save the show after its awful premiere and was prepared to "go along with any changes Sherman makes." Sherman never got the chance to make any changes. Gleason decided the show was too sick for heroic measures and it died a natural death.

The executive producer's vote of confidence proves Sherman still had a good reputation, but such contract assignments barely kept Sherman busy, could not match the predictability of his former salary at Goodson-Todman, and especially did not match the grand and expensive and needless new residence in Rye. "The kids didn't like to move," Golden said. "As soon as they made friends they had to move again." The major upheaval from Bronxville to Rye in June 1959 took place when Robert was nine and Nancy six, and it was an expanded version of Sherman's more run-of-the-mill instability. "Allan wasn't home much," Golden said of his years on *I've Got a Secret*. "Sometimes he came home, sometimes not. I would call him the next day. 'I slept on the couch.' Nothing was wrong. Never occurred to him to call to say he wasn't coming home." Others also found Sherman's behavior odd. Dee stayed in touch with her brother, Alex, and his family, and Dee's niece remembers that summertime trips from her home in St. Louis to the Sherman's in New York brought surprises. "Allan was home a lot during the day and he was always falling asleep and we always tiptoed around," said Terri Leamy. "If there is a male version of a prima donna, that was him. Always the most important person in the room."

One solution was to go into another room. That was where relatives and friends knew to look for Sherman's son, Robert. "Robbie was always in his room doing what he was doing," Leamy said. "Robbie was always distant. So bright that you couldn't even talk to him. When he was four years old he had wired a doorbell and light in a little log cabin. I don't know how he did it." Robert lived the same way when he got to California. "Robbie would go in his room and be Robbie," said Debbi Whiting, the daughter of Sherman's musical arranger, Lou Busch. "Very intellectual. He was in his own world." Robert was always fascinated with electronics and spent hours experimenting, building, and playing with games such as Geniac, an early computer kit. His father had been a hyper articulate and exhibitionistic boy that entertained his extended family. Robert was the opposite, and that had benefits. "My father was smart and mechanical and inventive, but even at age eight I knew electricity and he didn't," Robert said.

Between temporary television production jobs, Sherman invented a game show called *Matchmakers*, and he enlisted Robert's help to wire a buzzer for a tabletop version to demonstrate how the game worked. "It was to be played by a celebrity panel. There were two big visual game boards and what they were trying to do was match up clues from each board that related to each other somehow," such as an engagement ring and a picture of the often married Elizabeth Taylor, Robert said. *Matchmakers* never found a buyer, and these moments of father-son camaraderie could not outweigh Robert's apparent isolation. "He was very smart and high strung and he had a little black light and used to look at rocks and mica," said Bobby Rosengarden's son, Neil Rosengarden. Neil's brother Mark said, "I remember Robbie was really shy. I remember not being able to draw him out."

His parents also did not know how to draw Robert out, and when during the summer of 1960 they forced the ten-year-old to be with other children, they were sorry. "I should have let him stay in the basement," Golden said.

Camp Champlain was on the shores of New York's Lake Champlain, near the Adirondack Mountains, much further north than the Catskills region where many Jewish families sent their children to summer camp. In that distant location, some kids inevitably got homesick. "I never saw anyone as unhappy, though, as the boy we called Sherman," wrote Paul Lieberman in a *Los Angeles Times* story about the son of the man who wrote "Hello Muddah, Hello Fadduh," the world's most famous summer camp song. Robert's summer camp misery turned into anger at mealtime one day when during an argument he threw his knife — the dull butter knife that was classic summer camp cutlery — at a fellow camper. "It hit the other boy square in the chest," wrote Lieberman, who as a fellow camper witnessed the scene. The victim went down, unhurt but crying, and Robert Sherman was sent home.

That is not the way his mother remembers it, but her version might be worse. "The owner called after two weeks and said Robbie was demoralizing the other kids in his tent," Golden said. "He hated it so." Robert's memories of the experience are sketchy. "But I just hated it a lot," he told Lieberman.

The summer camp fiasco is the kind of event that makes parents wonder about themselves as parents, and it was not the only cause for concern. Robert and his younger sister, Nancy, fought constantly. Sherman was deeply troubled by it, and he later wrote an unpublished manuscript, *Every 600 Years, on a Tuesday (The Journey to the Perfectly Fair)*, that features his children as characters in a story that teaches them to look beyond life's unfair imbalances. The alternative is to make their unhappiness permanent. "This is Nancy, a girl. This is Robert, her brother. / Observe them refusing to talk to each other." The opening pages elaborate on the daily stresses in the Sherman household around 1960, when his children were young.

> Name-calling, blame-tossing, then hitting, then crying.
> Then milk began spilling. Then toast began flying.
> Then the hair-pulling started, and then it got rough.
> Mother yelled, "Stop!" and Dad yelled, "That's enough!"
> The siblings, still raging, exchanged a mean glare,
> And the parents thought, sadly, It just isn't Fair.

This family wretchedness was a variation on Sherman's own unhappy childhood that he tried to escape by renaming himself, instinctively embracing an old Jewish practice that saw parents rename children during times of illness so the angel of death would not find them. It did not work. Family dysfunction found him. In fact, he invited it in. "He was a lovely little guy, but abusive to his family," said Bill Loeb, who managed Sherman's career in the mid-1960s. "I used to see him at home sitting in his shorts and T-shirt, unglamorous like a little mogul in his chair, and barking orders. His wife would get rattled." Other visitors were also disturbed by Sherman's behavior at home. In the early 1970s, his daughter Nancy brought a friend to her father's Los Angeles apartment to help Sherman set up a quadraphonic stereo system. "My friend got so pissed," said Nancy. "She wasn't used to parents just sitting there and telling you what to do. And that's how he always was."

Sherman's regrets over his failings, and the similar failings he experienced at the hands of his own parents were always on his mind. His 1959 story "A Football for Grandma" begins with him losing his patience with his son Robert and Robert's angry response, which reminds Sherman of his own childhood anger toward his own mother. *Every 600 Years* is a message of love to his grown children that tries to redress earlier wrongs, when everyone in the family felt, "We do love each other, though no one would guess it. / Why can't we find some kind way to express it?" The tragedy of failed parent-child relationships always haunted him. Near the end of his life Sherman wrote in his 1973 book, *The Rape of the APE*, "Of all the people you are ever going to meet, you will know your own mother and father the least."

The family's unhappiness probably stemmed from Sherman's dogged insistence that childhood could be wonderful and innocent and joyful, if only people would do it right. "One thing my father had always been interested in was childhood schoolyard kind of games and those rhymes that you do while jumping rope and things," Robert said. That fixation led to the *I've Got a Secret* episodes that got him fired, and his children's bickering was another rebuke of his idealization. In his song parody "Headaches," Sherman accepts the mundane and disappointing realities of family life. It features a child issuing the laughably unreasonable demand, "Mommy! Can't you keep Daddy's car out of the driveway?" But Sherman reserved that healthy perspective for his comedy. "In his writing he wrote pathos, sympathetic," Golden said. "He didn't live that way." In life, whatever conflicted with his treasured vision of childhood had to go, or he did, and in 1961 he did. With a friend named Allie Singer, Sherman invented, pitched, and sold to CBS a new game show idea called *Your Surprise Package*. The network sent Sherman and Singer to Los Angeles to produce it, and Sherman left New York on February 12, 1961. He did not arrange for his family to follow him, or make plans to come home.

"Allan was having a very good time in Los Angeles, a very good time with bad companions," Golden said. She telephoned him at night but he was never in. That's because he was at PJ's, a new bar and nightclub on Santa Monica Boulevard in Hollywood that was named after New York's P.J. Clarke's. Golden later became familiar with Sherman's routine there. "He was friendly with the waitresses who told me, 'Every hooker that comes in, he makes them into a nun.'" Rose-colored glasses made childhood look better than it is, and it did the same for women.

Golden flew west with Robert and Nancy to visit her husband in the spring of 1961 during the Easter holiday school vacation. "He said, find me an apartment," Golden said. "A one-bedroom apartment. It was very hurtful." At the end of the Easter break, Dee and the children returned to Rye, but she was nervous. Her marriage and family life were in jeopardy, and just as in 1945 when Rose tricked Sherman into returning from New York to Chicago and pushed him to marry, the moment called for boldness. Otherwise, Sherman would drift away. This was clear to Sherman's Aunt Edith, widow of Rose's younger brother, Maury Sherman. Edith's long experience with Sherman family problems included her own husband's alcoholism, and she told Dee that to save her marriage she should withdraw her kids from school and move to Los Angeles immediately. Dee listened, and in May 1961 she pulled Robert and Nancy out of school, rented the Rye house, and went after her husband.

Ollavood!

For a few weeks the family lived together in Sherman's apartment, and in June they moved next door to Harpo. *Your Surprise Package* was on the air. It debuted on March 13, 1961. Reunited with his family, living in luxury, and working as a television producer, Sherman's life took on the appearance of healthy normality, but his behavior betrayed him. That summer the Sherman family visited Lake Tahoe on the California-Nevada border. Sherman gambled there, and he lost, big. "Well, Robbie will go to junior college," Golden remembers him telling her. She had no response to that. "What could I say? I was a little afraid of him."

Sherman's steamroller personality also showed up at work. "It was mad, absolutely mad," said Hal Cooper, director of *Your Surprise Package*. "He never stopped pushing the writers, pushing me, and pushing the whole show." It was, like *Secret*, another vehicle for "double entendre jokes," Cooper said. Panelists were given racy clues about what was inside a big gift-wrapped box on stage, and their responses allowed for off-color humor. For an electric dishwasher a clue was, "How your husband would like to see this: really stacked." The show had other weaknesses that proved Sherman underestimated the importance of the Goodson-Todman planning he detested. Panelists were confused by the rules and forgot to start or stop their time clocks. They were not entertainment professionals, as on *Secret*, but members of the general public trying to cope with material created on the fly by Sherman and his maniac friend Dave Vern. "Allan would suddenly get an idea to improve. His mind was always churning," Cooper said. "'Call the prop department and cancel shipload of something and get something else.' Sometimes it was impossible and I had to say, 'Allan, no!'" It had been the same during the summer of 1959 on *Perry Presents*. "We worked till 10 at night and I'd get a call at 2 AM and it was Allan," said Ray Charles. "'You know that thing we did? I fixed it.'"

This was not the Sherman of *I've Got a Secret* years that went golfing instead of to the office. In those years, his mania fed his revolving obsessions with golf, painting, photography, and antiques, other television shows, and his Jewish song parodies. Getting fired unsettled him. He had learned his lesson, but his new workplace hyperactivity was just as self-destructive as the earlier nonchalance. Before he left for California, *Variety* reported that Sherman had "half a dozen saucers in the air." In addition to the *Matchmakers* game, he supposedly had a deal to write a television special about *Life* magazine for its twenty-fifth anniversary, a contract to write an unnamed "hush-hush special," and was developing both a new television series and a comedy show. A happy medium was not available to him. Sherman swung from extreme to extreme.

A reminder why kicked off his return to Los Angeles. His parents and grand-parents were dead, but his criminal stepfather, Dave Segal, was still around, and he landed in Los Angeles on March 7, 1961, shortly after Sherman. Segal was not there to see his stepson. He came to town on criminal business, and on March 14 was in apartment 46 at the Fiesta Hotel on 7843 Lankershim Boulevard when two Los Angeles policemen arrived to arrest him. He was wanted for grand theft. They knocked on Segal's door. There was no answer. They opened the door with a passkey. Segal placed a .32 Colt pistol in his mouth and fired. In his wallet police found letters, notes, and other papers that connected him to "the syndicate" in Chicago, including information about attempts to legalize gambling in Chicago and Maryland where, Segal wrote, "New Governor with us." Sherman's stepbrother, Sheldon, flew in from Chicago to make the funeral arrangements, and on March 17 buried his father in the prominent Los Angeles Jewish cemetery of Hillside Memorial Park. Sherman did not attend the funeral, said Golden.

When Sherman was depressed, his mad, chaotic, and violent family legacy encouraged self-pity and self-destruction, usually achieved with the help of a menu. When he had his wits about him, he used them instead. Humor tamed what he called his "yo-yo" ups and downs and transformed his cockeyed experience into nutty charm. Others celebrated moving into a home with a housewarming. But since childhood, Sherman's many move-ins were just preludes to the inevitable move-outs, so when his summer rental of the Saltair house ended on Labor Day 1961 he celebrated his exit with a housecooling. "After Labor Day, I will live in a humble rented apartment and you wouldn't want to see me like that," Sherman's invitation read. "A modest dinner will be served. An hour later you will be hungry again. At which time another modest dinner will be served." Steve Allen and his wife, Jayne Meadows, had moved from New York to Los Angeles, and they were there, and so were Harpo Marx, "Bullets" Durgom, and Earl Wilson, who featured the party and quoted its invitation in his September 1, 1961, column. Another guest was Norman Corwin, a writer renowned for producing brilliant radio programming after the attack on Pearl Harbor, and for more recent triumphs. In 1957, his *Lust for Life* screenplay about Vincent Van Gogh was nominated for an Academy Award. In January 1961, he wrote remarks for the show business stars that performed at President Kennedy's inaugural gala.

It was not hard for Sherman to assemble these guests and dozens more. He was always gregarious, and as a television producer he had a working life that generated new connections, including comic actor Jim Backus and dramatic actor Everett Sloane, who played Mr. Bernstein in Orson Welles's *Citizen Kane*. If his show business networking failed, Sherman pulled out all the stops. "I had such a headache," Golden recalled. "He was walking down the street and inviting people."

Besides, by the late 1950s much of the television industry had migrated west, bringing many of Sherman's New York associates to Los Angeles. Another migration was also important to his future success. After World War II, Los Angeles became a magnet for Jews. When Sherman left the city in 1941, its Jewish population was only 130,000. Ten years later it was more than 300,000, and by the early 1960s it jumped again to nearly 400,000. "By the 1960s, only New York and Tel Aviv exceeded L.A. as the world's largest Jewish cities." It constituted a whole new audience for his "Goldeneh Moments" parodies, and to keep his repertoire fresh Sherman wrote new songs. "I would get a call from Allan literally at 11 or 12 at night. 'I need some help. I need someone to bounce some ideas off of,'" Hal Cooper said. "And I'd put my pants on and go over there and he'd make scrambled eggs, and I'd help him in writing a song for a party he was going to."

One of his new California songs was a Jewish parody of "Camelot," which premiered on Broadway on December 3, 1960. Sherman's version was called "Ollavood!"

> The movie stars all sit around the pool there
> The food at Nate 'n' Al's is very good
> And Sammy Davis Jr. goes to shul there
> In Ollavood!
> Where every girl can be a movie princess
> Where palm trees sway real good like palm trees should.
> Where Mrs. Eddie Fisher once made blintzes
> In Ollavood!

Sherman could be a hustler when he wanted, and his house party performances resembled the way he tried to make it as a songwriter when he was twenty. In the fall of 1944, while suspended from college, he became a regular at Gibby's, a Chicago piano bar, and on slow nights he plugged songs from his student musicals *Nothing Ventured* and *Mirth of a Nation*. It paid off with introductions to Lois Andrews, one of the Andrews Sisters, and singer Kitty Carlisle, who was reportedly interested in two songs from *Mirth of a Nation*, "Eleanor, Eleanor" and the lost "Dear Dr. Morgenthau." Skip Farrell, one of Chicago's most popular singing stars, even played *Nothing Ventured*'s "Lovely as a Lullaby" on his radio show. Now in Los Angeles, Sherman was doing it again, but at almost thirty-seven, he was running out of time. "Goldeneh Moments" was fun and games in New York while he worked on *Secret*, a hit show. *Your Surprise Package* was not a hit show. It would end on February 23, 1962, less than a year after its premiere. The show's bleak prospects must have been clear by September 1961, when Sherman moved out of the Saltair house. He needed a big break, and he got one.

Big Bad Jim

On September 27, 1961, he and Dee spent $75,000 on a four-bedroom, four-bath house with a swimming pool at 906 Chantilly Road in the luxury Los Angeles neighborhood of Bel Air. After the closing, they spent another $10,000 to build a home office and make other improvements. The $85,000 house, an unprepossessing ranch home, was more than five times the $15,000 median price of California homes, but it was not expensive for Bel Air, home to movie stars Cary Grant and Burt Lancaster. It was, however, expensive for the Shermans. They still owned the house in Rye and could not qualify for a mortgage large enough to swing the new purchase. A loan from Dee's mother allowed the deal to go ahead, Golden said.

Sherman and Dee sold the house in Rye a few months later on December 23, 1961. They had owned it for just two and a half years. Dee and the children went east without Sherman to pack it up, and because he was not there to oversee the move his instructions were to ship everything. "When we got back here to California we discovered that there were boxes that had firewood in them," Robert said.

Their new Bel Air home was a financial strain, but like the Rye house it was an advertisement as much as a residence. Sherman loved and needed to host parties for the influential show business people that could help him land jobs in television and perhaps even that music package he dreamed of, and for that he needed a display of affluence in accord with his image, if not his reality. He was a friend of Harpo's, had entertained Jack Benny and George Burns, was written up in Earl Wilson's column, and was buddies with television talk show star Steve Allen. Sherman had no choice. He had to look successful, and a summer rental in Brentwood and then a house in Bel Air helped. Shortly after the housecooling party Sherman got a call from personal show business manager Bullets Durgom. A former publicity man in the 1940s for the Glenn Miller and Tommy Dorsey orchestras, advance man for Dorsey's star singer, Frank Sinatra, and personal manager to Jackie Gleason, Durgom "was right out of Damon Runyon," said Bill Marx. "Everything got to Bullets sooner or later."

Bullets and Sherman had an earlier *I've Got a Secret* connection. Sherman's show needed celebrities, and Bullets managed them. But Bullets never heard Sherman's song parodies before the housecooling party, and they gave him an idea. The president of Warner Bros. Records, a straight-laced and charity-minded Mormon named Jim Conkling was retiring to devote himself to public service. Bullets was tone-deaf to such ideals, but he had perfect pitch when it came to making the most of a high-profile event, and in classic Bullets fashion he got himself named to the committee in charge of handling Conkling's October 25, 1961, send-off at the Crystal Room in the Beverly Hills Hotel. Affectionately known as the Pink Palace after the distinctive paint was applied in 1948, the hotel in the 1940s hosted stars such as Humphrey Bogart and Marlene Dietrich and the famous recluse Howard Hughes. Frank Sinatra and Dean Martin brought their impolite manliness to the place in the 1950s, and in that spirit Bullets asked Sherman to whip up for the Conkling party a bit of army barracks humor. It was a stag event, no women allowed, so the language could be rough. To the tune of country music singer Jimmy Dean's then hit song, "Big Bad John," Sherman gave Conkling the business in "Big Bad Jim."

Now Big Bad Jim was an ordinary slob
Till the day Glen Wallis come and give him a job
He was just a trumpet player when he was young
But all the ladies loved him for his triple tongue
That's Big Jim
Big Bad Jim.
Jim can still remember that bygone day
When he did a lot of blowing with Alvino Ray
First he blew the rhythm section
Then he blew the brass
Then he blew the rest of local 802 en masse

The crude and rude parody gets ruder and cruder. It goes on to portray Conkling as a homosexual slut that enjoys servicing the entire recording industry. Though Sherman attended the party, he did not sing it live. He and Bullets had visited a recording studio where Sherman sang his parody over the music to the original song, which can be heard playing in the background. At the Conkling bash, Bullets put the specialty record on a turntable. "The highlight [of the party] was the 'Big Jim' parody of 'Big John' which Bullets Durgom and Allen [*sic*] Sherman penned," *Variety* reported. It was far from Sherman's usual fare, but its success confirmed that Sherman knew his audience. He knew the men of his generation and the love of coarse language and jokes that lay under their sophistication and titles. Sherman had not been shocked by rule-breaking sexual behavior since junior high, and that early education was still paying dividends.

The Conkling event was an important showcase for Sherman's comic talents. Harpo's party introduced Sherman to legends that may have had more reputation than clout, but Conkling's introduced his voice and wit to 250 of the top men in the recording business, including the president of Warner Brothers Pictures and founder of Warner Bros. Records, Jack L. Warner, Sherman's future musical arranger, Lou Busch, and Mike Maitland, the new president of Warner Bros. Records and Sherman's future boss.

Those relationships were only about six months off, but they were preceded by events that brought Sherman to a new low, though they also testified to his good luck and determination. On November 6, 1961, two weeks after the Conkling party, Los Angeles suffered what the city's fire department called "the most disastrous brush fire in the history of Southern California." The Bel Air-Brentwood Fire destroyed 484 homes. Sherman's street, Chantilly Road, was at the center of it, but in the random manner of such fires his home survived. Three months later on February 23, 1962, *Your Surprise Package* aired for the last time, and Sherman went on unemployment. At night, depressed, he left the house to drink. "When he was sitting night after night in P.J.'s, Robbie asked, 'When's dad coming home?'" said Golden.

A Nation of Immigrants

Despite the self-pity he indulged and the hurt he caused, he doggedly kept his eye on the music package he breezily announced he was considering when he left *I've Got a Secret*. He continued to promote his "Goldeneh Moments" parodies at house parties, including one on April 10, 1962, at an unknown location that was important enough to record. At least some in the audience were regulars, and called out for Sherman to sing "The Riviera," a song to the tune of "Return to Sorrento" that lampoons the Los Angeles Riviera neighborhood, where the streets are named after Italian towns and regions, such as Amalfi, Napoli, and Corsica. "1481 Sorrento / Has three bedrooms and a maids room / And a lovely built-in kitchen / And a sliding glass lanai." But the rest of his performance was dominated by the "Goldeneh" repertoire of Jewish song parodies, including "Seventy-Six Sol Cohens," "When You Walk through the Bronx," "There Is Nothing Like a Lox," and a new one called "Chopped Liver" that parodied Johnny Mercer's "Moon River," from the movie *Breakfast at Tiffany's*. The night before the party the song won an Oscar Award, and on the spur of the moment, Sherman said, "I decided to desecrate" it.

> Chopped liver
> Rolled up in a ball.
> Too much cholesterol
> They say.
> You heart breaker
> You fat maker
> From now on I'm going the safflower way.

The party performance was a success. The crowd laughed loudly and applauded often, and the open enjoyment reflected the country's changing cultural climate that began to welcome ethnic identity. It was a change that had been building for some time, and then seemed to arrive all at once with the November 1960 election of President John F. Kennedy. As an Irish Catholic, his ascent represented "the mainstreaming not just of a man but of a cultural ideal, that of white ethnicity itself," and the idea that whites could be ethnics, could be culturally different from Wasp Americans without being locked into a racial or religious category was enormously attractive to Jews, whose allegiances to their group were not easy to sort out. The ties included religion, and also family, history, language, food, custom and humor. Ethnicity was the only idea big enough and vague enough to encompass the Jewish American experience, and in the 1950s Jewish social scientists Nathan Glazer, Daniel Bell and Seymour Martin Lipset worked out the particulars of this new idea in light of "the quite anomalous experience of Jews: that put family, education, assimilation at the center" of the story of how various peples fare in America. The Jewish story became the model ethnic-American story, and because of the Jews' success it was a story with a happy ending. Immigration was given the same Jewish twist by Oscar Handlin, a historian at Harvard who took his Brooklyn Jewish boyhood seriously and decided that immigrants were at the heart of the American story. His 1952 book, *The Uprooted: The Epic Story of the Great Migrations That Made the American People* won a Pulitzer. Jews were eager to find non-Jewish boosters of the same idea, and in 1959 the Anti-Defamation League published *A Nation of Immigrants*, Senator John F. Kennedy's pamphlet extolling the benefits of ethnic diversity.

Not all ethnic voices that year were made to order for the delight of official Jewry. In 1959, Philip Roth's *Goodbye, Columbus* presented stories about flawed and even unappealing Jews that incensed many in the community, and exposed how new and sensitive this business of being openly Jewish in America still was.

Frank expressions of Jewish ethnicity did not come only from academics and literary authors such as Handlin and Roth. Entertainers took laughter as a reliable sign their ethnic humor was getting cross. Their material did not always succeed.

The now legendary album, *2000 Years with Carl Reiner and Mel Brooks*, received mixed reviews. It was panned in *Billboard*. The weekly did not even mention the "2000 Year Old Man" routine, performed with a Yiddish accent. "Unfortunately, it is not very funny comedy," was how the trade dispatched the record on November 21, 1960. *Variety* liked it, and also the 1961 follow-up, *2000 and One Years with Carl Reiner and Mel Brooks*, which was nominated for a Grammy Award, but news stories announcing major sales never came. It remained in-group entertainment, and a delicate one. *Variety* avoided uttering

Jewish or Yiddish to describe the "2000 Year Old Man" bit, instead falling back on code that those in the know would get, such as "dialectician."

Anti-Semitism was dead, but decades of public silence about Jewish characteristics made their reappearance hard to accept. Leonard Bernstein became conductor of the New York Philharmonic in 1958, and in 1960 his strong Jewish identity made some people uncomfortable. Feeling "so damn guilty about being in Berlin, of *all* places, over Rosh Hashana" to conduct, he proposed beginning the concert with a prayer in Hebrew. The problem was, the performance was scheduled to be broadcast on American television on Thanksgiving, and after a television producer took an informal poll among friends "who are by no means stiff-necked," she told Bernstein "they think Thanksgiving is basically a Protestant holiday, and some people might be — well, not offended, but think it's bad timing." Bernstein went ahead with his Hebrew prayer. He had clout. Up-and-comers got rougher treatment. In March 1962, the *New York Journal-American* wrote that Barbra Streisand, then starring in *I Can Get It for You Wholesale*, her Broadway debut, "resembles an amiable anteater." A few months later on June 29, Warner Bros. Records president, Mike Maitland, received a telegram recommending Streisand for a recording contract. No other career was anticipated. "Due bad facial features extremely limited films."

Big celebrity was still reserved for Jewish comedians that either ignored Jewish identity, such as Mort Sahl, or those like Bill Dana that camouflaged it under an assumed ethnicity. Dana was a sensation as José Jiménez, a meek and bumbling Chicano with limited English. He appeared as Jiménez at President Kennedy's inaugural gala on January 19, 1961, alongside top stars such as Frank Sinatra, Gene Kelly, Milton Berle, Tony Curtis, Nat King Cole, and Ella Fitzgerald, and on May 5, 1961, the character became "something close to a national hero" when the Mercury Seven astronauts adopted him "as an informal mascot."

But despite resistance and reticence, the cultural restraints that held Jewish ethnicity in check were loosening up, and much of this new ease also emanated from the White House, where humor replaced grim earnestness, and comedy ushered in honesty. Song parodies were an especially good way to skewer official culture, and the entertainment at Kennedy's inaugural gala included "an 'Ode to the Inauguration,' a pastiche of popular songs with special parody lyrics." In January 1962, the *New York Times* applauded the return of high culture to the White House, but was forced to admit it was mostly Mrs. Kennedy's doing. The president "enjoys satirical comics, particularly Bob Newhart, Joey Bishop and Mort Sahl." Unselfconscious enjoyment was part of the Kennedy magic. "The food is marvelous, the wines are delicious, there are cigarettes on the table, people are laughing, *laughing out loud*, telling stories, jokes, enjoying themselves, glad to be there," is how Leonard Bernstein remembered a November 1961 White House dinner in honor of cellist Pablo Casals.

So many forces bombarded American culture with Jewish energy that by the time of Sherman's 1962 record contract a critical mass had been reached. The 1950s folk music movement was from the start internationalist, and Israeli songs performed partly or largely in Hebrew sold well. An example came in July 1950, when *Billboard* reported Decca records had "phenomenal success" with "Tzena, Tzena, Tzena." Folk music took off during the Kennedy years, when Harry Belafonte's 1959 recording of "Havá Nagila" made the tune a pop standard during the young president's abbreviated term. In 1960, Billy Wilder's Academy Award–winning film, *The Apartment*, has Jack Lemmon's character signal his transformation from go-along organization man to moral individual by having him adopt the values of his Jewish neighbor, who convinces him to be a mensch. In June 1961, Jackie Mason succeeded at New York's Copacabana club with a fast-paced comic delivery *Variety* was frank enough to state was "tinged with a Yiddish dialect," though some of his Jewish material fell flat. On March 25, 1962, a couple of weeks before the April 15 tax-filing deadline, Mason did a series of tax jokes on the *Ed Sullivan Show*, and got worked up that President Kennedy hosted a lunch for 300 at the Waldorf Astoria that cost $15,000. "My bar mitzvah didn't cost that much," Mason complained. That got a big laugh, but the next joke showed that Americans were unfamiliar with some Jewish concerns. Kennedy invited Egypt's President Nasser to the White House. Mason offered, "Let him invite Ben Gurion, I'll be glad to pay for it." The line bombed.

Like Mel Brooks and Carl Reiner, Jackie Mason tried to turn ethnic Jewish comedy into mainstream entertainment. There were signs the country was ready, but nobody had yet found the perfect formula.

SIX
MY SON,
THE FOLK SINGER

On August 6, 1962, Joe Smith of Warner Bros. Records was out to dinner in Los Angeles with his wife and father-in-law when he played a tape of Sherman's first album, *My Son, the Folk Singer*, recorded earlier that day.

"A guy at the next booth said, 'What is that? I want twenty-five of those. I'll write you a check,'" recalled Smith. "We thought we had something."

They had something big. Sherman's album hijacked a collection of folk songs, took them on a joyride through his Jewish imagination, and turned them into a hit album that left critics wondering what was going on in this country. When the record was released in October reviewers at *Variety* and *Billboard* agreed *My Son, the Folk Singer* was funny. They also agreed it ribbed an American world that would hardly feel the jab. Turning "Frère Jacques" into "Sarah Jackman" might be funny to *us*, but it would not be funny to *them*, was how the thinking went. *Billboard* predicted sales among "New Yorkers, Los Angelenos, and other big cityites." All were euphemisms for Jews. *Variety* agreed Sherman's customers were "mostly along the Miami-Catskills axis." Yet the album revealed that when no one was looking the line between Jews and everyone else had blurred. Everybody loved "Sarah Jackman."

Sarah Jackman, Sarah Jackman
How's by you? How's by you?
How's by you the family?
How's your sister Emily?
She's nice, too.
She's nice, too.

By the end of October 1962, three weeks after it appeared, *Folk Singer* had sold almost 400,000 copies and was one of the fastest selling albums in history. By early November sales hit half a million, and in December surpassed a million. When the album sold big in Atlanta, Georgia, *Billboard* had to admit that it was out of its depth. America was changing. "Today's mass-communications media — such as T V, movies, radios, newspapers, magazines — are raising sophistication levels, apparently, and removing some of the 'regional' or 'ethnic' limitation to national popularity."

The highbrow *Saturday Review* saw in Sherman's success evidence of something more profound. It opined that, "periodically a bard arises in the land whose hitherto uncelebrated talents seem a convulsive expression of a long-suppressed general emotion." That long-suppressed emotion was ethnicity, as the groundbreaking book *Beyond the Melting Pot* made explicit a year later. The ethnic revival of the 1960s and 1970s was on its way, but the country needed a volunteer. Some group had to lead the charge and wave the banner for those who had funny last names and relatives that spoke mangled English. *Folk Singer* said the Jews would take that job.

Sherman was just what everyone had been waiting for.

Too Perfect

Usually, anyone waiting for Sherman found him to be late. This time circumstances forced him to show up early.

In June 1962, Sherman was characteristically pursuing two career opportunities simultaneously and working to undermine at least one of them. To replace his *Your Surprise Package* producing job that ended in February, he contacted Steve Allen about producing the upcoming *Steve Allen Show*. On

May 23, 1962, *Daily Variety* announced "Allan Sherman Named Producer of New Steve Allen Show." A week later, on June 1, Sherman signed an Exclusive Artist's Recording Agreement with Warner Bros. Records.

"Bullets said to us that he had a guy, Sherman," said Joe Smith, then head of promotions at Warner. "I had heard Allan, and thought it was interesting. Stuff was Goldeneh." All of Sherman's hustling—the house party performances, the Harpo gig, the Conkling party—had paid off. He had a contract. The music package was within sight.

But it was hardly a guarantee of success, never mind stardom. His Warner contract, engineered by Bullets, was, understandably, modest. Sherman was an unknown, overweight thirty-seven-year-old performer of his own Jewish song parodies. Woody Allen's 1984 film *Broadway Danny Rose*, about a hapless talent agent, has clients like that. So did Warner Bros. Records. "We had no artists," said Stan Cornyn, a retired top executive who started at Warner as a writer of liner notes when the company was founded in 1958. "Stereo was a niche for us. Polka in stereo, Hawaiian stuff in stereo." The idea was to sell between 8,000 and 10,000 records.

Sherman's contract called for first album royalty rates that topped out at 5 percent for sales in excess of 30,000. A number beyond that was unthinkable. Warner guaranteed one record between July 1, 1962, and June 30, 1963, and two more over the next two years. A record a year is a meager output, and Sherman's royalty rate further limited the possibility of riches. If his first album sold 30,000 copies he would gross about $8,000. Then he would have to pay Bullets, who took Sherman to the cleaners on the deal, demanding 20 percent of his royalties. Ten percent was his standard fee as personal manager, and he argued for the additional ten percent because it would have gone to an agent if Sherman had one. He did not have one. So instead of that 10 percent ending up in Sherman's pocket, Bullets claimed it. In an echo of his mother's scheme to mastermind his marriage, Sherman could not defend himself against single-minded adversaries that pursued their goals without conscience or scruples. He did not even tell Bullets to talk with his lawyers in New York, at Becker and London. That firm took another 6 percent. Sherman's decision to remain childlike into adulthood was expensive.

Still, he found himself in an ideal situation. He was signed with Warner and was the producer for Steve Allen, creator and host in 1954 of the *Tonight* show and one of the most famous and respected men in television. Sherman had realized his dream of getting a record deal for his Jewish song parodies, and he also improved his position in the television industry. In the 1950s, he wrote and performed his "Goldeneh" parodies while producing *I've Got a Secret*. Now he could record a parody album a year for Warner Bros. while working for Steve Allen. Both his creative and fiscal needs would be fulfilled. It was perfect, which is a condition no self-destructive person can bear. Just like in college, and at Goodson-Todman, Sherman sawed off the practical limb that supported him.

"We did meetings during the day, and in the evenings Allan and I toured the clubs, listening mostly to jazz, ostensibly scouting talent for the show," said writer Jerry Hopkins about their time together on the *Steve Allen Show*. Hopkins was Steve Allen's "kook booker," the one who drummed up offbeat characters for the show. "When the bars closed at 2, we'd then go to a big club on Santa Monica Boulevard, for an early breakfast of bagels and cream cheese, scrambled eggs and lox. So it was closer to dawn than midnight when our day ended." This schedule was more than Allan could bear. He was not up to it, physically, and never arrived at work before 10, and then, Hopkins recalled, "seriously out of breath from the one flight of stairs, and threw himself on the couch in his office, where he gasped for breath."

That was not the worst of it. Sherman could not break his Vegas gambling habit, and after he started on the show he concocted a story about needing to speak to a bandleader there. "He lost his money, plane ticket, everything," said Golden. "Dirty, disheveled, he took a bus back. He called me to pick him up to take him to the meeting they were already having."

Despite these infuriating lapses, Sherman's affability and generosity made guest appearances. "He was extraordinarily friendly and kind to me," said Jerry Goldstein, who got into television production thanks to Sherman giving him a gopher job on the *Steve Allen Show*. And Hopkins counted himself as Sherman's "new best friend." But Sherman was not doing his job. "He sat there telling jokes but not telling us what to do," said Win Opie, the show's assistant director. "He had no creative input to the show at all." Not content with benign neglect, Sherman actively undermined Steve Allen. "He was sitting in the front row and yelling at Steve" during taping, remembered Milt Hoffman,

Sherman's associate producer. "Calling attention to himself while Steve was performing." Word got back to Westinghouse, and the show's sponsor sent Joel Chaseman, an experienced producer who had worked for newsman Mike Wallace to investigate. "When I got to the *Steve Allen*, to put it in the kindest possible light," Chaseman said, "Allan Sherman was just not terribly engaged with the process." The two men had lunch at the Formosa Café, a Chinese restaurant popular for decades with the Hollywood stars whose photographs blanket the walls. "And I asked Allan about a lot of this stuff and he had a variety of non-replies. He was funny and cordial and friendly and nonresponsive."

Three weeks after the announcement of Sherman's hiring came the announcement of his firing. "Oust Producer from Allen's New TV Alley" read a top headline on the front page of the June 19, 1962, *Daily Variety*. "Allan Sherman has been axed as producer of the new Steve Allen TV show after functioning in that capacity for first week of taping," was the lead. Sherman claimed in his autobiography that Westinghouse planted the story as revenge for his agent insisting Sherman receive full payment as per his contract, regardless of his brief engagement, and that the story left him stranded and alone as a disgraced pariah. The charge seems true. *Billboard* ran a benign report that Sherman resigned, and gave the minor news the minimal coverage it deserved. But Sherman ignored Westinghouse's efforts to salvage the Steve Allen situation when he was not doing his job, or even showing up. "In his book, he wrote that Westinghouse was evil," Golden said. "Quite the opposite. They called the house and asked for him." And he was no pariah. "He was really more interested in being a talent," Hoffman said.

That also had its problems. Sherman's new contract with Warner Bros. made him guarantee that his song material be either "wholly original" or "in the public domain throughout the world." The "Goldeneh Moments from Broadway" were out, despite the record company's efforts. Joe Smith and Sherman visited Meredith Wilson, creator of *The Music Man*, to get permission to record "Seventy-Six Sol Cohens." As head of promotions at Warner, Smith once arranged for 3,000 radio stations across the country to play *Music Man* songs on the same day. "Meredith loved me for that," Smith said. The love affair ended after Sherman started to sing his parody. "Meredith stood up and yelled, 'This is a joke. You're crazy! Get out of my house. Get out of my house.'"

By the end of June 1962, Sherman was faced with a bigger gamble than he ever placed in Vegas. He had no job, and he needed to write new song material immediately to record an album at the front end of his contract period, not the back. He did not have the money to last until the spring of 1963. As he later told *Variety*, the summer of 1962 "was a lean one." Sherman "had about $1,000 from June till August, when he would get a $1,500 advance for his first recording." After fame brought him new funds he kidded that he always lived beyond his means but that lately it was getting harder to do. But at this time his situation was no joke. Years of unsteady employment and steady spending threatened to ruin him, and Sherman was reduced to putting the touch on friends and acquaintances. "I knew him when he was in a real deep scuffle," said comedian Bill Dana about the weeks after Sherman left the *Steve Allen Show*. "He was in survival mode, looking for handouts."

Imp at Play

My Son, the Folk Singer was a rush job made possible by Sherman's nearly thirty years of preparation. He was a pro at writing Jewish parodies and expert at turning nursery rhyme tunes and other emblems of childhood into comic commentaries on adult life. Plus, Sherman had a certificate in writing under great pressure. It was the setting he liked best. So after he was fired from the *Steve Allen Show* and lost his income, Sherman hurried to record an album for Warner Bros. that required no copyright releases. Meredith Wilson's outburst was just the tip of the iceberg. Congress was revising the copyright laws, and music publishers were on the warpath against the kind of liberties Sherman took with their property. In a few months' time, Philip B. Wattenberg, attorney for the Music Publishers Protective Association, would single out Sherman's work as just the kind of thing that had to stop. "The changes I have suggested eliminate the right as now provided in the draft to arrange without limit and to *adapt*," Wattenberg emphasized on April 15, 1963. That right was not merely a commercial concern to publishers, Wattenberg asserted, but a moral one. It leads to "unauthorized adaptations which are beyond the limits of reason and good taste." For example, "Allan Sherman has made a record of the well known musical composition 'BEWITCHED' by Lorenz Hart and Richard Rodgers with an entirely new title 'TZIMISHED' and a parodied lyric."

The transcript of the hearing does not reveal whether anyone smirked. By April, Sherman was famous and had played two Washington, D.C., functions. But Wattenberg's willingness to stare down giggles was a sign of how determined publishers were to end such parodies.

Warner's president, Mike Maitland, suggested Sherman parody the folk music craze. Most of the songs were in the public domain. It was an inspired idea. By the early 1960s, the twenty-year-old folk music scene had deserted the gritty roots planted in 1941 by the ardently leftist Almanac Singers and other residents of Greenwich Village's so-called Almanac House, such as Pete Seeger and Woody Guthrie. Instead it had become bloated with solemn, sometimes beautiful but often just pretty renditions of antiquated classics performed by the Kingston Trio, the Limelighters, and Peter, Paul and Mary. Even the *Village Voice* was tired of the folk movement's forced earnestness, and on October 4, 1962, just as Sherman's folk parodies debuted on the radio, its front page lamented that the "1950s will probably go down as the decade in which folk music lost its purity and brought the Kingston Trio into the world." The paper sneered at "professional folksingers" that parleyed "the laments of poverty into such sizable insurance against the experience of it."

That atmosphere provided a wealth of folk material to parody, and Sherman, his wife, and his newly assigned musical director Lou Busch set out to find the ripest targets. Busch, also known as the ragtime pianist Joe "Fingers" Carr, was with lyricist Johnny Mercer's Capitol Records before Warner Bros., and at Capitol he worked with singers such as Nat "King" Cole, and Peggy Lee. He knew how to guide performers toward songs that would work for them, build a coherent album, and write the musical arrangements that determine an album's sound. "Lou would hold everything together because he was a pro," said Warner's Stan Cornyn. That talent made him perfect for Sherman, who needed holding together. "Lou disciplined Allan," Golden said. "He came to the house with a blank sheet of paper and made order out of chaos." And he knew how to establish the musical straight lines for Sherman's lyric punch lines. His grand orchestrations supplemented by a chorus of angelic voices set up Sherman's untrained voice for the biggest laugh. "If there had been no Lou Busch, it would not have been a hit," said Robert Sherman.

Busch was also a wised-up ladies man and joker who soon met his third wife through Sherman. "They were just having too much fun," said Busch's daughter,

Debbi Whiting, who watched her father and Sherman write the *Folk Singer* album when she showed up at the Shermans' Bel Air house after school. The two men sat together in the living room at a black baby grand piano where Sherman sang into a microphone hooked up to a tape recorder in his home office. The connection between the two locations was a sixty-foot extension cord. "The wire I hooked up went from the office, through the kitchen, through the dining room to the piano," said Robert. Busch played the piano. Sherman was so unfamiliar with the instrument that when he later recorded *Peter and the Commissar*, a live album that parodied classical music, an assistant put masking tape on the keys so he could play four notes of "How Dry I Am." But he was an ardent student of music and song and instinctively understood basics such as time and meter, Smith said. And he was in full possession of the charm that facilitated many relationships and friendships. "There was something lovable about him," Golden said. "He was impish." Playful naughtiness provided the chemistry between him and Busch. "They were constantly laughing and cracking each other up, and they got a little dirty," Whiting said. "It's like a bunch of musicians sitting in a band and they're laughing and you knew they were being blue. I grew up around musicians, and the rule number one was, don't marry one. I mean, hello?"

Sherman's wife already had enough experience to say amen to that lesson, but at least now she was enjoying the benefits of a husband like hers. She and Lou and Allan sat around a table on the lanai and "we played records and some we parodied," Golden said. She was not merely tolerated. Golden was a welcomed contributor who helped Sherman with many of his songs. In 1963, she and Sherman visited the University of Illinois, and Golden's niece, Terri Leamy, was at the breakfast table when Sherman and Dee wrote a song about their old school that he sang later that day. "He was making up the words and laughing and she really contributed some very clever lines and I was surprised, and they said 'Oh, that happens all the time.'"

Besides, there was no time for false pride. Sherman needed an album fast and could use all the help he could get. He was never averse to shortcuts. In their search for parody targets, Sherman, Dee, and Busch do not seem to have listened to very many folk records. Of the ten songs on *My Son, the Folk Singer*, three came from Harry Belafonte's live albums recorded in 1959 and 1960 at Carnegie Hall. These were "Jump Down, Spin Around (Pick a Bale o' Cotton),"

"Water Boy," performed by folk singer Odetta, and "Matilda," a Calypso-style song about an unfaithful woman that "take me money and run Venezuela." At his 1959 concert, Belafonte transformed "Matilda" into a twelve-minute group sing-along by calling on his musical trio, his conductor, the audience, and "everybody" to sing the chorus "a little louder." Belafonte even used a little Yiddish, calling on "the whole *mishpocha*," or family, to sing along. Sherman targeted the song and also Belafonte's schmaltzy performance in his parody, "My Zelda."

Two more songs parodied on the album — the sixteenth-century English ballad "Greensleeves" and the early twentieth-century American cowboy song, "The Streets of Laredo" — were easily plucked from the cultural ether. Folk-singer Theodore Bikel recorded both songs on his 1958 album, *Young Man and a Maid: Love Songs of Many Lands*, and "Laredo" got another boost in August 1961 on the *Best of Burl Ives* double album. Another idea came from the Mormon Tabernacle Choir, which in September 1959 had what *Billboard* called the "most unusual new pop singles hit today" in its recording of the "Battle Hymn of the Republic," the rousing nineteenth-century American standard that contributed the phrase "the grapes of wrath" to American history and literature, which Sherman tweaked to produce his greatest pun. Sherman's own mental storehouse of songs surely contained "Dear Old Donegal," the song about an Irish American's return to his hometown that was already popular in 1942, but in March 1962 it was recorded again, by Connie Francis, and its revival made it perfect for the Sherman treatment that turned it into "Shake Hands with Your Uncle Max." "Frère Jacques" became "Sarah Jackman." And finally his fascination and identification with childhood discovered possibilities in "Las Chiapanecas (The Mexican Hand-Clapping Song)," recorded in 1958 by Percy Faith on his *Viva! The Music of Mexico* album and in the summer of 1962 by Nat "King" Cole, which Sherman may have known about before the general public due to Busch's connections. But the inspiration for "Oh Boy" seems to be the simple version on the 1962 children's album *More Learning as We Play*.

Jewish Absurdity

"Not many in the audience knew what to expect," Cornyn said of the *Folk Singer* recording session. "Maybe half did." That was key, because Warner wanted the live album to capture the invited audience's laughter, which if everything went right would be raucous. But no matter how good the material, the crowd's reaction would not be at its greatest on a second hearing. Sherman had one shot to deliver the album.

Smith from Warner Bros. drove to Sherman's house on Chantilly Road to take him to the August 6 recording session, but they first stopped at the unemployment office. Sherman had to pick up his check.

They were on their way to Radio Recorders, a top Los Angeles studio where Elvis Presley recorded six times between September 1956 and January 1958. In the summer of 1960, it hosted Duke Ellington and his Orchestra. Sherman was booked into the studio's newest space, a room forty-five by seventy-five feet at 1441 North McCadden Place. It was more than big enough for the small orchestra of five musicians, a chorus comprised of three women and five men, and Sherman's need to lean back and spread his arms wide when bellowing out a tune, but it only just comfortably fit the more than one hundred folding metal bridge chairs set up for the guests and the impromptu bar stocked with liquor and food ordered from PJs, Sherman's favorite nightspot. He got to the studio about noon and rehearsed the album two or three times without an audience until about 4 PM, said Robert Sherman. Guests started to arrive at 5. "The studio had been converted into a nightclub, with tables and chairs and booze and food and wall-to-wall friends, a claque," Hopkins recalled. The setting was an expanded version of the house party entertainments Sherman had given for years. "He said, 'Get the friends and relatives,'" remembered Golden. "About a hundred to a hundred fifty people came. There were drinks. It was a party atmosphere." Bullets Durgom was there, and so was television producer Sheldon Leonard, actor Everett Sloane, comedienne and actress Pat Carroll, songwriter Harry Ruby, former child acting star Jackie Cooper, writing buddies Richard Gehman and Maurice Zolotow, and Theo Bikel, whose songs would be parodied. "The organizers knew that I appreciated Allan Sherman's Jewish sense of the absurd," Bikel said.

That is what Sherman delivered.

"We all laughed our asses off," Hopkins said. "When he stepped to the mike and sang, *'Sarah Jackman, Sarah Jackman / How's by you? / How's by you? / How's your brother, Bernie?'* and then his partner in the duet answered, *'He's a big attorney,'* and then Allan continued, *'How's your brother, Seymour?'*

and she answered, *'Seymour joined the Peace Corps'* we were falling off our seats with laughter."

Television actress Christine Nelson sang that famous song with Sherman. As a native New Yorker she knew how to deliver her lines with the unpolished outer-borough perfection required. But it was Sherman that delivered the key opening line that astonished the crowd. It could scarcely believe what it heard. When he sang the words, "Sarah Jackman, Sarah Jackman" to the "Frère Jacques" melody it took a moment until everyone grasped this wholly unpredictable parody. Then they roared. "I haven't laughed that hard in many a year," said Pat Carroll.

In two hours the recording session was over, Smith said. It may have been even less than that. Robert Sherman remembers the whole album was done in just ten minutes more than the released album, which clocks in at thirty-seven minutes. His father did all the songs in one take. "No stops, nothing."

Then life went back to normal. "We all but forgot about it," Golden said. "Months passed. Allan went back to creating television shows, game shows." Sherman did look for work, and was named producer of the first Writers Guild awards show for television and radio writers, scheduled for December 6 at the Beverly Hills Hilton. The show was not for broadcast. It was a roast strictly for invited insiders, and the producer role was a nonpaying gig that promised to put Sherman back in circulation. Yet despite Sherman's parody performances on the Hollywood house party circuit, his "Big Bad Jim" song for the Conkling roast, and his friendships with award show participants Everett Sloane, Jackie Cooper, and Carl Reiner, he needed the help of friend Jess Oppenheimer, creator of the *I Love Lucy* television show to get him the job. Things were still tough, so it is unlikely Sherman was casual about his album. Casual was not Sherman's style, and that is not how others remember it.

"When he made the record, and it was not yet released, he never stopped; the energy was amazing," said Hal Cooper, of *Your Surprise Package*. "He sent out records so that there was talk about it."

The effort turned out to be unnecessary.

Upside Down

"UNBELIEVABLE!!"

That was the headline on the October 31, 1962, *Call Board*, devoted to the Sherman phenomenon. "We have all just shared one of the most fantastic experiences in the history of the record business," the internal newsletter at Warner Bros. Records Sales Corporation announced to its staff. It had the facts to back it up. "It took [Bob] Newhart 23 ½ weeks to go over 300,000 (309,452); 36 weeks to go over 400,000 (412,000). It took Allan Sherman three weeks and one day to go to 390,000!" There was no precedent for such sales. *Folk Singer* only shipped to radio disc jockeys on October 4. It took a few days for the albums to arrive. But they got airtime immediately, and it seemed customers jammed the stores a few minutes later. On October 27, Warner Bros. Records president Mike Maitland ran an ad in the industry trade magazine *Cash Box* headlined, IN APOLOGY. "To the countless numbers of dealers, rack merchandisers and one-stops who are awaiting fulfillment of their orders, we humbly beg your patience." In Los Angeles and San Francisco, distributors sold the album dressed only in plain paper sleeves. Customers returned five days later to collect the cover. *Call Board* conceded that other recent artists from soul singer Ray Charles to Peter, Paul and Mary to Elvis Presley generated great excitement and rang up even greater total sales, "*but* never has a complete unknown turned the radio and record industry so completely upside down as our own rotund Allan Sherman."

The success turned Sherman face down. "He was always lying down. He was in shock," Golden said. "Robbie's friend's father came over, a psychiatrist, and Allan said, 'I don't know what to do.'" That was a problem others soon fixed. Bullets and the folks at Warner Bros. gave him plenty to do. Another album had to be produced right away to take advantage of all the excitement, and that meant his contract had to be rewritten, and he needed a publicist, an investment counselor, a talent agency, and a roadie, because he was going to do a national concert tour. Within a few weeks there was a meeting at Sherman's house with Bullets, agent Eddie Green from the newly hired United Talent Agency, and future superstar agent Jerry Perenchio to plan Sherman's life. "Allan was completely new to this and dependent upon the advice of Bullets," said Marvin Tabolsky, who came on as road manager. Sherman kept asking Bullets if he was taking the right steps, Tabolsky said. "Bullets gave the okay."

Family members might not have given the okay if they had known what was coming. "Things in so many ways starting with that fall of '62 just became crazy and different and it was a different life in a lot of ways," Robert Sherman said. In 1963, Sherman toured about 270 days, and of the 90 days remaining in the year 70 brought people to the house to play piano with Sherman and write songs, Robert said. "It did get very crazy very fast." Robert was almost thirteen, and his sister, Nancy, turned ten in November 1962 when their father's hectic new life descended upon them. The siblings responded with divergent strategies. Robert had his interests in technology and his room. Nancy's strategy was the opposite. "Nancy went to camp and loved camp, loved being away from home," Golden said. Her taste for life away from home only grew. She spent her high school years at a boarding school in Vermont. "She always wanted to be away — camp, school, adventure." Sherman was a great success, but his family endured the unsettling chaos he had experienced in his own childhood years under Rose's erratic direction.

There was little time to think about that. The world was behaving very strangely. On October 17, just as *Folk Singer* was taking off, Sherman received a note from an old Goodson-Todman colleague who was friends with lyricist Johnny Mercer. "Ole John Mercer is in town and sends regards; he dug the album the most too," wrote Bob Bach. Six months earlier in April at a Los Angeles house party Sherman sang "Chopped Liver," his parody of Mercer's Academy Award–winning song, "Moon River." The success of the Jewish version depended upon the unbridgeable chasm between Sherman's world and Mercer's. But now his comedy about that chasm was closing it.

Everything great and distant that Sherman once mocked now held out its hand to him. In his college play *Mirth of a Nation* he lampooned Washington politics, President Roosevelt, and First Lady Eleanor Roosevelt. Now Washington embraced him. On October 26, 1962, the chairman of the Federal Communications Commission, Newton N. Minow, wrote him a note of congratulations and almost misty-eyed thanks. "MY SON, THE FOLK SINGER has brought brightness into our lives in some difficult hours here." Minow was referring to the Cuban Missile Crisis that historians and movies say terrified the nation with the prospect of nuclear war with the Soviet Union. Left out is the public's simultaneous infatuation with Sherman's Jewish song parodies. "Why aren't you on television?" asked Minow.

The answer was because he was too scared. Ed Sullivan invited Sherman to sing "Sarah Jackman" for the Sunday evening show's audience of more than thirty million viewers, but he declined. Sullivan improvised. On October 28, he had comedy duo Norman and Dean come on the show and pantomime the song. A week later, Sherman received a note from the Kennedy White House. It was from Arthur Schlesinger Jr., special assistant to the president. "I can't say how much we have enjoyed the record — and how grateful I am to Kevin for suggesting you send it to me." The identity of Kevin is lost, but the sincerity of President Kennedy's enjoyment was confirmed when newspaperman John David Griffin told Bullets Durgom he heard Kennedy singing "Sarah Jackman" to himself in the lobby of the Carlyle Hotel, where the Kennedys kept a New York residence. "It would not surprise me," Minow said of the story Sherman included in his autobiography. "JFK had a wonderful sense of humor. I know that the songs were the talk in Washington, D.C." They were, in fact, a cause for amazement. Local radio station WWDC was "bug-eyed" that *Folk Singer* outsold singles. "We've checked record sales every week since 1955," the station told *Variety*, "and this is the first time anything like this has happened. It's unheard of. And what's more, the album is selling sensationally."

All this was wonderful, but another note of praise that made its way through the Irving network was even better. Irving Hoffman was described by a friend as "a thin, rumpled, nervous, breathless, entertaining eccentric" and "major theatrical press agent" who knew everybody, including Irving Berlin, the great songwriter Sherman admired and parodied for more than twenty years, since his "We Are Civilians '43" send-up of "This is the Army, Mr. Jones." Hoffman's note to Sherman was typed on stationery printed with Hoffman's name, New York business address, and the words "handy nervous breakdown avoider." Sherman could have used one of those. "Irving Berlin wants you to know that he thinks your album is great," Hoffman wrote. "He says he knows a great deal about 'the lost art of parody'... and he thinks... well, you call me when you get to N.Y. & I will tell you — or perhaps — have Mr. Berlin, himself — tell you."

Berlin may have been the son of a cantor, but he was not always so sanguine about being associated with Jewish material or Jews. When his *This Is the Army* stage show played during the winter of 1942–43, he complained there were "too many Jews in the show." Berlin feared the act would be viewed as a vehicle for Jews to avoid combat duty. That Jewish self-consciousness was a common affliction. It was what burdened Sherman's mother, Rose; distanced her from her original self; and split the family into Jewish and non-Jewish factions. Sherman joined his immigrant grandparents on the Jewish side of the divide, but he always desired to heal that childhood rupture by creating Jewish material everyone could love. He succeeded with *My Son, the Folk Singer*.

Sarah Jackman

Sherman's habit of writing under deadline pressure was a strategy that forced him to bypass his brain and access his substantial gut, which seems the only way he could have assembled the many successful elements of his first album's radio hit, "Sarah Jackman." The song's lyric rarely missteps as it roams over the Jewish American landscape to point out the sights then known only to insiders.

> How's your cousin Ida?
> She's a Freedom Rider.
> What's with Uncle Sidney?
> They took out a kidney.
> How's your sister Norma?
> She's a non-conforma.

The expression "How's by you?" that kicks off the song's dialogue between Jerry Bockman and Sarah Jackman is a perfect rhyme substitute for the original tune's "dormez-vous," and it is also an authentic bit of what linguists call Jewish English. It is a literal translation from the Yiddish, and it signals a subtle shift in values from the individual to the family and community. "How's by you?" invites a more expansive answer than the Standard English substitute "How are you?" The answer to "How are you?" is of limited interest. The answer to "How's by you?" affects everyone because it is about everyone, and so is the song. Just as importantly, this Jewish expression is uttered without self-consciousness. There is none of Jackie Mason's comic combativeness about his ethnic identity, and it is not the exaggerated Old World accent of Mel Brooks's "2000 Year Old Man." It is the voice of ethnic Americans talking naturally among themselves. This is what makes the song's dialogue structure key to its success. Jackie Mason's stand-up routine addressed an American audience. The 2000 Year Old Man explains himself to Carl Reiner's elegantly spoken newsman interviewer who represents the non-Jewish world's curious but bewildered interest in this Jewish phenomenon. In "Sarah Jackman," the characters talk on the phone to each other and do not address or acknowledge a non-Jewish audience — an approach that gives the writer the leeway to avoid pieties.

Avoiding pieties was paramount, because the whole idea of the album was to parody folk music pieties, and there was no point in substituting one set for another. It didn't. "The rhymes were just off the wall and a little hip, too," Warner's Cornyn said. Sherman's Jews are not cute or quaint and they do not live picturesque lives outfitted with colorful customs that non-Jewish Americans are meant to admire or envy. Sarah Jackman's friends and relatives, many of them bearing the stereotypical Jewish names Esther, Shirley, Ida, Nathan, Sidney, Manny, Seymour, Bernie, Moe, and Hy read the steamy popular fiction of John O'Hara and are attorneys, showbiz talent agents at William Morris, Peace Corps volunteers, and the civil rights activists known as Freedom Riders. They seem to be doing what everybody else is doing, but they are, more precisely, doing what Jews were most known for doing. Sherman's Jews, paradoxically, are the most representative Americans of their time even as they fulfill "Jewish American norms and expectations" — such as the law, show business, and civil rights.

This made "Sarah Jackman" Jewish folk music that could pass as American folk music. It documented the range of characters that made the moment fresh and distinct and gave it its recognizable flavor. This is folk music's traditional task, but it was a task the folk revival shirked. Peter, Paul and Mary did not sing about Manny working out at Vic Tanny, or Rita who was "a regular Lolita."

The sexual element was part of the hip attitude Cornyn recognized, and it not only worked against folk music pieties but Jewish ones, too. In 1963, Philip Roth responded to readers who objected to "Epstein," the *Goodbye, Columbus* story about an adulterous senior citizen. He recognized his angry public wanted to "rule Lou Epstein *out* of Jewish history." That same year Saul

Bellow noted the Jewish community's desire for simple, positive depictions of itself.

Sherman's parodies were hardly bruising, but they did not let the Jews off scot-free. His in-group humor allowed him to claim without argument that many Jewish families had teenagers who couldn't keep their pants on, and each had a Nathan whose name brought the rejoinder, "Him I've got no faith in." It permitted him to create a swearing garment factory owner that has lost his best salesman. On the *Folk Singer* track "Shticks and Stones," to the tune of "Jimmy Crack Corn," Sherman's businessman sings, "Gimme Jack Cohen / And I don't care." The trouble is, "the bastid's gone avay." Sherman's parodies are gentle, but they are not pap. They express suppressed truths, and that is a comic approach that offers a big psychological payoff. The "burden of lies is shaken off and the emotional result is a feeling of great relief." Relief from a burden of lies was what Sherman's life and humor were all about.

Two more elements contributed to the success of "Sarah Jackman." The nursery rhyme tune allowed Sherman to tap into the youthful innocence he preferred over adult worldliness, but he was worldly enough to realize that good comedy required him to pair that soothing childhood tune with adult lyrics. Irving Howe wrote that classic Jewish humor drew its wit from measuring "the distance between pretension and actuality." Sherman's song does exactly that. It produces laughs by exposing the childhood melody to the adult activities — both earthy and foolish — of the characters recounted in its lyrics.

Sherman's knack for arranging that clanging collision of two worlds was what made his debut Jewish material so explosively funny and winning. Jewish attitudes and accents were custom made to produce a comic effect when paired with folk tunes of oh-come-off-of-it seriousness. Sherman couldn't have written his comic send-ups if he had been of French or German heritage; as one critic noted, those are elevating languages. But the English spoken by Yiddish immigrants and their children is different. The life it represents is simple, direct, and unpretentious. With such qualities, the more serious the original material, the funnier the Jewish parody. The bigger they are, the harder they fall. This highlights the final reason why *Folk Singer*'s greatest hit was the "Sarah Jackman" parody of "Frère Jacques." The high-culture airs of the French original made the Jewish parody just that much funnier.

Welcome Home

It was no accident that Sherman's favorite comic device was parody. The technique is "almost synonymous with American Jewish humor itself," and he used it to bring down big targets and win an unembarrassed place for Jews in the public sphere, an aim that first energized him in his high school article about American humor's dearth of Jewish material.

"Dear Old Donegal" was a perfect example of the injustice Sherman intended to remedy. In it an Irish immigrant to America tells how he returns home to Donegal, is welcomed by his mother, invited to "shake hands with your Uncle Mike," marries his old sweetheart, and is joined in the church by "Branigan Flanigan Milligan" and many more. The sentimental song was already well known when Bing Crosby's brother Bob recorded it in 1942, and its appearance during wartime is a good measure of the Irish community's public comfort, a comfort Jews then could not hope to equal. It was at about this time the young Leonard Bernstein was encouraged to change his name to Burns to escape the anti-Semitism that might hinder his musical career.

Even in 1962, when Sherman parodied the song in "Shake Hands with Your Uncle Max," the studio audience's reaction to Sherman's bravura rattling off of Jewish last names in place of the Irish ones betrays a startled amazement, a can-you-believe-it excitement and grateful laughter that the burden of lies is over.

Meet Meyerowitz Berowitz Handleman Shandleman
  Sperber and Gerber and Steiner and Stone
Moskowitz Lupowitz Aaronson Berenson Fineman
  and Fierman and Friedman and Cohen
Smalowitz Wallowitz Teitlebaum Mandelbaum Levin
  Levinsky Levine and Levi
Brumberger Shlumberger Mincus and Pincus and Stein
  with an ei and Styne with a y.

Those Jewish names are the heart of the parody, and they are the perfect comic rebuttal to the embarrassment that induced some American Jews to change their names, but other changes were not strictly necessary and reveal Sherman's character more than they do the Jewish community. He had to alter the story line about an immigrant returning to his ancestral home. That was not an option for Jews, whose ancestral communities were destroyed in the Holocaust, and also were not fondly remembered. Sherman's traveling salesman returns instead to the old neighborhood. But the parody contributes a narrative of lonesome wandering absent in the original. The Irish immigrant returns home a success. Sherman's preamble about a traveling salesman is less triumphant. "Every night a strange café, a strange hotel, and then / Early in the morning I am on the road again." And Sherman could have retained the idea of the returning son's marriage to his sweetheart. Instead his hero is welcomed by his mother and wished farewell by his mother, who promises him that the whole extended family will always be there.

> Whenever you're on the road mine boy
> Wherever you may roam
> We'll all be here
> When you come back
> To wish you
> We-elcome home.

For Sherman, home was not the life he built with his wife and children but the lost world of his childhood. Everything else was exile.

There is pathos in many of *Folk Singer*'s parodies, but it only makes the comedy more memorable, satisfying, and funny. In "The Streets of Miami" there is a killing, just like in "The Streets of Laredo." But in Miami when one Jewish business partner shoots another, the wounded man crumbles "just like a piece halvah" and the shooter's punishment is worse than jail. It is a life sentence of cold winters.

> They came with a posse
> And took mine six-gun away
> The crowd was too angry
> To leave me in jail
> The sheriff said, "Outlaw
> I'm gon' let you run away
> But don't ever be seen
> South of Ft. Lauderdale."

In the "Greensleeves" parody "Sir Greenbaum's Madrigal," Sherman makes comic use of the traditional plaintive melody and the problems that, Greenbaum explains, "engendered my attitude bluish." He has had it with being a knight. "That's no job for a boy who is Jewish." The profession is more trouble than the fairy tales let on. "All day with mighty sword / And the mighty steed / And the mighty lance / All day with that heavy shield / And a pair of aluminum pants." This song does end in marriage, but the union is practical, not romantic. "I'll work for my father-in-law / When I marry Miss Guinevere Schwartz!"

The surface melancholy continues in the "My Zelda" parody of "Matilda," about a deserted husband whose wife "took the money and ran with the tailor." But tragedy yields the greatest comedy in "The Ballad of Harry Lewis" parody of "The Battle Hymn of the Republic," which tells the story of a garment worker killed in a fire.

> I'm singing you a ballad
> Of a great man of the cloth
> His name was Harry Lewis
> And he worked for Irving Roth
> He died while cutting velvet
> On a hot July the fourth
> But his cloth goes shining on.
> Glory, glory Harry Lewis.

Lewis "had the finest funeral / The union could afford." But his real reward is his association with one of comedy's greatest puns.

> Oh, Harry Lewis perished
> In the service of his lord
> He was trampling through the warehouse
> Where the drapes of Roth are stored.

What all these songs have in common are a cast of characters and themes devoid of traditional folk music's heroic aspirations and behavior. Sherman's parodies were a cultural breakthrough as well as comic masterpieces. He jostled American culture off its high horse and made it mingle with those who had recently arrived in steerage, giving a voice to Americans that had been too embarrassed to call attention to themselves. They spoke off-kilter English, worked low-class jobs, had large, unruly families and were crazy for bargain merchandise. This, too, was part of Sherman's appeal to the many non-Jewish buyers who made the album a national sensation. Their parents also spoke nonstandard English and struggled to make a buck. Sherman's acceptance by a broad array of Americans was unexpected, but it is a hallmark of the Jewish experience in America to be the exemplar of national trends. The stories of other ethnic groups have not had the same widespread resonance. After he became famous, Sherman tried to strike an ecumenical note. He told *Newsweek* that if *Folk Singer* had grown out of Chinese or Italian roots, it would have been just as big a hit. *Newsweek* didn't buy it. "He should live so long," it said.

No Rudder

Folk Singer had the comedy headlines to itself until late November 1962, when Vaughn Meader's *The First Family* album satirized the Kennedy White House and sold more than three million albums in four weeks, making it the fastest selling album of all time and pushing Sherman's album into second place in that category. But instead of eclipsing *Folk Singer*, the news media grouped the two records into one story about chart-topping comedy albums, and noted that both attracted imitators. Comedian Morey Amsterdam of the *Dick Van Dyke Show* talked of cutting an album called *My Son, the Jokeslinger* and Jubilee Records issued *More Folk Songs with Allan Sherman and His Friends* that included "Tzimished" and other song parodies Sherman wrote and recorded in 1951. Sherman asked retailers such as the Doubleday bookstore chain to pull the unauthorized record from their shelves.

There were other complications. Christine Nelson demanded compensation for her role as Sarah Jackman in the hit song. "Allan didn't make any deals before" the album came out, Golden said. "Allan said to me, 'I regret the whole thing.'" He gave Nelson 2.5 percent of his *Folk Singer* royalties. That did not end Sherman's need for attorneys. His "Seltzer Boy" parody of "Water Boy" generated a lawsuit for copyright infringement. It turned out it was not an anonymous folk song after all, and the music publishers demanded compensation. Sherman's wonderful parody transformed the agonies of the original Southern black work song, in which a rock-breaking prisoner calls for water, into the kvetching of a thirsty Jew. Its comic opening bellow and weak guitar strumming was a send-up of folksinger Odetta's dramatic "Water Boy" performance.

> Seltzer boy!
> Where are you hiding?
> If you don't come right now,
> I'm gonn' tell you boss on you.
> Oy.

And unlike Odetta's persecuted worker who thirsts for water, the humblest of beverages, Sherman's Jew is not so easily satisfied.

> Don't bring me water
> I'd rather have seltzer
> Cause water don't bubble
> And water don't fizz.
> Water I hate it
> Cause it ain't carbonated
> But a glass of seltzer
> On the other hand, is.

The problems posed by the various lawsuits did not amount to very much. They were minor irritations overwhelmed by adulation. *The Hollywood Reporter* wrote "the sure sign of a smash success comes when two deejays feud over which one first intro-ed the LP to listeners," as happened with *Folk Singer* when competing Los Angeles disc jockeys Gary Owens, at KMPC, and Bob Crane at KNX bickered over who was first. The dispute has never ended. "I was the first to play it because we were all friends," Owens said. The *Reporter* first heard it from Crane on October 1. Another indication of the bear-hug embrace that welcomed *Folk Singer* was its appearance not just in the White House, but also in Barbie's Dream House. The famous doll's living quarters had to be decorated with furniture and tokens of American pop culture. A miniature version of the *Folk Singer* album cover made the cut. In addition, the trade press gave Sherman the edge over Meader for continued success due to "the added promotional asset of a musical comedy LP over a straight talk item." Music fit better into radio playlists, and radio play led to sales and concerts. By early December, Sherman was booked to perform six times during the last six nights of the year. He would start in Hartford, Connecticut, on December 26 and move on to Boston, Newark, Baltimore, and two nights at New York's Carnegie Hall. Carnegie was originally planned as a one-nighter, but the December 28 show sold out so quickly another was added for December 31.

Meanwhile, Sherman had to produce the December 6 Writers Guild award show, a job he took on when he was down and out. "All kinds of pressures were brought on me to quit this show, after the record hit," he told *Variety*, but it is little wonder he kept the date. It put him back among his television colleagues as a star, and it gave him a chance to do more of the Broadway parodies he loved. Sherman sang his "Frank Cooper" parody of "Maria" and wrote a new one, "Desilu." Sung to the tune of *South Pacific*'s "Bali Hai," it is about "what happens when a writer gets a call from Desilu," the production company owned by Lucille Ball and her husband, Desi Arnaz.

Desilu will call you
Anytime, anywhere
They will say, You're a genius
Make a change, here and there.

This schedule exhausted Sherman, but it also satisfied his need to be over-extended and under deadline. New project ideas tumbled out of him. Within weeks of his notoriety he told various publications he was going to write a book for *Playboy* called *Impressions*, revive his college musical *Nothing Ventured*, produce a live television special called *The Palace: The Golden Years* to celebrate the fiftieth anniversary of New York's Palace Theater, write the song lyrics to a Broadway musical called *Grandma and the Girls*, and secure the rights to *South Pacific* so he could record his *South Passaic* parody. In November he bought a gold Lincoln Continental. In February 1963 he bought the film rights to the 1957 bestselling book, *Where Did You Go? Out. What Did You Do? Nothing*. It looks back at author Robert Paul Smith's 1920s childhood world of unscheduled game playing and underrated idling. Taken together these projects are a portrait of Sherman's turbulent mind, where obsessions with an idealized vision of childhood fought it out with a childish delight in expensive toys and sexy girls. "He was a ship without a rudder," Golden said. "I was the rudder."

She had help. Bullets Durgom and Warner Bros. made sure Sherman kept his eye on the ball. The top priority was to record another album.

Allan Copelon, Chicago, 1929. Courtesy of Syril N. Gilbert.

Sherman's mother, Rose (Sherman) Copelon, circa 1923.
Courtesy of Syril N. Gilbert.

Rose, on right, with sister Kate Sherman, 1926.
Courtesy of Syril N. Gilbert.

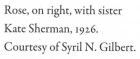

PERCY COPLON
"The Man On The Pole"
Stopped eating 7-25-49
Will eat again 12-4-49

Sherman's father, Percy Coplon, at the start of his 100-day fast. Courtesy of his daughter, Hilda Copelon Willard.

Allan's maternal grandparents, Esther and Leon Sherman, 1951.
Courtesy of Syril N. Gilbert.

Allan Segal while he briefly
attended high school in
Ohio, 1940. Courtesy
of Dee Golden, Nancy
Sherman, and Olan Mills
Portrait Studios.

Caricature of Allan
Copelon from the satirical
Satyr, University of
Illinois, 1942. Courtesy of
the University of Illinois
at Urbana-Champaign
Archives. Record Series
13/3/810, Box 1.

Allan and Dee wedding
photograph, 1945.
Courtesy of Syril N.
Gilbert and Dee Golden
and Nancy Sherman.

Sherman warming up the television studio audience as producer
of *I've Got a Secret*, June 25, 1956. CBS/Landov.

Recording session for
My Son, the Folk Singer,
August 6, 1962. Courtesy
of Dee Golden and
Nancy Sherman.

Jazz drummer Bobby Rosengarden made
home recordings of Sherman's "Goldeneh
Moments from Broadway" song parodies.
Courtesy of Sharon Rosier.

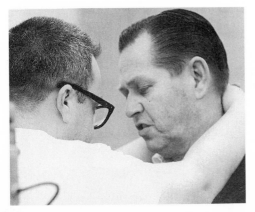

At recording session
with musical director Lou Busch.
Courtesy of Robert Sherman.

Belting it out at the *Folk Singer*
recording session. Courtesy of
Robert Sherman.

Posing before appearing
on The Garry Moore
Show, December 7, 1962.
CBS/Landov.

Steve Allen plays piano as Bullets
Durgom enjoys a November 6,
1962, performance at Sherman's Bel
Air home to celebrate the success of
Folk Singer. © Leigh Wiener.

The November 1962 party
performance was the kind of
venue Sherman played as an
amateur since the mid-1950s.
© Leigh Wiener.

Sherman at the Sands in Las Vegas, January 1963.
UNLV Libraries, Special Collections.

Sherman at the Sands. "He fell apart for pretty girls," said his road manager Marvin Tabolsky. UNLV Libraries, Special Collections.

"He went to Vegas. There were so many women around," said Joe Smith of Warner Bros. Records. UNLV Libraries, Special Collections.

At the Chi Chi in Palm Springs with Frank
Sinatra, Jill St. John, Chi Chi owner Irwin
Schuman, and Dee Sherman, April 1, 1963.
Courtesy of Dee Golden and Nancy Sherman.
With permission of Frank Sinatra Enterprises,
LLC, and Jill St. John.

"I have your record and I like it very much,"
President Kennedy told Sherman. March 4, 1963.
Courtesy of Robert Sherman.

The Sherman family
at home in Bel Air,
California, March 1963.
Courtesy of
Robert Sherman.

Allan and Dee with President Johnson following campaign
event, May 28, 1964. LBJ Library photo by Cecil Stoughton.
Provided by Dee Golden and Nancy Sherman.

Sherman with showgirls from the Sands at an October 11, 1965, "literary tea" for the publication of his autobiography, *A Gift of Laughter*. UNLV Libraries, Special Collections.

In 1965, Rod Serling cast Sherman as a sheriff in the television series, *The Loner*. CBS/Landov.

seven
MY SON, THE CELEBRITY

"Do you think we did it in there, in the control room?"

By the time Sherman asked the recording engineers if the *My Son, the Celebrity* album session was over, he had dutifully followed a friend's instructions to "get loaded." On outtakes from the session a shell-shocked and tipsy Sherman tells the assembled audience, "I don't understand the whole thing. I don't understand the whole thing starting on August 6 when we did the first session. . . . But I'm willing to accept it because from the first time I knew I was in show business I knew it was insane."

He had not seen anything yet. *Celebrity* was recorded over three days, including November 30, 1962, his thirty-eighth birthday. In late November Sherman's sales were tremendous and certainly warranted the celebrity status his second album's title both touted and lampooned, but there was more to come. *Folk Singer* was still picking up speed. It was number 28 on *Billboard's* Top LP's chart the week ending November 10, number 9 a week later, number 2 on November 24, and number 1 on December 1 and December 8. On December 15, *Billboard* reported sales hit 1 million, and on January 5, 1963, he was pictured smiling on the magazine's cover flanked by the president of Warner Bros., Jack Warner, and Mike Maitland, president of Warner Bros. Records. All three held aloft *Folk Singer*'s Gold Record award.

Celebrity furthered Sherman's rise. On December 26, *Variety* praised the second album as "a good deal sharper and more witty than the first effort." A week later *Billboard* asked, "Who says lightning never strikes twice?" Distributors agreed that it would and placed advance orders for 200,000 *Celebrity* albums. They were right. *Time* magazine kicked off media coverage of the new album in the New Year with a January 4, 1963, ovation. It delighted in Sherman's brand of nonsense and celebrated *My Son, the Celebrity* and its parody of "Comin' Thro' the Rye," the popular poem and song by the eighteenth century Scottish poet Robert Burns. Its exact meaning has been debated. Is the rye a river or a field of grain? Sherman's research, conducted at Jewish delicatessens across the country, discovered an overlooked meaning.

Do not make a stingy sandwich
Pile the cold cuts high.
Customers should see salami
Comin' thro' the rye.

Time also enjoyed "When I Was a Lad," an updated version of Gilbert and Sullivan's song from *H.M.S. Pinafore* that transposes the rewards of trivial accomplishments from the Queen's navy to the canyons of Madison Avenue. Sherman pulled this gem out of his desk drawer. He wrote it in June 1959 while he worked on the Perry Como summer television series, *Perry Presents*. The cheerfully superficial hero sums up his successful advertising career with a note of gratitude. "So I thank old Yale, and I thank the Lord / And I also thank my father who is chairman of the board." But the weekly's favorite was "Won't You Come Home, Disraeli," another reworking of the "Bill Bailey" tune Sherman used in 1942 for his college hit, "Don't Burn Down Bidwell's." The song features a lovesick Queen Victoria comically pining for Benjamin Disraeli, the late nineteenth-century British prime minister of Jewish ancestry. In "Disraeli," Sherman pulled off feats of wit that match up well with parody legends. The nineteenth-century American comic playwright John Brougham "was in the avant-garde of the demolition campaign" that finished off the old pieties of his time, and when he got going he sprinkled his parodies with "totally anachronistic elements such as telegraphs and railroads." Brougham's work "was not an academic exercise in literary parody." On the contrary, he "was very conscious of the contemporary interests of his audience, and he did not limit their laughter to a now obsolete genre."

The description is apt. Sherman had the same nonacademic inclinations and discovered for himself Brougham's technique of including in his parodies anachronisms that would delight his audience. Sherman's Queen Victoria complains to Disraeli,

> You claim official business
> Took you away
> To Egypt and Bombay and Rome.
> Well, I'm not so certain,
> Cause you're a 19th century Richard Burton
> Disraeli, won't you please come home?

The newsmagazine's circulation of more than three million made it influential enough, but *Time* was also the voice of Middle America. It once drove beat poet Allen Ginsberg crazy. "I'm obsessed by Time Magazine," he wrote in his 1956 poem "America." *Time*, Ginsberg said, insisted that everything and everyone in America was serious and in earnest except him. A lot had changed in the country and at *Time* in seven years. Its Sherman coverage did not just stick to the new *Celebrity* album but recognized that Sherman's Carnegie Hall concerts revealed an unofficial and unreleased third album, the "Goldeneh Moments from Broadway." It cited his *South Passaic* parody of *South Pacific* and other Broadway parodies, and the caption under a photograph of Sherman read, "In South Passaic, nothing like a lox." Regardless of how many *Time* readers knew what that meant, it was a sign of the country's widespread interest.

For the week ending February 16, 1963, *Celebrity* was the number 3 record in the country, with *Folk Singer* still at number 2 after sixteen weeks on the charts. *The First Family*'s extraordinary sales earned it the top spot, but Vaughn Meader's fortunes were on the wane. His January concert tour was "disastrous," reported *Billboard* in a February 2 story headlined, "Powwow to Decide: What Now for Meader after U.S. Bomb Tour." A month later, *Variety* reported that

Sherman's two albums had combined sales of almost 1.8 million, and on April 3 Warner Bros. Records president Mike Maitland handed Sherman his second Gold Record award. Sammy Cahn, the lyricist whose songs won four Academy Awards and were nominated for thirty joined in presenting the plaque. *My Son, the Celebrity* had delivered.

Warner Bros. had inadvertently discovered the key to success with Sherman: push him into a corner and do not give him any time to think. Tight deadlines were crucial to his productivity. The decision to record *Celebrity* was made in mid-October, when the success of *Folk Singer* became clear. That gave Sherman only five weeks to write ten new songs. It was a trick he pulled off in July for *Folk Singer*, and in November he did it again. Once more he and Lou Busch got together to listen to records, knock around ideas and rehearse and record, but these weeks were also filled with press interviews, lawsuits, concert planning, and new contract negotiations. Given the chaos, Sherman's ability to write the new album was remarkable. Everyone who knew him recognized his gift. "He was an immensely creative man," said Billy Goldenberg, a close friend and Emmy Award–winning composer. "He was creative as hell," said Jon Hendricks, founding member of the 1950s Grammy Award–winning vocal group, Lambert, Hendricks & Ross, known for putting words to jazz arrangements. "I think he was a genius at his work."

Parody ideas seemed to fly through Sherman's head with the speed of swallows, and sometimes all he could do was catch a few lines as they streaked by. Goldstone and Tobias were his agents after he was fired from the *Steve Allen Show*, and his ex-wife remembers him borrowing the tune of "Fly Me to the Moon" to create a timely parody. "Goldstone and Tobias / Said that I'll be working soon." The "shtick" medleys on *Folk Singer* and *Celebrity* gather up these fragments and put them to work. Others got away. "Allan had a tremendous poetic rhyming ability," said Jerry Perenchio. "He was brilliant," Bill Dana said. "I never had any question about his gift with language and word play." Joe Smith said, "Allan was as clever a guy as I've ever known. He could write so fast and knock out things, it was a wonderment. He said, sometimes I hear the song and hear the parody." A good example was when Sherman and Smith visited top Los Angeles deejay Bob Crane, who featured Sherman on his radio show. Crane asked about parody writing after he had played the song, "Golden Earrings," and Sherman demonstrated his ability with an instant parody.

> There's a gypsy
> Like one I've never seen
> She wore a pair of Goldman's earrings
> Her ears are turning green.

Another is his send-up of "The Oldest Established," the *Guys and Dolls* song that is an ode to Nathan Detroit. Sherman wrote it in the mid-1960s while he traveled with daughter Nancy on the subway from Manhattan to Coney Island, Brooklyn, to eat hot dogs at Nathan's.

> Why it's good old reliable Nathan's
> Nathan's Coney Island red hots
> If you're looking for hot dogs
> That taste really grand
> Take a bus or subway out to Coney Island.
> Get a hot dog provided by Nathan's
> Where it's beef not lamb and not pork
> It's the oldest established [missing lyrics] hot dog in New York.

Little David Susskind, Shut Up

In January 1963, Sherman took his act on the road and to the nation's airwaves, and over the next twelve months he repeatedly appeared on the most popular entertainment and variety shows on television, including twice on the *Garry Moore Show* and *Perry Como's Kraft Music Hall* and four appearances on the *Steve Allen Show*. He also showed up on television programs headed by singing stars Andy Williams, Edie Adams, country singer Jimmy Dean, and Vic Damone's *The Lively Ones*, but his greatest television coup was ten appearances on Johnny Carson's *Tonight* show, including the week beginning August 5 when he was Carson's guest host. At the same time, he performed more than thirty live concerts across the country and Canada in a wide range of venues for every strata of the population — nightclub crowds in Vegas, government officials and press at black-tie parties in Washington, D.C., and "fathers and mothers, sons and daughters, and young blades squiring their best girls out for an evening of family entertainment" at traditional concerts like the ones at Carnegie Hall that were held from Hollywood to Buffalo. This was the big time.

He was as ready as he would ever be. His talent was fully developed, but other parts of his personality were still locked in childhood. Show business was a business, and from a business point of view it was crazy to turn down an invitation from the *Ed Sullivan Show*. Nothing else came close to its power to make a star. It was "the gold standard for what mattered in show business." But Sherman made the decision to appear first on the *Garry Moore Show*, starring the former host of *I've Got a Secret*, out of a sentimental and almost certainly unreciprocated loyalty, a filial devotion that Sherman deployed naturally in order to generate a flow of family feeling in his direction. The wish fulfillment of his first album's full title, *Allan Sherman's Mother Presents My Son, the Folk Singer*, hid the truth with a joke. The now adult and orphaned Sherman had been a virtual orphan since he was eight, and he longed to extend that too-brief moment when he was a son. *Billboard* was on the money with its headline about Sherman's decision to stay true to the man he worked with more than four years before — "Loyal Son."

If that is what it took to make Sherman comfortable on television before an audience of millions, that is what it took, and his loyalty did elicit the warmth he needed. On the January 8 show, taped January 4, Moore gave Sherman a big build up, praised his "sensational album *My Son, the Folk Singer*," reminded the audience it had heard his songs "on every radio station in the country," took a swipe at Sullivan in a mention of television shows that had actors pantomime Sherman's songs, and finished his introduction by trying to put Sherman at ease. "He's still in a state of shock, but he's happy."

Sherman's television debut was a success. He was electrified and energized with enthusiasm and wonder. "This is ridiculous," he told Moore. Dressed in a tuxedo with off-kilter bowtie, he wore his signature black glasses and an expression that was the showbiz equivalent of the "wild surmise" the poet attributed to the first Europeans to see the Pacific Ocean, except what Sherman saw with the aid of his childlike imagination was even bigger. In less than a month he would tell a newspaper reporter, "I wouldn't be surprised if they told me I was going to be president." For Sherman, possibility became a realm with insanely expanded borders.

He sang "Sarah Jackman" with Dorothy Loudon, an actress he would work with again. They recited new lyrics Sherman composed for the show that did not match the originals, though he did get off one good topical rhyme. "How's your cousin Frieda? / Listening to Vaughn Meader." Then came the highlight of the evening, Sherman's rendition of *Celebrity*'s "Shticks" medley that culminates in "Don't Buy the Liverwurst." The number bristled with an absurd and zany giddiness. Sherman bounced around while he sang, unable to keep still as he practically hopped in place, while behind him were what Moore called "the kids," a choral troupe of twenty-two attractive, wholesome, and freshly scrubbed young men and women — a vision of un-Shermanesque perfection — who chimed in on the Jewish parody of the Negro spiritual, "Down by the Riverside," with a cheerful and rousing, "Don't buy the liverwurst, don't buy the liverwurst." Mahalia Jackson had helped make the song ubiquitous in the late 1950s with television performances on the Dinah Shore and Nat King Cole shows, and in 1963 Pete Seeger introduced such spirituals by claiming they are "so great that [they] must be able to cross any boundary." That's the kind of piety that keeps parodists in business.

Sherman saw his opportunities and took them. Many of *Folk Singer*'s "Shticks" take aim at the African American song repertoire that was more integrated into the nation's culture than were its creators. That irony was part of the comedy when Sherman turned "St. James Infirmary," made famous by Cab Calloway and Louis Armstrong, into "Mt. Sinai Hospital," transformed "Mama's Little Baby Likes Shortnin' Bread" into "Mama's Little Baby Loves Matza," and rewrote "When the Saints Go Marching In" as "When the Paintners Go Marching In," preserving, as the African American song tradition also does, the in-group dialect, in this case the Jewish *paintner*, which was "the standard Bronx pronunciation of 'painter.'" A layer cake of meanings, ironies, and in-jokes pile up in another such parody, Sherman's "Little David Susskind." The Negro spiritual, "Little David, Play on Your Harp," takes as its hero the great biblical Jewish conqueror and king. But Sherman's comedy, like that of Jewish poet Irving Layton, who imagines the statues of the Hebrew prophets Ezekiel and Jeremiah telling each other dirty jokes as they wait out eternity in the church of Notre Dame, uses Jewish irreverence to rescue David from his inappropriately pious Christian fans. His "Little David" is about the Jewish David of 1962, David Susskind, host of the television talk show *Open End*, dubbed "Open Mouth" by those who thought Susskind did not know when or how to shut up. Sherman and his audience were among them, but Sherman went further. He saw Susskind's verbosity as a Jewish trait, and imagines him as a literal little David, as a baby with his Jewish mother.

> Little David Susskind, shut up
> Please don't talk, please don't talk
> Little David Susskind, eat first
> Then you'll talk.

Part of the comedy in all these parodies is the recognition that no matter how much the blacks are despised, the Jews will never come close to having songs about their lives, problems, and traditions embraced by the country, leaving unsaid what that reveals about America's acceptance of the Jews. In a 1965 interview that touched on minority representation in American government, Sherman wondered, "it'll be interesting to see which one we accept first: a Jew or a Negro" in the White House. Sherman's parodies indicate he would not have been surprised by the eventual answer.

A Hero for Every Folk

The *Garry Moore Show* was an important entertainment variety showcase that in 1959 launched Carol Burnett on her television career. In May 1962, up-and-comer Barbra Streisand was a guest on the program, and it was where she sang "Happy Days Are Here Again" for the first time with the grim ironic delivery that made it "her first signature song." The show stood for quality acts, and Sherman benefitted from such associations just in time to spur interest in his upcoming concerts. His performance also indicated he had the energy for the months ahead. He would need it. Bullets arranged a schedule that put Sherman's penchant for juggling multiple projects to the test.

On January 6, he opened with singing star Vic Damone at the Sands Hotel and Casino in Las Vegas. His contract kept him there through January 22, but that did not mean he could not also appear in concert elsewhere during the same period. On January 18 and 19 Sherman was booked in Southern California to perform at the Santa Monica and Pasadena civic auditoriums. The bouncer-sized president of the Sands, Jack Entratter, gave him the nights off. They were busy. First, the Friday show in Santa Monica sold out. Another concert was added for the same day. Then the same thing happened to the Saturday appearance in Pasadena. Sherman was double-booked for that day, too. A *Variety* headline declared, "Allan Sherman Hottest 1-Niter Attraction in Calif. in Years." His friends wanted in on the act. At Carnegie Hall, singer Eydie Gormé had played Sarah Jackman to Sherman's Jerry Bockman. Now Christine Nelson, Jayne Meadows, and Edie Adams took turns in the role. In the summer, Rosemary Clooney would be paired with Sherman. He was a hot date. Steve Allen joined Sherman at the last Pasadena concert for a rendition of "My Zelda," and Harpo Marx revived his classic act at all four of the weekend's concerts, breaking character to speak at the last show in Pasadena, where he announced it was his last public appearance.

An unreleased recording of one of the Santa Monica shows affirms *Variety*'s review that though "Sherman at this point may not be the polished pro as usual concert performers are concerned, he has that informal, friendly, warm appeal that immediately strikes an empathetic response in his audience." He worked the same charm at his Carnegie concerts. "Sherman is a plump, crew-cut chipmunk man with black-rimmed glasses and a blinking diffidence that suggests he would like to make apologies throughout the harbor for the fact that his ship came in so fast," *Time* wrote. Jerry Hopkins saw that sheepish bewilderment, as well as a straining for acceptance.

His parodies were brilliant, yes, but he was also the sincerest comedian/ humorist I ever encountered. When he stood in a tux in front of an audience, and he slipped a hand inside his jacket like some lounge singer, closed his eyes and opened his mouth like a carp desperate for air, his double chin wobbling, presenting a comic parody of a café crooner to complement his lyrics, he was always stretching, not believing he was really there, knowing he had a rotten singing voice, couldn't even reach a note let alone bend one, we knew he was trying as hard as he could, it was clear he was really doing his very best.

Much of this amateurish appeal was on the level, but a healthy amount was calculated. Sherman had a lot of stage experience. In college he spent as much time performing in his own musicals and acting as emcee for every floor show and "Sing" as he did in class, and that does not count his time as a kid entertaining his extended family, or the countless times he belted out his "Goldeneh Moments" songs. He knew how to elicit applause and affection. *Billboard* closed its review of his Carnegie Hall performance with a prediction of Sherman's continued success and the rhetorical question, "What else could you expect from a neighborhood fella?" An unpretentious, chummy, vulnerable style inspired audiences to love him not with passion but as one of the gang, a family member, one of our own.

Sherman's ability to deliver that vulnerable style is on display in the Santa Monica recording. It captures Sherman in full control of himself, his material, and his audience. First the crowd heard a prerecorded announcement by Jack Benny. He pouts that Sherman, who "was a very good friend of mine until a couple of months ago," has now come to prefer "money and success to my friendship." Then Sherman addressed the audience.

I think it behooves me to explain what I'm doing here. I used to produce television shows and direct them and write them and stuff, and I had this nutty hobby of writing these songs. And a friend of mine about six months ago heard them and said, let's go and get somebody to make an album out of them, and he did, and the album sold millions of copies and made my whole life crazy. So what I propose to do here for these next number of minutes is to make your life crazy, if possible.

As part of his disarming and self-effacing introduction, he explains why he no longer looks "exactly like Cary Grant." Publicity consultants felt it was the wrong image for his songs, and they urged him to "just try looking short and fat and wearing glasses. If it works, we'll keep it." But if he made excuses for his looks, he made none for being Jewish. "I'm Jewish but I don't flaunt it nor do I apologize," he later told a reporter, and that unflinching ownership of his Jewish identity and confidence in his Jewish parodies was on display in Santa Monica. The Jews and their accomplishments, and his comic efforts to highlight both, were subjects he treated with pride and seriousness free of earnestness. It contrasted sharply with his opening humble act when five minutes into the show he said, "About six years ago, I wrote what I have always referred to as my masterwork, which is called, 'Goldeneh Moments from Broadway.' And what happened was, it occurred to me, what if all of the great hit songs from all of the great Broadway shows had actually been written by Jewish people. *Which they were.*"

It was a line familiar to his friends, but it was new to the audience, which enjoyed it and the "Seventy-Six Sol Cohens" parody Sherman then sang. The song parted with the rule he just pronounced, and he joked that Meredith Wilson came from "the Jewish section of Mason City, Iowa." But the other "Goldeneh Moments" songs he performed, including "There Is Nothing Like a Lox" and "When You Walk through the Bronx" adhered to the project's premise, as did "Small World" from *Gypsy*, by Jule Styne and Stephen Sondheim. Sherman's parody version, performed with "Sarah Jackman" partner Christine Nelson, imagines what the song written by Jewish people would be like if it was written by Jewish people.

NELSON: Funny,
    I got one son a doctor
    One son a CPA
SHERMAN: My son,
    Is a doctor, a dentist.
BOTH: Small world, isn't it?
NELSON: I live,
    On the Moshulu Parkway,
    Eighty-Eight, Forty-Three
SHERMAN: I live
    In the Kew Gardens, Gardens.
BOTH: Small world, isn't it?
    We have so much in common
    It's a phenomenon.
NELSON: I won't
    Act like a nudnik

SHERMAN: Or a no-goodnik
From now on.
NELSON: I have
A whole showroom of cloth coats
On Seventh Avenue.
SHERMAN: Funny,
I make linings for cloth coats.

What was new about all of this was Sherman's sense of ease, his frank pleasure in his Jewish identity that he learned from his grandparents. Sherman's Jewish persona was contemporary, not yet ready for nostalgia's rose-colored glasses, and one snubbed by the Jewish cultural elite that preferred to wrap itself in "the Jewish cultural spirit" of destroyed East European Jewry than "forge any connection to the Jewish community as it really existed." Conflicted Jewish identity was widespread and sometimes debilitating. In Saul Bellow's 1964 novel *Herzog*, Jewish characters adorn their conversation with Yiddish terms they get wrong, yearn for the immigrant *shul* of childhood, write themselves New Psalms, obscure their origins with elevated English diction, and convert to Catholicism. It was not clear what it meant to be a Jewish American, and Sherman's comic Jewish persona was helpful, calming, and healthy. He playfully but proudly stood up for Jewish names, cultural achievements, and habits. On the *Celebrity* album's "Horowitz," he parodies George M. Cohan's "Harrigan" that in 1907 rejoiced and poked sly fun at a perhaps lightly earned Irish pride that could be confused with mere boasting. "For I'm just as proud of my name, you see / As an emperor, Czar or a King could be." In "Horowitz," Sherman more modestly hauls out a Jewish giant, the classical pianist Vladimir Horowitz, and not incidentally the Jews who attend his concerts. Horowitz liked the song so much he asked for a signed copy of the *Celebrity* album.

H-O-R-O-W-I-T-Z spells Horowitz
Yesterday I took my girlfriend Peggy
To watch him play a concert at Carnegie.

That parody and the rest of Sherman's repertoire amounted to a pop culture version of the comical first line that *Herzog*'s Jewish hero thinks to himself after much confusion and heartache, "If I am out of my mind it's all right with me." Sherman commented on American Jewish cultural dilemmas and proposed nutty but charming solutions. In his introduction to "The Ballad of Harry Lewis" he made sure his audience understood he had a Jewish agenda fueled by an old grudge, but he used a light touch.

> I wonder, do you agree with me that every folk should have a folk hero? And what disappointed me when I was in school was that my folk didn't have a folk hero. I mean, Paul Bunyan, he wasn't Jewish. Tom Dooley, gentile. And big John Henry, it's no use even talking. So I waited till I got to be thirty-eight years old and we still didn't have a folk hero. So when I got a chance to write this first album I invented a folk hero for my folk. A nice folk hero, and he does everything in this song that a folk hero should do in one of these ballads. He dies and everything. Nice.

Of course, garment worker Harry Lewis is not a Jewish folk hero. Jewish life does not recognize the category. A Jewish John Henry had to be an anti-John Henry or the song would be laughable, not funny. Harry Lewis is a *schlemiel*, a Jewish mockery of non-Jewish folk heroes, and the song stands up for a Jewish point of view profoundly skeptical of the Christian impulse to make demigods of Tom Dooley, John Henry, and other doomed men.

> Although the fire was raging
> Harry stood by his machine
> And when the firemen broke in
> They discovered him between
> A pile of roasted Dacron
> And some French-fried gabardine
> His cloth goes shining on.

Ten Percent Jewish

Sherman's introductions to the "Goldeneh Moments" and "Harry Lewis" reveal he knew his funny songs made thoughtful points, and he was amused and pleased that others also understood there was more to his success than just laughs. "A whole sociological thing happened" with the success of "Sarah Jackman," Sherman told his audience. "There's a fellow at Harvard who is actually writing a thesis on why this song should become popular in this country at this time under these circumstances . . . And he's got a marvelous theory. His theory is that everybody is really part Jewish. Won't that be news for the New York Athletic Club?"

The punch line brings to mind Woody Allen's later bit about the Jewish couple dressed as a moose that are "shot, stuffed and mounted at the New York Athletic Club. And the joke is on them, because it's restricted." Social anti-Semitism had receded to the point that it could be openly ridiculed. But if anti-Semitism was a moldy and archaic holdover, Sherman's Jewish material was new, and its popularity demanded explanation. The fellow at Harvard, sociologist Herbert J. Gans, was actually at the University of Pennsylvania, and he did not quite say that everyone is part Jewish, though the misunderstanding is understandable. In his article about Sherman that appeared in May in *The Reconstructionist*, Gans interpreted Sherman's songs as "saying that the popular culture is by and large a Jewish product." If everybody was not part Jewish, they were anyway unknowingly absorbing Jewish culture through the Broadway stage and the movie musicals made of them.

A celebration of the fiftieth anniversary of the Anti-Defamation League in January 1963 was another opportunity to reflect on Sherman's fame as a milestone of social change. The *Washington Post* reported that the ADL's first target was vaudeville's "unshaven, derby-hatted Jewish tailor," and fifty years on the organization looked forward to a time when prejudice "can be reduced to a point of friendly competition," such as that between "Virginians and North Carolinians." The newspaper suggested Sherman represented a better ideal than the ADL's vision of a bland future. "Today, Jews are secure enough to enjoy [ethnic] jokes more than they resent them, and nearly everybody is laughing at the phonograph records of Allan Sherman."

The *Post*'s hip attitude might have been owed to inside information. By the time it published that story, the *National Press Club Record* had alerted the Washington press corps that Sherman was set to perform February 2 at the annual National Press Club Inaugural Ball, where he "will relate the experiences of 'Sarah Jackman' and her nice relatives." A new club president took the oath of office that night, administered by Supreme Court Chief Justice Earl Warren, and Sherman sat at Warren's table, alongside Vice President Lyndon Johnson and White House Press Secretary Pierre Salinger. Most of the other Press Club guests were just as unlikely Sherman fans. The seating chart reads like the original lyrics to the song Sherman turned into "Shake Hands with Your Uncle Max." There was McAndrew, McFarland, McCormack, McKelway, Hennessey, Corrigan, and Cullen and Moore. There were also two O'Briens and a Blair, a Boggs, and many other names not likely to show up in "Sarah Jackman."

Sherman began by ignoring the issue in favor of common ground. He had himself introduced as a former newspaperman, and for the room full of press the one-time *Daily Illini* columnist opened with "Just the *Times*," a parody of "Just in Time," a song that by 1963 had been recorded by Ella Fitzgerald, Nina Simone, Tony Bennett, and Frank Sinatra. "Just the *Times*" commemorates the 114-day New York newspaper strike of 1962–63.

Just the Times
I miss the New York Times
You just can't get the Times
Around my block
No one knows
If Taubman liked the shows
Or what James Reston thinks of Arthur Krock
No one knows
What's in that lovely crossword puzzle
Or if Scarsdale had a wave of crimes
Since last December eight
We've been illiter-ate
So please negotiate
And reinstate the Times.

Then Sherman got down to business. He did not jettison his Jewish material or otherwise kowtow to the august bunch. A recording of his performance reveals Sherman addressed the issue head on. "As to the rumor that I'm Jewish, the actual fact is I was raised by Jewish people — my mother and my father,"

Sherman told the crowd, fudging the facts, but their laughter proved it was exactly what they wanted and needed. The Jewish issue was the elephant in the room, and it was the subject of one of the many phone conversations that arranged his appearance. "On one call, the fellow said that it would be a good idea if I kept in mind that this was a mixed group and that the composition of this audience would be approximately 10 percent Jewish," Sherman said. "I'm actually delighted to hear that. For example, Chief Justice Warren, I didn't know you were any part Jewish at all."

It got a big laugh, the crowd relaxed, and the moment demonstrated another side of Sherman's societal value, especially among the powerful in Washington. His popularity suggests the audience was relieved that someone found a way to comically defuse the once taboo Jewish question at a time when the struggle for black civil rights generated conflict. Perhaps there was the hope that Sherman's humor might serve as a gentler model for black comedians. Dick Gregory was a star attraction in the early 1960s, and Sherman's joke about Warren being 10 percent Jewish found a counterpart in Gregory's act, but with a difference. "You really want to have some fun? . . . make out you're colored some day. I suggest you do it on a weekend. You do it *during* the week, you might get fired." Gregory was tougher on his audience and the country. His comedy was "a cataloguing of wrongs, a reading of indictments," wrote the *New York Times*. "He wouldn't mind paying his taxes, 'if I thought they were going to a friendly country.'" Yet some contemporaries detected an underlying similarity between the Jewish and black comics that Sherman welcomed. "Actually, our 'resemblance' stems from the fact that we both project an acceptance of what we are," Sherman said.

Their differences are even more instructive. Gregory attacked a hostile society in defense of his group. Sherman was an equal opportunity knock artist. He took on the country's un-Jewish folk repertoire, but when Broadway's Jewish creators hid their origins, Sherman called them on it, and when explicitly Jewish works slipped into the sentimental, he delivered the comic slap needed to bring them to their senses.

My Son, the Celebrity delivered such therapy to "Hava Nagila," a Hebrew song associated with the young and then romantically perceived State of Israel, though the infectious tune stems from a Hasidic community in Eastern

Europe. The melody was written down in 1915 by Jewish music researcher Abraham Zvi Idelsohn, and in 1918 he wrote its Hebrew lyrics. "Hava Nagila," or "Let us rejoice," was instantly popular in 1920s Jerusalem, and the folk music revival made it a standard in the United States after the war, but it was most closely associated with Harry Belafonte. He sang it as early as 1951 at New York's *Village Vanguard*, and it appeared on his 1957 album, *An Evening with Belafonte*, though the album's ad campaign touted cuts such as "Danny Boy" and "Shenandoah," not "Hava Nagila." By 1959, however, the song was considered a draw. Ads named "Hava Nageela" as a reason to buy *Belafonte at Carnegie Hall*.

The song was ready to be taken down with a send up, and in March 1962 Bob Dylan recorded "Talkin' Havah Negiliah Blues," not released until 1991. He introduces it by saying, "Here's a foreign song I learned in Utah" and ends it with a cowboy yodel. In between those two lines are the mispronounced title words, and that is the whole song. As one critic noted, its significance is Dylan's demurral. He chose "to not perform it as it should be performed." Sherman also put his foot down. In "Harvey and Sheila" he dished out the same treatment to "Hava Nagila" that he earlier reserved for the Broadway musical. Sherman's parody argues that "Hava Nagila" is a pretense, that it represents an inauthentic way to be Jewish in America. A scholar later confirmed Sherman's intuition, writing that Israel "has little meaning for American Jews at the times in their private lives when they feel most keenly Jewish," such as at Jewish weddings and funerals. When Sherman sang "Harvey and Sheila" on the *Steve Allen Show* he raised the stakes by announcing that, "the Christian name of this song is Hava Nagila." Proof that Sherman was right is the reaction of the National Press Club, which was underwhelmed by "Harvey and Sheila." Unlike the original, it was too Jewish for the largely non-Jewish audience.

Harvey and Sheila
Harvey and Sheila
Harvey and Sheila
Moved to West L.A.
They bought a house one day
Financed by FHA

It had a swimming pool
Full of H_2O
Traded their used MG
For a new XKE
Switched to the GOP
That's the way things go

The rest of Sherman's press club show repeated a good deal of what he did in Santa Monica, and his stage patter was so genuine that when he prepared to sit on the edge of the stage, a la Judy Garland, and sing "Overweight People," his parody of "Over the Rainbow," nobody could have guessed that he did the same act a few weeks before. "You think the world is ready for this?" is exactly what he said in Southern California.

Somewhere, overweight people
Just like me
Must have someplace where folks don't count every calorie
Somewhere, over the rainbow
Way up tall
There's a land where they've never heard of cholesterol
Where folks can eat just what they want
And still be slim and trim and gaunt,
You'll find me
Where every little thing I taste
Won't wind up showing on my waist, or worse,
Behind me.

When he finished, his dilemma was also the same as at the earlier concert. "Folks, you are looking at a person with a great problem. Did any of you see Judy Garland? How the hell does she get back on the stage?" It was all planned, as it should have been, and it was a crowd pleaser. Steve Allen helped him write the act, and Sherman carried it off. The crowd believed it was all done on the fly.

The Press Club engagement was a winner, and before the evening was over Pierre Salinger invited Sherman to dine at the White House the following night. The following day brought Sherman his first humiliating press coverage. "Sherman 'Marches' On" was a *Washington Post* photo essay that portrayed him as he looked in his hotel suite before the Press Club event, which was drowsy, droopy, unshaven, fat, and unhealthy as he lay on the sofa wrapped in a terry cloth robe and smoking a cigarette. The caption noted that he also sipped a Coca-Cola, "his 'breakfast.'" Remarks quoted under each of the four photographs were as grandiose as the pictures were repellent. "Did you know that I'm up for the same part as Tony Curtis in a movie?" The story delighted in its meanness, but it did catch Sherman's undisciplined and self-destructive side that was temporarily put on hold by fame and a tight schedule. It could not be postponed forever.

"Show business can be a dangerous thing," Jon Hendricks said. "Allan just wasn't suited for it. Allan was a decent man. He was a good cat, you know. Being a star will kill you."

Hymie's on the Moon

Stardom's dangers included easily available women, but even before Sherman indulged that dubious opportunity he pursued a destructive path. "He loved to gamble, he really did," said his road manager Marvin Tabolsky. Sherman's system at the blackjack tables was to win three hands in a row before pulling back to his original stake. "It didn't work all the time." When he was not losing his money, Sherman concentrated on losing his health. "He had asthma and smoked like a fiend," Tabolsky said. "He'd be wheezing, gasping, and I used to say to him, Allan, how can you sit there and smoke and hack and cough? And he used to say, 'don't worry, it'll be okay, it'll be okay.' It always amazed me how he would punish himself."

Also punishing was his concert schedule. From Washington Sherman flew to Chicago for concerts on February 9 and 10 at the Arie Crown Theater, and then traveled with his musicians and New Christy Minstrels back-up singers by bus and sometimes by air to Cincinnati, St. Louis, Detroit, Toronto, Buffalo, Rochester, New York, Montreal, Yale University, Bridgeport, Connecticut, and then back to Washington, where he played the Loew's Capitol theater on March 1. It was his twelfth show in twenty-one days, but Sherman found it more revitalizing than exhausting. "It kept him sane. He loved to entertain people," Bill Marx said. "Allan genuinely liked to see people laugh, to make that connection." "People really got into his act," Tabolsky said. "He lost his fright and became one with the audience and was able to connect, and they felt that. You could see people in the audience with big smiles on their faces, really having a good time. That fed back to him, and the more they did that the more he poured out his thing. . . . Nobody could understand this roly-poly guy as a concert performer, but it worked."

Friends who knew him from his days in television found it especially bewildering. "[H]e does not exactly look like the overnight-sensation type," wrote Maurice Zolotow. "In fact, he looks more like a short, fat headwaiter in a Chinese restaurant. He packs 225 pounds of blubber on five feet, six inches of frame attached loosely to a moon face with horn-rimmed glasses that do absolutely nothing for him."

Yet on March 4, 1963, the unlikely star met President Kennedy and received firsthand confirmation that the commander in chief was a fan. Sherman sang at the Department of Labor fiftieth anniversary dinner, his second gig for official Washington, and once again he sat at the vice president's table, which included Assistant Secretary of Labor Daniel Moynihan, Senator Barry Goldwater, and New York Congressman Adam Clayton Powell, among others. President Kennedy spoke at the dinner, and Sherman briefly met him during the festivities. Kennedy said, "I have your record and I like it very much."

Everybody did, and they did whatever they could to show it. After the Labor Department dinner, Sherman immediately flew to Los Angeles for a March 8 taping of the *Steve Allen Show* he had been fired from less than a year before. He was treated like royalty. Allen dispensed with an opening monologue and went right into a recitation of Sherman's credits, including his "fantastic meteoric rise" and the two albums that sold two million copies. On top of that Sherman was recently in Washington where he met the president, Allen crowed, and displayed a photograph of Kennedy greeting the entertainer. Finally, Allen smoothed any feathers that might have still been ruffled from Sherman's short stint with the show a year before. "Allan has been one of my personal friends for many years and he was when our series first started here the producer of the show," but Sherman found "greener fields," Allen said.

Only then did Sherman appear, and he was rarely off-screen for the rest of the ninety-minute show. Sherman was a star, but he claimed the first-night jitters of only a few months but many concerts before. "I'm in a state of terror," he told Allen. He did not look it, and sang bits and pieces of songs that would turn up on future albums, such as "I See Bones," a take-off on "C'est Si Bon," before introducing "Hymie's on the Moon," another whack at the "Fly Me to the Moon" song he toyed with before his fame. The new parody was the product of a passing fancy. The flight from St. Louis to Cleveland was only forty minutes, Sherman explained. If it were longer, the song would be, too.

> The little State of Israel
> Is quite a happy place
> For the little State of Israel
> Has conquered outer space
> And that's why,
> Hymie's on the moon,
> And little Seymour's in the stars
> Julius is on Jupiter
> And Marvin is on Mars.

Like "Just the *Times*" and many other Sherman songs, this one reacted to the news of the day. Sherman was in many ways still the journalist he was in college, only he now recorded contemporary goings on in his comic folk songs. In 1963, Israel established its National Committee for Space Research, and the idea of Jews in space must have seemed impossibly incongruous and irresistible to Sherman. It may also have appealed to Steve Allen's other guest, Mel Brooks. "Hymie's on the Moon" is his kind of Jewish humor. On his television show, *Get Smart*, Hymie was the secret agent given bum assignments like hiding in a mailbox. Sherman's parody seems to have lain dormant in Brooks's imagination until 1981, when it surfaced in the "Jews in Space" number in his *History of the World, Part I*.

Star-Father

The *Steve Allen Show* brought Sherman home for his first break in more than two months of touring, but true to what Robert Sherman remembers, it seems to have been a working vacation. On March 6, *Daily Variety* reported Sherman was preparing a third album, and the three weeks after the Steve Allen taping is likely when he began working with Lou Busch on *My Son, the Nut*. It was one of the longest periods Sherman spent away from concert and nightclub stages before its release in late July.

That nonstop schedule bred tensions in the family, sometimes expressed by his son. "Hello, star-father. Greetings, magnificence of stardom," was one of Robert's quips. He had grown out of the stage that saw him holed up in his room and now resembled his father. "Robbie would say why don't you do it this way, why don't you do it that way," Tabolsky said. "He was show-biz oriented." Intelligent and persistent, Robert also apparently refused to acknowledge any special respect owed his elders, and that earned him a reputation. "Robert is as cheerfully and appealingly obnoxious as ever," Richard Gehman wrote in his liner notes to *My Son, the Celebrity*. It was a running gag. Sherman assured an interviewer that fame had not changed him or his family. "Friends tell me that my twelve-year-old son Bobbie is still obnoxious." It was a backhanded compliment, code for a mouthy but undeniably smart kid. Robert declared his love for his father in the same barbed way. "You'll never amount to anything unless you cut an album and appear on an Ed Sullivan TV show," he taunted before Sherman's fame hit. "Robbie was always Allan's alter ego," Golden said. Nancy, then twelve and still living at home, seems to have left the field to the two of them. Gehman's liner notes do not mention her. "Nancy was not involved," Tabolsky said. "Always quiet." She "is still the sweet cheerful self she was in our pre-fame days," Sherman told an interviewer. That was an evasion of the complexities of family life. Evasion was the way he wanted it. "They were not part of his life," friend Billy Goldenberg said of Sherman's family. Sherman loved his wife and "he adored his children," but he needed distance from them, Goldenberg said. "He wouldn't have them around."

Dinner with Sinatra

On March 27, Sherman started a ten-day engagement in Palm Springs, California, at the Chi Chi. "Bigger than Ciro's, better than the Trocadero, and more fun than the Mocambo that jammed L.A.'s Sunset Strip, the Chi Chi was a veritable shrine to 'live' entertainment," remembered *Palm Springs Life* magazine in 2007. The club had a Polynesian décor, and in 1948 its new Blue Room was festooned with "palm tree murals, full-size portraits of nubile island girls, plush red leather banquettes, doll-faced cigarette girls, handheld telephones, and a five-piece rumba band." Restraint was not the point. "They had a maitre d' and a front desk with three or four bell captains in tuxedos," bandleader Bill Alexander told the magazine. "It was a real Vegas-style operation."

Owner Irwin Schuman expanded the Chi Chi in 1950 with the new $100,000 Starlite Room, big enough to seat five hundred at the classic little nightclub tables covered in white linen. He also contracted with the Las Vegas Flamingo Hotel's booking agent to share acts and insisted his club operate under a "name talent policy." The Starlite Room was a hit; in 1954 Schuman enlarged it to seat 800, and the larger venue helped make the Chi Chi and Palm Springs a "worldwide tourist resort" and a top destination for star acts such as Milton Berle, Sarah Vaughn, Julie London, Mel Tormé, and Nat King Cole. Despite the tourists, there were often more stars in the audience than on stage, as entertainers from Cary Grant to Frank Sinatra arrived to watch their peers put on a show.

Sherman was just in time to enjoy the last of these glory days, before rock and roll ended the Chi Chi's reign, and he made the most of it. By the time he and Tabolksy drove down from Los Angeles, Sherman had already written "Chi Chi," a parody of "Gigi," the title song to Lerner and Loewe's movie musical, and he made sure the word got out and found the right audience. "Fritz Loewe delayed his Japan trek to catch Allan Sherman at the Chi Chi" and hear the "Gigi" parody, reported *Daily Variety*. That was Sherman's hope, but it was untrue. Before he sang his parody he told the Chi Chi audience that Loewe "saw fit to leave for China the day before I opened here . . . I wish he could have stayed to hear this."

Chi Chi

Are you a club or just a joint where people come and sit and point

At Don Ameche?

Oh Chi Chi

What is it made you Palm Springs' greatest club by far?

Chi Chi

Even though you're very large you've got such warmth and style.

Chi Chi

When your waiters over-charge they smile, they smile.

Chi Chi

Where all the very finest folks sit in the smoke and nearly choke

And think its peachy.

Oh Chi Chi

What is it made you Palm Springs' greatest club by far?

Is it the food? The drinks? The show here?

Or there's no place else to go here!

That's the miracle that made you the way you are.

Sherman was a hit, reported *Variety*. He "is now an old pro and a polished performer. . . . He gave the old bistro its best night in years." There was no better proof than the stamp of approval he got that made up for Loewe's absence. "I think one of the biggest thrills of his life was . . . Sinatra came in, and Sinatra invited him to have dinner with him," Tabolsky said. "That really was a big thrill." Sherman first came within range of the star's orbit back in January when *Daily Variety* reported, "Sinatra, Dean Martin and Davis Jr. surprised Allan Sherman and Vic Damone on the Sands stage." But this time was different. On April 2, 1963, the local *Desert Sun* newspaper ran a photograph of a beaming Sinatra flanked by Sherman and actress Jill St. John as they sat crowded together at a table, Sinatra's left arm draped over Sherman's shoulder. The published photograph was a cropped version of the original. It left out Chi Chi boss Schuman and Sherman's wife, Dee.

Over the next two months Sherman remained at star altitude. His last night at the Chi Chi was April 5, and then he flew to Miami for an April 10 to 21 booking at the Diplomat Hotel, a stint that coincided with the influx of New

Yorkers coming down with their families for the spring holiday. While he was there, *My Son, the Folk Singer* was nominated for a Grammy Award. On April 20, 1963, the album was still doing great business at number 16 on the *Billboard* "Top LP's" list of the 150 best-selling mono albums, a chart it had been on for twenty-five weeks. *Celebrity* was number 13 after fourteen weeks on the chart. On May 1, the *Perry Como Show* put Sherman front and center, with Como explaining that his guest "is responsible for the style of our show tonight. In his whole career he's only made two albums and they've sold a million each, the rotten kid." The hostility may not have been a joke. Como introduced him as Alvin. The next night Sherman was on the *Andy Williams Show*; the day after that he opened for a week in Los Angeles at the Crescendo Club; and when that was done he flew to New York for a May 15 appearance, his first, on Johnny Carson's *Tonight* show. Luckily for him, the show was a rare dud, and that made him shine all the brighter. "Comedian Allan Sherman's routine from his hit album was hilarious and the interview that followed was equally entertaining," wrote *Billboard*. He did not spend much time in New York. Steve Allen needed him in Los Angeles for a May 24 taping that aired June 6, the same night Sherman opened a three-week run at the San Francisco Fairmont Hotel's Venetian Room, a venue music journalist Joel Selvin called the "last elegant supper club on the West Coast." It was where Tony Bennett first sang "I Left My Heart in San Francisco," and it hosted all the top acts, from Lena Horne and Ella Fitzgerald to Marlene Dietrich.

In the midst of this public acclaim and jet-setting, Sherman was able to pause and reflect that not all was what it seemed. A machinery of illusion and fraud surrounded him, he told *Variety*. "Agents, press agents, Warner Bros. records promotion people, they all gathered around. It was overwhelming. I didn't know what they wanted. All of these people convinced me I was rich, which isn't necessarily so. They said it so they would get heavy commissions and such, and by the time you pay them, you're no longer rich." Not only that, but fame could be as hard to hold on to as money. "If you can get this lucky all of a sudden, you can get that unlucky, too."

That time would come, but not yet.

EIGHT
MY SON, THE NUT

Reports of 1960s music fans "actually breaking down doors" of record stores to buy a star's latest hit song sound like news about a teen sensation, but in the summer of 1963 they were about overweight sensation Allan Sherman's smash single, "Hello Muddah, Hello Fadduh! (A letter from camp)." The song was a hit as a single record, and when *Billboard* on July 27 reported on the behavior of overwrought customers, the song was so new the publication got the title wrong, calling it "Dear Muddah, Dear Fadduh." It was included on Sherman's *My Son, the Nut* album, his third in just ten months, and *Billboard* likely did not yet have a review copy. *My Son, the Nut* did not top the magazine's "Album Reviews" lineup until August 10. But the mistake was telling. Everyone was playing catch up. Sherman was moving too fast. *Variety* scooped *Billboard* with a July 31 review of *Nut*, but its story was obsolete before it went to press, and it had to inform readers that "Hello Muddah" was "already scoring in the singles market."

"When he was hot he was hotter 'n' hell," said Jerry Perenchio. Joe Smith remembers that Sherman "was idolized." Jon Hendricks believes Sherman deserved it. "'Hello Muddah' is a great American masterpiece."

Sherman's ten months in the public eye had been success after success, and when "Hello Muddah" soared it seemed a flight powered by all the momentum that came before. The weeks prior to "Hello Muddah" were especially eventful. On July 11, *Variety* announced Sherman would guest host the *Tonight* show the week of August 5 for Johnny Carson, who took over the late-night program less than a year before, in October 1962, at the same time Sherman grabbed the spotlight. On an average night, seven and a half million people watched Carson, and Sherman proved himself before that audience first on May 15 with a performance that got applause in the press, and apparently again on July 10, the day before he was named guest host. "Sherman was always known as an upper guy," said Sheldon Schultz, *Tonight's* talent coordinator. "We chose him and went after him." A week later on July 18 Sherman was on the *Steve Allen Show*, where the audience gave him a welcome beyond what stage hands can cajole out of a merely polite audience. The crowd applauded, whistled and yelled out its approval, and Sherman won the same reception again the next night when on July 19 he played the Hollywood Bowl to a record-breaking capacity crowd of 16,076, a victory he trumpeted on July 24 in a full page *Variety* advertisement that boomed, "ALLAN SHERMAN MAKES HISTORY AT HOLLYWOOD BOWL." The crowds stopped traffic on the freeway, remembered Golden. "What impressed me most was that people came in stretchers and wheelchairs. People want to laugh." That triumph encouraged Sherman and his agents to repeat it, and on July 26 he played the Bowl again and performed the song that became his classic, his signature, and over time his albatross. "His newest, a take-off on a homesick boy at camp, is his best," wrote the *Los Angeles Herald-Examiner*. "It is belly-laugh material and parents will revel in its so-true-to-life barbs."

Billboard reported Warner Bros. shipped 70,000 copies of the "Hello Muddah" single in two days. *The Hollywood Reporter* said it was 100,000 in four days. By August 4 the record had been out two weeks and the *New York Times* wrote that sales were 300,000. By September it was a hit in Australia. In October it was on the charts in Great Britain and, somehow, the Philippines. By then sales had reached 700,000. New Zealand came on board in November, and so did Hong Kong, and over the next few years, songwriters in Sweden, Norway, and Israel did their own versions of the song to Sherman's inspired choice of melody, a segment from the "Dance of the Hours" by nineteenth-century Italian composer Amilcare Ponchielli. Its playfulness caught Sherman's attention at least as early as 1958, when he included it in an unused skit he wrote for the Victor Borge special. Unlike most other Sherman songs, "Hello Muddah" adds lyrics to a tune that originally had none, and it may have been a trick he learned from his friend Jon Hendricks, who as the inventor of "vocalese" created lyrics to accompany jazz instrumentals.

The hit single helped *My Son, the Nut* streak to the top. On August 17, it was number 90 on *Billboard*'s "Top LP's" chart. A week later it was number 5, and on August 31 it was number 1, the best-selling album in the country. "Every Sherman Release a Number 1 Seller" was the headline in trade magazine *Cash Box*, which noted that Sherman's perfect score of three records in a row to hit number 1 put him in "such select company as Elvis Presley and Frank Sinatra, both of whom have had a string of number 1 LP's." At the end of September, *Nut* was still number 1, and Sherman's first two albums were in the top 100. *Celebrity* was at number 39 nine months after its debut, and *Folk Singer* was at 89 after forty-seven weeks. Warner Bros. was ecstatic. At a convention for its record distributors company president Mike Maitland brought out Sherman for "10 minutes of hilarity" before outlining his marketing push for the company's new releases. For Sherman, Maitland promised to go all out. *My Son, the Nut* would be promoted with skywriting.

Sherman also was flying high.

"He had everything then," said Golden. "Life was a bowl of cherries. He was a big star."

Why Did We Move Here?

The success of "Hello Muddah" and the third album were astounding wins, because as *Billboard* noted, *My Son, the Nut* "was even faster moving than his original successes, and this after a second album which never built up the same kind of steam as the first." *Celebrity*'s more than respectable sales of over 600,000 were just half *Folk Singer*'s. The second album was a bit of a hodgepodge, with Jewish song parodies such as the biting and brilliant "Harvey and Sheila," a lackluster protest song against the telephone company, and the enjoyable absurdities of "Mexican Hat Dance" and "Me," which like his earlier song about Los Angeles real estate parodies the Italian-language hit "Come Back to Sorrento," recorded by Dean Martin and others. "Counting both feet, I have ten toes / They're not lady toes, they're men toes / And I keep them as mementoes / For I love them tenderly." *Celebrity* also engages in more satire than Sherman's reputation as a gentle parodist admits. "Al 'n Yetta," sung to the tune of the French children's song "Alouette" (Sherman loved to puncture the French and Italian songs Americans embraced but could not understand) rips into a housebound couple transfixed by television. The song takes down inane shows like *Mr. Ed*, about a talking horse, and also features a cutting insight about so-called cultural programming. "Al 'n Yetta watched an operetta / Leonard Bernstein told them what they saw." In "The Bronx Bird Watcher," a parody of Gilbert and Sullivan's "Titwillow" from *The Mikado*, itself a send-up of operatic melodrama, the clueless Blanche living in a split-level ranch is immune to a songbird's beguiling "titwillow," and with the cold bloodedness of the profoundly dim recalls only one thing about her husband's gift. "As I fricasseed him / He let out a yell."

In contrast with this loose assortment, Sherman's first and third albums offered coherent themes rooted in his childhood, and when he tapped into the powerful emotions of his early life and transformed them into comedy he produced hits. *My Son, the Folk Singer* did comic battle for the world of his beloved immigrant Jewish grandparents, and *My Son, the Nut* grew from the heartbreaks inflicted by his parents. He never forgot those rotten experiences or threw them away. They made good fertilizer. In "Hello Muddah," he turned child abandonment and the pitiful pleading of a little boy for his parents into comedy. There is an "eternal war that goes on between children and parents," Sherman said about "Hello Muddah's" international success. "Children and parents have this invisible war going on all over the world at all times."

Take me home
I promise I will not make noise
Or mess the house with other boys
Oh please don't make me stay
I've been here one whole day.

"If you listen real close to a number of his songs, there is always a hint of anxiety," said his cousin Morris Coplon. "The anxiety in Allan's work is always there." But the point is that one must diligently look for the anxiety, because the triumph of "Hello Muddah" is how it blends childhood fear and misery with a deft humor that owes its comic effect to the anxiety it quickly dispatches. Like all good children's stories, "Hello Muddah" introduces suffering and unhappiness to heighten the relief of the happy ending, and like all good children's stories it touched a nerve.

As a children's song addressed to adults, to mothers and fathers, it invites them back into the frightening world of childhood they can now safely visit with Sherman as their amusing guide. At the same time, it assuages parental guilt with the assurance that the pain they cause their children is unserious and ephemeral. For adult listeners, Sherman, the adult pretending to be a child, is on their side. On the other hand, for children Sherman is the sympathetic adult that understands them better than their own parents. He accepts as valid both a child's fear and its fickle shift to joyous activity in the song's famous ending.

Wait a minute
It stopped hailing
Guys are swimming, guys are sailing
Playing baseball, gee that's better
Muddah, Fadduh, kindly disregard this letter

"Hello Muddah" skillfully works both sides of the street, divining, expressing, and dispelling the anxieties of both children and parents. Childhood and the child-parent relationship, overcharged with love and suffering, was, along with Jewish identity, Sherman's greatest subject.

It is also the subject of *My Son, the Nut*. The album as a whole is a children's record for children and adults. *Nut* seesaws between the universal childhood preoccupations that dominated Sherman's childhood — family happiness or the lack of it and the discovery of the world through language. "Hello Muddah" and also "Headaches," "Here's to the Crabgrass," and "Hail to thee, Fat Person" comically monitor the loneliness, disappointment and misunderstanding between parents, and between children and parents. "I See Bones," "Hungarian Goulash No. 5," and "One Hippopotami" revel in a child's discovery of novel words to say, the wonderful rhymes they can make, and the large world they represent. The latter songs followed a wonderful tradition of irreverence. "Hungarian Goulash" offers a whimsical tour of the world's foods, and it uses the melody of Johannes Brahms' "Hungarian Dance No. 5" in the same way Warner Bros. employed Richard Wagner's "Ride of the Valkyries" in the classic 1957 Bugs Bunny cartoon, "What's Opera, Doc?" Both comic bits secretly celebrate classical music, finding a way to feed it to their audiences by diverting them with a delightful story, like a mother coaxing a baby to eat by turning a spoonful of applesauce into an airplane landing in the infant's mouth.

If you like Hungarian food
They have a goulash which is very good.
Or, if you wish, a dish that's Chinese
Somewhere down in column B there's lobster Cantonese.
Hey!

"One Hippopotami" takes the same tack to inculcate a delight in words.

Singulars and plurals are so different, bless my soul
Has it ever occurred to you, that the plural of half is whole
A bunch of tooth is teeth
A group of foot is feet
And two canaries make a pair
They call it a parakeet.

But "Hello Muddah," written as a letter from a homesick boy at Camp Granada, overshadows the album's other songs. "'Hello Muddah' came to him so fast I couldn't write that fast," Golden said of the brainstorming sessions that saw Sherman spouting out the lyrics while Golden jotted them down. His creative speed caught everyone's attention. "All you'd have to do is give him a pencil and he could come up with stuff," said Al Lerner, a musical arranger who worked with Sherman on later albums. "He could do more in an hour of writing than someone else could do in a month," said Bill Loeb, Sherman's manager after Bullets Durgom. "He was a really bright man." Cleverness was certainly part of it, but his songs were also the product of years of rumination.

"Hello Muddah" did not come to him, as he claimed in his autobiography, on the spur of the moment as he considered the prospect that his daughter, Nancy, was about to attend camp. That story in the book was made up afterward, Golden said. His son Robert's miserable camp experience likely came into play, but Sherman had more than enough material of his own.

In the song, Sherman's child persona relates an account of camp that is part *Perils of Pauline* and part Battle of Iwo Jima. "All the counselors hate the waiters / And the lake has alligators." But in addition to the ambiguity that allows it to work for children as well as their parents, it also combines ethnic and American elements to create a comedy that is, in a sense, bilingual. By retaining a Jewish sensibility and speech patterns ("Now I don't want / This should scare ya") and marrying them to summer camp and the middle-class activities promoted there ("Guys are swimming / Guys are sailing") Sherman spoke to Jewish and general audiences simultaneously in a language both could understand in their own way. It was a comic invention American Jews were in a unique position to create. They were members of their own group and also such avid consumers of American life that aspects of that life became associated with Jews. This was especially true of summer camps. Jews were "at the epicenter of the summer camp marketplace" and "sent their children to camps in disproportionate numbers compared to their Christian peers." The allure was powerful because at camp Jews learned American activities such as sailing not easily accessible to Jewish city dwellers, and at the same time constructed "a new brand of ethnic Americanism." Sherman's song gave voice to the common and ethnic aspects of Jewish camping, and while he was at it invented a new Jewish humor that left behind ethnic dialect comedy and paved the way for the mainstream Jewish humor later mined with spectacular success by Jerry Seinfeld. This comedy did not erase Jewish names, styles of speech, or typical activities, but it was also not concerned with immigrants or Jewish religious matters, and so could be read as Jewish or not, depending upon the audience's degree of familiarity with Jewish life.

Sherman managed the same trick with *Nut*'s other comic songs about familial unhappiness and misunderstanding. In "Hail to Thee, Fat Person," Sherman addresses the audience with comic solemnity to "explain how it came to pass that I got fat." With musical strains of "America the Beautiful" building in the background, he tells the story of how "when I was a child my mother said to me, 'Clean the plate, because children are starving in Europe.'" Sherman obeyed, became fat, and because the children in Europe kept starving, Sherman and his fellow hearty eaters are inadvertent national heroes other Americans should greet with a respectful and patriotic, "Hail to thee, fat person / You have kept us out of war." This works comedy's magic on the truth that Sherman's mother was to blame for her son's condition. Sherman transforms his and Rose's profound misunderstanding of one another into laughter at a parent-child miscommunication problem that is universal. It also describes a family scene Jews recognize as their own, with the overbearing mother, obsessed with the welfare of community and perhaps family members still in Europe, urging her child to eat. But other white ethnics were also able to read it as a reflection of their own experience. As a researcher in Chicago found, Italians, Irish and Jews all claimed their mothers were central and unique. The Jews, however, because of their prominence in creating entertainments, became the country's ethnic representative, supplying a "narrative for immigrants across the board." Sherman was a key player in this Jewish cultural ascent that saw other groups claim the Jewish story as representative of their own.

"Here's to the Crabgrass" turns family misery into comedy as it parodies that hymn to domestic paradise, "English Country Garden," and turns it into its weedy and mundane opposite. "Here's to the crabgrass / Here's to the mortgage / In fact, here's to suburbia." The song tracks the dream of suburban life as it quickly devolves from, "Come let us go there / Live like Thoreau there" to "Why did we move here?" Americans were going through the same stages of grief as they realized suburban life could be a hectic disappointment with its Cub Scout meetings, dance classes, lawns, Little Leaguers, and search for status, a message "Crabgrass" makes wonderfully comical through the contrast between the lament of the lyrics and the underlying music's incessant cheerfulness. "Can't keep a maid here / No matter what they're paid here / The place has bad publicity." Other Jewish comedians worked the same suburban territory. In 1962, Alan King wrote *Anybody Who Owns His Own Home Deserves It*, and in 1964, *Help! I'm a Prisoner in a Chinese Bakery*. The latter's back cover billed King as America's "angry man of the suburbs." The search for Eden in suburbia also fed the writing of Jewish novelists. Philip Roth's *Goodbye, Columbus*, Bruce Jay Friedman's *Stern*, and Saul Bellow's *Herzog* all addressed the search for a perfect life away from the city. It was a disaster for Moses Herzog. "Oh, he had really been asking for it," Herzog thought to himself as he remembered the idealized life in the country that resulted in so much unhappiness. Sherman's husband and wife in "Crabgrass" also reap distress, and the song closes with them pledging to return to the city for another inevitable round of disappointment.

> Back to the city where life is gay and witty
> Back to the noise there that everyone enjoys there
> Back to the crush there, hurry let us rush there
> Back to the rat race, don't forget your briefcase
> Back in the groove there, say why don't we move there?

Jewish writers did not have the suburban subject to themselves. From the somber John Cheever to Jean Kerr's lighthearted *Please Don't Eat The Daisies*, non-Jews wrote about the loneliness and absurdity of suburbia, but there was good reason that it, like summer camp, was a favorite Jewish subject. "Jews suburbanized to a far greater degree than other Americans," and the Jews' suburban experience was the model for the country. Levittown, founded by builder Abraham Levitt and his sons, opened on Long Island in 1947 and was soon copied by builders across the nation. This put Jews at the center of the new national life. Concentrated in the New York metropolitan area, they were among the first to experience suburban life and live it *as* a community. Sherman was part of this typical Jewish and American life in both New York and Los Angeles, and he had the indispensible talent of every good social observer, which is to grasp the significance of the obvious. Nothing was more obvious than postwar suburbanization. The "great American land rush after 1945 was one of the largest mass movements in our history," wrote urban historian Kenneth T. Jackson. It was also a perfect fit for Sherman's themes of a lost home, and of wandering. "Hello Muddah's" plaintive "take me home" was his childhood dream. The poignant "why did we move here?" of "Crabgrass" was the question.

All Day, All Night, Cary Grant

With "Hello Muddah" a hit and Sherman about to begin his week as guest host of *Tonight*, the most important newspaper in America finally gave in and recognized his existence. On August 4, 1963, the *New York Times* ran a fastidious feature on the performer that somehow managed to avoid using the word Jewish. The *Times* could almost be seen to grimace as it held Sherman's parodies at arm's length and described them as the "odd-ball adaptation of well-known songs." The less refined *New York Post* profiled Sherman the same day, and that article by future film director Nora Ephron did not turn away from the "unmistakably Jewish overtones" of his breakthrough *Folk Singer* album. Both papers, however, reported Sherman's complaint that he was not in touch with reality. The childhood themes of his new album, and their origins, were on his mind. "My parents divorced when I was 6 and I spent the rest of my life at Fred Astaire and Dick Powell movies," he told Ephron. "This caused me to lose my grip on reality."

Acting crazy is a comedian's forte, and claiming a distance from reality can be a form of bragging, but Sherman's stint on *Tonight* proves it was not an empty boast. The control he exhibited in January at his Santa Monica concert came and went. His performer's mask kept slipping. As someone who found it difficult to sustain one personality, the burden of two was a strain. On his *Celebrity* album Sherman sang the ditty, "All day, all night, Cary Grant / That's all I hear from my wife is Cary Grant / What can he do that I can't? / Big deal, big star Cary Grant." That showed admirable confidence and cool, and the bit had wit when in Santa Monica he claimed his true appearance made him a dead ringer for the movie star. More than half a year later on the *Tonight* show the routine still had legs, so long as it was clear Sherman knew it was a joke. It was not always clear. "He wasn't just going for a laugh," recalled friend Jerry Hopkins. "He truly did want to be Cary Grant."

It was Sherman's running gag for the week, and on Monday, August 5, his first night as guest host he challenged Grant to "let the public decide who is prettier." This was followed by a non sequitur delivered with a bit of nastiness. "First of all, did you ever have a hit record in your life?" And then it was back again to self-aware cleverness. "Void in states where challenges to Cary

Grant are not legal." When contestants in the International Beauty Pageant appeared on the show, Sherman leveraged the Cary Grant act to tiptoe the line that divides comic from uncomfortable behavior. Sherman arranged for Miss Ireland to give him a passionate kiss, a move obviously motivated at least as much by the real Sherman as by his persona. "He loved pretty girls," remembered Tabolsky. "He fell apart for pretty girls." Then he quickly dispelled the ambiguity and got back into character. After the kiss Miss Ireland was supposed to say, "Who's Cary Grant?" She didn't, and Sherman alertly turned this to his advantage. "She forgot the line. That'll give you an idea, Cary baby."

There were other gaffes, too, driven by his need to say something profound about childhood. "It's true," he insisted when the audience did not respectfully welcome his insight that all adults are eight years old inside. "When you were a child you were all the things you were going to be, except later you have a beard." This was a core idea for Sherman, and his earnestness made it a conversation killer, but the missteps that signaled his submerged character flaws were for the time being overshadowed by his successes. Cary Grant played along and sent a telegram Sherman read on Wednesday night that admitted Sherman was the more adorable. "You're right, you talented man." Then Sherman, wearing a beret and carrying a cigarette holder, descended with exaggerated suavity into the audience to kiss some women. "I'm sorry, there isn't a great deal of time," he said. "I'll take care of the rest of you after the show." The same night he elevated typical talk show chitchat in a conversation with television actor Robert Stack, who played federal agent Eliot Ness on *The Untouchables*. When Stack mentioned that Italian Americans were sensitive to the Italian names of the show's criminals, Sherman defended ethnic honesty. "It takes the juice out of a story to call everyone Smith and Jones."

"He was great, he was gabby, he made the role easy," said *Tonight*'s Sheldon Schultz. "I'm sure he was a bit nervous, but he knew he wasn't Olivier. He felt that every day that this happened to him was a fucking miracle."

Another miracle was his opportunity to book Bill Cosby. The comedian's agent, Roy Silver, had tried and failed to get his client on the *Tonight* show but saw an opportunity to bypass the usual channels when Sherman guest hosted. He was right. Schultz said Sherman went downtown to Greenwich Village to see Cosby perform at the Bitter End and fought to put him on the Monday,

August 5, show. Tabolsky remembers Cosby coming to see Sherman in Carson's office. "Cosby did the Noah routine. Talk about rolling on the floor. Allan couldn't wait to get his name on the board." Both agree Sherman pushed for Cosby. "Who turned this guy down? He's killer," Schultz recalled Sherman saying. "Allan was all for him. Cosby came on and he killed 'em, and Allan was just great to him." Sherman's next step proved he did not always need directions to find reality. He pulled a fast one. "We used to get the Carson show a day late" in California," said Warner Bros.' Joe Smith. "Allan called to tell me there's a guy he had on and we gotta sign him." That is, sign Cosby before his *Tonight* show spot airs in California, when everyone in the business will know how great he is. "We signed Cosby and had seven incredibly successful albums with him," Smith said. Sherman shared in that success. On August 15, just ten days after Cosby's appearance on *Tonight*, Sherman struck a deal with Warner Bros. for "a royalty of one percent (1%) on all records sold by us recorded by Mr. Cosby." "We made lots of money from the Cosby records," Golden said.

Child Is Father of the Man

It was money he would very much need. The tension between his fame and his insecurities drove Sherman to make awkward public confessions that were one of the many missteps that eventually lost him the opportunities he had won. Just a week after hosting *Tonight*, Carson brought Sherman back on the show August 16 to promote *My Son, the Nut*. His appearance proved he was slipping. Sherman did not know when enough was enough. Again he wore the beret, behaved with faux sophistication and nonchalance, kissed a woman in the audience, and then lay down on the couch. "What is all this?" Carson asked. "Dr. Carson, you've got to help me." "I believe that, yes." "I keep dreaming I'm short and fat but in real life I'm Cary Grant." "Oh, you going to do that again!" Carson exclaimed. It was getting old, and Sherman's references to psychoanalysis had lately become an embarrassing tic. He told a newspaper in Rochester, New York, "Sigmund Freud said that a pun is merely an extension of words." The polite response to that is confused silence. In the *New York Post* profile, Nora Ephron quoted him saying, "Freud once said, just because two people like each other doesn't mean they have to be glued together. What I mean is, you can try to understand someone who's half way around the world." Yet another Freud attribution was not so trite, but like his other comments it was also wrong. When he hosted the *Tonight* show Sherman gave Freud credit for the poet William Wordsworth's insight that anticipated much psychology, "The child is father of the man."

Childhood and its psychological repercussions in adulthood consumed him, and though in his autobiography Sherman dismissed psychotherapy as a scam practiced by quacks crazier than him, he needed help. In New York in the 1950s he had sought treatment from Dr. Edmund Bergler, a psychiatrist from Vienna who studied with Freud and who specialized in the problems of creative people, specifically writers and creators of comedy. Bergler would not have been surprised to learn that before Sherman visited him he told his friend Maurice Zolotow, "What psychiatrist would want to treat me? I'm no good. I'm rotten to the core." For Bergler, humorists "are on the border-line of psychotic depression with a saving grace of occasional manic-defense." That manic defense is wit, which tries "to debunk the [negative] internal images imprinted long ago by the authorities of the nursery."

On the August 16 *Tonight* show, Sherman abandoned wit and crawled back into the nursery. He brought out a blanket he claimed was his childhood security blanket, his *nana*, put some in his mouth, and then humorlessly lectured Carson and the audience on its significance. "All of us, up till we were two or two and a half years old, we had a nana," and it "makes you feel warm and secure and good." After that, adulthood is one long search for a replacement. "All your life you spend, and this is true, looking for some other kind of nana." He put a corner of the blanket in his mouth and cajoled Carson into doing the same until Carson had enough. "Allan, how would you like to do a song from your new album, *My Son, the Nut,*" Carson said, giving the last word the emphasis Sherman's behavior deserved.

Sherman had a taste for lecturing but no talent for it and was irritatingly pedantic. Entertainment took a backseat to the psychological truths he felt compelled to utter. But the defense of childishness offered Sherman a payback that made the cost worthwhile. It gave him a license to wallow in sexual indulgence and obliterate unhappiness through ecstasy, because for him childishness was not the same as innocence. In *Rape of the APE*, Sherman's idealized depiction of perfect sexual union involves childlike "playing, rolling in the jungle grass, giggling, laughing, screaming," and leads to the antidote to all pain, all problems, all consciousness. "There were no more Fears now; there were no thoughts . . . the big world was gone." Sherman made this link between childishness and sex explicit when he pushed Carson to join him in chewing on the blanket. "It's group *nana*." It took Carson a moment to register this allusion to group sex, but it was not the first time Sherman made jesting references to some pretty far-out sexual practices. After his performance at the Ford Auditorium in February 1963, the *Detroit Free Press* reported that upon viewing his small hotel room Sherman complained, "'How can we hold a bacchanalia or an orgy in here?' Then signaling to the bellhop with a grand wave: 'The orgy room, please!'" He was not entirely kidding.

"God help us all, he discovered humping," said Hal Cooper. Like many of Sherman's show business colleagues, Cooper believed this erotic adventuring was something new for Sherman. "He discovered girls and girls discovered him," Perenchio said. "Here was this fat, pudgy unattractive Jewish guy who probably got laid five times in his life and now he had groupies." Sherman's college experiences would have surprised them, but they were right that fame allowed Sherman to take his pursuit of pleasure to more outrageous lengths than before. "Great looking chicks showed up," said Joe Smith. "He went to Vegas. There were so many women around, leggy blondes. Well, Vegas, in those days, everything was for sale."

It was a world Sherman had imagined since his adolescent poems "Catastrophe" and "The Physics Student's Valentine," and now his fame — and a disregard for his marriage vows — made this fantasy come true. It didn't matter that he was married, had kids, responsibilities, said friend Mark Rosengarden. "People go crazy with too much freedom and too much power." Sherman's college buddy Sherman Wolf played the beard for him by escorting Sherman's girlfriend as Wolf's date to events that included Sherman's wife. And as his group *nana* joke hinted, he also engaged in more unusual escapades, such as an orgy that was popular in New York with the best people, "the sort of women you might meet at Elaine's," and the writer George Plimpton, and Sherman's friend, the classical pianist Leonid Hambro.

"I think I was unique in his life," Hambro said. It was Hambro that introduced Sherman to the orgy he attended once at the ten-room Manhattan apartment of publicity man Jim Moran, renowned for publicity stunts such as selling a refrigerator to an Eskimo, and sitting on an ostrich egg for nineteen days until it hatched to publicize the 1947 film, *The Egg and I*. "One of the rooms was devoted to costumes" donned by orgy participants, Hambro said. "There were all sorts of inducements to become sexually aroused."

These shenanigans seem to have started in January 1963, when Sherman first played the Sands in Las Vegas, and it went on for years. "He lived a life of excess. Burned the candle at both ends," said Sherman's former protégé Jerry Goldstein. "It was just excess, total excess." In April 1965, Goldstein was in a position to name Sherman the guest host of the *Nightlife* television talk show. It paid ten thousand dollars a week and Sherman stayed at New York's Plaza Hotel. "I get me a bottle of champagne and I go up to the hotel," Goldstein said. "Knock on the door. 'Who is it?' 'J. Goldstein.'" Sherman answered the door wrapped in a bed sheet. "I see racing in the background a naked lady, followed by a naked guy, followed by a naked lady." Sherman gave Goldstein a big hug and big kiss. "Is this a bad time?" Goldstein asked. Sherman did not think so. "Leave it alone. It'll take care of itself," was his answer.

That breezy attitude toward the boundary many felt should separate the private from the public had its drawbacks. In mid-1963, Sherman was in conversations with the great composer Richard Rodgers. The legend sufficiently respected the parodist's accomplishments to consider joining him in writing a musical version of that book about the simple joys of childhood, *Where Did You Go? Out. What Did You Do? Nothing*. Rodgers asked Sherman to keep their discussions quiet, said Golden. That was something he could not do. "Allan Sherman Fathers Musical" headlined a story in the *New York Times* on August 8, 1963, and it reported that though no composer had been chosen for the proposed show, it "is understood that Richard Rodgers may create the tunes." Their relationship survived that minor mention, but on August 9, 1964, the *Times* ran another story on the unlikely pair, who were then thinking of turning the novel, *Father of the Bride*, into a musical. "Allan and I have had two or three discussions, but so far we have nothing to report," Rodgers said. "It's been kind of a meeting of a mutual admiration society; he likes my stuff and I like his." That compliment from the partner of lyricists Lorenz Hart and Oscar Hammerstein was perhaps the greatest Sherman ever received, but the public intrusion ended their talks. "Rodgers got mad, so Rodgers said goodbye," Golden said.

Sherman's personality and career were founded on comically exposing the facts denied or ignored during his early life with his mother, such as the family's Jewish identity. Frankness was not something he could finely regulate. His need for full disclosure was permanently set to the on position. "He'd tell anything," Golden said. This ensured conflict not only with others but also his own creations and image. Even before the popularity of "Hello Muddah" had peaked Sherman chafed at the limitations its wholesomeness threatened to impose. He was right to sense trouble coming. In October he sang the tune on the *Perry Como Show*, and on his head he wore a beanie equipped with a twirling propeller. His song, rich in subtleties, had become a goof. The blame was partly his. Antics such as chewing on a blanket paved the way. But that behavior alternated with Sherman defending his right as an adult to use a more direct, rougher though far from blue vocabulary. When he hosted *Tonight* he complained about censorship to guest Edie Adams, "I want to say hell and damn." Whether he was giving voice to his infantile or mature selves, restraint was not his style.

Too Jewish

For the remainder of 1963, many of the venues Sherman played offered him the latitude he needed. He was at the Nugget hotel and casino in Sparks, Nevada, for two weeks in September and returned to the Sands in Las Vegas for three weeks in October. In between, Sherman performed at his alma mater, the University of Illinois, and got off some wonderful wisecracks. "I'll always remember the first time I went to register. I reported to a window marked 'Row thru Smack' — that's the sort of thing that stays with you." The college revived his penchant for Groucho-esque humor. Sherman claimed he was thrown out of the university because he refused to inform on an ROTC student that cheated. "I could reveal his name now, but I can't remember it. . . . Besides that, he has gone on to become governor of a great state." In concert, he sang new lyrics to "Hello Muddah."

Take me back, Ole Alma Mater, take me back
I promise I will not cut class
This time I won't cut class
At least I'll go enough to pass.

On November 14, Sherman opened at New York's Copacabana to strong reviews. The next day "My Son, the Copacabana Smash" was the headline in the *New York World Telegram and Sun*. *Variety* was more subdued. "Allan Sherman is a funny fellow but too much of a good thing can be overdone." The trade weekly suggested his act would be better briefer, but this was a quibble. He was a star, and fellow comedian Shelley Berman at the Basin St. East club suggested his fans also take in Sherman's act. More did than might have been expected, given that Sherman was still playing the Copa on Friday, November 22 when President Kennedy was assassinated.

On November 23, "the Copa was packed," Sherman wrote in his autobiography. After countless hours glued to their television sets, people needed to get out of the house, and Sherman performed the act he did for the president at the Department of Labor.

A month later, Sherman headlined at the Diplomat Hotel in Hollywood, Florida, for the Christmas holidays. He was in good form, and offered one of the better explanations for the power of comedy. "Comedy is a fundamentally serious thing. It's a way you and the audience agree on the truth of something."

The year closed on that high note, and when he looked back on 1963 there was only one concert experience that rankled. The one for Jews.

"They have a kind of inside Jew thing there," Sherman said of New York's Catskill Mountain resorts. "I don't understand it — it's too Jewish for me." Sherman played Grossinger's on August 10 and then on August 31 its arch competitor and glitzier rival, the Concord Hotel. The Concord was then at the top of its game, the Copacabana of the Borscht Belt. Judy Garland performed there before her April 1961 Carnegie Hall concert, and in 1962 the hotel opened the Monster, its championship golf course. But in his autobiography Sherman haughtily called it a ghetto and condescended to reassure the prosperous Jewish businessmen, executives, doctors, and attorneys they had nothing to fear from the larger world. "Jump in, the water's fine in the human race."

This was not Sherman at his best. He was showing off, and his obnoxious condescension proved he had no more achieved a perfect level of Jewish comfort in America than those he lectured. "To be too Jewish is too much," he wrote in his autobiography. On the other hand, to try and escape it, well, "that's too much, too." His parodies grew out of his public effort to find the proper Jewish-American middle ground, but his success attracted many Jews wrestling with the same problem, and that large Jewish audience threatened to tip Sherman's hard-won balance to the too Jewish side. It was a new paradox and problem many openly Jewish writers and entertainers soon faced. The Jewish celebrities that changed their names and submerged their Jewish roots did not have to manage their relationship with their Jewish audiences. Sherman, however, was among the first to experience the ambivalence that would trouble the careers of many public Jewish figures whose Jewish audiences expected, or were perceived to expect, or whose mere presence implied to observers and the public figure himself the expectation of an unreasonable level of Jewishness. "I've had an enormous amount of criticism from Jewish groups," Woody Allen told one journalist. A critic wrote that Saul Bellow was "rather edgy about being considered a Jewish writer." Partly, the problem grew out of all the different ways Jews could use Jewishness to make a claim on Jewish celebrities. The categories include religion, family, history, culture, language, peoplehood or any combination of the above. Maintaining a balance while juggling or fending off so many claims is not easy. Sherman was caught in what one writer called the "power of Jewishness . . . to make people go completely crazy with the complexity of the terms it asks them to juggle."

nine
ALLAN IN WONDERLAND

On February 9, 1964, the *New York Journal-American* ran a profile of Sherman while he toured England. International concerts were the logical next step. Over the past year he had blanketed the American market with an extensive tour and television appearances, and he had fans in London, Leeds, and Manchester. *My Son, the Folk Singer* sold 200,000 records in England and "Hello Muddah" was also a hit. So on January 31, Sherman flew to London for a two-week stint of live concerts, BBC television appearances, and bouts of sumptuous indulgence. He and his small entourage from home, just road manager Marvin Tabolsky and a substitute musical conductor, Joe Guercio, travelled from concert to concert in a Jaguar. In London, Sherman's room with a fireplace was in the posh Dorchester Hotel, "a fortress propped up with moneybags" built in 1931 as a "gilded refuge of the rich." At dinner, Sherman ate without restraint, his usual approach, at the exclusive White Elephant Club, a show business redoubt where actors and producers talked, ate, drank and waited for reviews in the morning papers. "We would go out to these fancy restaurants and have these great meals," Tabolsky said. "Allan never held back.

He ate everything, escargot, whatever was served he wanted to experience. Smoked salmon and capers for breakfast with the diced onions. It was a whole new experience." Part of this abandon included visits to prostitutes, Guercio said. The concerts were a success, too. "He was funny every night," remembered Guercio. "He was the in thing. Beautiful." But despite the accolades, and underneath the hedonism, Sherman was worried. From the beginning of his fame he was haunted by the idea that it could suddenly vanish like an easily won gambling haul, and he told the newspaper that he was girding himself against this possibility. "I'm pledged not to get desperate."

It would not be an easy pledge to fulfill. While Sherman was in England, the Beatles landed in America, and the day the Sherman story ran was the same day the group debuted on the *Ed Sullivan Show*. Beatlemania was the first of several cultural shifts that in 1964 began to loosen Sherman's grip on fame and success.

Bigger stars than Sherman were worried about the Beatles. Between songs on their Sullivan debut, Elvis Presley wired them a welcome that Sullivan announced on the air. That was one way for Presley to keep his name before the multitudes of teenaged girls that once had screamed for him. Presley knew enough to be scared, but many in the mainstream media, such as talk show pioneer Jack Paar, had no idea what was going on and scorned the shaggy-haired group. Meanwhile, the Beatles' television audience was forty-one million, 20 percent of the country, and the adoration that followed them astonished disinterested observers. Sherman got a chance to witness it firsthand. On August 21, 1964, he was in Seattle, Washington, to play benefits for the local Variety Club and Children's Orthopedic Hospital. Traveling as usual with his road manager Tabolsky, Sherman stayed at the Edgewater Inn. The hotel's other guests were the Beatles, in town to perform at the Seattle Coliseum. "I got up one day and I saw all these workers putting up barriers, and police on horseback," Tabolsky said. He and Sherman wondered, "Is the president in town, some dignitary? No, it was the Beatles. It was pandemonium."

A writer for the *Saturday Evening Post* understood it. The Beatles were selling pure happiness. Those recent pop culture kings of the sneer and the curled lip, Marlon Brando, Presley, and James Dean were out. "Exuberance is in. . . . Self-pity is out, whooping with joy is in." In late 1962, Sherman had hit it big with the same product. His parodies were a celebratory overturning of stale and self-important icons. But now he allowed himself some spite and meanness toward the young. That struck a chord among adults in a culture beginning to feel the strain of the still-nascent generation gap, but it worked against the comic instincts and reputation that made him a success.

Sherman's fourth album, *Allan in Wonderland*, went on sale in March 1964 and on April 10 *Time* magazine, which the year before enjoyed "There Is Nothing Like a Lox," now publicized the new album's "The Drop-Outs March," a number it professed to believe "may do more to keep kids in school than hours of sermonizing by principals and parents." The song was topical. At the outset of the 1963–64 school year, the *New York Times* reported that, "The most fashionable concern is over 'drop-outs.'" President Kennedy set the tone in his 1963 State of the Union address, which deplored the fact that "4 out of every 10 students in the 5th grade will not even finish high school." Sherman's song took a sardonic view of the problem, and he performed it March 27 on the satirical television news show *That Was the Week That Was*. Though he recorded it for the *Wonderland* album on January 20, before the Beatles arrived, it had special appeal in the wake of the teenage screaming the rock stars unleashed. *Time* found in "Drop-Outs" a handy weapon against bad kids. The song has venom.

> Soon dropouts very soon
> You'll wear a different hat
> Soon you will be in the army
> Just try dropping out of that!

The *Time* story was a natural news hook when Sherman appeared on the *Tonight* show April 16, and he again sang "Drop-Outs." A very different kind of song from the new album was "Green Stamps," which roasted the behavior of parents, not teens. "Green Stamps" transformed the 1941 "Green Eyes" from a song about the mesmerizing power of love into one about the mesmerizing power of the retail loyalty program that encouraged mindless consumerism. The former television game show producer knew Americans loved to win prizes and own the latest gadgets. That love of shopping showed up on his first album's "Jump Down, Spin Around (Pick a Dress o' Cotton)." Sherman's criticism then was veiled. Only the laughter is apparent. "Here's what I've been searching for / A genuine copy of a fake Dior." On "Green Eyes" the criticism is more pointed but without a sting as Sherman's persona implicates him in the national foolishness of spending to save money.

All day and night I'm dreaming
I'm dreaming of redeeming
My Green Stamps for a toaster
So gleaming and deluxe.
Oh how it will thrill me.
And please me and fulfill me
To know that my toaster only cost me
Fourteen hundred bucks.

Also superior to "Drop-Outs" is *Wonderland*'s nimble and silly "Skin," a parody of "Heart" from the musical *Damn Yankees*.

You gotta have skin
All you really need is skin
Skin's the thing that if you got it outside
It helps keep your insides in.

In stark contrast to "Drop-Outs," the song revisits a favorite Sherman theme of welcoming forgiveness for all human types, including those he addressed in "Hail to Thee, Fat Person" as "either skinny or in some other way normal," because in addition to keeping your insides in, skin has democratic values.

It fits perfectly
Yours fits you and mine fits me
When you're sitting down it folds and looks grand
And then when you stand it's where it's been.
Ain't you glad you got skin.

However, there were not many good songs on *Wonderland*, and the record never rose above number 32 on the *Billboard* charts. In a roundup review of comedy albums, the *New York Times* panned it. "If you like what Mr. Sherman is doing, you will have no trouble understanding the words. They are only all too clear." *Variety*'s review was gentler out of respect for Sherman's stature. "Although the humor doesn't hit as hard as past sessions, there's considerable levity here." The best example is "Good Advice," an eight-and-a-half-minute jazzy romp through a range of famous inventions and discoveries made possible through the good advice of the fatheaded storyteller. It delivers the energy and delight of Sherman's earlier shticks medleys.

> Alexander Graham Bell was building a fence
> With some wood and a long piece of wire
> He said there's something strange going on around here
> I keep hearing the voice of Uncle Meyer
> I said Mr. Graham Cracker (that was my little joke)
> With that wire you've got the world in your power
> Just get a mouthpiece and an earpiece and a piece in between
> And you'll sponsor the telephone hour!
> And that was
> Good advice, good advice
> Good advice costs nothing and it's worth the price.

The reference to Uncle Meyer is the album's only Jewish material, and the record's title indicates the break with his earlier songs by departing from the *My Son* formula. Sherman was casting about for a new direction. His first idea was to call the album *The Real Allan Sherman*, with cover art showing him looking into a mirror that reflects the image of Cary Grant. That tired joke was shunted aside in favor of *Allan in Wonderland* and an unflattering close-up photograph of Sherman's heavy face striking a pose somewhere between mock innocence and obnoxious self-absorption. It was not a good sign of what was happening to him. "He got very arty, talking down to people," said Joe Smith. "You and I, *we* knew how to do and nobody else knew how." Despite the changes occurring within him, the new album title continued a key *My Son* idea. *Allan in Wonderland* still identified Sherman as a child living in a childhood world.

Sherman had, in fact, gone through the looking glass into an alternate universe where a short, fat man with glasses could sing about Jews and meet the president. But that topsy-turvy world was coming to an end. He was running low on good Jewish material, and he was rapidly aging. *Wonderland*'s liner notes informed customers that the album does not include "about 30 seconds of tape where Allan was checking to see if his oxygen had been brought in (it had)." He was thirty-nine years old. His health was terrible. He told Maurice Zolotow he had a heart blockage. A photograph taken when he landed in London showed him looking far heavier than he appeared on his *My Son* album covers. His face was inflated with fat.

A benign interpretation is that like a child in the grip of terrible habits, Sherman did not know how to take care of himself. Another is that he knew how to take care of himself, but only if "take care" is imbued with the malevolent meaning implied by Hollywood gangsters. Sherman took a contract out on himself. "I remember telling him he was going to kill himself, and he did," said Faith Dane, the actress who stole the show in the stage and movie versions of *Gypsy* as the stripper Mazeppa in the number, "You Gotta Have a Gimmick." She was one of Sherman's early girlfriends in the 1950s when he lived in New York. "He was a genius. Some geniuses are motherfuckers. Ally happens to be a nice guy." But Dane gave him hell about the eating habits she predicted would doom him. "He said, 'Stop trying to scare me.' I was screaming at him. I'm a very hysterical person." Even reasonable people agreed with her assessment that Sherman was determined to ruin himself. Sheldon Keller told Steve Allen that Sherman "was the most self-destructive person I've ever known . . . some people aren't very nice, and their attitude toward the world is 'f— you.' Well, it always seemed to me that Allan's motto was 'f— me.'"

Others were more than willing to help. "He gave away money," Golden said. "He cosigned loans for someone he knew only casually at Goodson-Todman. Everybody had a sob story and he gave away money. He fell for sob stories." A woman who lost her job when *Your Surprise Package* folded approached Sherman after he became famous. She needed money to send her children to Los Angeles's private Oakwood School, and Sherman shared this explanation with his wife. Golden recalled her reasonable reply. "I said, 'your kids go to public school.'" Sherman did not deprive himself, either, and never tired of telling reporters of how after his first album hit it big he bought a gold Lincoln Continental without even bothering to visit the dealership. He ordered it by phone. "The startled salesman asked: 'Don't you want to come in and see it?' Allan said: 'No. Just send it over.'" It was an extreme example of typical habits. "He was a spendthrift," said Leonid Hambro. "His living quarters were extravagant, big tipper, loose with money. Always the host at dinner." And the meals were not modest. "Dinner was a bacchanalian feast. He would order a lot of stuff. He really liked to enjoy himself," said cousin Mickey Sherman. Fun was enjoyable in itself, and also part of the master plan for self-destruction. "He went from being in dire need financially, to fame, and then throwing it away," said Bill Dana.

On top of his extravagances were unavoidable expenses. Six percent of Sherman's income flowed to his New York lawyers at Becker & London, a leading entertainment law firm that represented Frank Sinatra, Dinah Shore, and actor George C. Scott. Business manager Alexander Tucker, a former Internal Revenue Service man who specialized in helping show business clients such as the Marx Brothers and Gregory Peck, also had to be paid. Tucker put Sherman into exotic investments such as the cattle company Oppenheimer Industries, oil drilling outfits, and 59 King Wharf, a resort development in the Virgin Islands. "It was a completely different world in those days," said Larry E. Martindale, who worked for Tucker as a CPA when Sherman was a client. Tax rates were as high as 90 percent, but the government allowed many deductions. "Every investment we made had a tax angle," he said. When it came to capturing a percentage of Sherman's assets, only the government topped Bullets Durgom, who owned 20 percent of *Folk Singer*'s revenues and 10 percent of *Celebrity*, *Nut*, and *Wonderland*. In June 1964, Sherman got rid of Bullets with a reported buyout of $45,000.

But Sherman's fame allowed him to absorb every financial blow he and others could land on him. He was not easy to do in. "Money was coming in from all sides then," Golden said. By December 1963, Bill Cosby's first album, *Bill Cosby Is a Very Funny Fellow, Right*, was one of *Billboard*'s "Breakout Albums," and a year later *I Started Out As a Child* was another. Sherman was credited as coproducer on both, and both featured his laudatory liner notes. His financial interest in the albums was not common knowledge. At the same time, a huge sum of deferred payment was building for Sherman at Warner Bros., which in 1964 was contractually required to pay him only $7,500 each quarter. This enforced savings plan was perfect for a spendthrift, and it also kept him in a lower tax bracket. By the end of 1966 Sherman's deferred compensation account was $325,183.51, an amount equal to more than $2 million today. In addition, tens of thousands of dollars were held by Curtain Call Productions, a business formed to exploit "copyrights owned by Allan Sherman," and Allan Sherman Enterprises, "a production company which makes the services of Allan Sherman available for personal appearances." In 1965, Milton Bradley produced Allan Sherman's Camp Granada Game, a board game for children inspired by Sherman's hit song. The object was to escape from camp and go home, and by the end of 1966 it earned Sherman $26,416. On top of that, he was still collecting from Goodson-Todman a $250-per-show royalty as creator of *I've Got A Secret*, which stayed on the air until 1967.

Plus he was still performing. On February 20, 1964, he appeared at the Cork Club in Houston, and on March 6 and 7 he was in Des Moines, Iowa, and then St. Paul, Minnesota. The provinces loved him, with the *Houston Post* exclaiming, "Allan Sherman is about the most refreshing thing to hit the nightery circuit in years." In the summer he played a state fair in Great Falls, Montana, and he was also in demand at the swankiest cabarets in the country. On April 1, Sherman opened in Chicago for a week at the Empire Room in the Palmer House, Chicago's greatest and oldest hotel. The Empire Room was one of the country's grandest supper clubs, with "24-karat gold leaf finishes, mirrored walls and French crystal and gold chandeliers." During his hometown stay he was invited to a luncheon with Mayor Daley to celebrate Chicago's designation as one of America's cleanest cities, and Chicago's papers gave him multiple write-ups and top-notch reviews. "Sherman Elevates Parody to a Minor Art Form" was the *Tribune's* headline. The *Sun-Times* published a spoof that imagined a trio of show business sharpies that decline to take on Sherman's ethnic act. "Hey, that sounds Jewish!" says a character called Cuff Links. "Are you making fun of the Jews, tubby?" The story ends with Cuff Links also rejecting the Beatles.

Publishing advances added to Sherman's money pile. In May 1963, Atheneum Press handed over $5,000 for him to begin work on an autobiography.

A year later Sherman apparently realized the project was beyond him and on April 1, 1964, brought in Maurice Zolotow as an equal partner. Zolotow ghostwrote the book, said his daughter Crescent Dragonwagon. Harper & Row wanted illustrated children's book versions of "Hello Muddah" and "I Can't Dance," an *Allan in Wonderland* song about adolescents at a co-ed social, and both books appeared in 1964 with art by Syd Hoff. Sherman got a $2,500 advance for *I Can't Dance*, and an unknown but probably much greater amount for *Hello Muddah, Hello Fadduh!*

In June 1964, he shared a $4,000 advance from G.P. Putnam's with television writers Arnold and Lois Peyser. Together they wrote *Instant Status; or, Up Your Image*, an oversized softcover novelty book filled with easy-to-remove phony letters from famous people and organizations. The joke is that customers can address the letters to themselves to boost their reputations. Decades before reality television and the virtual reality of Facebook, Sherman detected that Americans were losing interest in ordinary life. They wanted to aggrandize and publicize themselves. This book was for them. "Nowadays, if you have a good enough *image*, you don't need a person there at all," the book assured readers. A letter from the Reverend Martin Luther King says, "Thanks, Man!" and is signed "Marty" for those who want to be an instant liberal. To enhance the letter's effect, the book advises, "When your friends read the letter, blush coyly and say, 'I did what I *could*.'" A letter from Hugh Hefner on *Playboy* letterhead establishes a young man as a swinger. "Dear Tiger . . . Sounds crazy! *How* many girls and *how* many waffle irons?" There is even a letter from Mount Neboh Temple to achieve instant Jewishness. As the letter's introduction notes, "Among some segments of our society it is now considered a status symbol to be Jewish. . . . If you are one of those, or if you just happen to like the food, use this letter." On the November 20, 1964, *Tonight* show, Sherman told Carson, "If you buy this book you can have an image overnight," because "what an image is is just that people think you're something that you aren't."

Sherman was growing unhappy with his own image as harmless man-child. Newspaper stories said he had a "devastatingly sweet smile," and described him as boyish, a pixie, a cherub, and elf. He had earned the endearments. Not only the *My Son* and *Wonderland* album titles but also Sherman's overweight round face gave him a boyish appearance, and there was truth to the image. Children were a special interest. "He came to our fifth-grade class at Bellagio Road School and spoke to us for an hour about being a comedian," remembered Michael Abrahams, a classmate of Nancy Sherman and a neighbor on Bel Air's Chantilly Road. The kids submitted jokes and Sherman reviewed them. "Mine was a bomb but he was kind about it." Emmy Award–winning actor Jay Thomas had a similar experience in March 1966 as a seventeen-year-old budding comic in his hometown of New Orleans. "I read in the paper that 'Hello Muddah' is coming to the Roosevelt Hotel and I approached Sherman, left him a note and said I want to show you my act. I get a phone call at my house from Sherman's secretary. Allan is willing to see you." Thomas went over to the hotel, performed his act, and Sherman took the young man seriously and gave him constructive advice. "He said, 'You've got something. You're funny, you're brave, you've got energy. You talked a little too fast. You have to give us a chance to laugh.'" Sherman also invited Thomas and three guests to see his performance in the hotel's Blue Room cabaret, so Thomas brought his father, brother and a friend to the show, which included Sherman announcing "we have a new young talent with us tonight." The spotlight landed on Thomas and he got a hand from the audience. "He was the guy who said it's okay to pursue my dream," Thomas said.

So the boyish image was a good fit, but it was far from perfect. There were troubling complexities of Sherman's character it could not accommodate. At the Roosevelt Hotel, Sherman had a girlfriend with him. "She was a hot young thing," Thomas said. More disturbing than his sexual affairs was his unseemly slovenliness. Neighbor Michael Abrahams remembered Sherman at daughter Nancy's sixth-grade graduation party. "Allan came out in his underwear to say hi." This penchant for walking around in his boxer shorts caught people's attention. "He sat in his shorts, belly hanging out at home," said manager Bill Loeb, who replaced Bullets. Warner's Stan Cornyn recalled Sherman "obscenely dressed in boxer shorts." The source of these distasteful antics was a self-hatred that wanted the world to agree that his worst feelings about himself were right. "I sing like an idiot," he told the *Miami News*. "I'm ugly," he told another reporter. In "Hail to Thee, Fat Person," "Overweight People," and *Wonderland*'s "Little Butterball," a parody of Gilbert and Sullivan's "Little Buttercup," Sherman turned his self-hatred into comedy.

I'm called little butterball
Dear little butterball
Though I could never tell why
My calories mount, my cholesterol count is as high as an elephant's eye.
They told me to diet
I promised I'd try it
Yet somehow my weight would not budge
Each Metrecal cookie
To me tasted ookie
So I covered it with hot fudge.

"Butterball's" baby talk did nothing to move his image to the mature side of the ledger. It also worked against the depths his greatest songs managed to include on their way to the laughs. Absent is the traveling salesman's sorrowful introduction to "Shake Hands with Your Uncle Max," Harry Lewis's death by fire among the drapes of Roth, or the lament in "The Streets of Miami" as Marvin contemplates the penalty for shooting his partner.

So now I can never
Go back to Miami.
And New York is so cold
That a person could die.
I'd be better off dead
Like my late partner Sammy
Cause he's in that big Fontainebleau in the sky.

Sherman was running out of steam and tiring of the hard work required to transform misery into memorable humor, and in the spring of 1964 he found a more direct outlet in "His Own Little Island," a decidedly noncomic tune from the failed 1961 Broadway musical *Let It Ride*. The song's bleak depiction of people as isolated islands separated from each other by oceans suggested the walled-off areas of Sherman's personality that distanced him from normal community, and announced and bemoaned his strangeness and estrangement. "Wish someone special / Would come to my island," sang Sherman.

This retreat into earnestness marked the limits of Sherman's comic talents.

He could not create what at the same moment Woody Allen was becoming famous for, a new comedy that addressed adult psychological and sexual problems. "I think I will review for you some of the outstanding features of my private life and put them in perspective," was the Allen line that summed up his approach and let him make comedy out of his alleged personal agonies. In the early 1960s, after years as a television comedy writer for Sid Caesar and others, he began performing this kind of material in clubs across the country, and by 1964 he was a top act with admiring reviews in the *New York Times* and a performance salary of $5,000 a week.

Sherman and Allen crossed paths twice that year. On May 26, 1964, they shared a stage when they were part of a large cast of entertainers gathered to perform at a Washington, D.C., fundraising event for President Lyndon Johnson's 1964 election campaign. Allen was Sherman's opposite in every way. Thin and angular to Sherman's rounded heft, Allen at twenty-eight was eleven years younger than Sherman but sophisticated, knowing, and verbally agile, with none of the thirty-nine-year-old Sherman's boyishness. "Allen told about his hard times in New York on a lean income when he couldn't afford a psychiatrist," reported *Variety*. Allen explained, "I had to take group analysis. . . . At recess, we would divide into teams to play games. It would be the bed wetters vs. the finger nail chewers." He was a hit with the audience. Sherman was, too. He sang, "Skin," "Hello Muddah, Hello Fadduh," and what *Variety* called "the evening's showstopper," a number created especially for the event called "Once in Love with Lyndon." Its dull boosterism, sung to the tune of Frank Loesser's "Once in Love with Amy," could only be a hit at a political convention.

Once in love with Lyndon
Always in love with Lyndon
And on the Tuesday of the big election
Guess who my selection will be.
November third it's Lyndon
It's Ladybird and Lyndon
And on the morning of the inauguration
What a happy nation you'll see.

A few months later on July 8, Sherman and Allen met again on the *Tonight* show. Woody Allen was Carson's guest host and his opening monologue displayed the gifts that would soon make him one of the most famous humorists in the world. He gobbled up territory Sherman had successfully worked, from Jewish adjustment in a non-Jewish world to jokes about his far-from-perfect physical appearance to childhood terrors. Allen did his bit about working for an advertising agency that hired him to be the firm's show Jew, and then fired him for taking off too many Jewish holidays. There was the one about him surfing the waves, "my body a bronzed miracle" as his wife ahead of him "rowed frantically." And he told the story of how as a boy he was force-fed his violin by the neighborhood tough. When it came to sharing shameful weakness and cowardice, Allen could not be topped. "In the event of war, I'm a hostage."

Allen gave Sherman a warm introduction. "Listen, there's a fellow here tonight and everybody says it's phenomenal how he was such a sensation but it's not phenomenal because he's really one of the warmest people and one of the funniest people that I've ever met. And he's extremely witty and slightly overweight but adorable. Allan Sherman."

The appearance should have been a breeze. This was Sherman's fifteenth time on *Tonight*, and by all objective measures he was riding high. On May 12, his "Hello Muddah" song won the 1963 Grammy Award for best comedy performance, and on May 27 he performed an updated version of the hit on *Tonight* that was recorded live. The new single shipped just days before he sat with Woody Allen on July 8, and by the end of July the updated camp song climbed onto *Billboard*'s "Hot 100" list. But Sherman was touchy. He did not have the confidence of a winner. When the audience laughed at the news he was going to conduct symphony parodies with the Boston Pops Orchestra at Tanglewood, his Don Rickles–type response lacked the humor of the master. "You people with your low class taste. You make fun of somebody who writes three symphonies, but I wrote three symphonies in one week." It was an absurd statement and an uncomfortable moment. Woody Allen's years on the nightclub circuit taught him that success in front of a live audience required more than great material. He had to like the audience.

Sherman knew the rule and had applied it in his concerts, but like other pursuits he sometimes lost interest in it. "He thought of himself as a writer-creator person," said his son Robert. "That's what he enjoyed doing most. The performing was kind of a means to an end." Sherman managed to salvage the evening. His story about buying toilet plungers so the Boston Pops' trombonists could play jazz notes got laughs. "I don't need the sticks," Sherman told the store clerk. "Oh yes you do," the clerk replied. But he was most relaxed when he could ignore the audience and sing a new song as he read the lyrics. Sherman wrote it just hours before the show and had no tune for it, so he sang it to the *Tonight* show orchestra's improvised cha-cha.

She wore a bathing suit without a top
Because she found it was not against the law there
And then some angry person called a cop
When he arrived he enjoyed what he saw there.
She wore a bathing suit without a top
While lying down on the sand for her siesta
They told the cop that he should make her stop
And he said when I finish looking I'll arrest her
The beach was so crowded
They were standing in the ocean
She wore an itsy bitsy teenie weenie bottom half of a bikini
That's what was causing the commotion.
She wore a bathing suit without a top
And she went walking on the beach for a breather
And the most fascinating thing about her suit without a top
Is that it didn't have a bottom either.

It was the first and one of the better sex songs Sherman would continue to write in the years ahead, but it also shares their weaknesses. In them Sherman is either the observer of a new world he does not fully understand or approve of or, as in this song, a tittering onlooker. It does not lead the audience into new territory, and as the 1960s sexual revolution gained steam his sexual material seemed increasingly clichéd, childish, and antique. At the same time, Woody Allen's sexual material helped define the new moment. In one routine, he fantasizes about baseball to postpone orgasm during sexual intercourse. Allen soon finds himself in a "first and third situation." He does not know whether to "squeeze or steal." Sherman, faced with the young Woody Allen, seemed intimidated, and did not know whether to bluff, call, or fold.

The irony was that while Sherman's sexual comedy could not catch up with society's new permissiveness, he was engaging in acts that would have made Allen's audiences blush. "He entered the sexual scene with such enthusiasm, first as a voyeur and then as a participant," remembered Hambro. On July 4, just days before his *Tonight* show appearance Sherman wanted some action. He knew whom to call. "Sherman says, 'Leonid, get me a woman. If anyone can do it, you can.' I knew this girl from the Dominican Republic. Sensational girl. Sensational girl." She was available, for a price, and Hambro brought her to the Hampshire House on Central Park South where Sherman often stayed when he was in New York. He rented actor Jerry Orbach's penthouse apartment. "It was all done in 1930's [style]," Tabolsky said. "It was beautiful. Panoramic view of Central Park." When the woman met Sherman she "went up to him and said, 'You're a fat little fuck, ain't ya,'" said Hambro. "That instantly put him at ease because he was always sensitive about that." Hambro had sex with her on the living room floor. Then Sherman did the same.

Sherman never made peace with his sexual conflicts and drives. He would always veer between prudery and promiscuity.

Bye Bye Blumberg

By 1964, Arthur Fiedler had conducted the Boston Pops Orchestra for thirty-five years and had made it a nationally known and loved institution. When he invited Allan Sherman to perform classical music parodies before the summer audience at Tanglewood, Fiedler was not taking much of a risk. His reputation could withstand almost anything. Sherman's could not, but the concert was a victory for him. In June 1964 Sherman performed *Peter and the Commissar*, his version of Prokofiev's *Peter and the Wolf*, with orchestras in Syracuse, New York, and Baltimore before presenting a final version with the Pops on July 22. Warner Bros. wanted no part of it. "His ambitions changed him," said Cornyn. "He wanted to be taken more seriously. He eventually turned to repertoire of such remoteness that we said go ahead Allan, but not on our label."

With Warner's good riddance Sherman recorded the Pops concert for RCA Victor's Red Seal, the top label for classical recordings, and it did surprisingly well.

Sherman's Peter is a composer of beautiful music, and the commissar is Sherman's old enemy since college days and his years at Goodson-Todman, the organization man that meddles with the man of genius. Commissars, also known as "junior executives," are the kind of people that "sit on the handlebars while everybody peddles," Sherman says. At first, the commissars adulterate Peter's compositions, but in the end his original work triumphs. "It was played on all the Russian TV shows / And Siberians whistled it as they froze."

Those were the best lines of the *Peter* parody. The album's other two numbers, "Variations on 'How Dry I Am,'" and "The End of a Symphony" did not match even this modest level of wit, but Sherman's star power was strong enough to make the concert a success. "In all fairness it must be noted that Allan Sherman was very well received," admitted an unimpressed concert reviewer for the *Berkshire Eagle*.

When the album was released in October, *Billboard* pegged it as a likely winner, a "Spotlight Pick." Red Seal was taking no chances. It organized "an all-out campaign" of radio promotions, advertisements, and a contest to make the record "one of the top sellers in Red Seal history." The marketing blitz leveraged the image Sherman yearned to achieve with his topless bikini song. Red Seal targeted the college market with ads in *Esquire* and *Playboy*, and its contest promotion included a coupon in *Cavalier*, one of several *Playboy* competitors that published nude pictorials of young women alongside celebrity profiles, including one on Sherman in September 1963. Another *Cavalier* feature in August 1964, "My Son, the Gesticulator," consisted of photographs of Sherman hamming it up, and it was perfectly timed to help the hip marketing effort. The album's sales peaked on January 16, 1965, when *Peter and the Commissar* reached a respectable number 53 of the *Billboard* charts, where it spent fourteen weeks before disappearing in late February.

Sherman seemed to have left behind his original Jewish material without regret. *Allan in Wonderland* and *Peter and the Commissar* paid little attention to the subject, and at an August 14, 1964, concert he sang nothing from the very Jewish *Folk Singer* album. Instead the Hollywood Bowl audience heard

"Skin," "Green Stamps," "Overweight People" and apparently the entire Tanglewood concert, which clocks in at three-quarters of an hour. In another case of overdoing it, Sherman sang both versions of "Hello Muddah."

That must have been all the new Sherman anyone could handle, but the public's appetite for his Jewish material was not sated. In October 1964, someone released a bootleg recording of Sherman's *My Fair Lady* parody. Exactly when and where it was recorded is still a mystery, but it filled a need. "You're not IN, you don't swing if you don't have this album," wrote Hollywood columnist Sidney Skolsky of the bootleg release. "It's Sherman at his funniest."

That hunger for his Jewish comedy made *For Swingin Livers Only!* serendipitous. Released in November 1964 on the heels of the *My Fair Lady* bootleg, Sherman's fifth album for Warner Bros. was his most Jewish since *Folk Singer*. On the cover, he and a blonde sip chopped liver through two straws. And though *Variety*'s review began with the deadly, "This is not one of Allan Sherman's better music parody items," the album did well. It was a *Billboard* "Spotlight Pick," became one of the magazine's "National Breakout" albums, reached number 32 on the chart — where it spent sixteen weeks — and in March 1965 was nominated for a Grammy for Best Comedy Performance alongside albums by Bill Cosby, Woody Allen, Jonathan Winters, and Godfrey Cambridge.

Quality does not explain its success. *Variety* was right. Of the eleven new songs, only the ironic "Bye Bye Blumberg" can still deliver laughs. "Your Mother's Here to Stay" is an inspired one-liner. It gives Irving Berlin's "Our Love Is Here to Stay" the pie in the face it seemed in retrospect to be begging for. And "Shine On, Harvey Bloom," about a Jewish astronaut, is also a one-trick pony that offers little to laugh about after the "Shine On, Harvest Moon" parody hits home. The album's other songs, including "Pop Hates the Beatles," "Beautiful Teamsters" ("Beautiful Dreamers"), "Kiss of Myer" ("Kiss of Fire"), "J.C. Cohen" ("Casey Jones"), and "Grow, Mrs. Goldfarb" ("Glow Worm") are complete failures. But "Bye Bye Blumberg," about a lonely traveling salesman who misinterprets the send-offs that accompany his many departures as signs of affection instead of wishes he get lost, is excellent humor. The "Bye Bye Blackbird" parody tees up its joke with pathos, allowing Sherman to hit it dead-on.

My name is Charlie Blumberg
And I travel everywhere
Cause I'm a traveling salesman
So I fly from here to there
In every town I visit
Folks must think I'm really swell
Cause every time I leave a town
I get a fond farewell.
Every time I fly away
People cry, and they say
Bye bye Blumberg.
It's a shame I have to go
Seeing as how they miss me so
Bye bye Blumberg.
Once I took a trip with Irving Cohen
No one even noticed he was goin'
Me they smashed across the head
With champagne, and they said
Blumberg, bye bye.

As good as it is, the song could not carry the whole album, and the *My Fair Lady* bootleg was by definition a very limited release and not widely known enough to lift *Swingin' Livers*. Instead, the album seems to have owed its popularity to the Broadway musical starring Zero Mostel that opened a few weeks before on September 22, 1964, and became a sensation. Critics attacked *Fiddler on the Roof* as a betrayal of the Sholem Aleichem stories it was based on, as well as for its sentimentality and supposed lack of authenticity, but the public loved it and kept it on stage for almost eight years. When it closed in 1972 it was the longest-running show in Broadway history at the time. And Broadway did not mark the border of its appeal. "[M]iracle of miracles — success occurred everywhere." Instead of being "too Jewish," as its creators feared, *Fiddler* was Jewish material with universal appeal, just like a certain Jewish song parody album of two years before. So if *Fiddler* gave the unworthy *Swingin' Livers* a boost, it was only fair. Sherman's *Folk Singer* helped prepare the ground for *Fiddler*.

Tevye communicated what a scholar called a "generosity of spirit, an ambivalence toward the obligations of tradition." So did Sherman. The two jolly Jewish fat men made being Jewish familiar and fun, and though Sherman's new album was lousy, it was indisputably Jewish. In the mid-1960s that was often good enough. The Jewish experience that "only yesterday" was seen as "at best marginal or exotic and as at worst grubby and rather shameful" was now "somehow more meaningful, more interesting, more relevant, more *central* than the experience of most other groups in our society." The general feeling regarding ethnic groups had shifted from the early twentieth century's why can't they be like us to, "If only we could be like them!"

But this new mood, exemplified by *Fiddler*'s success, was not good news for Sherman. In 1962, he had stuffed Jews into non-Jewish songs and smuggled them into the national conversation like contraband. Two years later, *Fiddler* proved that Jewish material could now be sold openly. It also proved that Jewish material could leave behind a Jewish "sensibility that was tragic and ironic." *Fiddler*'s great tearjerker songs "Do You Love Me?" and "Sunrise, Sunset" bid "Blumberg's" irony bye-bye.

And you'll see
When I'm really gone
In neon lights on Forest Lawn
Blumberg, bye-bye.

Ten

PEYTON PLACE, U.S.A.

"I'm not supposed to be Jewish," Sherman told the *New York Times* on the eve of his first television special. "I was Jewish three seasons ago. Then it was avant-garde. I have to come out like 'Romeo and Juliet' and forswear my forefathers. NBC felt that it was all right for a few million records, but they want me to be understood by thirty million viewers in Council Bluffs."

Sherman's ambivalence about television was no match for its allure. It promised prominence and money and on January 18, 1965, Sherman was the star of "Funnyland," a one-hour pilot that had the potential to become a regular series. It was his "Desilu" moment, and just as in his "Bali Hai" parody that zeroed in on the irresistible television sirens that flatter and entice men to "make a change, here and there," Sherman agreed to play down the ethnic angle. The new success of *Fiddler* on New York's Broadway did not yet mean that television, with its nationwide audience, could follow suit. But Sherman's complaint about it was as much reflex as disgruntlement. He could not resist looking down on the people lifting him up. Peter had his commissar and Sherman had Goodson-Todman, the Westinghouse people on the *Steve Allen*

Show, and now NBC. "I did not think up the title 'Funnyland,' and I wish to apologize to all those for whom it created a chip on the shoulder," he told the *Times*, which noted Sherman placed the blame "deftly on unnamed NBC forces." That must have pleased the executive suite.

Broadening his scope for the *Los Angeles Times*, Sherman took on the whole television industry. "Allan feels very strongly about television. He thinks it has lost its momentum from its early live days," the paper reported on the day of the special. "'It's thinking is backward,' he says. 'It tries to play to millions of people in their living rooms. Listen, the living room is the one place people want to get out of. The thinking should be to make shows that take them out of the living rooms.'"

For Sherman, television was unfinished business, and stardom gave him a chance to prove that his instincts about the medium's special ability to transmit a sense of immediacy and spontaneity was right, and Goodson-Todman and Westinghouse's need for planned perfection was wrong. His life was built on the same premise. Sherman did not plan for a career as a television star. But fame of whatever origin led to television, and from the moment his albums sold big he was a regular guest star and an item on the agendas of television networks loath to miss out on whatever was next. As early as May 10, 1963, before the "Hello Muddah" phenomenon, a *Daily Variety* headline announced, "ABC, NBC Pitching TV Offers to Allan Sherman." He also continued to tout his television expertise, telling *Variety* that the size of the summer television audience was substantial and "people in the trade don't realize it."

If his three 1964 albums did not come close to matching his first three in originality or sales, it was at least in part because Sherman was focused on getting back into television, this time in front of the camera. On March 4, 1964, less than a month after his return from England, news broke that BBC-2 wanted him to host one of its new "International Cabaret" shows. In July, NBC was thinking of him to host *That Was The Week That Was*, but in late September signed him to "write, produce and star [in] a special hour-long comedy show." Having "Funnyland" in the bag did not halt his search for other opportunities. In November Sherman was in talks with playwright and television producer Irving Elman to star in "Paradise Cove," a comedy that never made it to the screen, and the same month he got a favorable mention for a bit part in the series, *Mr. Novak*. Good reviews also followed Sherman's October appearance on *Hello Peapickers*, an unlikely match starring country singer Tennessee Ernie Ford. His November act on "NBC Follies of 1965" with singer Steve Lawrence went less well. "Sherman fluttered about trying to be funny," complained *Variety*, something he managed only when "Sherman, garbed as a Puritan, barged into Indian country and announced he'd come to settle."

But even all this activity does not capture how desperately Sherman wanted to have his own show. The prospect of "Funnyland" persuaded him to live like he wanted to stay alive. Health problems had dogged him for months. After another campaign event for Lyndon Johnson, this one on October 31 at New York's Madison Square Garden, Sherman was wiped out. He was too weak to accept an invitation extended to the celebrities to come down to the Johnsons' Texas ranch for a preelection bash, and by November 5 he was in New York's Doctor's Hospital for "peace and quiet" and a physical. That was probably where he heard he was "a perfect candidate for a coronary." On December 1, 1964, he checked into Hollywood's Cedars of Lebanon hospital determined to lose fifty pounds. A photograph of Sherman in his Cedars hospital bed supports the diagnosis. His body, swollen with fat, was a bulbous, distended mass. There was no way he could keep his December dates at the Nugget in Sparks, Nevada, and the Chi Chi in Palm Springs. Those engagements were sacrificed. He performed instead for the reporters covering his weight-loss regimen. The hospital was the perfect setting for one of his favorite routines — Sherman as infant. "He was an unshaved cherub swaddled in pink pajamas, having just finished a hearty breakfast of stewed prunes and black coffee," wrote the *Los Angeles Times*. "On one wrist was the hospital's official bracelet; on the other, the identification he insisted upon: 'Sherman, baby boy.'"

Besides, there was a television show to write, and he could do that in the hospital while he consumed his 500 calories a day. "It was bizarre, but in Hollywood that never stopped anyone," said Sam Bobrick, one of four "Funnyland" writers that visited Sherman at Cedars to prepare the show. Some days there were also "the producer, the director, the publicity man and a secretary gathered around the hungry comedian's bedside," wrote one reporter. It made great newspaper copy, but Bobrick was not amused. "They'd give him uppers, downers, and writing that show was a mess because he was always glassy-eyed," he said. "Allan was so scattered at the time that you'd start on one thing and then he decided on something else. You kind of knew this was going nowhere."

Yet it almost did. Once again, blessed with the frantic commotion and tight deadlines that were his favorite working conditions Sherman produced comedy that won critical applause on his own terms. "It was an unorthodox production that followed no rules," wrote *The Hollywood Reporter* in a review titled, "Sherman's 'Funny Land' a Smash Television Show." Rule-avoidance television was the kind he had always championed, said Robert Sherman. "Goodson-Todman preplanned for all contingencies. My father's view was set up a fun situation and if something went wrong those were the most fun moments." *Variety* also recognized and liked the show's deviation from the norm. It was "as different as any show since the late Ernie Kovacs and it was a rib-tickler if not an outright howler."

Americans in what Sherman called Council Bluffs were interested in what Sherman had to offer. They tuned in based on Sherman's reputation. "Funny-land" won the ratings war for its time slot. Then they agreed with the industry insiders. "The best show of its kind this season," wrote the *Daily Oklahoman*. The reviewer for Columbus, Ohio's *Dispatch* decided, "Allan Sherman's Funny-land was not only a nice place to visit, but I wouldn't even mind living there." In thoughtful Boston, the *Record American* called the show "about as clever, imaginative and amusing a TV comedy offering as I've seen in a long time. It was also 'different' and even experimental — a couple of characteristics which television programmers ordinarily shy away from as 'unsafe.'"

Sherman knew what he was doing. His advance comments to the press were impolitic but they were also right. Comedy was his territory, and so long as he did not try any cross-border raids on profundity he was on solid ground. Instead of the overblown television productions Sherman lambasted that featured "thousands of dancers and Taj Mahals of scenery," "Funnyland" bet everything on a barrage of wordplay vignettes and song performances involving just Sherman and his three disparate costars Lorne Green, star of *Bonanza*; movie actress Angie Dickinson; and Broadway actor Jack Gilford, who had recently wrapped up his stint playing Hysterium in *A Funny Thing Happened on the Way to the Forum*. It was a formula the Smothers Brothers in 1967 and *Rowan and Martin's Laugh-In* in 1968 ran amuck with in the far more anarchic social climate of the late 1960s, but Sherman's show already had their self-aware irreverence and love of absurd silliness. "The character of Allan Sherman is fictitious and should not be confused" was the mock serious notice that prefaced the show, and Sherman's opening bit continued in the same vein.

When NBC said that I could have a one-hour show, they said there were certain things that I would have to guarantee them. First, they said, it must get a high rating. And second they said, it must not offend anybody, and then they said it must win an Emmy Award. And so I said, would you fellas mind if it's a good show? And they said that's optional.

"Funnyland" went after its sponsor, the Timex watch company, whose commercials demonstrated its products' resilience by placing them in extreme situations, often under water. Sherman dropped a watch into Angie Dickinson's water glass. "They only work under water, you know." Later in the show Sherman asked for the time. "I drank my watch." In a skit with Lorne Green, Sherman looked in his ear and reported what he saw. "The Ponderosa. They're subdividing it." Television's censors were also lampooned.

Let's go sailing on a ship called censorship
To the land where TV censors clip
Any words they fear
Might offend your ear
With a rip rip rip and a button-your-lip
And a no no no no no
And if you ask why
They reply oh my
Because it is a family show
A typical clean-cut
Guaranteed wholesome
Charcoal filtered
Television family show.

Sherman managed to deliver some light sexual material in a winning off-hand manner. "If I may suggest something," offered the beautiful Dickinson. "You do, you do," replied Sherman. In another bit, Sherman explained that in childhood he often escaped to imaginary worlds such as Pirate Land and others less innocent that made him late for dinner. "Now how could I tell [my mother] that I had spent the afternoon in Doctor Land with Geraldine from next door. I mean I was making a house call." In the show's visit to "If Land," Lorne Green said, apropos of nothing, "If Abdul Nasser played football for Vassar, he'd be known as Nasser the Vassar Passer." This kind of "If" scenario became a running gag on *Laugh-In*.

Jewish material, as Sherman predicted, was absent, except for one joke about the fictitious Mr. Teitlebaum, in charge of thinking up NBC show titles. Its absence did not cramp Sherman's style. He did not come out with any earnest declarations about his Jewish identity like those about childhood that generated uncomfortable silences on the *Tonight* show. Nothing Jewish escaped through the cracks in his character because there were no Jewish pressures building under the surface. The *My Son* albums had solved that problem for him, and he produced very little Jewish material for the rest of his career.

So the public looked elsewhere. Jewishness was hot in 1965. In September, the comedy album *You Don't Have to Be Jewish* was a hit, with sketches such as "The Reading of the Will" that features Jack Gilford as the attorney running the proceedings. "To my beautiful daughter Jayne, with a y," got a laugh it owed to Sherman's "Stein with an ei and Styne with a y" from "Shake Hands with Your Uncle Max." The same year the parody album, *James Blonde, "The Man from T.A.N.T.E.,"* took on both the popular film secret agent, James Bond, and the *Man from U.N.C.L.E.* television show. Blonde was secret agent 006.95, marked down from 007.00. Mel Brooks had the same idea, and in 1965 his *Get Smart* television series also parodied the secret agent craze. But the biggest Jewish hit of the year was Dan Greenburg's book, *How to Be a Jewish Mother: A Very Lovely Training Manual*. It was the top-selling nonfiction book of 1965 and also inspired a successful record album of the same name.

Sherman helped break open the Jewish mother comedy category in 1962 with his first album, *Allan Sherman's Mother Presents, My Son, the Folk Singer*, but he was unqualified to celebrate Jewish mothers. He had tapped into something he did not actually experience, and when it took off it inevitably left him behind. Greenburg's Jewish mother book offered a list of "Basic Sacrifices to Make for Your Child." Sacrifices were not Sherman's mother's specialty. He lived the stereotypical Jewish boyhood only intermittently when he boarded with his grandparents. Sherman's Jewish parodies released a tidal wave of Jewish comedy material he did not have the know-how to surf.

The insistence on nonethnic material in "Funnyland" was just what Sherman wanted. However, NBC did not develop the pilot into a series. No paperwork survives that may have revealed why the network passed on the show, but Sherman gave NBC plenty to worry about, from his health to his undiplomatic remarks in the press to antics such as writing the show from his hospital bed. Still, he was eager to move from Jewish humor to a comedy that touched on Americans' common life, including that greatest of common denominators, television, and the maddeningly unreal mirror of reality it offered.

He was already headed there. *My Son, the Celebrity*'s "Al 'n Yetta" humorously documented the new affliction of television addiction, and on *My Son, the Nut*'s "Headaches" parody of "Heartaches," Sherman skewered television commercials. "Headaches / Headaches / Aspirin commercials give me headaches." Television had been officially recognized as a problem on May 9, 1961, when Newton N. Minow, chairman of the Federal Communications Commission and future Sherman fan, called television "a vast wasteland." *Mad* magazine got there before both Minow and Sherman with a 1955 parody ad for Bofforin. "Headache? Cold misery? Why wait for old-fashioned relief? Go Kill yourself!" Sherman's headache remedy had an active ingredient that was more to the point. "Today I swallowed the best cure yet / I ate my TV set." Television advertising was such a pervasive and annoying part of modern life that in 1965 it became the irritation that interfered with the Rolling Stones' satisfaction. Keith Richards and Mick Jagger could not stand the man that explained, "How white my shirts can be." But the group's real message was its rock medium that divided Sherman's generation from the teenagers driving record sales. On June 6, 1964, when the Stones appeared on *The Hollywood Palace* television show, even the cool and raffish Dean Martin helplessly confessed, "I don't know what they're singing about, but here they are at." By the time Sherman's "Funnyland" aired in January 1965, rock music dominated *Billboard*'s ranking of the nation's top 10 records, which on January 16 included three albums by the Beatles and one each by the Supremes, the Beach Boys, and the Rolling Stones.

This new youth culture held a silver lining for Sherman. He was now in demand as a hip but clean representative of the teenagers' parents' generation. "Allan Sherman's opening brought out the crowd — and earned plenty mitts," reported *Variety* when he kicked off a stint at the Chi Chi on March 2, 1965. "Material is fresh, whimsical, and Sherman's 'Hello Mudder' [*sic*] is still the favorite. And it might be noted the sock act has no blue notes." Despite the lackluster performance of his 1964 record albums, in 1965 he enjoyed one of his greatest periods as a hot entertainment property, and Sherman shared with friends and relatives his good mood and good fortune. In early 1965, his Aunt Edith, widow of his Uncle Maury Sherman, was very ill with a heart aneurysm. The only one who could help her was the great surgeon Dr. DeBakey in Houston, Texas, who in December 1964 had just operated on the Duke of Windsor. Edith's daughter, Carol Selsberg, remembered, "My mother writes DeBakey, 'You're the only one who can do it.' DeBakey says come, I won't charge." Edith told Sherman she had to fly to Houston for the surgery and he bought her a plane ticket, Selsberg said. That generosity would not have surprised Sherman's friends. "You had to know that at this time in his life, there was always a cherubic smile," said Jerry Goldstein. "When Allan was feeling good you knew it. He made you smile. When that was going on in Allan's life he was a happy guy."

There were plenty of reasons to be happy. His brain's parody-making apparatus was soaring, and it had just spotted its next victim. "Downtown" by Petula Clark was a huge hit single in January 1965 that celebrated the city as an enchanting antidote to loneliness and more obscure sources of the blues. Its youthful exuberance is innocent of the inescapable sexuality of the Rolling Stones. Clark's city scene imagines folks doing the bossa nova. This was too wide-eyed for Sherman, and in "Crazy Downtown" he turned a skeptical parents' eye on what was really going on.

> You don't come home till 4 a.m. cause you're roaming
> In the streets somewhere,
> Downtown.
> We would feel swell if only someone would tell us
> What goes on down there,

Downtown.
But every time we ask you what you're doing after dark there
You just say that you were frugging to Petula Clark there
That's what I mean
So, kids, give your folks a break
Cause you're driving us crazy, we sit here all night and take
Miltown,
Swallowing pills so we'll
Calm down.

Variety spotted it as a winner on March 19 and less than three weeks later it had sold 250,000 copies. The *Washington Post*, which in 1963 had dished out Sherman's first public whipping in its mean-spirited photo essay, gave Sherman credit for the timely send-up. "Like so many innovations, it seems a wonder that nobody thought of it before. It's all right to kid 'The Dance of the Hours,' as Sherman did previously with 'Hello Mudduh, Hello Fadduh.' But how much more effective it is, to lampoon a song that was popular recently. And what better time to do it than right on the heels of that popularity?" Starting in the 1970s, Weird Al Yankovic built a successful career on Sherman's idea.

"Crazy Downtown" got Sherman back on television. He sang the parody on *The Hollywood Palace* show on March 27, and again on NBC's *Hullabaloo* on April 20. That show taped April 16, while Sherman was in New York guest-hosting *Nightlife*, and it might have been in celebration of "Crazy Downtown" and his upcoming television appearance that Sherman planned the sex party Goldstein stumbled upon when he visited Sherman that April week at the Plaza. Whatever the kids meant when they said they were frugging, it is a sure bet they were not doing what Sherman was doing.

Hiding that licentiousness was good for business, because Sherman's image as a comical would-be lover had television calling him for dates. He signed a deal in November 1964 to appear in television ads for Brillo dishwashing pads, and shot two of them in January 1965 for $90,000, an astounding fee for a few days' work that attests to his appeal. To the tune of "Fascination," a song he parodied in *Nut*'s "Automation," a beret-wearing Sherman serenades a woman with, "It was Brillo soap pads, I know / Darling that's what made all your pots and pans glow." He signed another sponsorship deal in 1965 with the container division of the Scott Paper Company to write six song parodies about the firm's paper cups. The 2,000 records, called *Music to Dispense With*, were given away to Scott Paper customers. Certain unpaid appearances were worth attending for the publicity. On April 25, 1965, the Friars Club in Beverly Hills honored Jack Warner, and Sherman's name appeared beside those of Jack Benny, Milton Berle, George Burns, Danny Kaye, and other stars in a *Hollywood Reporter* advertisement urging readers to buy tickets to the dinner. Press coverage of the evening mentioned Sherman's performance of his "never-to-be-released" *My Fair Lady* parody popular with entertainment insiders.

Sherman's new manager, Bill Loeb, engineered these opportunities, and in May 1965 he put Sherman in a room with comic strip artist Al Capp, creator of "L'il Abner," to discuss creating a new television series. Nothing came of it, but in July and August Sherman was on the "Celebrity Game" television show, hosted by Carl Reiner and often featuring Mel Brooks. On the inane program, a contestant tries to guess what a celebrity will answer to questions such as, do movie stars like playing love scenes. To that question, a contestant guessed Sherman would say "love is where you find it." It seems a prearranged straight line that allowed Sherman to deliver an apparently instant parody. "Love is where you find it / Look beneath it / Look behind it / And you'll find it."

The Loner

On "Funnyland," Sherman had battled his image as lovable and sexually unthreatening. When Dickinson tells him "I think you're so adorable I just want to pinch your cheeks," Sherman screams. "Ahhh! Pinch my cheeks. Adorable. Ever since I was eight years old every girl I ever met wanted to pinch my cheeks. On my honeymoon, five days and nights of getting my cheeks pinched. Ahh! I hate adorable." But in "Crazy Downtown" and the "Brillo" ads Sherman accepted it and milked it for all it was worth. He was having it both ways, playing a role the public liked while secretly getting his kicks. "Allan at the time would still hit the mark," Goldstein said of the "Nightlife" gig. "If he stayed out all night, no one gave a rat's ass." But a different Sherman image occurred to Rod Serling.

On "Funnyland" Lorne Green sang his 1964 hit song "Ringo," a sentimental cowboy song that wore a taciturn disguise, and then Sherman, dressed in cowboy gear and wearing a Beatles wig sang a terrific parody.

> He sat me down in the desert sand
> With a comb and scissors in his hand
> As he cut my hair he said, I'm the best,
> The fastest barber in the west.
> I asked him where he'd gone to school
> He said, I studied in Liverpool
> I met four kids called the Beatles there
> And I'd give my life to cut the hair of Ringo.
> I met him next in the old town square
> A voice was calling numbers there
> The crowd was tense, listening hard
> Each one had some beans and a card
> The voice called 5, then 14
> They covered each number with a lima bean
> Five beans in a row means a bullet in the head
> Because way out west you can wind up dead playing Bingo.

He played it straight, the audience went wild, and Sherman carried off a self-consciously pugnacious, hard image that apparently caught Serling's eye. *The Twilight Zone* had gone off the air in 1964 after five years, and in 1965 Serling was writing *The Loner*, "a half-hour post–Civil War Western about a wandering, introspective cowboy in search of life's meaning." Serling wrote an episode for Sherman, who played a sheriff hailed as a Civil War hero, having captured thirty-three Confederate soldiers single-handed. The story is a fabrication. "They used to call me fatty. Now they call me sheriff," Sherman's character explains to The Loner, played by Lloyd Bridges. But in the course of the episode Sherman's character is put to the test and displays courage. Sherman was put to the test as an actor and displayed talent. He lost himself in the character and was by turns comic, sympathetic, and tough. For a moment, when "The Sheriff of Fetterman's Crossing" aired on November 13, 1965, Sherman revealed a side of himself that was adult, capable, and even formidable.

He hated this adult aspect of his character and regarded it as a flaw to be overcome or resisted. Childhood and a child's sensibility was Sherman's ideal, as his autobiography made clear when *A Gift of Laughter* was released in October. Almost forty-one, his view of his unhappy and destructive family origins was fit for a nursery rhyme. "Everybody in my family was crazy. Not *crazy*-crazy. *Nice*-crazy. *Sweet*-crazy." Harpo Marx was a treasure because he "was a child who never grew up." If children instead of adults ran the world, "there would be less fear and less crime and less war and less status-seeking and less embarrassment and humiliation and shame. And prejudice and genocide just simply wouldn't exist at all." Sherman recalled one time he played and won the adult world's game. When he and Harpo appeared in concert together, Sherman successfully used his star power to demand better marquee billing for Harpo. This victory was in his eyes a failure. "I swear to you that I have never done this to gain anything for myself," wrote Sherman. "But I have done it several times, and I am ashamed that I ever did it all."

It was sentiments like these that *Newsweek* in its review of *Gift* felt Sherman "ought to be the first to parody." Adults were not buying his sentimental philosophy. And there were other signs his judgment was off. When *Gift* appeared Sherman was playing the Sands in Las Vegas, and with the help of the public relations firm McFadden, Strauss, Eddy & Irwin he organized a "literary tea" there on October 11, 1965, to publicize and discuss his book. "He got laughed at," remembered Golden. That was understandable. The literary tea idea and setting were absurd, and so was Sherman's choice of panelists. "Allan has made arrangements for four Sands show girls to participate in the tea as part of a panel on the book," publicist Ben Irwin informed the Sands. The *Saturday Review* covered the event and conveyed its hollowness with a few choice quotes. The book proves "that somebody can still become a star overnight," said one of the showgirls. "It holds out hope."

The autobiography was not as bad as the tea held to celebrate it. Ghostwriter Maurice Zolotow was an experienced pro and knew how to put together a fast-paced and entertaining story. The *New York Times* dispatched it with a quick write-up but admitted "Mr. Sherman is a very honest and a very funny man." The honesty was probably a reference to the stories about his early sexual adventures, and how as an adolescent in California he was sick with the mumps and disobeyed doctor's orders to stay in bed until he regained his health because he could not resist ogling the beautiful teenage girl his mother had hired to clean the house. As a result, one of his testicles atrophied. So "there I was, a mere youth of fifteen, with only one ball left, and *still* a virgin," Sherman wrote. That kind of language ended a lucrative advertising deal Sherman had signed with General Mills, which cited a morals clause in Sherman's contract when it fired him. That the book's "Puberty Revisited" chapter appeared in *Playboy* magazine in July 1965 as "Sex and the Single Sherman" was small consolation. "The sex scene cost us $50,000," Golden said. "I told him not to, but he said it's the truth and I've got to tell it." His child's sense of honor prevailed over adult realities.

Peyton Place

Sherman was at his worst when he thought or wrote about himself. He was much better at covering the American scene around him, as his best albums proved, but with the October 1965 *My Name Is Allan*, his first album in a year, he switched cultural teams. Where he was once the outsider mocking the castle, unmasking the ethnically agnostic Broadway musical and updating the safely antiquated folk repertoire to include contemporary Jews, he now defended the established order as it crumbled around him. On March 7, 1965, police attacked black civil rights marchers in Selma, Alabama. "Bloody Sunday" was a national news story, and it soon brought the Rev. Martin Luther King to Selma for another march and precipitated a speech by President Johnson in favor of the voting rights act that became law in August. That summer Barry McGuire's "Eve of Destruction" cataloged the unsettled moment and dared listeners not to worry, and Bob Dylan's "Like a Rolling Stone" began, "Once upon a time," turning the classic introduction to a children's story into the ironic opener to a snarling tale of humbled privilege.

My Name Is Allan treated far lighter topics, from fad diets to name-dropping celebrity culture to television commercials touting scientific-sounding gobble-dygook. Some of the songs survive their time because Sherman spotted aspects of American life that turned out to be as evergreen as they are foolish. *The Drinking Man's Diet*, an insidious little book by Gardner Jamison and Elliot

Williams, was published in 1964, translated into thirteen languages and sold more than two million copies. The key was, liquor has no carbohydrates. Sherman got it. "If pounds you would burn off / Then turn on your Smirnoff / And drink, drink, drink." In "Chim Chim Cheree," he parodies the *Mary Poppins* song to skewer advertising that intimidates consumers with pseudo-science.

> Chim Chiminey Chim Chiminey
> Chim Chim Cheree
> Those are three words that don't make sense to me
> But I'm used to words that don't make sense to me
> From all those commercials I see on TV
> When I see an ad that can't be understood
> I know that the product has got to be good
> Those words may be crazy, but I think they're great
> Like sodium acetylsalicylate
> Sodium acetylsalicylate.

But when Sherman ventured into more controversial subjects he took a conservative stand. Off-Off-Broadway theater was new when he addressed it on the October album's "It's a Most Unusual Play." The *New York Times'* first in-depth article on the underground theater world would not appear until December, when it noted that "sex, in an impressive variety of forms, is popular on the OOB circuit. Homosexuality, incest, and sado-masochism are treated frequently and sometimes humorously." The *Times* was open-minded about it. Sherman was not. To the tune of "It's a Most Unusual Day," he sang,

> It's a most unusual play
> Feel like throwing my tickets away
> Cause the boy gets the boy and the girl gets the girl
> And it's way too far off Broadway

Another song also championed sexual conformity. "Peyton Place, U.S.A." disapproves of the television series that in 1964 brought soap opera themes of sex and illicit relationships to the prime-time evening hours. The *Peyton Place* brand was hardly new. The 1956 novel was made into a 1957 movie, and a film sequel appeared in 1961, but Sherman treated it as a cultural watershed.

"Everyone's moral fiber's in complete decay there / They've got a problem cleaning up the P.T.A there / Peyton Place, U.S.A." This moral grandstanding on a passé sexual issue was paired with a moral complacency about something that actually mattered, when in December 1965 Sherman performed in South Africa. In 1964, authorities there deported singer Dusty Springfield because she refused to promise she would not entertain multiracial audiences. Sherman promised South Africa's *Sunday Express* newspaper, "I'll not do a Dusty Springfield." Nothing could have made Sherman more aligned with the generation the 1960s sought to overturn than his hypocritical sexual puritanism and passivity on racial justice. *My Name Is Allan* topped out at number 88 on *Billboard*'s "Top LP's" chart and disappeared from the charts after eight weeks.

As the veteran of an orgy and other freewheeling practices, Sherman was an odd champion of conventional sexuality, but in 1965 his frequent criticisms of sexual liberties were moral pep talks he directed at himself, an unwilling listener. In a June 1965 interview with the new *Penthouse* magazine, Sherman complained about people whose sex lives celebrate "sex without individuality — and it doesn't seem to make any difference whose sex organs are involved. There is no personality involved in it."

In Sherman's case, that was an over simplification. His sexual liaisons involved one important personality, his own, that he could not control.

eleven

ODDBALL

"He wanted the divorce," Sherman's ex-wife Dee Golden remembered. "He was in love with a girl. It came to a very sad end. She left him abruptly. He had several girlfriends and he never remarried."

In 1966, Sherman ended his marriage and followed in the self-defeating footsteps of his unbalanced parents. To try and apply the brakes to his downhill slide, he sometimes sought the advice of friends about new girlfriends. "He would call up and say, 'What did you think?'" said Billy Goldenberg. Almost without exception Goldenberg's answer was the same. "This person doesn't care for you so why are you interested? I don't know what you're looking for."

The simplest answer is Sherman was looking for what he got, which was rejection and loneliness. They were the conditions that had formed him, and now he returned to them.

A turning point occurred shortly after January 12, 1966, when he began a three-week engagement in the Venetian Room at San Francisco's Fairmont Hotel. At the outset, Sherman displayed a masterful control of his business.

"One thing that impressed me was I put him in the Venetian Room with the orchestra at 2 PM," and he said, "'I don't like my show. I'm going to write a whole new show,'" recalled his manager, Bill Loeb. By 7 PM Sherman was done. By the end of the month he had planned a whole new life, but it turned out the skills he applied to the stage were not transferable.

In San Francisco he met a twenty-five-year-old woman named Lynne Martin, who lived in the San Francisco Bay Area. Martin had an interest in show business. In May 1961, when she was a "pert, auburn-haired" twenty-year-old student at Oakland's Mills College she was a bit player in the movie, *The Pleasure of His Company*. "Everybody knew her. She goes with all the celebrities," Golden said. In March 1966, she was the "hot young thing" Jay Thomas met in New Orleans when Sherman played the Roosevelt Hotel. However, she was not the woman Sherman bedded a month later in April, when he played two weeks at Houston's Cork Club. "We went to Houston and I said, 'Allan you'll have no problem getting a gal here,'" said Al Lerner, a musical director who was one of several Sherman used after he split with Lou Busch because he said he wanted more lush arrangements. In Houston, Sherman found a young woman and he called Lerner and told him to come down to his room. "He wanted to show me what he had captured."

This behavior hardly indicated a commitment to his new love, or stability of any kind, and in late April Sherman returned home for two weeks before he opened May 8, 1966, at the Nugget in Nevada, where he recorded his seventh album for Warner Bros., *Allan Sherman Live!! (Hoping You Are the Same)*. "It was very crazy," Lerner said. "He said we should do a live album from here. 'Good idea; when?'" The answer was tomorrow. The album was recorded May 20 and released in July, but his slipshod work habits were no longer redeemed by a lively humor, and the album became his first that never made it onto the *Billboard* charts. The *New York Times* dismissed it as "mostly more of the same," but not "as convincing as on previous efforts." A few songs are sharp and socially incisive, and reveal Sherman's growing disenchantment with suburban family life. "Taking Lessons" zeroes in on the American obsession with self-improvement, made possible by the dubious new luxury of leisure time. To the tune of "Makin' Whoopee" Sherman sang,

The modern family
Has time to burn
We all take lessons
We try to learn
The latest new things
We never do things
We just take lessons.

"Second Hand Nose," a parody of "Second Hand Rose," takes the quest for self-improvement to its logical conclusion.

I'm calling Dr. Max Rose
That's who I chose
He's gonna make me a second hand nose
I went to his office once or twice and
All his patients looked like Barbra Streisand
Then I'll get second hand hair, second hand teeth
And contact lenses in a baby blue
And elevator shoes and then I'll melt the girls' hearts
They can't resist a man with interchangeable parts.

These and less successful numbers put him either out of step or in opposition to the 1960's emphasis on change and defiance and freedom, sometimes with a spite that first showed up in "Dropouts." "Dodgin' the Draft," to the tune of "Ballin' the Jack," looks forward to draft dodgers being classified 1-A, and "The Rebel" gleefully anticipates a time when a statue in honor of student rebellion is forgotten by all except pigeons. The young were popular scapegoats, but Sherman's unhappiness grew from his own sense of victimization. In "Sorry 'bout That" he is a sap that gets taken advantage of by everyone, and in "Taking Lessons" he resents paying for children's ballet and karate lessons. A parody of "A Taste of Honey," called "A Waste of Money" catalogs his failed efforts to buy love before he met the woman who loved him for himself alone.

On June 3, 1966, soon after the Nugget gig, Sherman told his wife he was leaving her. "He rang the doorbell and Maxine [the maid] answered door," Golden said. "He came in and said go in the bedroom, and he said I want a divorce. I was sitting on the bed. I fell off. He kept on talking but I didn't hear him. I said if you're going, go."

"It was the saddest day of my life, and I'm sure his," said Tabolsky. "I got a call from Bill Loeb, 'You got to meet me at Allan's house. He's got to move out.' So I met him, and Bill and I carried his clothes out of the house. And I got to tell you it was awful, awful. The kids were standing there." Loeb and Tabolsky stuffed everything into Loeb's car and drove to Sherman's temporary Los Angeles apartment in the Fountainview West, a high-rise on La Cienega just below Sunset known as "the halfway house," the place men lived after they left their wives.

Sherman had only a month to consider his new life before he left California to perform at London's Savoy Theater from July 7 to 16. Reviews of his performance there hinted he was drinking. "Sherman's delivery of patter, even with mike, is not well projected, for he slurs words and phrases." After London, his son Robert, then sixteen years old, joined him in Europe for a hectic vacation. They spent the four days from July 18 through 21 in Rome and Copenhagen before arriving in Germany on Friday, July 22, where Sherman spent the weekend performing for American troops in Wiesbaden, Mannheim, and Frankfurt. Originally the plan was for the whole family to join him in Europe, but after the split, his wife and daughter instead flew to Hawaii. This first formal separation and the stay in Germany unsettled him, and he made dark jokes about the Nazi murder of the Jews. "He used to say, 'I haven't been here before but parts of my family are here,'" said Laurie Holloway, Sherman's piano man at the time. The personal and historical grief did not throw him off his sexual feed, however. Neither did the presence of his son. "One night he said, 'we're off,'" Holloway said. "Where are we going? 'We're going to a brothel.' And I said I'm not interested, and I wasn't. So I sat and read a magazine or whatever while he went inside."

Sherman flew back to San Francisco on July 25 to reunite with his new girl-friend. At the airport she insulted him, a "very bad insult," Golden said. "He socked her in the eye. She sued . . . that's how it ended." According to Martin's legal complaint, Sherman struck her in San Francisco's Fairmont Hotel, and she sued him for $425,000. The case was settled out of court for an undisclosed amount. The new life he had left his wife to pursue lasted less than two months.

Then began an odd and unhappy period. "I became the girl on the road," Golden said. She took the place of the numerous women Sherman found while touring. "I wanted to keep the relationship going, yes. Two kids!" Apparently, so did Sherman. "He was ambivalent. He called like we're old friends," Golden said. "He couldn't make up his mind." She accompanied him to a show he gave at the Kahala Hilton in Honolulu on August 9, and on August 11 joined him in Australia where he had club dates in Sydney and Melbourne. "In Australia he was seeing a psychiatrist twice a day," Lerner said. Both Sherman's misery and his wife's were apparent to the Australian newspapers. "Reporters called us the sad-eyed Shermans," Golden said. "They saw right through us." Golden returned to Los Angeles after one week and left Sherman behind until the August 30 end of his Australia tour, which was followed by another stop in Honolulu. The Kahala Hilton wanted him back for a September 6 show. By October his marriage was over. *Variety* reported he and his wife had separated and that he had moved to New York.

New York offered a number of advantages. It put Sherman close to the *Ed Sullivan Show*, which in 1966 featured him as a guest eight times. As a history of the show noted, it often functioned as a "final resting place for America's biggest headliners in their twilight years," and that is what it was for Sherman, after his two most recent records did poorly. New York had other benefits, including nightclubs that offered Sherman employment. In October 1966, shortly after he arrived in town, he played the Basin St. East, a venue on East 48th Street off Lexington Avenue that offered top-name entertainers such as singers Peggy Lee and Barbra Streisand. But most importantly, the city was the right place for him to take one more shot at his dream of landing a musical on Broadway.

There were early signs he did not have the emotional or creative stability it would take. On October 16, 1966, he was the star of the one-hour television series, *Something Special*. Unlike "Funnyland," this was no pilot. There was no potential it would turn into a Sherman television series, and the tantalizing possibilities that in 1965 drove him in search of a television property had faded. In 1966, he appeared on *Sullivan*, and on shows hosted by Andy Williams, Dean Martin, Mike Douglas, and Merv Griffin, but there were no meetings with networks or producers for *Variety* to report. His hour on *Something*

Special, recorded much earlier in the year on February 11, was part of a ten-show package, with each focusing on a name entertainer, such as Pearl Bailey and Leslie Uggams.

On his show, Sherman performed an amusing British version of "Hello Muddah" that began, "Hello Mater, Hello Pater," and gave good renditions of "Bye, Bye Blumberg" and "The Painless Dentist Song," a parody of "The Continental" from *My Name Is Allan* that borrows the original song's theme of growing intimacy between lovers to explore the strange intimacy demanded by dentistry. "This is Miss Klinger / You've met her finger / So open wide and Miss Klinger will squirt." But even the best numbers, such as the opening effort that featured Sherman as a dashing playboy adored by three gorgeous women showing plenty of cleavage and leg were hackneyed. He hammed it up, to make the ladies' man joke clear, and sang, "Call Me," another song from *My Name Is Allan,* that parodies "Call Me Irresponsible." It is a funny and clever piece of work that ridicules the pseudo-sophistication of celebrity name-dropping, and Sherman's appearance as a Hugh Hefner knock-off perfectly complemented the lyrics.

Call me, Efrem Zimbalist
Get me, Bobby Kennedy
Then call Dave Ben-Gurion, too
Then tell Carol Baker I'm home now
Tell her Mastroianni sends love from Rome now
Then get Hank Mancini
And tell him Fred Fellini
Is waiting, where the heck is the song?
Order Scotch and ice and then
Ring up Barbra Streisand and then
Set up a conference call
With Sammy Davis and Charles de Gaulle

But the show's most memorable moments were the uncomfortable and distressing ones. To build a loose structure for the special, Sherman used his songs, some with updated lyrics, to tell the story of his life. The changes he made to "Sarah Jackman" allowed him to vent his self-hatred at the moment he took up with his new girlfriend and contemplated the end of his marriage. In "Sarah Jackman" he plays a college student phoning Sarah, played by his original song partner, Christine Nelson, for a date. College is where Sherman met his wife, Dee, who broke up with him before their reunion and hastily arranged marriage, and the new "Sarah Jackman" seems a confession that Dee should not have married him, that he never deserved her, and was a bad husband. Sherman begins the song's dialogue.

> I met you last Thursday
> That was my bad news day
> Gee I'd like to date you
> No because I hate you
> I would love you always
> Yes in different hallways
> I'll buy you a Coke dear
> But you're always broke dear
> Then I'll get a job dear
> Who would hire a slob dear?

That was the uncomfortable. The show closed with the distressing, as Sherman proved his immature idealization of childhood made him painfully incapable of communicating with real children. He serenaded a seven-year-old girl from the audience with his original composition, "Oddball," a good song with excellent music by Tony Award–winning composer Cy Coleman that like the great "My Funny Valentine" professes love for an imperfect but charming woman. The little girl, however, was unable to read between the lines, and as Sherman sang to her she struggled not to cry.

> Oddball
> You're something else, that's the rumor
> Little oddball
> With that wild sense of humor
> Why do you do those strange and peculiar things you do?
> Everyone else in the world is in step, but no not you.
> You're just an oddball

All the time nonconforming
Tell me oddball
What makes you so heart-warming?
You're not too good-looking
You're way out of style
And even when you make a serious face I've still gotta smile
Cause you're an oddball
Is there no one to love you?
Little oddball.
Do they all make fun of you?
Well you're one of a kind
And that's what I find refreshing and new
And I guess I'm an oddball, too
Cause little oddball, I love you.

His last album for Warner Bros., *Togetherness*, released four months later in February 1967, displayed even more of Sherman's instability and bad judgment. The album's first song parody is "Westchester Hadassah." The title is a great one-line takeoff on the 1966 hit song, "Winchester Cathedral." Sherman should have stopped there, because he sings his parody in a voice weary with exasperation and contempt for the Jewish women's organization, and wit takes a backseat to a tasteless denial of everything he once valued and represented.

Westchester Hadassah
I'm trying my best
Enclosed is one dollar
I'll owe you the rest.
No more of my dough
No more of my dough
No more of my dough de-oh dough
Remember that raffle
When you held your monster bazaar
I bought all the tickets
All but one
And that was the one that won the car.

Westchester Hadassah
How wrong can you be?
I'm not even Jewish
Stop pestering me.

When he was not lashing out he wallowed in nostalgia. "Down the Drain" bemoans the disappearance of "the sweetest things in life," that somehow includes the "Czar of all the Russias," German zeppelins, and other supposed treasures of the recent past. "Turn Back the Clock" pretends to defend contemporary youngsters against complaints by reminding older listeners of the things they said when they were kids, but the song concentrates on a bygone age's preteen juvenilia, such as "your mother wears army shoes," which were clearly not analogous to the chants and slogans of "Make Love — Not War" and "Black Power!" that made the 1960s a period of historic social disruption and transformation. "Turn Back the Clock" was Sherman's white flag of surrender. Four years earlier he was, as he once accurately stated, avant-garde. In 1967, he was old hat.

But Sherman could still occasionally produce an amusing invention. "Signs" is a collection of commonly posted announcements and warnings Sherman strings together into a mock romantic pastiche of American life. The song comically insists that our culture's most important communications are these trivial ones, not the heartfelt utterances of love that usually accompany the parody's sultry music.

Keep off the grass
Children at play
No deposit no return
No casting today.
Wait for the dial tone.
Do not fold do not bend
Do not open till Christmas
Open other end.
No checks cashed
Make deliveries in the rear
Shake well before using

This end up, my dear.
Close cover before striking.
Do not push do not shove
No shorts in the dining room
Dump no rubbish, my love.
Made in Japan
Slippery when wet
Save this wrapper to dispose of gum
All sales final, my pet.

And Sherman could still craft a comic trapdoor for a pretentious song to fall into. With "If I Were a Tishman," his last Jewish parody of a Broadway musical, he took on the most famous and successful Jewish show of them all, *Fiddler on the Roof*. In *Fiddler*, Jewishness is out of the closet and apparently quite removed from the earlier Broadway musicals written by Jews that kept mum on the subject. But the price of this openness is sentimentality. Jewishness in *Fiddler* is celebrated for its quaint historical flavor. That made it similar to the antiquated folksongs popular in the 1950s, a formula that never sat well with Sherman.

Sherman's "Tishman" parody brought things up to date. It zeroed in on the spectacle of middle-class and affluent Jews identifying with the impoverished and charming Tevye, and made things uncomfortable for them. In "If I Were A Tishman," Sherman introduces the very wealthy and less charming Tishman family, whose billboards were once ubiquitous at construction sites throughout Manhattan. The parody reminds American Jews that they have reached the heights of financial power, and that people dream of being in *their* shoes. Here again, as with his "Harvey and Sheila" parody of "Hava Nagilah," Sherman's Jewish sense of irony corrects the American Jewish community's sentimentality with a dose of reality. Sherman's Tevye, complete with sighs and a frequent *oy*, imagines life as a Tishman.

I'd build the 6-6-6 Fifth Avenue building
Right in the middle of the town
One block wide and forty-eight stories high
And I'd have eighteen elevators going up

And twenty-seven more going down
All of them express to pass you by.

Togetherness went nowhere. It did not hit the charts and was not reviewed or otherwise noticed, but Sherman's name still had currency, and on June 24, 1967, *Billboard* reported that he and Tony Award–winning Broadway composer Albert Hague were at work on a Broadway musical called *Birth Is the Coward's Way Out*. Sam Fox Publishing Co. had signed Sherman and Hague and set about licensing the team's songs. Steve Lawrence was Fox's first customer. When the story broke, Lawrence had already recorded Sherman's affecting, "Did I Ever Really Live?" The song was also recorded by jazz singer Joe Williams, and performed by Gloria Loring.

You're born, you weep,
You smile, you sleep.
You cling, you crawl,
You stand, you fall.
You stand again, and try,
And then you walk.

The spare lyric continues to trace the arc from infancy to early childhood and youthful independence, after which Sherman's imagination sees not a long middle life but the approach of death, and uncertainty about how he conducted his life.

Too soon you'll hear a distant drum
Too soon the time to go will come
And time won't wait
Is it too late to ask,
Did I ever love?
Did I ever give?
Did I ever really live?

The song was for Sherman and Hague's Broadway musical that later took the name *The Fig Leaves Are Falling*, and both were inspired by Sherman's divorce. The show and the divorce were linked in other ways, too. He divorced in order to write it. In an interview he said, "It occurred to me suddenly that maybe I'd bought my freedom to write a musical." That insight rings truer than the conventional explanation he offered his wife that he fell in love with another woman. Loving another was not his strong suit. "After our divorce, he said I loved you as much as I could love anybody," Golden said. "He meant limited."

That did not stop him from pursuing women. In April 1967, he moved into a two-bedroom, one-bath unfurnished rental apartment at 118 East 60th Street, and from his twenty-second floor windows he had a view of New York's Playboy Club at 5 East 59th Street. "He would stand at the window with binoculars and when he saw something he liked he went shopping," said Mark Rosengarden. That might have been how he met a girlfriend remembered by friends and family only as Linda. She was a Playboy bunny. "Linda was a real good lady," Goldenberg said. "She was right there for him. She loved him for Allan." Family members disagree. "I think Linda was after his money," Nancy Sherman said. But Sherman's flightiness posed a challenge to gold diggers. At some point in late 1967 or early 1968, he left Linda for someone new. Later, after this new woman left him, he returned to Linda.

Crescent Dragonwagon does not remember which of Sherman's women she met when she visited him one night with her parents, Maurice and Charlotte Zolotow, but the girlfriend was young and beautiful and from Sherman's apartment's the city lights made a dazzling show. It was a paltry consolation for a terrible evening. "The main clear event I have is when we went to Allan's apartment when he was with the girlfriend and the sense of outrage in the house," Dragonwagon said. "My mother is supposed to go to the house and behave, but Sherman had deserted the woman who supported him and this could happen to us."

It was a terrifying prospect. Sherman's life was in a tailspin. On May 11, 1967, he was one of thirteen comedians featured on NBC's *Colgate Comedy Hour*. The *Los Angeles Times*, usually a reliable fan, reported Sherman was "not so funny." His behavior was also unfunny when he played the Hungry i in San Francisco the last week in September. Billy Goldenberg played piano, and Goldenberg's friend, David Kreitzer, came to a show and afterward hung out with Sherman, who was with a girlfriend. "He had his hand down the front of her dress and was massaging her chest," Kreitzer said. "You just ignore that. I never saw that behavior before."

Sherman may have been high. "I remember he had his joints made by Nat Sherman," New York's tony tobacconist, Kreitzer said. "They were rolled in pink paper and had gold tips with his name stamped in gold. He'd invite me over to do a 'pinkie.'" Marijuana, prepared in unusual ways, had become a regular diversion. "He would marinate his marijuana in Scotch, dry it out, and smoke it," Mark Rosengarden said. "Branch of marijuana in Johnny Walker, like thyme in vinegar . . . big huge buds soaking up the Scotch."

The marinade probably did not go to waste. By the end of 1967, intoxication was indispensible. Life had become too painful to live without it. On September 18, 1967, he and his ex-wife agreed to a division of assets that gave her the Bel Air house, a 1966 Lincoln automobile, a guaranteed payment of $50,000 upon the sale of his investment in cattle, and approximately half of his assets, including his deferred compensation held at Warner Bros., deferred royalty payments due Curtain Call Productions, and royalties from the sale of the Bill Cosby albums. In addition, he had to pay $3,000 a month in alimony. When children's book writer Stoo Hample, famous for his 1961 *Silly Book*, met Sherman in December 1967 he was a mess. "He was very lonely and very sad drinking lots of Scotch," Hample said. "Big tumblers full of brown liquid." The Zolotows introduced Hample to Sherman. They thought Hample could help him write the *Fig Leaves* musical, but nothing came of it. "I'd come to New York at noon but he wasn't up," said Hample, who lived in Larchmont. "I'd pound on the door. There were sleep marks on his face." Then instead of working, Sherman wanted to go shopping. "He did the real baby talk. 'No! Let's go to Bloomingdales and buy some presents for our friends.'"

Irresponsible spending was a lifelong habit, but he could no longer afford it. Sherman had to earn money, and in 1968 he went on the road to play whatever performance dates he could land. In January he was in Chicago at Mister Kelly's, in February it was the Hotel Tropicana in Las Vegas, and in March he played Miami's Deauville Hotel. In mid-June he was the emcee at the Daytop Music Festival on New York's Staten Island, and at the end of the month he was booked into the Cape Cod Melody Tent. Meanwhile, bad news kept coming. On June 11, 1968, his relationship with Warner Bros. Records ended. "We have decided not to exercise our option for an extension of the term of your contract," Warner Bros. wrote Sherman, who kept on touring. In August he again played the Catskill Mountains. This time he was not at the top tier Concord Hotel but the humbler Stevensville, and in September he was back in Miami to close a series of summer lawn parties sponsored by the city's tourist bureau. He also landed some television appearances. From August until the end of the year, as the January 1969 Broadway opening of *Fig Leaves* neared, Sherman appeared on the *Merv Griffin Show*, *Tonight*, the *Mike Douglas Show*, and a program called *Showtime*, hosted by comedian Godfrey Cambridge.

Sometime during 1968, Sherman took Linda to London, where he visited his friend Jon Hendricks. "He complained about his girlfriend," Hendricks said. "We felt that he was very unhappy and this unhappiness was going to kill him. And he needed to find a woman who really and truly loved him, and I don't think that was happening." Nevertheless, by the end of 1968 Sherman announced he planned to marry Linda, an event that would never take place. "They drove up to see me to tell me at the end of 1968," said Nancy Sherman, who was then a sixteen-year-old high school student at the Woodstock Country School, a boarding school in Woodstock, Vermont. She chose the location in part to be closer to her father in New York, and he helped his daughter with the school application. "At my junior high we had the 440[-yard] run. Most people did it in two to three minutes but I did it in four," she said. "My father said on my application to private school I should say, 'no one came near me in the 440.'"

That was charming and decent. Sherman's wit helped him express love. But such endearments were nearly all the power his wit had left. It could not energize his musical, *The Fig Leaves Are Falling*.

TWELVE
HALLOWED BE THY GAME

Sherman's rightly forgotten musical is preserved only in works such as *Not Since Carrie: Forty Years of Broadway Musical Flops*, but at least one of its songs is worth remembering.

The Fig Leaves Are Falling opened on January 2, 1969, at New York's Broadhurst Theater and closed after four performances. The idea for it was lifted directly from Sherman's life, but the show itself did not embody an idea at all, just tired sentiments and urges that sunk the work and exposed his personal failings. Like Sherman, the play's middle-aged hero, Harry Stone, has a wife, Lillian, of twenty years; a son and a daughter; and a mistress twenty years his junior named Pookie that the *New York Times* described as "a mini-skirted mini-brain." During the course of the show, Stone must choose between Lillian and Pookie, but their names alone relieve any tension surrounding the eventual decision, which the actors sometimes called upon the audience to help solve. Sherman unwisely brought some of his game show background to the stage. In the 1950s, part of his job as a television producer was to whip up audience enthusiasm, and Harry Stone tries the same, at one point asking all the men in the audience that "have been unfaithful to their wives to raise their hands." A reviewer assures his readers, "Don't worry, they don't have the nerve to go through with it. But there are enough other things to be embarrassed by." One of these, noted the *New Yorker*, was a "*very* low point" when Stone, played by Barry Nelson, "awarded a roast chicken to ticket-holder B-3 — a lady from Sarasota, who sounded understandably dismayed by her good fortune."

Witless gimmicks were not the worst *Fig Leaves* had to offer. "Oddly enough, the show is not as exasperating as its attitude," one critic wrote. The offending attitude was familiar to the ever-fewer listeners Sherman's albums found after 1964. It was fear of "America's youth revolution. The whole business of young idealism. . . . But there is one part of this revolution that this mentality finds very appealing and that, of course, is sexual freedom. Now THERE is something that appeals to [Stone and his ilk] — all those mini-skirts willing to be lifted." This attitude was merely immaturity, and it was deadly. "All the innuendoes, leers, the self-conscious coyness is unbearable," a reviewer wrote. It was more proof that by the late 1960s Sherman was completely out of touch. A review in *The Hollywood Reporter* had no trouble diagnosing the problem.

The people in Larchmont, from whence Sherman's hero and the bulk of his potential audience come, know by now that their kids didn't just march for the sake of marching or blast the establishment in the same way that daddy used to swallow a goldfish. They're also beginning to discover that they're more than sex-deprived pinheads. But these are the bizarre premises of the "Fig Leaves" book, and nobody, not even in Larchmont, ever bought humor without an anchor in reality.

The musical's saving grace was the actress Dorothy Loudon, who played Lillian, the show's most intelligent and sympathetic character. Sherman realized, at least in the part of himself that wrote, that he should not have left his wife. *Fig Leaves'* second act, which even its severest critics admitted was entertaining, came to life because it centered on Lillian, who is celebrated in the rousing, "Lillian, Lillian, Lillian," and permitted to blossom in her delivery of "All My Laughter," which expresses her awakening after her husband leaves her for Pookie but before he returns home. Some reviewers hated the show so much they could not bother to praise Sherman for the songs they liked, but *Variety* recognized that though the story was terrible, "one outstanding element . . . are the lyrics by Sherman." In "All My Laughter," he got across the endless desire for sensation he satisfied through the stimulants of performance, sex, gambling, eating, drinking, and laughter.

> I want to laugh
> All of my laughter
> I want to cry
> All of my tears
> I want to turn on the lights
> And see all of the sights
> And hear all of the music before it disappears.
> I want to sing
> All of my love songs
> I want to drink
> All of my wine
> I want to ride on a skylark
> And fly a giraffe
> This life is my lark
> And I won't take half.
> I want to laugh
> All of my laughter before I go.

The trouble with the wish expressed in the song is getting the timing right. After *Fig Leaves* closed Sherman had laughed nearly all his laughter, but he was still around.

The weeks following the end of his Broadway dream brought the end of his marriage. His divorce had been generating paperwork and legal fees for two and a half years, but finally on January 31, 1969, Sherman signed the application for final judgment of divorce, and on February 6 his marriage to Dee was dissolved. That ending did not lead to a new beginning. His girlfriend Linda left him. "After the play flopped she was out of there," Nancy Sherman said. His former musical arranger, Lou Busch, told Stan Cornyn at Warner Bros.,

"If ever I saw success ruin a guy, it was Allan. He blew the wife, the kids, and eventually, the money, too." Extended family and friends also drifted away. Rose Hackman was Sherman's cousin on his mother's side, and in the early 1960s the Hackmans lived near the Shermans in Los Angeles and socialized with them often, but "once Allan and Dee split up we lost touch," said Rose's son, Michael Hackman. "My mom was Allan's relative but we wound up being closer to Dee." Morris Zolotow made the same choice. "My father became friends with Dee," said Crescent Dragonwagon. "Every Wednesday they went to the movies along with Alvin Toffler and Betty Friedan." Sherman's ex-wife moved in more elite circles than Sherman did as an ex-celebrity.

At first, Sherman appeared to weather the divorce and *Fig Leaves* failure well. He did not let his Broadway disaster become a humiliation that drove him from public view. Instead, he seems to have forced himself to appear in public, whatever the venue, because his first post–*Fig Leaves* performance was February 7 in suburban White Plains, New York, where Catholic Relief Services sponsored a small benefit for the people of Biafra. He soon landed higher profile gigs and appeared on the *Joey Bishop Show* in March and April and the *Tonight* show on March 17. On April 25, 1969, Sherman then returned to Los Angeles where he taped an appearance on the popular *Dating Game* television show that aired May 3. It was an odd setting for the forty-four-year-old parodist, but he looked better than he had in years. In a dark suit, white shirt, and necktie that had a multicolored psychedelic print, Sherman's color was deep his weight noticeable but under control, and a post-divorce goatee and receding hair were well trimmed. The show opened with him singing his parody of "Spanish Flea," the *Dating Game*'s theme song and a hit for Herb Alpert & the Tijuana Brass. Sherman recorded the parody on his 1967 *Togetherness* album. It had a lighthearted romantic theme that suited the television show.

> I've got a sweetheart flea, cute kid.
> Lives on a beagle near Madrid.
> If she can sublet her beagle
> I'll make her my legal first wife
> And we'll live a dog's life.

"Most women are crazy. Most people in general are crazy," was Sherman's opening statement to the three bachelorettes, and he wanted to know how crazy they were on a scale of 1 to 100. He also wanted to know how pretty each thought the others were, and he volunteered that his nose was straightened and so he had false cartilage there. Were any of them wearing anything false? The former game show producer knew how to spice up a show, but most interesting is the woman he chose as his date. She was the most giggly and girly of the three and certainly not the audience's favorite, which was the beautiful, good–humored, and self-confident bachelorette number three. With regard to the attractiveness of the contestants she told Sherman, "I would say you've got a pretty good choice here." And her response to his question about what false item she might have was, "What I've got false I'm not about to tell you." That stopped the show as the audience laughed and applauded, but Sherman was not having any. *Fig Leaves'* Harry Stone returned to the sensible and adult Lillian. Sherman preferred Pookie.

By the summer he was hustling to get back into show business. In June 1969 his manager Bill Loeb reportedly arranged for Sherman to work with London-based record producer Shel Talmy, famous for his work with rock bands such as the Who. "I wish I could tell you that was true," wrote Talmy about the purported arrangement. "I would have loved to record Allan, but unfortunately was never contacted by Bill Loeb or anybody else about doing it." In August, Sherman claimed to have a number of projects in the works that are more obviously fictitious, such as a television pilot for a "situation comedy in which he's to appear" and another for "an adult 'Laugh-In,'" but said what he really wanted to do was direct film comedies. What came through for him was more modest and disappointing. On January 8, 1970, he was part of the television special, "A Last Laugh at the Sixties," which featured great comic acts of the decade such as Mike Nichols and Elaine May. Their coffin-salesman routine was as fresh as ever, wrote *Daily Variety*, but Sherman's "Sarah Jackman" was "a tedious hangover." In March he performed at the Writers Guild Awards "minishow," a scaled-down version of the formerly bigger productions, but in April he had a chance to relive the perks of stardom when he was on a guest list that included Rod Serling and actors Candice Bergen and Dennis

Hopper. They all were invited to Hugh Hefner's Chicago mansion for an anti-Vietnam War dinner that found itself picketed by anti-*Playboy* magazine protesters from the growing women's movement. Sherman was reliably liberal. During the politically charged summer of 1968, he performed at a rally in Washington, D.C. to support Eugene McCarthy, who unsuccessfully sought the Democratic nomination for president. But when it came to women and sex, he sided with Hefner.

Sherman ended 1970 singing at Miami's Carillon Hotel during the Christmas holiday, and in March 1971 he performed for the second time at the Writers Guild Awards show, which was evidently a bigger event than the previous year. He found himself alongside comics Don Rickles and Jack Carter. Though he had not displayed any interest in Jewish material for years Jewish venues offered him work, and he took it. On June 13, 1971, he sang at Los Angeles's Wilshire Ebell Theater for the B'nai B'rith's "Salute to Israel's 23rd Anniversary." He did a decent acting job in the miserable low-budget 1972 movie, *Pepper and His Wacky Taxi*, but unsurprisingly the bit part led to nothing. By October of that year, Sherman's obscurity warranted him an appearance in *Newsweek*'s "Where Are They Now?" column.

As his diminished stature began to sink in, Sherman's physical condition worsened. Jerry Goldstein met up with him in 1971 and did not like what he saw. "Not well. Pasty-faced, no color. Already in major decline." One night at a Chinese restaurant with Morris Zolotow and Zolotow's daughter, Sherman was drinking and "collapsed face down in the soup," Dragonwagon said. His drinking was out of control. "Allan became alcoholic," Golden said. His old road manager, Tabolsky, ran into Sherman in an office building on Wilshire Boulevard. "I was standing in the lobby waiting for the elevator and Allan walked in. Didn't know what to say to him," Tabolsky said. "He just let himself go, and that's what killed him."

At least Tabolsky's sighting proved Sherman left his apartment. That was not the impression Tommy Smothers of Smothers Brothers fame got in 1971 when he and Sherman both lived in the Empire West condominium at 1100 Alta Loma Road. "It was sad. He was up there in his room. I don't think he ever went out." Sherman was writing, and he handed Smothers a manuscript.

"I could not put it down. I thought it was the best thing I ever read," said Smothers, who eventually purchased the rights to the work. "I don't know why it struck me so much. I really got deeply into the book."

Sherman's intelligent and amusing *Every 600 Years, on a Tuesday (The Journey to the Perfectly Fair)* was inspired by the children's story, *The Cat in the Hat*. An animated version of the Dr. Seuss book appeared on television March 10, 1971, with the voice of the cat supplied by Sherman. A reviewer called the show "an atrocious rendering," but the child-centered story with absent parents and a magical visitor spurred Sherman to create his own version about and for his own children. As in the Seuss story, at the start of *Every 600 Years* Robert and Nancy are frustrated, but boredom is not their problem. They are angry with their parents, unhappy with each other, and vexed at the unfair way the world seems to work.

> The children felt they'd been unfairly thrown out,
> And as a result, they were sulking about,
> Making faces, insulting, and teasing each other —
> And deeply resenting their father and mother.
> Their sad little hearts felt a hopeless awareness:
> In this Cruel World, there's a rareness of Fairness.

To the rescue comes a troll named Whatsizname that once every 600 years on a Tuesday has an unusual job.

> I'm the Chief Make-Up Man at The Perfectly Fair!
> Little Nancy said, "Lipstick and powder and such?"
> The Troll almost fell down, from laughing so much.
> "No not that kind of make-up — false rouge and fake lashes!
> Real Make-Up — for Fights, Disagreements and Clashes.

The sentimentality that was an embarrassment in his autobiography, and also in "Summer's Magical Music," a July 1971 article he published in *Reader's Digest* that humorlessly touts the "rhapsody of being alive, the mad waltz of energy and joy," works well in his unpublished children's story. Robert and Nancy learn that despite appearances to the contrary, there is fairness in life, and that even death is just payment for the gift of life. And the children, diverted by Whatsizname's antics and lessons, forget their animosity. "Thus the sweet sibling dears / Exchanged civil words for the first time in years."

Crucially, Sherman does not forget to be entertaining and funny. As every good children's story should, his contains adventures with villains that hate children, and at the hands of these Robert and Nancy hear a list of the crimes children commit. They are the injustices Sherman felt he suffered as a child, and that as an adult committed to the virtues of childhood he never forgot.

> "You climbed over the fence," the Chief said, "but that's mild.
> The worst crime you've committed is Being A Child."
> "Do you mean," asked the children, "you actually punish
> Human beings for being not yet twenty-oneish?"
> That's right," the Chief said. "Kindly listen with awe
> As I read you the text of The Anti-Child Law:
> First: Be it herein set forth as disclosure
> That babies go naked. (Indecent Exposure).
> Furthermore, when in need of emotion-release
> They cry rather loudly. (Disturbing The Peace).
> Whereas they stay up, full of vigor and zest,
> Until long past their bedtimes. (Resisting A Rest).

Daily Variety reported on August 9, 1971, Sherman's claim that *Every 600 Years* was "being prepped for animation." There is no evidence this was true. Its value was as a gift of love to his children. It was Sherman's attempt to teach something and perhaps make amends for his shortcomings as a parent, which were then in the spotlight. On October 22, 1971, his ex-wife filed notice with Los Angeles Superior Court that he was not paying alimony or child support. Their original agreement called for him to make $3,000-per-month alimony payments from October 1, 1967, until September 1, 1968, when the amount was reduced to $2,000. But on January 1, 1970, Sherman missed a payment. The same thing happened in March, May, June, July, October, November, and December, and all of 1971. Child support for Nancy was $250 per month, a payment he missed four times in 1969, nine times in 1970, and every month in 1971. Robert's support payments were also erratic. All together, with interest penalties on missed payments, Sherman owed Dee $53,635.95. He did not have it, and beginning on January 1, 1972, in recognition of his reduced circumstances, his alimony payments were set at the symbolic $1 a year.

Child support payments for Nancy continued. In the spring of 1970 she was seventeen and still at the Woodstock school in Vermont. Her decision to attend it to be nearer her father in New York left her isolated when in the spring of 1969 he returned to California. She graduated in June 1970 and came home to attend the University of California at Santa Cruz, and then Irvine. She soon became used to her father's deteriorating health. "One night the phone rang late and he said he was sick," Golden said. Sherman was at the Los Angeles Playboy club when he was rushed to Century City hospital. Nancy went to the hospital to look after her father, and when she returned her mother wondered why she had been gone so long. Nancy explained there was the usual ton of paperwork to complete. "She did it so many times," Golden said. "She was a kid!" Nancy continued to show her father great care and consideration. When in the summer of 1973 he was hospitalized to lose weight, she visited him on weekends to take him to the movies, Golden said. "I said to Nancy, you don't have to do that. Live your own life. She said, I want to."

Robert's support payments did come to an end. In 1971 he turned twenty-one, and a year later he went to work for his father's old boss, Mark Goodson. Robert had left college without a degree after several years of classes at Brandeis University, California State University at Northridge, and Santa Monica College. He was more interested in the world of television production his father once inhabited, and in the life his father continued to lead. With Sherman back in Los Angeles, father and son spent time together in unusual ways. "He met someone who worked for RAND who said, why don't you join MENSA, so we took the test and joined together," Robert said. The high-IQ pair also made excursions to the Los Angeles suburb of Gardena, a center of legal gambling. "I had never played poker for real money before that," Robert said. "I was not familiar with the rules and caused grumbling around the table." His father did not have that problem. "He knew it cold."

All of Sherman's interests were still in evidence. He wrote about children in *Every 600 Years*, frequented the Playboy club, and gambled, and in 1971 he revisited for the last time the theme of Jewish identity that made him famous and generated his greatest comic accomplishments. In the unpublished essay,

"My Moment of Truth Happened 29 Years Ago, but I Didn't Understand It until Last Thursday," he remembered the September 1942 fraternity rush week at the University of Illinois when a non-Jew mistakenly applied for and was accepted into Sherman's Jewish fraternity. The moment of truth arrived when the error was discovered. "'Just a minute,' I said. 'Dink has been here all through Rush Week. Didn't anybody ever mention the fact that we're Jewish?' We all looked at each other and shrugged our shoulders. The depth of our tragedy began to dawn on us. We hadn't mentioned it. Why should we, when we were all so busy being Gentile?" That was when Sherman realized how much of themselves Jews regularly submerged. "American Jews of my generation had a gentleman's agreement, a tacit conspiracy to kill off our own heritage. We grew up obsessed with one goal, to *assimilate*." In the essay, Sherman connected this hidden life to his life's work. At his all-Jewish Boy Scout troop in Los Angeles, "we all had an inner sense of absurdity; a little voice that kept telling us, You are *not* a Troop of Boy Scouts. You are a *parody* on a Troop of Boy Scouts." This is his answer to the frequently asked question, why are so many comedians Jews. The Jewish double inside the assimilated citizen views himself and the general life he participates in as ridiculous.

The essay did not inspire Sherman to write any new Jewish comedy. He had already written the songs that undid his assimilation, and the assimilation of the millions who laughed. Instead, he wrote about sex, a topic that fascinated him since junior high school.

His youthful poems about sex were often better than pieces he wrote as an adult. As early as 1967, when Sherman began singing *Fig Leaves* songs in night-clubs, a reviewer saw the problem. "He turns out to be surprisingly tasteless with several parodies concerned with sex." The reviewer might have heard, "Sex Is Better," which Sherman intended but did not include in his musical. "Chopin's Polonaise / Rates the highest praise / I know thirty ways / Sex is better." It is a testament to Sherman's obsessive determination to create something comic and original in this vein that after *Fig Leaves* tanked he kept at it. In December 1971, *Playboy* published his "Griselda and the Porn-O-Phone," a short story about an innocent from Puritan Ethic, Wisconsin, whose sexual hunger is awakened when she is the accidental recipient of an obscene phone call. She then subscribes to an obscene phone call service to ensure a steady supply. It was not a bad comic premise, but Sherman's story is as ambivalent as its creator. He slept around and then condemned Peyton Place, and "Griselda" is unhappy with sexual repression and also liberation. Griselda's male counterpart discovers Porn-O-Phone and becomes "hopelessly addicted." Sex is an unsolvable problem, which could have been a powerful theme, but Sherman's story does nothing more than point at it, while also trying to juggle another unresolved idea about the superficiality of a sexy image.

Despite these weaknesses and loose ends, the story generated a contract for Sherman to write a book for Playboy Press about the decline and fall of Griselda's hometown. *The Rape of the A*P*E** appeared in August 1973 and explained itself in an unwieldy subtitle as *The Official History of the Sex Revolution, 1945–1973, the Obscening of America, an R*S*V*P* Document.* The asterisks point the reader to the meaning of the acronym and abbreviation. A*P*E* stands for American Puritan Ethic and R*S*V*P* for Redeeming Social Value Pornography. All this hot air unintentionally revealed the book's weaknesses. It is often a rambling and strained comic effort stuffed with earnest, tiresome, and faux hip rants against conventional morality. "The APE made us ashamed of our bodies, our thoughts, our feelings. The APE robbed us of certain inalienable rights, and among these rights were sex, nudity and the pursuit of horniness."

However, for the dogged reader a discovery awaits. The middle section of the book is funny. As one patient reviewer discovered, "cloaked in disappointing opening and closing sections, this is a book in disguise. Its central 310 pages are neither stupid nor hypocritical" and is not so much for promiscuity as honesty and humor. Sherman treats the Magic Fuck, an idea that Erica Jong called zipless in her *Fear of Flying* that appeared a few months later in November 1973, with the comedy it deserves. "The Magic F**k will just happen, spontaneously," and "will seem to be happening with unusual speed and efficiency. No time will be wasted on the old dull preliminaries such as introductions, social amenities, flirtation, courtship, romance, seduction or foreplay." In addition, one's partner "will remain awake throughout." Finally, "you and partner will enter orgasm at precisely the same instant, as measured by the nuclear chronometer at the U.S. Naval Observatory." But in the book's last pages he did an about face and presented the same scenario straight. His idealized lovers experience a "sweet serenity such as neither of them had ever known." Sex remained a maddening conundrum for Sherman until the end of his life. Its ecstasies seemed to him to prove "that living is magic," a romantic idea his comic instincts undercut, but the comic shrewdness he exhibited since adolescence often deserted him now as he grew more desperate for life to come out right. As a review of *Rape* noted, "Sherman has a sense of aggrieved innocence, and he is genuinely upset that the emperor wears no clothes."

In 1973, however, his problems were more than philosophical. During a September interview with the *Chicago Daily News*, Sherman was "more concerned about his health than his humor." He had good reasons. To prepare for his book tour he spent fourteen weeks during the spring and summer of 1973 in the Motion Picture Hospital to lose thirty pounds. His old friend Jerry Hopkins visited him there and found Sherman entranced by the televised Watergate hearings that were bringing down the Nixon presidency. "Haldeman, Erlichman, all the names rhyme," he told Hopkins as he jotted ideas for song parodies that do not survive.

His weight loss brought limited benefits. In photographs, a full and bushy beard largely obscured his face, but he was obviously much heavier than he was four years earlier on the *Dating Game*. And the *Chicago Daily News* noted his voice "was husky, wheezy asthmatic." He took medication constantly. Plus there was another terrible health problem that brought the threat of death close to home. In 1973, his son Robert was diagnosed with acoustic neuromas, tumors in his inner ears. Robert knew something was wrong. At work producing game shows for Mark Goodson he was dizzy, and he went from doctor to doctor for advice until he visited Los Angeles's House Clinic, a center for ear diseases. Surgeries saved his life, but Sherman distanced himself from the specter of death that hung over his son. He was in the waiting room during Robert's surgery when a doctor "still covered in blood" approached him and Dee and told them Robert probably only had six months to live, Golden said. Sherman's response was bizarre. "He asked the surgeon, 'Do you know of a good place to eat?' The doctor said, 'we eat in the hospital.'" Sherman went to a local deli. Dee remained at the hospital to phone family. "He thought we got lost" because she did not show up at the deli, Golden said.

After a lifetime of bad habits his inexcusable behavior seems to reveal that his self-destructive tendencies shrank to nothing in the face of death. Or perhaps his decision to consume deli was an unconscious embrace of death, a wish to hurry it along. Life had become less attractive than ever. In January 1973 his ex-wife announced she would marry again, and on February 25 she wed Bill Golden, a public relations executive at MGM. "He was a wonderful man," Golden said. This hit Sherman hard. His attitude toward his relationship with his ex-wife was typically immature. It resembled a child's toward his parents. "He thought I'd always be there," Golden said.

On March 24, 1973, Steve Allen produced a comedy show at Carnegie Hall called "Steve Allen & His Friends." Sherman was not there in person, presumably because he was too weak and fat to travel. He could no longer get behind the wheel of a car and had to be driven by friends, Golden said. But the audience saw a film clip of Sherman in a parody advertisement for saki that was well received. In October another animated Dr. Seuss show put Sherman's voice back on television as the narrator of "Green Eggs and Ham" and other stories.

These trivial achievements made his *Rape of the APE* book all the more important to him, and on November 19 he complained to friend and public relations pro Sol Zatt that *Playboy* was not doing enough to promote it. Zatt gently hinted to Sherman that the book was not doing well because it was not very good, and the conversation headed in a new direction. Sherman was excited about a new project, a record album. "It's going to be to golf what 'Casey at the Bat' was to baseball."

"Hallowed Be Thy Game: The Gospel According to St. Andrews" is a re-telling of the biblical creation story to account for the existence of golf, which delivers heavenly satisfactions and hellish frustrations. It is not set to music and is not a rhyme. It is a stand-up comedy routine Sherman began performing live on July 14, 1972, when he appeared at Southern California's posh La Costa Country Club, which attracted golf pros and star amateurs such as Frank Sinatra, Bing Crosby, and Bob Hope. The subject played to Sherman's interests and strengths, and he pulled off a one-liner almost equal to his great "drapes of Roth" pun.

God intended golf to be a pleasure, Sherman informed his audience, but the devil created sand traps and water traps and all manner of lies, including "the downhill lie and the uphill lie and the sidehill lie and that unspeakable abomination the unplayable lie." But to save the game's players from eternal torments, God invented "the opponent who is a better player than you but needs your friendship for business reasons," and also "the unputtable putt, which he called the gimme." Golf's Ten Commandments guide players to the right path, ordering them to "replace thy divots as thou wouldst have others replace their divots before thee." The routine culminates in a golf contest between God and the Devil, and when the Devil stands in front of God on the putting green, God says, "'Thou knowest thou art not supposed to stand in front of me whilst I putt.' And the Devil said, 'Whither shall I go, oh Lord?' And the Lord said, 'Get thee behind me, Satan.'"

Sherman performed this excellent routine again on May 20, 1973, when it was recorded live for Warner Bros. Records. Joe Smith gave Sherman a $5,000 advance for the project, and after Sherman completed his *Rape of the APE* book tour he looked forward to the golf album he talked about with Sol Zatt on November 19. Sherman did not waste time. He asked Warner sound engineer Rudy Hill to bring a tape of the golf performance the next day to his new apartment at 1155 La Cienega Boulevard. Sherman wanted to review it, and Hill brought Sherman the tape at about 5 PM on November 20. Hill was still with Sherman three hours later when Sherman suffered a heart attack. "I called the doctor and began to give him mouth-to-mouth resuscitation," Hill told Warner's Stan Cornyn. "He regurgitated in my mouth, and then he died." When emergency medical personnel arrived they tried but failed to revive Sherman. He died ten days shy of turning forty-nine.

Over the next two days Sherman received more press than he had in years. Obituaries ran in newspapers across the country, with the *New York Times* outdoing all competitors. Its article with a photo treated Sherman and his comic creations with respect and appreciation, and delighted in reminding readers how his "antic wit transformed such songs as 'Frere Jacques' into 'Sarah Jackman,' [and] turned 'The Battle Hymn of the Republic' into the saga of a garment center cutter who trampled 'through the warehouse where the drapes of Roth are stored.'"

A memorial service was held November 23 at Hillside Memorial Park, and a notice that morning in *Daily Variety* attracted about two hundred "friends, relatives, and admirers," wrote Steve Allen, who in his eulogy said of Sherman, "if there are such things as heavenly music, as choirs of angels, the possibilities of parody are already occurring to him." Sherman was cremated and interred at Hillside Memorial Park on November 26, 1973.

Questions soon arose about Sherman's will. His New York lawyer from Becker & London was in California when Sherman died, and he told Golden the will was on his desk but he did not know if Sherman had signed it, Golden said. The fear was that he left his money, and more importantly his interest in his song properties to a lover he had at the end of his life. He did not. His only directive was a four sentence, hand-written will he had written on October 7, 1963, that left everything to his "beloved wife, Dolores (Dee)."

Golden's second husband died on January 14, 1986, and she died on July 17, 2012, at age 87 in Salt Lake City, where she had moved in 2003 to live near her daughter, who is married with three children. Robert Sherman recovered from his surgeries and worked at Mark Goodson Productions until 1989, when he moved on to the Family Channel and eventually his own production company. He also manages the Sherman estate.

A friend told Stoo Hample that he was in a record store when Sherman died. "Allan Sherman's *geshtarben*," the owner told a clerk in Yiddish. "Put his records out front."

THIRTEEN
HAIL TO THEE, FAT PERSON

By the time Sherman died, his descent from stardom was complete. All of his albums were out of print. In the early 1970s, after a tumultuous decade of mass peace and civil rights demonstrations, riots, political assassinations, and the public spectacle of Watergate the country could not respond to his clever but nonabrasive comedy and was ready for the hard stuff. Richard Pryor and Joan Rivers were among the new comics that delivered. On Pryor's 1974 album, *That Nigger's Crazy*, the "Have Your Ass Home by 11" routine revisits his teenage years with an abusive father. "Be home by 11! You understand '11' don't ya nigger? You can tell time, can't ya? What's that clock say in the kitchen, nigger. The clock, motherfucker, what's that clock say?" Joan Rivers was mild by comparison, but she never let the sentimentality of Sherman's *Fig Leaves* distract her from the conviction that the battle of the sexes was war. "Face it darlings, it isn't easy being a woman. No man's ever made love to you because you cleaned the linoleum." As an unmarried woman in her mid-twenties, she was an embarrassment and a burden to her family. "My mother had two of us at home that weren't, as the expression goes, moving." As a result, anyone was good enough for her. "Oh, Joan, there's a most attractive young man down here with a mask and a gun." But no one captured the new mood or garnered the success to prove it like George Carlin, whose 1972 *Class Clown* album included the "seven words you can never say on television" bit that became part of the language. By the end of 1976, *Class Clown* had sold almost 775,000 units. Sherman sold more copies of *My Son, the Folk Singer* in about four months, as opposed to Carlin's four years, but Carlin's career was still going strong. "When someone sells 1000 a month on a catalogue item . . . that shows what a solid following he has," his manager told *Variety*. Such longevity was exceptional, and the best contrasting example of a defunct act was Allan Sherman. "'The real big (comedy LP) hits [of years ago] you couldn't give away today,' he says, 'even though they were tremendous, like Allen [*sic*] Sherman.'"

The rise of Woody Allen and Mel Brooks in the late 1960s and early 1970s also helped diminish Sherman's reputation, though the two Jewish filmmakers shared the outlook of the song parodist. Unlike Pryor or Rivers, Brooks and Allen were too absurd for anger, and they agreed with Sherman that parody was the best way to shatter genres that had become a bore. *Blazing Saddles* did to the movie western what *Folk Singer* did to folk music, but the 1974 film admitted that Jews were peripheral to the classic and typically sanitized story. Sherman's "The Streets of Miami" put Jews in a cowboy gunfight, but it shed more comic light on the bad blood between Jewish business partners than nineteenth-century Americans. Blacks were the important overlooked minority of the Hollywood western, and the frank racism of *Blazing Saddles'* white townspeople was the movie's joke on the genre. Jews would not have made a satisfactory substitute.

Woody Allen's parodies of the crime caper in *Take the Money and Run*, science fiction movies in *Sleeper*, the hardboiled Humphrey Bogart hero in *Play It Again, Sam*, and the historical drama in *Love and Death* all followed the Sherman pattern by substituting a Jewish everyman for the stoic and heroic male lead. In each case, Allen's characters look around their worlds and see an inventory of drapes where they were told there would be grapes. "Science, I don't believe in science. Science is an intellectual dead end. It's a lot of little guys in tweed suits," his character says at the end of *Sleeper*. But Allen added a new ingredient to the parody formula. His characters are on the make. They want to bed the female lead and are frank about their sexual hunger. All are on the lookout for *Sleeper*'s orgasmatron, the ultimate sexual high. Brooks also made sex generate laughs simply by recognizing its existence where it had been denied, such as in Frankenstein's monster. If he is a man, he must have the sexual drives of a man. "Oh, sweet mystery of life / At last I found you," sings Madeline Kahn as she has sex with the monster in *Young Frankenstein*. Sexuality became the new firepower Jewish parodists used to blast pop culture products that were suffocating on their own dignity. It was the new frontier. The comic payoff of placing Jews in scenarios that once excluded them was meager. It had been done. Sherman also turned away from it after his first three albums and tried to make comedy out of sexual material, but he never found the right approach.

For years, Sherman's songs were relegated to offbeat corners of the radio universe, most prominently on the successful and proudly bizarre Dr. Demento radio program. "Two hours each week of ABSOLUTE INSANITY featuring the music and comedy of Monty Python, Tom Lehrer, Spike Jones, Frank Zappa, Allan Sherman," promised a 1982 advertisement. That year, Demento's weekly radio program was heard on 150 rock 'n' roll stations across the country. "I didn't really push Allan Sherman on my listeners," Dr. Demento said. "They asked for him." Demento's eclectic playlist was the kind of loose collection that became a refuge for Sherman's creations, though it was often the same creation over and over, "Hello Muddah." In 1977, Warner Bros. included the hit on *25 Years of Recorded Comedy*, a three-disc set that included virtually every name act, from Lenny Bruce to Nichols and May. Another collection in 1979 to mark Warner Bros.' twentieth anniversary included both straight music and comedy. "Sarah Jackman" was on the six-album set.

For die-hard fans, the all-Sherman alternative was the "best of" albums that began appearing in 1965 with *The Best of Allan Sherman*, a record that reveals how his reputation had changed from Jewish song parodist to creator of assorted novelty songs. Its ten songs included only one from the *Folk Singer* album, "Sir Greenbaum's Madrigal," ignoring the far better "Shake Hands with Your Uncle Max," "The Streets of Miami," and "The Ballad of Harry Lewis." The "Hello Muddah" hit was a requirement, and the other cuts skipped from his role as a comic journalist that pointed out the country's bad habits ("Green

Stamps" and "Little Butterball") to madcap creator of fun nonsense ("Mexican Hat Dance," "You Went the Wrong Way Old King Louie," and "Skin"). Another Sherman collection did not appear for eleven years, when Warner Bros. released *The Very Best of Allan Sherman* in 1976. The title protested too much. Its selections, which included duds such as "The Twelve Gifts of Christmas," "That Old Back Scratcher," and "A Waste of Money" were not the very best, or even very good, though its twelve songs allowed for increased representation from *Folk Singer*. *Very Best* offered "My Zelda" and "Sarah Jackman."

In 1979, Rhino Records produced *Best of Allan Sherman*. It was the first Sherman compilation to include "Harvey and Sheila," one of his greatest creations, and it rescued from obscurity the rollicking "Good Advice," but despite its roomy twelve-song roster it snubbed every *Folk Singer* tune except "Sarah Jackman." Rhino's audience was young people excited by the company's talent for "the discovery and promotion of contemporary weirdness." That audience was less likely to be fans of Allan Sherman than of a new breed of Jewish comedian like Robert Klein, whose 1975 "I Can't Stop My Leg," a musical parody of blues music and musicians, owed a debt to Sherman that Klein fans were unlikely to trace. They might, however, get a kick from *My Son, the Nut*'s zany, "Eight Foot Two, Solid Blue," about a Martian's infatuation with his extraterrestrial girlfriend. "Her steering wheel / Has sex appeal / Her evening gown is stainless steel / Has anybody seen my gal."

The 1979 album apparently sated the market's minimal Sherman appetite for seven more years. *A Gift of Laughter (The Best of Allan Sherman, Volume II)* did not appear until 1986, but it was quickly followed by the 1988, *My Son, the Greatest: The Best of Allan Sherman*. *Greatest* took advantage of the compact disc medium to offer customers nineteen songs. Aficionados were nonplussed. "The re-issued compilations on Sherman have helped fill the gap somewhat," wrote a comedy record expert of the 1979 and 1986 Sherman albums, just before *Greatest* was released. "A re-issue of 'My Son, the Folksinger [*sic*] would have been a better beginning." That criticism was still valid after *Greatest* went on sale. It did not include "The Ballad of Harry Lewis."

Few made the distinction between Sherman's best and lesser works. By the early 1990s, Sherman had no cachet and critics seemed to try and outdo each other in putting the parodist down. In a December 9, 1992, review of the Off-Broadway musical revue *Hello Muddah, Hello Fadduh!* the *New York Times* wrote Sherman's song material "often feels quite musty," though it liked "The Ballad of Harry Lewis" and "One Hippopatami." A year later on December 19, 1993, the *Times* decided the show, which employed Sherman's songs to tell the life stories of Barry Bockman and Sarah Jackman was worse than musty. The paper warned Jewish audiences that "[h]aving the ethnic sensibility to respond to [Jewish] references without needing elaboration guarantees comprehension, but does not insure enjoyment." Sherman's "Sarah Jackman" was easily dissected and dismissed. "[S]ing her name, repeat it, add 'How's by you' and that's what happens to 'Frere Jacques.'" A few months later on April 22, 1994, *Commonweal* magazine published "Shine on, Harvey Bloom: Why Allan Sherman made us laugh." The answer had more to do with the cultural moment than Sherman himself. Alienation made modern man the "Jewish man and modern man looked silly in the guise of old heroes. . . . By demonstrating how hilarious the Jew might look in classic heroic situations, Sherman demonstrated how irrelevant any of us would look." Now that times had changed, Sherman was finished. "In 'Shine On, Harvey Bloom,' Sherman wished the Jewish lunar explorer 'a lovely seder in your crater'; today Jewish astronauts ride the space shuttle and there is nothing the least bit dissonant about that."

That did not explain the rising star of Mickey Katz, whose 1950 Jewish song parodies inspired Sherman to write his own. Katz's parodies, delivered with healthy dollops of Yiddish, should have been even less interesting to contemporary listeners than Sherman's, but the klezmer musician was attracting new fans, suggesting that Sherman's unpopularity was, in the language of stock market analysts, more cyclical than secular. A predictable shift in tastes, more than a permanent realignment of the culture, accounted for the Sherman phobia.

Beginning in the 1970s, young Jewish musicians on the lookout for authentic cultural antecedents that could supply a joyous antidote to conventional Judaism's assimilated respectability discovered the East European Jewish klezmer tradition and its vivacious but also witty and worldly-wise sound. A founder of the Berkeley, California–based *Klezmorim* that in 1976 started the klezmer revival was drawn to the music's "rollicking, vodka-soaked sound." As the revival gathered steam in the 1980s and 1990s with the success of Andy

Statman, Henry Sapoznik, the Klezmer Conservatory Band, and others, it inevitably led to a rediscovery of Katz, who said of his 1958 album, *Mickey Katz Plays Music for Weddings, Bar Mitzvahs and Brisses*, "Every note of the album breathes the flavor of the old but little-known *happy* Jewish music of the old country." By 1999, Katz was a Jewish hero valorized for his "aggressively unassimilated interlingual parodies," and Sherman was seen as a virtual enemy collaborator that sold out the Jews to the majority culture. He offered "no Yiddish, no dialect accents, no uproarious klezmer frailachs," said one critic. This overstatement was more proof that Sherman's accent-laden *Folk Singer* album had been almost completely forgotten.

But the 1990s also saw the rise of a far greater cultural phenomenon than klezmer, and it followed the path of the more assimilated but still recognizably Jewish entertainment Sherman pioneered. The *Seinfeld* television show, starring a "Jewish male who spoke of personal lives rather than social problems, who made small observations and not large pronouncements," was virtually a televised version of Sherman's *My Son* records. It cast its comic eye on the trivial events that fill most of life, and its characters could have been lifted from "Sarah Jackman," which cataloged the Jewish American types that populated *Seinfeld*. That was a problem. Almost thirty years after Sherman proved Jewish material could succeed with non-Jewish audiences, television executives feared Seinfeld was "too Jewish." Instead, early ratings proved "it wasn't just a New York show, and for the people who had articulated, a number of times, 'it's too Jewish'" Seinfeld established what Sherman demonstrated a generation earlier. Jewish dissatisfaction and disgruntlement and despair generated by forced association with beloved but crazy relatives, the suburbs, the city, television, food, work, and one's insufficiently perfect self made for very popular comedy. The show ran from 1989 through 1998 and was "one of the most commercially successful sitcoms in the history of television." Despite the advent of Jewish astronauts, Jewish maladjustment was still America's favorite comic representative of the general condition.

After *Seinfeld* came Larry David's *Curb Your Enthusiasm* and Jon Stewart's *The Daily Show*, two television shows with even stronger Jewish elements than *Seinfeld*. On *Curb*, "the Jews in the show are not inferred or crypto," as on *Seinfeld*, but unambiguously identified. Stewart's book, *America*, was advertised with the help of a Shermanesque parody of "The Star Spangled Banner." The headline was "Oy vey, can you see!" In this cultural climate, the *New York Times* on August 3, 2001, reviewed the "Hello Muddah" musical for the third time, and now it seemed Sherman's original fans were right. He was an extraordinarily skillful parodist that deserved to be remembered. "Almost 40 years ago, a pudgy parodist took a lyric from a well-known patriotic song, dropped a silent W, changed a G to a D and put an O where an A was," and the result was the drapes of Roth pun the *Times* praised for the "sneak-attack brilliance of the wordplay." Sherman's "sense of timing and ear for incongruity," the *Times* continued, "put his best material far above the usual, where it remains even now." Several months later in January 2002, another *Times* reporter referenced Sherman as a shrewd amateur sociologist. In an article about the overscheduled children of baby boomer parents the reporter wonders, "Has so little changed since Allan Sherman" sang "Taking Lessons?"

> My daughter, Linda, she takes ballet.
> Her first recital was yesterday.
> She dropped her tutu, and her left shoe, too.
> She needs more lessons.

No, not much had changed, and one of Sherman's talents was to discover the new elements of American life that were destined to become permanent. The very qualities that caused Sherman to be considered less serious than other comics of his time — he was not overtly political, controversial, or provocative — made him an evergreen funnyman. Too ardent a commitment to relevance always carries with it an early expiration date, but children's ballet lessons are eternal, and so are unhappiness in the suburbs ("Here's to the Crabgrass"), the comic glory of the hapless workingman ("The Ballad of Harry Lewis"), summer camp, advice-givers ("Good Advice"), and extended families filled out with no-goodniks, dreamers, and teenagers that can't keep their pants on ("Sarah Jackman" and her motley crew of relations).

The *Times'* about-face on Sherman made it a good time for Rhino in November 2005 to issue *My Son, the Box*, a six-CD boxed set and fifty-page liner note booklet that included all eight of Sherman's albums for Warner Bros., previously unreleased songs such as his "Chopped Liver" parody of "Moon

River," and even promotional songs about paper cups and Encron polyester he wrote for the Scott Paper Company and American Enka Corporation, respectively. But the boxed set's most important new material was Sherman's Jewish parody of *My Fair Lady* that had only been available in very limited quantities as a bootleg record. The parody includes Sherman's narration of the story line and him singing five songs, including "Wouldn't It Be Lovely," "With a Little Bit of Lox," "On the Streets Where We Live," "I Got the Customers to Face," and "Get Me to the Temple on Time."

Sherman's twist on "I've Grown Accustomed to Her Face" is a triumph of his ability to make small adjustments in sound that result in momentous differences in meaning. In "Customers," the Jewish language teacher tells his non-Jewish female student, who has not yet achieved her full victory by being named president of Hadassah, that their relationship must end. The Jewish community cannot accept her, and a boycott of his candy store threatens to ruin him.

> I got the customers to face
> They used to flock into the place
> But when they heard the things you say
> They turned and ran away
> Where did they go?
> Where's Jake, where's Moe?
> They saw a shiksee and they ran
> That's how the Exodus began
> Where's Marvin Cohen and Seymour Harris
> And some others I could name
> Oh I'm so embarrassed
> For the neighbors it's a shame
> They looked at me and they said shmuck
> She don't know how to talk
> The customers I face.

True to the theme of *My Fair Lady*, Sherman makes it clear that language difference, not religious difference, is what threatens to doom their relationship. The former subsumes the latter. Talking Jewish is the same as being Jewish. Her mastery of Jewish English would be a sign of her inner transformation, and that is what happens when her teacher, having apparently lost the bet that he could transform Liza into a Jewish woman, prepares to pay up. "Wait! Don' pay de money," she hollers at the last moment in a way that leaves no doubt she now belongs.

That ending represents the triumph of ethnicity over more fixed forms of traditional identity, and it is the reason why the Jews have been such passionate salesmen for their culture on the national scene. The new American category of ethnicity allowed the Jews, for the first time, to win friends and influence (non-Jewish) people to accept and even adopt the Jews' comic, ironic, and irreverent view of non-Jewish culture. Sherman's *My Son, the Folk Singer* album was the first Jewish work to prove it could be done, and it showed how.

That achievement received its first important nod of recognition in 2006, shortly after *My Son, the Box* appeared, when Prof. Jeffrey Shandler of Rutgers University delivered a talk on Sherman as part of the National Foundation for Jewish Culture lecture series. Sherman's three "My Son" albums "are key texts of American Jewish culture," Shandler argued. His "Goldeneh Moments from Broadway" parodies "presaged later interest in the Jews of Tin Pan Alley," and his folk song parodies gave a meaning to American Jewishness, itself a new form of identity. For Sherman, Jewishness is "defined by a self-conscious difference in relation to the sensibilities of others, with which Jews are familiar and against which they take measure of themselves. To be an American Jew, then, is to be parodic." That may not have been new. The Jews were always aware that their sensibilities were different. In a Passover Haggadah from 1478, the wicked son "is depicted as a Christian knight, wearing armor and holding a sword and lance. This image, so familiar even today as the embodiment of chivalric virtue, appears to the Jews as a symbol of vice." What was new was Sherman's popularity among Jews and non-Jews. That indicates what Shandler called "an integration of Jewishness into the national repertoire of national popular culture and serves as a sign of Jews' sense of 'at-homeness' in America."

Sherman survives not just as a symbol of that "at-homeness," but part of it. Over the course of fifty years, his popularity has waxed and waned with changes in the cultural climate, but his best work has earned a permanent place in the country's musical repertoire and memory. When in 1977 telephone numbers finally dropped the letters that once formed part of the three-digit prefix, the *Los Angeles Times* remembered Sherman's mock protest song against the trend, "Let's All Call Up A.T.&T. and Protest to the President March," which included chants of "Plaza 9" and "Murray Hill 8." A *New York Times* story on the 1979 seltzer revival of course included lyrics from Sherman's "Seltzer Boy" parody, and upon the death in 1989 of the piano virtuoso Vladimir Horowitz, the *Washington Post* recalled Sherman's "Horowitz" tribute. In recent years, his reputation has if anything ascended. In 2008, *Freakonomics* coauthor Stephen J. Dubner called "Hello Muddah, Hello Fadduh" "one of the best songs ever written," and dubbed Sherman a "certified genius," citing as evidence, "Hail to Thee, Fat Person." Two years later, the *New York Times* realized that Sherman was here to stay. "Not long ago it would have been inconceivable that Allan Sherman would ever seem timely or topical again," and then in September 2010 Collectors' Choice records reissued his eight Warner Bros. albums in the midst of the giddy excitement surrounding the new "Mad Men" television series. Suddenly, Sherman's songs "can be read as both lighthearted crowd pleasers and glimpses into a culture of rat-race conformity," as on his "When I Was a Lad," about the advertising business. "I learned who was going out with whom, and who had the keys to the powder room / For the keys to the powder room, you see, is the key to the structure of the agency."

Shandler recognized that as parodists, the Jews sometimes feel at home in America only as official outsiders. But even with that caveat, whatever degree of comfort the Jews may feel is due, in some small way, to Sherman's success in making a place for them. As he sang in the final verse of "Harvey and Sheila,"

> Oh, that Harvey he was really smart
> He used his noodle
> Sheila bought a white French poodle
> Went to Europe with a visa
> Harvey's rich they say that he's a V.I.P.
> This could be
> Only in the U.S.A.

aCKnowLeDGmenTs

My father is fond of the expression, "One hand washes the other." In other words, nothing can be accomplished without assistance. That goes double for biographies, which depend upon the memories, papers, letters, and insights of others. Many people who knew Allan Sherman shared theirs with me.

At the top of the list of people that deserve my gratitude are the members of Sherman's immediate family, including his children, Robert Sherman and Nancy Sherman, and his ex-wife, Dolores "Dee" Golden, who passed away in July 2012, not long after my last conversation with her. All three generously answered countless questions, searched through papers and photographs, and with great hospitality welcomed my visits. I could not have written this book without their endlessly patient consideration and help, or their permission to quote from Sherman's plays, books, songs, unreleased recordings, and unpublished papers.

Members of Sherman's extended family also contributed greatly to my understanding of his complicated childhood. On the Sherman side of the family, I extend my thanks to relatives Michael Hackman, Vivian Mailand,

Evelyn Raden, and Helen Stricker. Sherman's first cousins, Mickey Sherman, Gerry Sherman, and Carol Selsberg were enormously helpful. Sherry Segal, a stepsister to Allan Sherman, very kindly shared stories about her and Sherman's parents. My thanks go also to Dee Golden's niece, Terri Leamy. Above all, Sherman's first cousin Syril Gilbert was a fantastic storehouse of information who never tired of answering my questions or rummaging through her memory for answers. She and her son, Arthur Gilbert, were crucial to the completion of this book.

Relatives on Sherman's father's side, the Coplons, were just as generous and contributed information available only to them. I am happy to thank Nancy Brodzki, Louise Goldstein Cole, Lee Cooper, Morris Coplon, Barry Hertz, Daniel Isenberg, Dorothy Macarus, and Jackie Scheinberg. I owe special thanks to Allan Sherman's stepsister, Hilda Willard, for the rare photographs of her and Allan's father, Percy Copelon. Family friend Joe Resnick offered key insights into Percy's character and upbringing.

Sherman was a very social man, and many of his friends were happy to share their memories with me. His buddies from college told me great stories and sang to me otherwise lost Sherman parodies. I am happy to thank Ed Dessen, Bill Hamer, Arte Johnson, Sheldon Keller, Bill Pilkenton, Larry Stewart, Dr. Henry Swain, Seena Swibel, and Sherman Wolf. I am especially indebted to Bruce Clorfene for spending hours telling me of his and Sherman's college friendship, adventures and mishaps. For information about Sherman and Camp Ojibwa, I am grateful to Steve Katz, Denny Rosen, Mickey Schwartz, Steve Simon, and Ellen Weinberg. Friends and colleagues from Sherman's days as a television producer and a recording star offered me invaluable help. I am happy to thank Michael Abrahams, Audrey Adams, Steve Beverly, Theo Bikel, Steve Binder, Sam Bobrick, Ray Charles, Joel Chaseman, Hal Cooper, Stan Cornyn, Bill Dana, Crescent Dragonwagon, Betsy Gehman, Billy Goldenberg, Jerry Goldstein, Joe Guercio, Leonid Hambro, Stuart Hample, Barry Hansen (aka Dr. Demento), Milt Hoffman, Laurie Holloway, Jerry Hopkins, Dick Hyman, Marty Ingels, Al Lerner, Don Lewis, Lawrence M. Mandel, Bill Marx, Kevin McCarthy, Adrienne Merrill, Newton Minow, Win Opie, Gary Owens, Jerry Perenchio, Thomas Peyser, Tony Peyser, Mark Rosengarden, Neil Rosengarden, Sheldon Schultz, Joe Smith, Randy Sparks, Marvin Tabolsky, Jay Thomas, Donn Trenner, and Debbi Whiting.

Additional thanks are due to Ray Charles and Mark Rosengarden for providing me home recordings of Sherman's "Goldeneh Moments from Broadway" song parodies made at the home of Bobby Rosengarden in the late 1950s.

I am very grateful to Tom Smothers for his generous permission to quote from Sherman's unpublished manuscript, *Every 600 Years, on a Tuesday (The Journey to the Perfectly Fair)*, to which he owns the rights.

I benefitted from conversations with many people who were kind enough to consider my questions. These include Tyler Alpern, Prof. Arnold Band, Barbara Bonfield, Hugh Brown, Rory Brown, Murray Horwitz, Howard Leib, Devra Hall Levy, Barry Mitchell, Laurence Roth, Ronald L. Smith, Fred Wostbrock, and Rabbi Eytan Yammer.

Gerald Nachman was a special help and inspiration. Prof. Ted Merwin's invitation to speak about Sherman at Dickinson College encouraged me in this project. Prof. Jeffrey Shandler allowed me to read and quote from his unpublished lecture on Sherman.

Librarians, archivists and others guided me to and handed over important items, including Hana Field at Chicago's Harold Washington Library and Rob Hudson at Carnegie Hall. Special allies in my research were Leith Adams, Ned Comstock, and Sandra Garcia-Myers, who helped uncover items in the Jack L. Warner Collection at USC's Cinematic Arts Library; Jonathon Auxier at USC's Warner Bros. Archives; Mark Quigley at the UCLA Film & Television Archive; Aimee Rendell of Freemantle Media; Lindy Smith at the University of Illinois at Urbana-Champaign's Archives Research Center, and Edward Zimmerman at Sony.

Many people at Warner Music Group's Rhino Entertainment offered me great assistance. I am happy to thank Erin D'Angelo, Charles Comparato, Tracie Parry, and Mason Williams. I am deeply indebted to Kris Ahrend, who was the indispensible and always cooperative key to crucial Sherman papers and correspondence at the Warner Music Group Archives. Mike Johnson, a longstanding champion of this project who introduced me to "the vault" and let me gaze upon its riches, was my secret weapon, my man on the inside.

When I was preparing my book proposal, blurbs praising Sherman greatly improved the odds of finding a publisher. For those blurbs I thank Jason

Alexander, Theodore Bikel, Bill Cosby, Dr. Demento, Prof. Josh Kun, Gerald Nachman, Ronald L. Smith, and Weird Al Yankovic.

Special thanks to my agent, Ted Weinstein, who believed in this project, guided it in its crucial early stages, and led me to Brandeis University Press and my excellent editor, Stephen Hull.

It is a pleasure to thank family members that put me up (and put up with me) while I visited libraries in Los Angeles. Thanks go to David and Alison, Ziv and Suzann, Anat and Jeff, and my brother Neil and his partner, Claude.

Profound gratitude to my father for his unwavering support and love (and that great lunch at Café Vasca).

And to my wife, Danielle, I award the as-yet-to-be-created but desperately needed Presidential Medal for Exceptional Matrimonial Bravery, with Oak Leaf Cluster for Outstanding Love and Patience in the Face of Spousal Madness.

appendix

"GOLDENEH MOMENTS FROM BROADWAY"
AND OTHER PARODY SONG LYRICS

In the 1950s, Allan Sherman wrote at least the twenty Jewish parodies of Broadway musicals included here. According to his autobiography, *A Gift of Laughter*, he wrote "How Are Things with Uncle Morris," a parody of *Finian Rainbow*'s "How Are Things in Glocca Morra," in 1953. That date likely makes it the first of his "Goldeneh Moments."

"HOW ARE THINGS WITH UNCLE MORRIS?"
(To the tune of "How Are Things in Glocca Morra," from *Finian's Rainbow*)

How are things with Uncle Morris?
Does he still work in the candy store?
Does he still run like he always did
To get some kid
Fa nickel halavah?
Is Aunt Bea with Uncle Morris?
Do they still live on the second floor?
Do they still live in the same old flat?

Is he still fat?
And does he walk around in his *gatkes* there   [long underwear]
Eating latkes there?
Since I moved away to Scarsdale,
And I joined a country club
I lost touch with them and they lost touch with me
How are things with Uncle Morris and Aunt Bea?

"TZIMISHED"

(To the tune of "Bewitched, Bothered, and Bewildered" from *Pal Joey*)
This is the lyric Sherman sang in September 1957 at the Vernon Hills Country Club Little Theater in Eastchester, New York. Tzimished (befuddled), fachottered (confused, messed up), fatroshket (bewildered), and fablongett (completely lost) are good parody substitutes for bewitched, bothered, and bewildered. They convey the original's sense of disorientation without the least hint of sexual infatuation.

I'm wild again
Beguiled again
A whimpering tsimpering tsild again
Tzimished, fachottered, and tzebulbet am I.
Can't sleep a wink
I lay and think
She's wearing my mink while she's out with Fink
Tzimished, fatroshket and tziboorjet am I.
I should tell her I'm leaving
But I can't—I'm afraid
If I tell her, she'll tell me
To *gay gezintehaid.*   [go in good health]
I say "Dot's all"
Walk down the hall
Then I turn around and say, *noch a moll*   [again]
Tzimished, fachottered and fablongett am I.

"ONE FOR MY BABY (AND ONE FOR TWO CENTS PLAIN)"

[To the tune of "One for My Baby (and One More for the Road)"]
Harold Arlen and Johnny Mercer's "One for My Baby" is associated with
Frank Sinatra, who recorded it in 1954 and 1958. Sherman's parody might
have been inspired by either performance. The expression "two cents plain"
refers to a small glass of seltzer without any added flavoring.

It's quarter to two
I'm feeling very *shwach*, I'll tell you the true   [faint, feeble]
So set 'em up, Moe
I got a couple things I want you should know
Mine future looks *shvartz*   [dark, black]
In mine hearts is a terrible pain
So make it one for my Sadie
One for two cents plain.
It's quarter to three
Don't know what's gonna be with Sadie and me
We had such a fight
The same old goddam fight we have every night
When I'm in the mood
Sadie tells me, *"Ich hob derr in bood"* ["I have you in the bath" or "Go drown"]
So make it one for my Sadie
One for two cents plain.
Now listen, Morris
I know you got your own kind *tzoris*   [trouble]
But Morris, I feel so ashame
So please console me
I can't believe my Sadie told me
That I should *gay ahayme.*   [go in the ocean, i.e., jump in the lake]
It's quarter to four
I know you wanna close the whole candy store
But Moe, can't you see
You simply gotta have *rachmonis* on me   [mercy]
I feel so alone
Sadie, please, won't you call on the phone?
Make it one for my baby
And one—
(Spoken) So long you making it, put a little chocolate sauce, okay?

"THUNDERBIRD"
(To the tune of "Wunderbar" from *Kiss Me, Kate*)
The Cole Porter musical, *Kiss Me, Kate*, opened on Broadway in 1948, and the film version appeared in 1953, but the Thunderbird from Ford did not appear until 1955.

Thunderbird, Thunderbird
What a fancy schmancy car
Have you seen, have you heard
Of the brand new Thunderbird.
Thunderbird, Thunderbird
Cheaper than a Jaguar
I am moved, deeply stirred
When I see a Thunderbird.
Oh it moves me sentimentally
In my throat there comes a lump
Neither Rolls Royce or the Bentley
Has a hump, dear
Near your rump, dear.

"THE FURRIER'S LAMENT"
(To the tune of Johnny Mercer's "Autumn Leaves")
"Autumn Leaves" was featured in a 1956 movie of the same name. Sherman sang his parody during one of the three *My Son, the Celebrity* recording sessions in late November and early December 1962. He introduced it by saying, "There's a cafeteria named Siegel's where the furriers are in New York, and there when they stand next to each other they ask questions, and those of whom the questions are asked will not answer. And this one does and he sings,"

The autumn haze
Stays in my window
I don't know why
It just don't sell.
The autumn haze
Has been there so long
It has an *ois-ga-mottered* smell.   [stale, worn out]

I sold the breath-of-spring
The natural, too.
I even sold
The silver blue.
But what takes me out the heart
This season
Is no one pays
For autumn haze.

"YOU'RE A NUDNIK, SONDRA GOLDFEIN"

> (To the tune of "You're A Queer One, Julie Jordan" from *Carousel*)
>
> A movie version of the 1945 musical *Carousel* was released in 1956, when
> Sherman was working on his Broadway song parodies.

You're a *nudnik*, Sondra Goldfein	[nuisance, annoying]
You are quieter and deeper than a *shisl*	[basin]
But I love you, Sondra Goldfein	
Not so much I only love you just a *bisl*	[little]
With your nagging and your kvetching	
And your *chaynik hocking* I'm a nervous wreck	[endless talking]
And I'll tell you, Sondra Goldfein	
I kinda sorta wish you'd *gay avek*.	[go away]
But I love you, Sondra Goldfein	
And some day up to the *chuppeh* we'll be led	[marriage canopy]
In the meantime, Sondra Goldfein	
Let's get up and let the *shvartze* make the bed.	[black person (derogatory)]

"WHEN YOU WALK THROUGH THE BRONX"

> (To the tune of "You'll Never Walk Alone" from *Carousel*)

When you walk through the Bronx
Hold your head up high
And look for a sign, "Fordham Road"
Soon you'll come to a store that sells pizza pie
Then you'll know that you're near my abode.
Turn right, walk two blocks
Turn left, cross the street

And no matter where you roam
Walk on
Walk on
Walk on through the Bronx
'Cause you'll find I won't be home.
Tonight I won't be home.

"AROUND THE WORLD"

(To the tune of "Around the World in 80 Days")
In late 1956, Bing Crosby sang "Around the World in 80 Days," which was
connected to the movie of the same name released the same year.

Around the world I looked for you
I gave a look in every nook on Second Avenue
I'm searching for the one I love
I haven't seen the one I love since *erev tisha bov*   [mournful Jewish holiday]
Your new address you didn't leave
Was it New York or County Cork
Or was it Tel Aviv?
And all the time I looked around for you
You was in the ladies' room.

"SEVENTY-SIX SOL COHENS"

(To the tune of "Seventy-Six Trombones," from *The Music Man*)
The Music Man opened on Broadway in December 1957, and this parody
probably dates from shortly thereafter, in 1958.

Seventy-six Sol Cohens in the country club!
And a hundred and ten nice men named Levine
And there's more than a thousand Finks
Who parade around the links
It's a sight that really must be seen.
Seventy-six Sol Cohens lead the big parade
With a hundred and nine Irv Kleins right behind
But the loveliest men I've known
Are the men they call Sol Cohen
At that good old country club of mine.

Oh, there's Sol the drugstore man, and Sol the furrier
Sol from coats
Sol from shoes
Sol, the builder, too
And one Sol Cohen is known as Sol the Worrier
He's so rich, what else has he got to do?
Oh, there's Sol who manufactures ladies' lingerie
Sol from shirts
Sol from ties
Sol, the commodore
The country club is full of Sols
And all the Sols are living dolls
But who's staying home to watch the store?
Seventy-six Sol Cohens in the country club
Seventy-six Sol Cohens playing gin
But they're hard to identify
'Cause as time goes passing by
One by one, they change their name to Quinn!

"CHANGE PARTNERS"

(To the tune of Irving Berlin's "Change Partners")
Ella Fitzgerald recorded this Berlin song in 1958, which might have
reminded Sherman of the tune, which dates from 1938. (When Sherman
sang his parody on a recording made by Bobby Rosengarden, he could not
remember the entire lyric.)

Must you write
Every script
With the same fortunate man?
You've already got twenty-six in the can.
Won't you change partners and write with me?
You and me
Heaven knows
What we could become.
If you just get rid of that no talent bum
Then you'll change partners

And write with me.
I'll buy the paper and do all the typing, Max,
We'll work at your place
So you can deduct if from your income tax.
You and me
Can't you see
We'd be like two George Bernard Shaws
Won't you change partners because
[unfinished performance]

"HOW DEEP IS A BIRDBATH?"

(To the tune of "How Deep Is the Ocean" by Irving Berlin)
Ella Fitzgerald also recorded this song on her 1958 album of Berlin tunes.
Sherman's parody imagines what the song would be like if Irving Berlin had
not loved his wife.

How much do I love you?
I'll tell you no lie . . .
    How deep is a birdbath?
    How high is a stump?
How many times a day do I think of you?
    How many fire engines are painted blue?
How far would I travel
To be where you are?
    How far would I travel?
    I ain't got a car
And if I ever lost you
Would I feel chagrin?
    How deep is the ocean?
    Why don't you fall in?

"THERE IS NOTHING LIKE A LOX"

(To the tune of "There Is Nothing Like a Dame," from *South Pacific*)

The 1949 musical, *South Pacific*, was released as a movie in 1958, when Sherman was fully engaged with his *Goldeneh Moments* project. He called his *South Pacific* parody *South Passaic*. He wrote parodies of three songs from the show—"There Is Nothing Like a Lox," "Younger Than Springstein," and "Desilu," a fragment of a parody of "Bali Hai."

We got herring, sweet and sour,
We got pickles, old and young,
We got corned beef and salami and a lot of tasty tongue
We got Philadelphia Cream Cheese in a little wooden box,
What ain't we got?
We ain't got lox!
We got cole slaw, freshly made,
And chopped liver, also fresh,
And a lot of things to please a man
Whose name is Moish or Hesh.
We got plenty pumpernickel,
We got bagels hard as rocks,
What ain't we got?
We ain't got lox!
We got plenty of food which is known as kosher
With the possible exception of smoked salmon,
Which is occasionally referred to by the upper classes, as Nova Scotia
There is nothing like a lox
Nothing in this world.
Wrapped in paper or a box
That is anything like a lox.
Men who manufacture frocks,
They go wild for lox
Men who speculate in stocks
Are investing their stocks in lox.
There is no dish like a lox
No other fish like a lox
And nothing smells like a lox
Or repels like a lox

There's nothing smart like a lox
That burns the heart like a lox
There ain't a thing that's wrong with any man here
That can't be cured by putting him near
A salty, pinkish
Slightly stinkish
Lox!

"YOUNGER THAN SPRINGSTEIN"

(To the tune of "Younger Than Springtime" from *South Pacific*)

Younger than Springstein are you,
Gayer than Klingstein are you,
Better than Goodstein
Finer than Feinstein, too, are you
Greener than Greenstein are you,
Tanner than Brownstein are you,
Smarter than Einstein
Franker than Frankenstein, are you.
And when your hair has turned to Silverstein
You'll still be rare as Goldstein, too.
So burning like Bernstein am I
Whining like Weinstein am I
Horney like Hornstein
Wilder than Wildenstein am I.

"DESILU"

(To the tune of "Bali Hai," from *South Pacific*)

Desilu will call you
Anytime, anywhere
They will say, you're a genius
Make a change, here and there.

"SUMMERTIME"

(To the tune of "Summertime" from *Porgy and Bess*)

A movie version of *Porgy and Bess* was released in June 1959, and that is likely what gave Sherman the idea to parody the work. On an undated home recording made by his friend Bobby Rosengarden, Sherman sets up his Jewish parody by saying,

You are about to hear an opera entitled *Solly and Shirl*. It takes place in the mid-Thirties, in a small village in the Catskill Mountains called Smoked Fish Row. And as we first see this little village and we see all the porches of the little *kuchaleins* [bungalows], and sitting on one of them is Sarah. And she's sitting with her little baby, Bubbie. And she's rocking on the rocking chair, and there's a fat lady sitting next to her, and the fat lady looks at her and she says, "My husband is not here this week. Is yours?" And the woman pays no attention and she sings to her little baby,

Summertime	
Everybody is *shvitzing*.	[sweating]
Schmaltz is melting	[rendered chicken fat]
And the Catskills is high.	
Oh, your Daddy's sad	
He'll come up for the veekend.	
So hush little Bubbie,	
Please don't cry.	
Next Monday morning	
He's going back to the garment	
He'll be selling	
Every sample and svatch	
Your momma also	
Gunn' give out a few samples.	
So sleep little Bubbie	
For God's sake don't vy [cry].	

"THERE'S A JAGUAR LEAVING SOON FOR THE CONCORD"

(To the tune of "There's a Boat Dat's Leaving Soon for New York"
from *Porgy and Bess*)

The only other *Solly and Shirl* song Sherman wrote, or that survives, is
"There's A Jaguar Leaving Soon for the Concord." In the fourth line,
"hamentash with moon" are the traditional Purim cookies with poppy
seeds. Moon is poppy seed, from the Yiddish, *mun*.

There's a Jaguar leaving soon for the Concord
Come with me
We gung be alright, Shirley
They got hamentash with moon at the Concord
Come with me
We gung leave tonight, Shirley
You'll wear all your fancy dresses
We'll be there three nights, two days
All your blues you'll be forgettin'
While we'll be settin'
And you'll be sweatin'
In new Autumn Haze
We'll dance in the fancy nightclub
The Cha Cha and Merengue
While we'll take a dancing lesson
We'll do some *fressin'*   [eating]
The delicatessen is not far away
Come along with me
Dot's the place
Let's go right now
Come alo-ong.
Dere's a Jaguar leaving soon for the Concord
Come with me
Dere we can't go wrong
Shirley,
That's where we belong.

"SMALL WORLD"

(To the tune of "Small World" from *Gypsy*)

The 1959 musical *Gypsy* opened in May 1959, and Sherman wrote at least two version of his parody of "Small World." This is the version Sherman sang at his Santa Monica concert on January 18, 1963, with Christine Nelson.

NELSON: Funny,
> I got one son a doctor
> One son a CPA

SHERMAN: My son,
> Is a doctor, a dentist.

BOTH: Small world, isn't it?

NELSON: I live,
> On the Moshulu Parkway,
> Eighty-Eight, Forty-Three

SHERMAN: I live
> In the Kew Gardens, Gardens.

BOTH: Small world, isn't it?
> We have so much in common
> It's a phenomenon.

NELSON: I won't
> Act like a *nudnik*   [nuisance, annoying]

SHERMAN: Or a no-goodnik
> From now on.

NELSON: I have
> A whole showroom of cloth coats
> On Seventh Avenue.

SHERMAN: Funny,
> I make linings for cloth coats.

BOTH: Small world, isn't it?
> Small, and funny and nice.

In an alternative version, Sherman has the man and woman more even explicitly embrace their common Jewish heritage.

WOMAN: We have so much in common,
MAN: It's a phenomenon,
WOMAN: Darling, let's say a *brocha*   [blessing]
MAN: And be *mishpocha*, from now on.   [family]

"OLLAWOOD!"

(To the tune of "Camelot," from *Camelot*)

Camelot opened on Broadway in December 1960, and when Sherman recorded this at Bobby Rosengarden's house in Great Neck, New York, the chatter with his listeners makes it clear he was already famous for his 1962 *My Son, the Folk Singer* album. He was then living in Los Angeles, and he sarcastically described "Ollawood!" as being "in honor of my new home."

The movie stars all sit around the pool there
The food at Nate 'n Al's is very good
And Sammy Davis Jr. goes to *shul* there   [synagogue]
In Ollawood!
Where every girl can be a movie princess
Where palm trees sway real good like palm trees should.
Where Mrs. Eddie Fisher once made blintzes
In Ollawood.
Ollawood.
I know it sounds a bit way out but in Ollawood.
That's what's all about.
When Mr. Khrushchev came to California
And looked around this gorgeous neighborhood
He said to Mrs. K
Let's sign with MCA
And get a series of our own
And stay in Ollawood.

"FRANK COOPER"

(To the tune of "Maria" from *West Side Story*)

This parody appears on the same recording as "Ollawood!" and was written about the agent who handled Sherman when he worked on the Steve Allen show in 1962.

Frank Cooper
I just met a man named Frank Cooper
He looked at me with eyes
So wonderful and wise to see
Frank Cooper
What god can I thank for Frank Cooper?

And how could I have known
He'd throw in Joel Cohen for free?
Frank Cooper
Say it loud and there's music playing
Say it soft and it's almost like praying
Frank Cooper
I'll never stop paying Frank Cooper.

"YOU'RE THE TOP"

> (To the tune of Cole Porter's, "You're The Top")
> This famous song from 1934 was the target of many parodies, some quite
> risqué, according to the biography *Cole Porter*, by William McBrien.

You're the top	
You're a dozen *chales*	[challah bread]
You're the top	
You're Chaim Weizmann's *tallis*	[prayer shawl]
You're the fins in back of a Cadillac that's new	
You're a house by Levitts	
A Manischewitz	
A Fontainebleau!	
You're a dish	
That was sent from Himmel	
You're a knish	
Made by Yonah Shimmel	
I'm a poor schlemiel who would like to steal a *khop*	[squeeze, feel]
But if Becky I'm a *shmendrick*	[fool, nincompoop]
You're the top!	
You're the talk	
Of a Lindy's waiter	
You're the walk	
On the first day *cheder*	[religious school]
You're the kosher wine when they toast	
"zoll zein mit glick"	[may it be with luck]
You're a piece of *flanken*	[prized beef dish]
And *gott zu danken*	[thank God]
You're *pesachdick*!	[food fit for Passover]

You're the top
You're the feast of *sukkus*   [festive Jewish holiday]
You're the top
Ava Gardner's *tuchus*   [backside]
Won't you have *rachmones* and say you're gonna stop   [mercy]
being mean to me, cause Becky
You're the top!
You're the smile
When they sing *Hatikvah*   [Israeli national anthem]
You're the tile
In a brand new *mikvah*   [ritual bath]
You're an egg cream soda and getta load-a this
You're a soup with noodle
You're apple strudel
You're *gribinniss*!   [chicken skin cracklings]
You're the gas
In a seltzer fizzer
You're the class
You're the *moile's* new scissor   [a *moile* performs ritual circumcision]
I'm a macaroon from a poor non-union shop
But if Becky I'm an *oomglick*   [loser]
You're the top!

Other unreleased parodies

"THE NIGHT THAT LEON TROTSKY DIED"

(To the tune of "The Night That Paddy Murphy Died")
This parody was sung to me by actor Arte Johnson, who attended the
University of Illinois when Sherman was also a student there. Sherman
wrote this nutty song for a student stunt show.

Olga, Olga, on the Volga
Striptease for the czar
Olga, Olga from the Volga
I wonder where you are
On the night that Leon Trotsky died

I never shall forget
The Russians got so stinking drunk
That some aren't sober yet
There are some things they did that night
That gave me quite a jar
They took the buckshot from the corpse
And called it caviar.
That's how they showed their respect for Leon Trotsty
That's how they showed their honor and their pride
That's how they showed their respect for Leon Trotsty
On the night that Leon Trotsky died.

"THE CONSCIENTIOUS OBJECTOR OF COMPANY Z"

(To the tune of "Boogie Woogie Bugle Boy")

Sherman wrote this parody of the Andrews Sisters' 1941 hit in November
1942 for a University of Illinois event in honor of the Good Neighbor policy toward Latin America that President Roosevelt instituted in the 1930s
and that continued during World War II.

THE CONSCIENTIOUS OBJECTOR OF COMPANY Z

There was a touch of Latin in his family
And when they called up his numbah,
He started to rhumba
So they put him in company Z.
He taught the second lieutenant to swing and sway
And when he started to conga they took him away
He didn't let them have peace
While in the kitchen police
So they put him in company Z.
He made the barracks jump
He did the rhumba and the conga
The captain saw him bump
And couldn't stand it any longa, the conga!
They put him back in the army, maraccas in hand,
Went out and drafted a real South American band
With all the rest at hard labors,
He's making good neighbors
Cause he rhumbas in company Z.

"ELEANOR, ELEANOR"

This parody of the nursery rhyme, "Pussycat, pussycat, where have you been?" is typical of Sherman's interest in children's songs and rhymes. He wrote it for his original 1943 college musical, *Mirth of a Nation*. The Eleanor of the title is First Lady Eleanor Roosevelt.

Eleanor, Eleanor, where have you been?
I've been to London to visit the queen
I've been to Manchuria
And I can assuria
I've been to more places than you've ever seen!
Eleanor, Eleanor, why did you go?
Life at the White House was boring me so
Have you forgotten?
My husband goes yachtin'
Sometimes with Winston and sometimes with Joe!
When people criticize me
Because I gad about
They really do surprise me—
'Cause hasn't a lady the right to go out?
Eleanor, Eleanor, whither away?
I'm getting tired of this USA
I'm off to Algeria
To gather materia'
For my newspaper seria, which is known as MY DAY!

"THEIR DOLL, SOL"

(To the tune of "My Gal, Sal")
The obscure original, written in 1905 by Paul Dresser, was featured in the 1942 film *My Gal, Sal*.

They call him frivolous Sol
To the girls in the Bronx, he's a doll
And no handsome young punk'll
Take girls from my uncle
He's their doll, Sol.
The girls know that they can relax

When with Murray or Melvyn or Max
Sol's kisses are sweet-a
He's the Bronx dolce vita
He's their doll, Sol.

"THE RIVIERA (NEIGHBORHOOD OF LOS ANGELES)"

(To the tune of "Return to Sorrento")

On the party recording made April 10, 1962, Sherman explained he wrote
this about the beautiful Riviera neighborhood of Los Angeles, where many
of the streets have Italian names. "And we were looking around there for a
house, and I wrote the following song in honor of where we were looking
for a house. 'Cause I'm the kind of person that writes songs in honor of
where he's looking for a house," he said. After he sang it he joked, "It's a sad
song about real estate."

1481 Sorrento
Has three bedrooms and a maid's room
And a lovely built-in kitchen
And a sliding glass lanai
756 Amalfi
Has a pool shaped like a kidney
And the owner's name is Sidney
Eighty thousand, you could try.
1242 San Remo
That's the dream house of your dream-o
You don't have to look and see mo'
That's the one you should buy
In the Riviera
Live near Maureen O'Hara
And Theda Bara
Till the day you die.

NOTES

PROLOGUE: OVERWEIGHT SENSATION

xi   *There were two days*   "The World on
     the Brink: John F. Kennedy and the
     Cuban Missile Crisis," John F. Kennedy
     Presidential Library and Museum,
     http://microsites.jfklibrary.org/cmc
     /oct26/ (accessed June 16, 2012).

xi   "Dear Allan Sherman"   Newton N.
     Minow to Allan Sherman, October 26,
     1962. Allan Sherman Papers (ASP).

xi   *In the Camelot*   Arthur Gelb and
     Barbara Gelb, "Culture Makes a Hit
     at the White House," *New York Times*,
     January 28, 1962, http://select.nytimes
     .com (accessed June 16, 2012).

xii "I can't say how much"   Arthur
     Schlesinger Jr. to Mr. Sherman,
     November 5, 1962. ASP.

xiii *As an account*   Stan Cornyn, *Exploding:
     The Highs, Hits, Hype, Heroes, and
     Hustlers of the Warner Music Group* (New
     York: HarperEntertainment, 2003), 210.

xiii "the competing impulses"   Eli
     Lederhendler, "Rereading the
     Americanization Narratives of Antin,
     Zangwill, and Cahan" in *Imagining
     the American Jewish Community*, Jack
     Wertheimer, ed. (Waltham, MA:
     Brandeis University Press, 2007), 259.

xiii "brought so much enthusiasm"   Saul
     Bellow, "Cousins," in *Him with His Foot
     in His Mouth and Other Stories* (New
     York: Penguin Books, 1998), 282.

INTRODUCTION: HUMPTY DUMPTY

1   "roly-poly"   *Far and Near*, November 18,
     1937, 4.

1   "Listen, World"   *Far and Near*,
     February 24, 1938, 2.

1   "The Passing Parade"   *Far and Near*,
     June 23, 1938, 1.

1   *Segal's funny*,   *Far and Near*, May, 26,
     1938, 1.

2   *They were an elite group*   "Hancock
     Park," Los Angeles Department of City
     Planning, Office of Historic Resources,
     http://preservation.lacity.org/hpoz/la
     /hancock-park (accessed May 8, 2012).

2 "Humpty Dumpty sat on a train" Allan Segal, "Mother Goose of 1938," *BURR* (Los Angeles: John Burroughs Jr. High, 1938), n.p.

2 "My grandmother" Evelyn Raden, telephone interview by author, February 7, 2005.

3 "He screwed" Lee Cooper, telephone interview by author, January 18, 2006.

3 "It didn't take" Morris Coplon, telephone interview by author, April 7, 2005.

3 "Anything that was" Mickey Sherman, telephone interview by author, February 27, 2005.

ONE. WITZ-KRIEG!

8 *Between 1906* For Anna (Lustig) Strowiss, see *Thirteenth Census of the United States: 1910 Population*, Chicago, Illinois, Ward 15, Sheet No. 19, line 2. For Abe Lustig, see "List or Manifest of Alien Passengers for the United States Immigration Officer at Port of Arrival," S.S. *Samlund*, Antwerp to New York, arrival of May 15, 1907, List 29, Line 3. For Saul Lustig, see *Fifteenth Census of the United States: 1930 Population Schedule*, Chicago, Illinois, Ward 35, Block No. 184, Sheet No. 7 A, Line 43. Fanny Lustig information in e-mail message from Syril Gilbert to author, April 21, 2011.

8 *Their sister Esther* Passenger records for Esther Sahermann, Riwke Sahermann, and Kreindel Sahermann. The Statue of Liberty—Ellis Island Foundation, Inc., Ellis Island Port of New York Records. www.ellisisland.org.

8 "To Grandma" Allan Sherman, "My Moment of Truth Happened 29 Years Ago, but I Didn't Understand It until Last Thursday," [1971], 2. ASP.

8 *Most Stashev Jews* "Staszow—History," *Virtual Shtetl: Museum of the History of the Polish Jews*, www.sztetl.org.pl/en /article/staszow/5,history/ (accessed May 8, 2012).

9 *Leib Lustig was* Leib Lustig, "List or Manifest of Alien Passengers for the United States Immigration Officer at Port of Arrival," S.S. *Latyia*, Danzig to New York, arrival on September 14, 1921, List 7, Line 26.

9 *The Lustig family's search* Leib left Ozarow sometime between Esther's birth there in 1881–82 and Abraham's birth in Stashev on August 1, 1883. For Leib's age and birth in Ozarow, see Leib Lustig, "List or Manifest." For Abraham's birth in Stashev, see Abe Lustig, "List or Manifest." For Abe's birth date, see Abe Lustig, World War I Draft Registration Card, www.ancestry.com. For Esther's birth in Ozarow, see Leibush Sherman, Petition for Naturalization, Chicago, November 5, 1914, National Archives and Records Administration (NARA). For Esther's birth in 1881–82, see *Fourteenth Census of the United States: 1920 Population*, Chicago, Illinois, Ward 16, Sheet No. 13 B, Line 97.

9 *Three slept* Rosalie Wise Sharp, *Rifke, an Improbable Life* (Toronto: ECW Press, 2007), 204.

9 *Jews in the Ozarow* Alexander Beider, "Names and Naming," *YIVO Encyclopedia of Jews in Eastern Europe*, www.yivoencyclopedia.org (accessed May 8, 2012).

9 *One name for* Jean Baumgarten, "Badkhonim," *YIVO Encyclopedia*, www.yivoencyclopedia.org (accessed May 8, 2012).

9 "He called my mother" Syril Gilbert, e-mail message to author, May 4, 2012.

9 *In the mid-nineteenth* Hillel Adler, *Memories of Ozarow* (Montreal: Ozarow Press, 1997), 8.

9 *That number* "The Rabbinic Dynasty of Ozarow," Ozarow Cemetery Restoration Project, http://ozarow.org/Letter_from _Rebbe.shtml (accessed April 30, 2012).

9 "divine authority" Morris M. Faierstein, "Ya'akov Yitshak Horowitz," *YIVO Encyclopedia*, www.yivoencyclopedia.org (accessed May 8, 2012).

9 "by citing" Sharp, *Rifke*, 208.

9 "taking the right" Adler, *Memories*, 166.

9 *It was not* "Staszow—History."

10 *Marriages in Ozarow* Sharp, *Rifke*, 208.

10 *First, Esther's* For Leibush Sherman's

birth in Ozarow, see "Petition for Naturalization."

10 *Leibush meant* Beider, "Names and Naming."

10 *Ozarow's revered* "The Rabbinic Dynasty of Ozarow."

10 *Allan Sherman wrote* Allan Sherman, *A Gift of Laughter* (New York: Atheneum, 1965), 27.

10 *gramen zogn* Baumgarten, "Badkhonim."

10 "My Grandfather" Sherman, *Gift*, 27.

10 *Leibush Sherman landed* Shermann, Leibusch, "List or Manifest of Alien Passengers for the United States Immigration Officer at Port of Arrival," S.S. *Kroonland*, Antwerp to New York, arrival on October 30, 1907, List 25, Line 15.

10 *Leibush worked* Leibush Scherman, "Declaration of Intention," Chicago, September 21, 1910, NARA.

11 *Nine months* Leibush Sherman, "Petition for Naturalization."

11 "steeped in" Sidney Sorkin, *Bridges to an American City: A Guide to Chicago's Landsmanshaften, 1870 to 1990* (New York: P. Lang, 1993), xi, 7.

11 "Leon was a smart" Gilbert, interview, February 14, 2005.

11 "Esther screwed around" Carol Selsberg, telephone interview by author, March 9, 2005.

11 "Esther necked" Dee Golden, telephone interview by author, February 17, 2011.

11 "a mechanic" Sherman, *Gift*, 41.

11 "She was ruthless" Golden, interview, February 8, 2011.

11 *Esther sneaked* Sherman, *Gift*, 23.

11 "understood that" Ruth Gay, *Unfinished People: Eastern European Jews Encounter America* (New York: W.W. Norton, 1996), 243.

12 "They fought" Gilbert, interview, April 15, 2005.

12 "They hated" Selsberg, interview, March 5, 2005.

12 "It was several" Mickey Sherman, telephone interview by author, February 27, 2005.

12 "He walked" Helen Stricker, telephone interview by author, February 28, 2005.

12 "He started drinking" Vivian Mailand, telephone interview by author, July 20, 2011.

12 "Morris had burns" Selsberg, interview, March 9, 2005.

12 "Everybody reached" Golden, interview, February 23, 2011.

12 "Esther was a" Gilbert, interview, February 14 and April 15, 2005.

12 *Rose and Kate soon* Sherman, *Gift*, 19. For Chicago's Jewish population, see Seymour Jacob Pomeranze, "Aspects of Chicago Russian Jewish Life, 1893–1915," in *The Chicago Pinkas*, ed. Simon Rawidowicz (Chicago: College of Jewish Studies, 1952), 119. For Jewish population of Northwest Side, see Louis Wirth, *The Ghetto* (Chicago: University of Chicago Press, 1956), 278. For Sherman family addresses, see Leibush Sherman, "Petition," and Leon Sherman, *Fourteenth Census*.

12 "stay clear" Jenna Weissman Joselit, "'Harness My Zebras': American Jews and the Pursuit of Pleasure," in *American Judaism in Popular Culture*, ed. Leonard J. Greenspoon and Ronald Simkins (Omaha, NE: Creighton University Press, 2006), 8.

12 "wild sense" Eli Lederhendler, "Guides for the Perplexed: Sex, Manners, and Mores for the Yiddish Reader in America," in *East European Jews in America, 1880–1920: Immigration and Adaptation*, Part Two, ed. Jeffrey S. Gurock (New York: Routledge, 1998), 541.

12 "constitutes a crisis" "personal disorganization" Louis Wirth, *Culture Conflicts in the Immigrant Family* (Chicago: University of Chicago Press, 1925), 33, 53.

13 *America filled them* Andrew R. Heinze, *Adapting to Abundance: Jewish Immigrants, Mass Consumption, and the Search for American Identity* (New York: Columbia University Press, 1990), 39.

13 *Newspapers serving* Maxine S. Seller, "World of Our Mothers: The Women's Page of the *Jewish Daily Forward*," in Gurock, *East European Jews*, Part Two, 525.

13 *Jewish immigrants* Simon Kuznets,

"Immigration of Russian Jews to the United States: Background and Structure," in Gurock, *East European Jews*, Part One, 60, 88; Lloyd P. Gartner, "Jewish Migrants en Route from Europe to North America: Traditions and Realities," in Gurock, *East European Jews*, Part One, 97.

13   *Margaret Sanger's guide*   Lederhendler, "Guides," 540.

13   *In 1920, Chicago's*   Pomerenze, "Aspects," 119.

13   "low comedy songs"   Harley Erdman, *Staging the Jew: The Performance of an American Ethnicity, 1860–1920* (New Brunswick, NJ: Rutgers University Press, 1997), 152, 150.

13   "long excruciating"   Hana Wirth-Nesher, "The Accented Imagination: Speaking and Writing Jewish America" in *Imagining the American Jewish Community*, ed. Jack Wertheimer, (Waltham, MA: Brandeis University Press, 2007), 288.

13   "were bound to be"   Eli Lederhendler, *New York Jews and the Decline of Urban Ethnicity, 1950–1970* (Syracuse, NY: Syracuse University Press, 2001), 45.

14   "kissed a Mazuzah"   Sherman, "My Moment of Truth."

14   "This is the great"   Alfred Kazin, *Contemporaries* (Boston: Little, Brown, 1962), 271.

14   "a sort of moral"   Stephen F. Brumberg, "Going to America, Going to School: The Immigrant–Public School Encounter in Turn-of-the-Century New York City," in *East European Jews in America, 1880–1920: Immigration and Adaptation*, Part One, ed. Jeffrey S. Gurock (New York: Routledge, 1998), 431.

14   "The immigrant is braced"   Wirth, *Culture Conflicts*, 126.

14   "beautiful-looking"   Sherman, *Gift*, 19.

14   "She had the mentality"   Coplon, interview, April 7, 2005.

14   "Rose liked"   Gilbert, interview, April 15, 2005.

15   "Rose was like"   Mailand, interview, July 20, 2011.

15   *Rose Sherman was born*   Leibush Sherman, "Petition."

15   "Esther entered"   Gilbert, interview, February 14, 2005.

15   *On July 17, 1922*   Rose Sherman and Jack Carp, Marriage License, Bureau of Vital Records, Cook County Clerk's Office, Illinois.

15   *Though of Russian*   Jack Carp, Certificate of Death, February 18, 1930, Registered No. 5648, Bureau of Vital Records, Cook County Clerk's Office. Also see, Jack Carp, *Fourteenth Census of the United States: 1920 Population Schedule*, Chicago, Illinois, Ward 18, Sheet 3B, Line 89. According to Carp's death certificate he was born in Manchester, England. The census shows he arrived in the United States when he was sixteen.

15   *Some Russian Jews*   Gartner, "Jewish Migrants," 94–95. Gartner claims the numbers of Jews immigrating via England is unknown. Others put the numbers at the relatively small 5,000 per year from 1906 to 1910. See Kuznets, "Immigration of Russian Jews," 3.

16   *There is no record*   Rose Sherman and Perry Coplon, Marriage License, October 18, 1923, Bureau of Vital Records, Cook County Clerk's Office.

16   "wild wind"   *Illustrated Souvenir of the Birmingham Storm, Monday Morning, March 25, 1901*, Birmingham Public Library Digital Collections, http://bplonline.cdmhost.com/ (accessed May 8, 2012).

16   *Three months later*   "List or Manifest of Alien Passengers for the United States Immigration Officer at Port of Arrival," S.S. *Pennsylvania*, Hamburg to New York, arrival on June 21, 1901, Sheet 3, Lines 23–26.

16   *In 1880*   *Birmingham's Plain Statement for the Homeseeker, the Investor and the Manufacturer* (Birmingham, AL: The Commercial Club, September 1893), http://bplonline.cdmhost.com (accessed May 8, 2012).

16   *Miners dynamited*   For Moses Coplon's arrival in America, see Copeland, Moses, *Twelfth Census of the United States—1900*, Jefferson County, Birmingham City, Alabama, Precinct 21, Ward 5, Sheet No. 9, Line 61.

16　*Two additional*　Gadalje and Sime Kaplan, "List or Manifest of Alien Passengers for the United States Immigration Officer at Port of Arrival," S.S. *Palatia*, Hamburg to New York, arrival on June 8, 1900, Sheet 46, lines 13–14.

16　*He joined*　Daniel Isenberg, telephone interview by author, May 14, 2004.

17　*"gentlemen whose devotion"*　Mark H. Elovitz, *A Century of Jewish Life in Dixie: The Birmingham Experience* (Tuscaloosa: University of Alabama Press, 1974), 56.

17　*"Percy was strictly"*　Joe Resnick, telephone interview by author, February 23, 2004.

17　*"the most offensive" "assimilation was highly"*　Stephen Whitfield, "The Braided Identity of Southern Jewry," in *Anti-Semitism in America*, ed. Jeffrey S. Gurock (New York: Routledge, 1998), 688–89.

17　*Though prejudice*　Howard N. Rabinowitz, "Nativism, Bigotry and Anti-Semitism in the South," in Gurock, *Anti-Semitism in America*, 655–57.

17　*"One I remember"*　Sara S. Sewelovitz, "The Call to the Open," *The Mirror* (Birmingham, AL: Birmingham High School, 1911), 12, http://bplonline.cdmhost.com (accessed May 8, 2012).

17　*"Percy was one"*　Coplon, interview, April 7, 2005.

17　*"You want to write"*　Resnick, interview, February 23, 2004.

17　*Percy channeled*　Randal L. Hall, "Before NASCAR: The Corporate and Civic Promotion of Automobile Racing in the American South, 1903–1927," *The Journal of Southern History* 68 (August 2002): 661, 667.

17　*"could take a metal"*　Coplon, interview, April 7, 2005.

18　*"In my mind"*　Isenberg, interview, May 14, 2004.

18　*By the time*　Percy Coplon, *Birmingham City Directory, 1913* (Birmingham, AL: R.L. Polk & Co., 1913), 466.

18　*"mechanician"*　"Big Race Full of Spectacular Thrills, Katz Seriously Injured in the Hundred-Mile Race," *Birmingham Age-Herald*, October 30, 1913, 7.

18　*"he didn't reckon" "Sensational Crashes at Big Race Meet, Auto Races Most Exciting Ever; Three Injured,"* *Birmingham News*, October 30, 1913, Sports, 1.

18　*He remained*　Percy Coplan, World War I Draft Registration Card, Serial No. 171, Registration No. 140. Registered June 5, 1918, Birmingham, Alabama, http://search.ancestry.com/search/db.aspx?dbid=6482 (accessed May 8, 2012).

18　*Percy wasn't satisfied*　Sherman, *Gift*, 18.

18　*"Percy said he"*　Coplon, interview, April 7, 2005.

18　*After the war*　Percy Coplan, Business Entity Search by Officer, Government Records, Alabama Secretary of State, http://arc-sos.state.al.us/CGI/CORPAGENT.MBR/INPUT (accessed May 8, 2012).

18　*A year later*　Percy Coplan, Business Entity Search by Officer, Government Records, Alabama Secretary of State, http://arc-sos.state.al.us/CGI/CORPAGENT.MBR/INPUT (accessed May 8, 2012).

18　*"led the race"*　"Thousands Enjoy Labor Ceremonies," *Birmingham News*, September 7, 1920, 4.

18　*The local paper*　"Chevrolet 490 That Cleaned 'Em Up at Fair Grounds in the Big Races on Labor Day," *Birmingham News*, September 19, 1920, 4; Coplon, Percy, *Birmingham City Directory, 1922* (Birmingham, AL: R.L. Polk & Co., 1922), 515.

19　*The place to go*　Register of Licensed Dentists, 1881–1886; 1903–1951, Record Group 208, Department of Registration and Education, Illinois State Archives.

19　*"My dad was"*　Dorothy Macarus, telephone interview by author, March 29, 2005.

19　*"I could have"*　Lee Cooper, telephone interview by author, January 18, 2006.

19　*Percy had a new*　Roco Motor, *Chicago Telephone Directory*, June 1923.

19　*"Roco" was a composite*　Isenberg, interview, May 14, 2004.

19　*"facsimile southerners"*　Stephen J.

Whitfield, "Is It True What They Say About Dixie?" *Southern Cultures* 8, no. 2 (Summer 2002): 11.

20 *Allan Sherman was born* Allan Copelon, Certificate of Birth, November 30, 1924, Bureau of Vital Records, Cook County Clerk's Office, Illinois.

20 "Rose started" Jackie Sheinberg, e-mail message to author, November 15, 2004.

20 *She gave birth* Irving Cutler, *The Jews of Chicago: From Shtetl to Suburb* (Urbana: University of Illinois, 1996), 156–60.

21 "As a child" Golden, interview, February 24, 2011.

21 "Allan mentioned" Leonid Hambro, telephone interview by author, October 16, 2004.

21 *On April 23, 1925* Roco Motor & Garage Company, Articles of Incorporation, Office of the Illinois Secretary of State.

22 *By then the Copelon family* Perry Coplon, and Leon Sherman, in *Chicago Telephone Directory*, November 1926, 1928 and 1929.

22 *Roco Motor officially* "The People of the State of Illinois at the Relation of Oscar E. Carlstrom, Attorney General, vs. Roco Motor & Garage Company," General No. in Chancery, 49414, June 14, 1929. Office of the Illinois Secretary of State.

22 "Mrs. M. Coplon" *Sentinel*, August 23, 1929, 23.

22 *After Chicago* Abe Lustig, *Los Angeles City Directory, 1929*, 1404.

22 "triumph of motor" Robert M. Fogelson, *The Fragmented Metropolis: Los Angeles, 1850–1930* (Cambridge, MA: Harvard University Press, 1967), 153.

22 "gigantic improvisation" Jules Tygiel, introduction to Tom Sitton and William Francis Deverell, ed. *Metropolis in the Making* (Berkeley: University of California Press, 2001), 4.

22 "post-Judaic" Moses Rischin, foreword to *The Jews of Los Angeles, 1849–1945: An Annotated Bibliography*, compiled by Sara G. Cogan (Berkeley, CA: Western Jewish History Center, 1980), viii.

22 "spacious, affluent" Fogelson, *Fragmented*, 145.

23 *They were in* Perry Copelon, *Fifteenth Census of the United States: 1930 Population Schedule*, Los Angeles, California, Assembly District 57, Sheet No. 13 B, Lines 98–100.

23 *Rose claimed* Rose Copelon vs. Percy Copelon, Complaint for Divorce, No. D103508, Los Angeles Superior Court.

23 "'Allan,' she said," Sherman, *Gift*, 40, 308, 309.

23 "when there were no hang-ups" Allan Sherman, *Rape of the APE* (Chicago: Playboy Press, 1975), 90.

23 "indecision and disorganization" Sherman, *Gift*, 40.

24 *Allan's whereabouts* Sherman attended school in New York City prior to May 10, 1933. He was in Chicago after May 10, 1933, and he left for California after September 18, 1933. See, Allan Copelon, Student Registration Card, Department of Compliance, Former Student Records, Chicago Public Schools. For Audubon Avenue, see Sherman, *Gift*, 54, and Max Lustig, *Manhattan Telephone Directory*, Summer 1933. Max Lustig was Ether Sherman's cousin. Gilbert, interview, April 20, 2011.

24 *On May 10 he moved* Allan Copelon, Student Registration Card, and Leon A. Sherman, *Chicago Telephone Directory*, September 1933.

24 "He was the love" Gilbert, interview, February 14, 2005.

24 *Before he died* Sherman, *Gift*, 40; Golden, interview, February 8, 2011.

24 *After Dave died* Allan Copelon, Student Registration Card.

25 *He spent his* Cutler, *Jews of Chicago*, 236.

25 "At Grandma's big" Sherman, *Gift*, 30.

26 "My grandma's love" Sherman, *Gift*, 28.

26 "I never knew Rose" Golden, interview, February 24, 2011.

26 "I loved her" Sherman, *Gift*, 23.

26 *Grandpa Leon took* Sherman, *Gift*, 26–27.

26 "stories of abandoned" Gay, *Unfinished People*, 48.

26 *shund* Nina Warnke, "Immigrant Popular Culture as Contested Sphere:

Yiddish Music Halls, the Yiddish Press, and the Processes of Americanization, 1900–1910," *Theater Journal* 48, no. 3 (1996): 323–24.

26 *Rose changed* Golden, interview, February 24, 2011.

26 "grandfather complex" Werner Sollors, *Beyond Ethnicity: Consent and Descent in American Culture* (New York: Oxford University Press, 1986), 230, 231.

27 "Dave Segal was" Gilbert, interview, February 14, 2005.

27 "Dave Segal was quite" Mailand, interview, July 20, 2011.

27 "Dave Segal was just like" Golden, interview, February 8, 2011.

27 "People liked him" Sherry Segal, telephone interview by author, April 26, 2011.

27 *Dave Segal, aka* Dave Daniel Segal, FBI file, Memorandum of May 8, 1961, from SAC, Los Angeles, to Director, FBI.

27 "Segal has hooked" "Gang Suspect Kills Self as Police at Door," *Los Angeles Herald-Express*, March 15, 1961, in Dave Segal, FBI file. For Poller's activities, see Michael D. Lyman and Gary W. Potter, *Organized Crime* (Upper Saddle River, NJ: Prentice Hall, 2000), 448.

27 *Segal was not* Helen Segal vs. David Segal, Final Judgment of Divorce, No. D-136541, February 9, 1937, Registrar-Recorder/County Clerk, County of Los Angeles.

28 *Like Jacob Carp* For Segal's birth, see Isaac Segal, Petition for Naturalization, Chicago, March 8, 1912, NARA. For physical description, see Segal, Dave, FBI file, report of May 8, 1961, 6. For description of Coplon, see Rose Copleon vs. Percy Copelon, Complaint for Divorce, Section VIII, paragraph III.

28 *Segal was born* Isaac Segal, Petition for Naturalization. For Segalowitz name, see "List or Manifest of Alien Passengers for the United States Immigration Officer at Port of Arrival," S.S. *Arabic*, Liverpool to Boston, arrival on May 5, 1906, List C.

28 *By 1908* Isaac Segal, Declaration of Intention, Cook County, Illinois, June 25, 1908. For seven children and Chicago address, see Isaac Segal, Petition.

28 *When Segal was eight* Sarah Siegel, Certificate of Death, March 30, 1914, Bureau of Vital Records, Cook County Clerk's Office, Illinois.

28 *In 1930* Dave Segal, FBI file, report of May 8, 1961, 6.

28 *He was single* David Segal, *Fifteenth Census of the United States: 1930 Population Schedule*, Chicago, Illinois, Ward 38, Block No. 502, Sheet No. 19 A, line 30.

28 *Segal married five* Sherry Segal, telephone interview by author, April 26, 2011.

28 *Helen Toppel, née Mandel* Louis Toppel, *Fifteenth Census of the United States: 1930 Population Schedule*, Chicago, Illinois, Ward 35, Block No. 423, Sheet No. 5 A, lines 36–41.

28 *Helen divorced* David Segal and Helen Toffel, Marriage License, October 3, 1932, Bureau of Vital Records, Cook County Clerk's Office, Illinois.

28 *On August 16, 1933* Frederick Mandel Segal, Certificate of Birth, August 16, 1933, Bureau of Vital Records, Cook County Clerk's Office, Illinois.

28 *Helen had walked* Helen Segal vs. Dave Segal, Complaint for Divorce, 2.

29 *When Segal married Rose* David Segal and Rose Sherman, Certificate of Marriage, May 10, 1936, Registrar-Recorder/County Clerk, County of Los Angeles.

29 *Less than eight* Sheldon Harvey Segal, Certificate of Birth, January 1, 1937, Registrar-Recorder/County Clerk, County of Los Angeles.

29 *After graduating* "History of Fairfax High School, The Early Years as Written by the Los Angeles Times in 1985," Fairfax High School, www.fairfaxhs.org (accessed May 8, 2012).

29 *Groves of trees* "Photo Album, History," Fairfax High School.

30 *The Segals lived* David (Rose) Segal, and Saml (Anna) Strowiss, *Los Angeles City Directory 1939*, 1874, 2020.

30 *In the fall of 1938* Allan Sherman,

"Scholarship Record," Los Angeles
Unified School District.

30 *On November 22, 1939* Dave Segal,
FBI file, report of May 8, 1961, 5.

30 *Fairfax High records* Allan Sherman,
"Scholarship Record."

30 *No city or school* Photograph taken in
Springfield, Ohio, provided by Nancy
Sherman.

31 "Witz-Krieg" *Colonial Gazette*, library,
Fairfax High School.

31 "The curse of Achmed" Allan Sherman,
"Witz-Krieg," *Colonial Gazette*,
November 8, 1940.

31 *Physics Student's Valentine* Allan
Sherman, "Witz-Krieg," *Colonial Gazette*,
February 14, 1941.

31 *In one piece of doggerel* Sherman,
"Witz-Krieg," *Colonial Gazette*,
October 25, 1940.

TWO. COLLEGE IN SEX ACTS
(PRINTER'S ERROR)

33 "And had the judges" *Daily Illini*,
October 8, 1941, 4.

34 "Sherman was so bright" Arte Johnson,
telephone interview by author, January
27, 2005.

34 "Allan was different" Bruce Clorfene,
telephone interview by author, February
2, 2005.

34 "look down on" Marianne Sanua,
"We Hate New York," in *An Inventory
of Promises: Essays on American Jewish
History in Honor of Moses Rischin*, ed.
Jeffrey S. Gurock and Marc Lee Raphael
(Brooklyn, NY: Carlson Publishing,
1995), 259.

34 "He was aloof" Sherman Wolf,
telephone interview by author, March 1,
2005.

35 "If he didn't" Clorfene, interview,
February 2, 2005.

35 *Sherman applied* Allan Sherman,
Scholarship Record, Los Angeles Unified
School District; "Farewell Senior A
Edition," *Colonial Gazette*, June 20, 1941,
4.

35 "Semitic school" "Harvard's
restrictions" David O. Levine, *The
American College and the Culture of*

Aspiration, 1915–1940 (Ithaca, NY:
Cornell University Press, 1986), 157, 150.

35 "His brightness" Dr. Henry Swain,
telephone interview by author, January
27, 2005.

35 *In the fall of 1941* "74 Pass Rhetoric
Proficiency Exams," *Daily Illini*,
September 20, 1941, 1.

35 *By the end of October* "Union Building
Committees Appointed," *Daily Illini*,
October 1, 1941, 1; "Debating Season
Opens November 8," *Daily Illini*,
October 29, 1941, 2; "Tomahawk 1945,"
Daily Illini, March 28, 1942, 1.

35 "Al Sherman, natural" "Frosh
Entertainers to Present Floor Show at
Frolic," *Daily Illini*, February 19, 1942, 1.

36 "First 29 readers" "Campus Scout,"
Daily Illini, March 14, 1942, 2.

36 "Since there are few" "Campus Scout,"
Daily Illini, April 26, 1942, 4.

36 *Before his freshman year* Margalit Fox,
"Sheldon Keller, TV Comedy Writer,
Dies at 85," *New York Times*, September
4, 2008, C12.

36 "a refreshing five minutes" Bob
Hathaway, "Acts from League Show
Highlight Sing; Seniors Give Farewell
Dance in Gym," *Daily Illini*, May 15,
1942, 1.

36 "Ten Top Men" "The Looking Glass,"
Hillel Post, May 14, 1942, 2.

36 *He was not* "Freshmen Eligible for
Honorary Listed," *Daily Illini*, April 5,
1942, 1.

36 "An Introduction to Literature" Allan
Gerald Sherman, Transcript, University
of Illinois.

36 "in keeping with" Merrill Prichard,
"P.E. Department Erects Display," *Daily
Illini*, September 24, 1942, 3.

36 "the most important" "Campus Scout,"
Daily Illini, April 26, 1942, 4.

37 *At the start* Sherman, Transcript.

37 *Crucially* Cutler, *Jews of Chicago*, 248.

37 "Nobody [in the family]" Golden,
interview, February 9, 2011.

37 "immediately after rendition" Helen
Segal vs. David Segal, No. D 136541,
"Order to Show Cause and Affidavit in
Re Contempt," September 30, 1946.

37   *By the end of*   "Pledged," in *The Octago-nian of Sigma Alpha Mu*, July 1942, 22.

38   *Two armed men*   "Bandits Make Cold Night Extra Chilly for Victim," *Chicago Daily Tribune*, December 14, 1943, 18.

38   "He opened a tavern"   Clorfene, interview, February 2, 2005.

38   "Allan's mother found"   Louise Goldstein Cole, e-mail message from Jackie Sheinberg to author, October 23, 2004.

38   *Percy put his talent*   Percy Coplon, Magic City Armature Works, *Birmingham City Directory 1937* (Birmingham: R.L. Polk & Co., 1937), 596, 1428; *Birmingham City Directory 1938* (Birmingham: R.L. Polk & Co., 1938), 224, 843, 1468.

38   *Sandlin was out*   There is no record of Percy Coplon's (Copelon) marriage to Mulkin. See "Certificate of Failure to Find," State of Alabama, Department of Public Health, Center for Health Statistics, Office of Vital Records, October 19, 2004. Paper held by author.

38   *Percy's mother died*   Mrs. Kate Coplon, Certificate of Death, File No. 25020, Bureau of Vital Statistics, State of Alabama. Mose Coplon, Certificate of Death, File No. 21809, Bureau of Vital Statistics, State of Alabama.

38   *Percy and Flora*   Hilda Willard, telephone interview by author, May 14, 2004; e-mail message from Sheinberg, November 15, 2004.

39   "My mother said"   Sheinberg, e-mails to author, November 10 and 15, 2004.

39   *Sherman wrote*   Sherman, *Gift*, 69.

39   "By Allan Copelon"   Allan Copelon, "Campus Scout," *Daily Illini*, September 24, 1942, 4.

39   *October 24 was*   "900 Fathers Register," *Daily Illini*, October 25, 1942, 1.

39   "As Glaugus Bleevitch"   Copelon, "Campus Scout," *Daily Illini*, October 24, 1942, 2.

39   "dashed to Chicago"   Bob Lahlein, "Campus Scout," *Daily Illini*, October 31, 1942, 3.

39   "My God"   Sherman, *Gift*, 70.

40   "He was his own"   Bill Hamer, telephone interview by author, February 28, 2005.

40   "He drank"   Clorfene, interview, February 2, 2005.

40   "It disturbed him"   Larry Stewart, telephone interview by author, January 25, 2005.

40   "He didn't like"   Clorfene, interview, February 2, 2005.

40   "Everybody in his family"   Golden, interview, February 9, 2011.

41   *On September 5, 1942*   Allan Sherman, "Campus Scout," *Daily Illini*, September 5, 1942, 2.

41   "over and over again"   Golden, interview, February 8, 2011.

41   "He played records"   Robert Sherman, interview by author, Malibu, CA, August 24, 2011.

41   "to facilitate dating"   Sherman, "Campus Scout," *Daily Illini*, September 10, 1942, 4.

41   "There are, if one"   Sherman, "Campus Scout," *Daily Illini*, September 17, 1942, 4.

42   "Shore 'an I"   Copelon, "Campus Scout," *Daily Illini*, October 17, 1942, 3.

42   "He would call up"   Hamer, interview, February 28, 2005.

42   *On Saturday evening*   "Stunt Show to Present Varied Acts; Satires, Ventriloquist Will Compete," *Daily Illini*, October 7, 1942, 1; Bill Cole, "Annual Dance, Stunt Show Are Today," *Daily Illini*, October 10, 1942, 1.

42   "It was laugh"   "Homecoming Show Predominates in Laughs," *Daily Illini*, October 11, 1942, 1.

42   "Al (Just Call Me a Genius)"   *Hillel Post*, October 23, 1942, 2.

43   "Burn down"   Sherman, *Gift*, 65.

43   "Sherman was an extraordinary"   Leonid Hambro, telephone interview by author, October 15, 2004.

44   "On the other hand"   Sherman, *Gift*, 66.

44   "from the wrong"   Sanua, "'We Hate New York,'" 242.

44   *Cosmic Fraternal Order*   Marianne R. Sanua, *Going Greek: Jewish college fraternities in the United States, 1895–1945* (Detroit: Wayne State University Press, 2003), 69–70.

44   "characteristic smooth"   Sanua, *Going Greek*, 111.

44 "Tau Lambda Tau" *Hillel Post*, October 23, 1942, 2.

44 "Allan would stay" Hamer, interview, February 28, 2005.

44 "The campus was loaded" Clorfene, interview, February 2, 2005.

45 "The Girl with the Golden" Ed Dessen, telephone interview by author, January 19, 2005.

45 "Aha!" Allan Sherman, "Campus Scout," *Daily Illini*, November 29, 1942, 3.

45 "Al Sherman Copelon" "The Looking Glass," *Hillel Post*, November 20, 1942, 2.

45 *Minkus was a well-known* "Carnival King and Queen," *Hillel Post*, April 8, 1943, 3.

45 "He was very gregarious" Seena Swibel, telephone interview by author, February 16, 2005.

46 "He was an erotic" Clorfene, interview, March 5, 2005.

46 "These letters were" Hamer, interview, February 28, 2005.

46 "Zeta House Murder" I. Feltastein, "Who Killed Bud Thud, or The Zeta House Murder," *Satyr*, October 19, 1942, 2.

46 *The* Satyr *featured* Al Sherman, "Are You the Half Human," *Satyr*, September 14, 1942, 1.

47 "you don't look Jewish" Sanua, *Going Greek*, 256.

47 *Sherman braved* Sherman, *Gift*, 55.

47 "It seemed as if" Sherman, "Campus Scout," *Daily Illini*, November 26, 1942, 2.

47 "Alice in Rhumbaland" Arnold Ostwald, "Campus Night Club Returns with New, Entertaining Show," *Daily Illini*, November 28, 1942, 1; "Commons Presents 'Good Neighbor' Latin Revue," *Daily Illini*, December 5, 1942, 1;

48 "He taught the second lieutenant" ASP.

48 "six curtain calls" Nick Shuman, "Humor, Melodious Score Highlight 'Nothing Ventured' Production," *Daily Illini*, February 20, 1943, 1.

49 "This is the road" ASP.

49 "I hated the Army" "I was allergic" Sherman, *Gift*, 72.

49 *After he was honorably* Military record for Allan G. Sherman, Service number 16-121-278, National Personnel Records Center, NARA.

49 "of Al Sherman's allergies" Sgt. Jack Adams, "Illini War Chant," *Daily Illini*, September 30, 1943, 4.

49 "When we got married" Golden, interview, February 8, 2011.

50 "Tomorrow, and tomorrow" Sherman, "Campus Scout," *Daily Illini*, December 5, 1943, 2.

50 "He lost interest" Golden, interview, February 8, 2011.

50 *The war made* "Cases of Cutting of Required Physical Education" and "Cases of [deleted], Allan Sherman, [deleted]," February 4, 1944, Record Series 2/9/1, Arthur C. Willard General Correspondence, 1934–46, University of Illinois Archives.

50 *He was readmitted* "Case of Allan Sherman, [deleted]," February 25, 1944, Record Series 2/9/1, Arthur C. Willard General Correspondence, 1934–46. University of Illinois Archives. Also see, Allan Sherman to the Assistant Dean, February 12, 1944, Record Series 15-1-16, Box 10, Liberal Arts & Sciences, Dean's Office, Student Correspondence, 1932–73. University of Illinois Archives.

50 "we had the same" Irene D. Pierson, Social Director, to Dean Fred H. Turner, September 20, 1943, Record Series 41/1/1, Box 2, Dean of Students Correspondence file, 1943–66. University of Illinois Archives.

50 "a bad mistake" "completely sincere" Allan Sherman to Dean Turner, September 15, 1943, Record Series 41/1/1, Box 3, Dean of Students Correspondence file, 1943–66. University of Illinois Archives.

51 *First Lady Eleanor* Laurence Bergreen, "This Is the Army," *Prologue Magazine* 28, no. 2 (Summer 1996): 98–99.

51 "draped as the 'Blue Fairy'" Pat Huber, "Sigma Alpha Mu, Tri-Delt, Evarts Win Top Honors in Stunt Show," *Daily Illini*, October 31, 1943, 1.

52 "We are civilians '43" Hamer, interview, February 28, 2005.

52 "Sherman was a brilliant" Sheldon

Keller, telephone interview by author, March 8, 2004.

52 "one of the big events" *Rhomer*, New Series, IV, no. 2 (December 1943): 2.

52 *It also won* "Stunt Show Sends Hillelites; Keeler Klub, SAM Skits Win Top Honors," *Hillel Post*, January 14, 1944, 1.

52 *Sherman continued* Sherman, *Gift*, 75–76.

52 "Allan called New York" Clorfene, interview, February 2, 2005.

53 *The* Daily Illini *ran five* "Hilarious Lyrics, Dialogue, Lilting Melodies to be Featured in Union Show," *Daily Illini*, February 24, 1944, 1; "Illini Union Show Pictures Capital During Twelfth Term of President," *Daily Illini*, February 27, 1944, 1; "Carnival Includes Union Show Skits," *Daily Illini*, March 3, 1944, 1; "'Mirth of a Nation,' Illini Union Show, Hits Campus This Week," *Daily Illini*, March 5, 1944, 1; "Curtain Goes Up on Illini Union Show Tonight," *Daily Illini*, March 11, 1944, 1.

53 "contained real wit" "Student Show Presents U.S. Life during Roosevelt's 12th Term," University of Illinois Alumni News, April 1944, n.p.

53 "Remove the sentimental music," "Eleanor, Eleanor" ASP.

53 *In April 1944* *Rhomer*, New Series, Vol. IV, no. 4 (May 1944): 1.

54 *On May 1, the Student Discipline* "Case of Allan Sherman," May 1, 1944 and May 10, 1944, and "Cases of Excessive Cutting in Physical Education," May 31, 1944, Record Series 2/9/1, Arthur C. Willard General Correspondence, 1934–46. University of Illinois Archives.

54 *But the registrar's office* G. I. Wallace to Dean Newcomb, June 22, 1944, Record Series 2/9/1, Box 80, Arthur C. Willard General Correspondence, 1934–46. University of Illinois Archives.

54 *Then on July 23* "Case of Allan Sherman, [deleted] and [deleted]," July 26, 1944, Record Series 2/9/1, Committee on Student Discipline, Arthur C. Willard General Correspondence, 1934–46. University of Illinois Archives.

54 *Clorfene helped Sherman* Clorfene, interview, February 2, 2005; "About Camp Ojibwa," Camp Ojibwa for Boys, www.campojibwa.com/about_adults .html (accessed May 10, 2012).

54 "Don't come back" Ellen Weinberg, telephone interview by author, May 6, 2010.

54 *Sherman applied for* "Case of Allan G. Sherman," August 31, 1944, Record Series 2/9/1, Committee on Student Discipline, Arthur C. Willard General Correspondence, 1934–46.

54 *He applied again* Sherman, "Special Reports," Transcript.

54 *Finally, on January 23* Sherman, "Special Reports," Transcript.

54 *While awaiting readmission* Hamer, interview, February 28, 2005.

55 "We all dressed up" Johnson, interview, January 27, 2005. Song lyrics provided by Johnson.

55 *His "Don't Take My Pin"* "Over A Coke," *Hillel Post*, March 13, 1945, 3.

55 *For the next twenty* "Don't Fence Me In" *Party Songs of Alpha Sig* (1956), www.horntip.com/html/books_& _MSS (accessed May 10, 2012); *Illinois Wesleyan University Magazine*, Winter 2002, www.iwu.edu/magazine/2002 /winter/anderson.html (accessed May 10, 2012).

55 "If I should drink" Sanua, *Going Greek*, 347.

55 *He had pinned* *Rhomer*, New Series, Vol. IV, no. 3 (March 1944): 3.

56 "They didn't come" Golden, interview, February 7, 2011.

57 "having an on-again-off-again" *Rhomer*, New Series, Vol. IV, no. 2 (December 1943): 2.

57 "learned many secrets" "The Looking Glass," *Hillel Post*, October 29, 1943, 2.

57 *After Sherman's summer* "Campus Scout," *Daily Illini*, December 15, 1944, 2.

57 "who his next pin-up" "Over a Coke," *Hillel Post*, March 13, 1945, 3.

57 *In April 1945* "Over a Coke," *Hillel Post*, May 10, 1945, 3.

57 *It probably happened* Sherman, "Special Reports," Transcript.

58 "Chopped liver!" Bud Burtson and Allan Sherman, *The Golden Touch, A Fable*, 35, 55, 61–62.

59 *Sherman cowrote* For Bud Burtson see, Paul Denis, *Your Career in Show Business* (New York: E.P. Dutton, 1948), 152.

59 "represents the influence" Deborah Tannen, "New York Jewish Conversational Style," *International Journal of the Sociology of Language* 30 (1981): 147.

59 "ethnic-religious" Lederhendler, *New York Jews*, 13, 28.

60 "the Jewish Camelot" Lederhendler, *New York Jews*, 13.

60 "deepened and intensified" Arthur Goren, *The Politics and Public Culture of American Jews* (Bloomington: Indiana University Press, 1999), 190.

60 "There will be a series" Allan Sherman to Bill Pilkenton, postmarked June 24, 1945. Provided to the author by Pilkenton's daughter, Pamela Pilkenton Hammil.

60 *In December 1944* "Two Illini Join Forces to Produce Tons of Tantalizing, Torrid Tunes," *Daily Illini*, February 28, 1945, 3.

60 *Sherman did not realize* Sherman to Pilkenton, June 24, 1945.

60 "Allan was in New" Golden, interview, February 8, 2011.

61 *He hid it* Golden, interview, April 4, 2011.

61 "I see people" Golden, interview, February 23, 2011.

61 "She worried" Gilbert, interview, February 14, 2005.

61 *Dr. Ben Lichtenstein* Gilbert, interview, February 14, 2005; Larry R. Squire, *The History of Neuroscience in Autobiography*, volume 5 (Amsterdam: Elsevier Academic Press, 2006), 667.

61 *Sherman married* Allen [*sic*] Sherman and Dolores Chackes, Certification of Marriage, Office of the County Clerk, Cook County, State of Illinois. Gilbert, interview, February 14, 2005; Gay, *Unfinished People*, 268.

62 *He had a weakness* "Moses Silverman, at Synagogue 46 Years," *Chicago Tribune*, May 17, 1986, http://articles. chicagotribune.com (accessed May 11, 2012).

62 *His mother-in-law* Helen Segal vs. David Segal, "Affidavit in Support of Motion for Issuance of Execution after Five Years and for Temporary Restraining Order," No. D-136541, October 8, 1946, 3, Los Angeles Superior Court. Also see, Segal vs. Segal, "Counter-Affadavit of David in Opposition to Motion for Issuance of Execution after Five Years and Restraining Order," October 17, 1946, 1–2.

62 "decades-long" Erdman, *Staging the Jew*, 160.

62 "ancient rivalries" Stephen J. Whitfield, *In Search of American Jewish Culture* (Hanover, NH: Brandeis University Press, 1999), 73.

63 "Failure, smailure" *Golden Touch*, Act Two, Scene 2, 9.

63 "pseudo-formal society" Lauren B. Strauss, "Staying Afloat in the Melting Pot: Constructing an American Jewish Identity in the *Menorah Journal* of the 1920s," *American Jewish History* 84, no. 4 (December 1996): 326.

63 "customs and standards" Seth Korelitz, "The Menorah Idea: From Religion to Culture, from Race to Ethnicity," *American Jewish History* 85, no. 1 (March 1997): 93.

63 "the ethnic character" William Toll, "Horace M. Kallen: Pluralism and American Jewish Identity," *American Jewish History* 85, no. 1 (March 1997): 63.

63 "I'm Jewish oriented" "Sherman 'Marches' On," *Washington Post*, February 3, 1963, A7.

64 "a moral obligation" Toll, "Horace M. Kallen," 71, 70.

64 *On August 28* Louis Calta, "'Heiress' to Bow on Rialto Sept. 29," *New York Times*, August 28, 1947, 28; Louis Calta, "'Ballet Ballads' Due at Music Box," *New York Times*, May 18, 1948, 27.

64 *In June*, Billboard "Golden Touch for Fall," *Billboard*, June 5, 1948, 44.

64 *The same month* Louis Calta, "Wiman

to Offer Connelly Comedy," *New York Times*, June 17, 1948, 28.

64 "A woman across" Golden, interview, February 9, 2011.

64 "Hey fats" Jerry Lester to Sherman at 340 E. 66th Street, New York, NY, n.d. ASP.

65 "Think of how many" Golden, interview, February 10, 2011.

65 "He loved food" Golden, interview, February 9, 2011.

65 *Sherman first made* Golden, February 9, 2011

65 "I played the part" "Leave It to Mike," My Old Radio, www.myoldradio.com /rare-shows/leave-it-to-mike (accessed October 10, 2011); John Dunning, *On the Air: The Encyclopedia of Old-Time radio* (New York: Oxford University Press, 1998), 390.

65 "a piano lad" "Balti. Op Woe: Acts Too High, No $ to Buy," *Billboard*, February 12, 1949, 39–40.

65 "witty ditties" Wally Griffin, telephone interview by author, November 23, 2009.

65 "That was his" Golden, interview, February 9, 2011.

66 "the godfather" United Press International (UPI), "Admitted Land Swindler Offers to Aid Arizona," *The Hour*, March 25, 1977, 37.

66 *Wildberg, a legitimate* Lester Bernstein, "London Premiere for 'Golden Touch,'" *New York Times*, July 16, 1948, 15.

66 *Warren and Steuer were* "Admitted," UPI, 37. J. P. Shanley, "Ben Grauer Plans Stint as Producer," *New York Times*, July 20, 1957, 37; Dorothy Kilgallen, "Broadway Bulletin Board," *Toledo Blade*, July 14, 1947, 28.

66 "Storywise the play is weak" *Variety*, May 2, 1951, 68.

66 "Its failure broke" Golden, interview, September 22, 2011

66 "I remember" Dorothy Macarus, telephone interview by author, March 29, 2005.

67 "prove that anything," "Original Mr. Five-By-Five Embarks On 100-Day Fast to Trim Waistline," *Mobile Register*, August 26, 1949.

67 "It took Coplon" Roland Dopson,

"Birmingham Faster Asks Visitors to Skip Food Talk," *Dothan Eagle*, September 4, 1949, 10.

67 "Newspapers carried" Edwin Strickland, "Tarrant 'Fatty' To Try 100-Day Fast on Pole," *Birmingham News*, August 25, 1949.

67 "Rose said, 'I thought you knew'" Golden, interview, February 23, 2011.

68 *In late 1949* Sherry Segal, telephone interview with author, April 26, 2011.

68 "It was a total" Gilbert, interview, March 18, 2005.

68 "She couldn't stand" Golden, interview, February 8, 2011.

68 "My sermon for today" ASP.

69 "did their best" Ken Bloom, *Broadway: Its History, People, and Places: An Encyclopedia* (New York: Routledge, 2004), 287.

69 "a capitalized Human" Whitfield, *In Search*, 119.

70 *In 1950, only* Gary R. Edgerton, *The Columbia History of American Television* (New York: Columbia University Press, 2007), 103, 170.

70 *In early 1950* Sherman, *Gift*, 109–10.

70 "aspired to be smart" Edgerton, *Columbia History*, 120.

70 "Well—it's dirty" Sherman, *Gift*, pp. 124.

71 "The Gameshow King" David Marc and Robert J. Thompson, *Prime Time, Prime Movers* (Boston: Little, Brown and Co., 1992), 251.

71 "the most popular of all" Bernard M. Timberg, *Television Talk: A History of the TV Talk Show* (Austin: University of Texas Press, 2002), 243.

71 *The median income* U.S. Department of Commerce, "Current Population Reports, Consumer Income, Family Income in the United States: 1952," April 27, 1954, www2.census.gov/prod2 /popscan/p60-015.pdf (accessed May 11, 2012).

71 "the hardy perennials" Jack Gould, "Quiz Programs," *New York Times*, January 23, 1955, X13.

71 "artifice" *Variety*, June, 25, 1952, 36.

71 "so frail" "TV Follow-Up Comment" *Variety*, July 3, 1957, 38.

71 "I have the world's" "Tele Follow-Up Comment," *Variety*, June 20, 1956, 23.

72 "capital of love" Dan Wakefield, *New York in the 50s* (Boston: Houghton Mifflin, 1992), 195.

72 *Writer Calvin Trillin* Wakefield, *New York*, 229.

72 "Due to the unprecedented" Sherman, *Gift*, 148–49.

73 "Not Bronxville" Golden, interview, February 9, 2011.

73 "I'm not exaggerating" Golden, interview, February 11, 2011.

73 "It was not being" Golden, interview, February 17, 2011.

73 *Rose died* Rose Segal, Medical Certificate of Death, State File No. 34010, May 20, 1953, Bureau of Vital Statistics, Cook County, State of Illinois.

73 "Allan took her death" Gilbert, interview, February 14, 2005.

73 "was an active member" *Oak Leaves* (River Forest, Illinois), May 27, 1953, 53.

74 *maker of plastic dishes* Sherry Segal, interview, April 26, 2011; American Plastics appears in the Illinois Secretary of State's Certified List of Domestic and Foreign Corporations only in 1953 and 1954, per e-mail message from Hana Field, Harold Washington Library, Chicago, July 28, 2008.

74 "She could be very ingratiating" Golden, interview, February 24, 2011.

74 "a foot-operated buzzer" Segal, interview, April 26, 2011.

74 *Allan's mother* Golden, interview, February 24, 2011.

74 *He tried to apply* Sherman, *Gift*, 176.

74 "Allan and I were in Chicago" Golden, interview, February 8, 2011.

74 *The fire marshal* "Thousands See Firemen Fight N.W. Side Blaze," *Chicago Daily Tribune*, October 17, 1954, 1.

74 "One amusing story" Segal, interview, April 26, 2011.

74 "lousy life" Gilbert, interview, April 20, 2011.

74 *He died* S. Segal, Social Security Death Index, ancestry.com (accessed August 23, 2012).

75 "I like all" Golden, interview, February 8, 2011.

75 *He moved* Golden, February 11 and 15, and October 12, 2011.

75 "Allan was a joy" Hambro, interview, October 15, 2004.

75 "improvising genius" Daniel J. Wakin, "Leonid Hambro, 86, Pianist with an Astounding Memory, Dies," *New York Times*, October 26, 2006, A23, www.nytimes .com/2006/10/26/obituaries/26hambro. html (accessed May 11, 2012).

76 "timing, mugging, dialects" Albert Goldman, *Ladies and Gentlemen, Lenny Bruce!* (New York: Random House, 1971), 112.

76 "Dave Vern was a very" Golden, interview, February 24, 2011.

76 "our folk heritage" Sam Levenson, *Everything but Money* (New York: Simon and Schuster, 1966), 7.

76 *In the fifties he* Gerard Jones, *Men of Tomorrow: Geeks, Gangsters, and the Birth of the Comic Book* (New York: Basic Books, 2004), 313.

76 "sensitive and skilled" Wakin, *New York Times*, October 26, 2006.

76 "I was an orgy man" Hambro, interview, October 15, 2004.

76 "I'd like to be" Golden, interview, February 15, 2011.

76 "a lot of drinking" Crescent Dragonwagon, telephone interview by author, December 8, 2009.

76 "the Boswell" "Maurice Zolotow, 77, Show Business Writer," *New York Times*, March 16, 1991, 29.

77 "Zolotow and Sherman" Betsey Gehman, telephone interview by author, May 5, 2010.

77 "she had dark" Wakefield, *New York*, 197.

77 *The same mistake* Jerry Perenchio, telephone interview by author, March 30, 2005. Perenchio thought Bullets was Jewish.

77 "People call me" Richard Gehman, "The Hanneler," *TV Guide*, March 16, 1963, 19.

77 *Allen came to New York* Edgerton, *Columbia*, 170.

77 "We like you, too" *Steve Allen Show*, 1963-03-22. UCLA Film and Television Archive.

77 "By coincidence" Golden, interview, February 23, 2011.

78 *Regulars included*   Mark Rosengarden, telephone interview by author, September 30, 2009.

78 *He took the name*   Tim Brooks and Earle Marsh, *The Complete Directory to Prime Time Network and Cable TV Shows, 1946–Present* (New York: Ballantine Books, 2007), 1071; Michael Lydon, *Ray Charles: Man and Music* (New York: Riverhead, 1998), 67.

78 "My father and him"   Neil Rosengarden, telephone interview by author, October 23, 2009.

78 "Sherman would come"   Ray Charles, telephone interview by author, April 1, 2005.

78 *On Secret's fifth*   "*I've Got a Secret* [1957-06-19, 5th anniversary show]," UCLA Film and Television Archive.

78 "If I come in"   Golden, interview, February 9, 2011.

78 "I was a Disorganization"   Sherman, *Gift*, 147.

79 *The three-act play*   Allan Sherman and Eugene O'Sullivan, *The Happy Medium* (unpublished manuscript), Yale Collection of American Literature, Beinecke Rare Book and Manuscript Library, Yale University Library.

79 "Sometimes it is quite funny"   *Variety*, April 23, 1952, 50.

79 *In September 1954*   "New Comedy at East Eden," *Chicago Daily Tribune*, August 29, 1954, E8.

79 "Nichols: Then you"   Sherman and O'Sullivan, *Happy Medium*, Act II, 19.

80 "a challenge in ingenuity"   "What's Going On?" *Variety*, December 1, 1954, 35.

80 *It bombed and Sherman*   "Television Reviews" *Variety*, October 4, 1956, 15; "Tuesday Now TV's 'Bluesday,'" *Variety*, October 31, 1956, 25.

80 "delightful entertainment"   J.P.S., "Borge Deftly Blends Music and Comedy," *New York Times*, February 20, 1958, 51.

80 *In March he was in*   "Phil Silvers' Special," *Variety*, March 19, 1958, 24.

80 "100 choir-boy types"   Gil Fates, *What's My Line? The Inside History of TV's Most Famous Panel Show* (Englewood Cliffs, NJ: Prentice-Hall, 1978), 74–75.

80 "Allan would defend"   Fates, *What's My Line?* 73, 78–79.

80 "handkerchief parachute"   Fates, *What's My Line?* 79–80.

81 *But the show did not*   Sherman, *Gift*, 182. A copy of this episode was provided to the author by Freemantle Media.

81 *After Goodson-Todman*   Sherman, *Gift*, 184–86.

81 *On June 12, 1959*   "Bargain and Sale Deed," recorded June 15, 1959, Liber 5917, Page 275, Office of the Westchester County Clerk, Westchester, New York.

81 "gorgeous Dutch"   Golden, interview, February 9, 2011.

81 *A month later*   "Bargain and Sale Deed," recorded July 23, 1959, Liber 5931, Page 178, Office of the Westchester County Clerk, Westchester, New York.

81 "he wanted to show"   Golden, interview, February 9, 2011.

82 *Grandpa Leon died*   Leon Abraham Sherman, "Medical Certificate of Death," State File No. 3042, Bureau of Vital Statistics, Cook County, State of Illinois.

82 "'It's beautiful, no?'   Allan Sherman, "A Football for Grandma," *Readers Digest*, February 1960, 125.

82 "Be a Jew at home"   Efraim Sicher, *Jews in Russian Literature after the October Revolution: Writers and Artists between Hope and Apostasy* (Cambridge; New York: Cambridge University Press, 1995), 6–7.

FOUR. THERE IS NOTHING LIKE A LOX

83 "Handicaps"   ASP.

83 *Respected golf course*   "Lake Isle Country Club," GolfNow.com, www.golfnow.com /course-directory (accessed May 12, 2012).

83 *Brooklyn-born Milton*   "Milton Farber, 81, Retired Head of Farberware Company, Is Dead," *New York Times*, November 15, 1991, D18; "This is Golf?" *The Bee: Danville, Va.*, May 18, 1953, 7.

84 "Cadillac Row"   John Sturner, telephone interview by author, September 6, 2008.

84 "When you are Golfing"   Sherman, *Gift*, 169.

84 "I'm wild again"   ASP.

84 "a destroyer"   "Unquote," *Billboard*, May 4, 1963, 15.

84 *In the early twentieth* Whitfield, *In Search*, 62.

85 "fine balancing act" Gay, *Unfinished People*, 60.

85 *Marilyn Monroe got* Jonathan Freedman, *Klezmer America: Jewishness, Ethnicity, Modernity* (New York: Columbia, 2008), 138.

85 *Elizabeth Taylor married two* C. David Heymann, *Liz: An Intimate Biography of Elizabeth Taylor* (New York: Carol Pub. Group, 1995), 203–4. Also see, Stephen J. Whitfield, "Movies in America as Paradigms of Accommodation," in *The Americanization of the Jews*, ed. Robert M. Seltzer and Norman J. Cohen (New York: New York University, 1995), 83.

85 "fatal and monotonous" Fred Matthews, "Louis Wirth and American Ethnic Studies," in *The Jews of North America*, ed. Moses Rischin (Detroit: Wayne State University Press, 1987), 137.

86 "You know what it cost" "Brooks and Reiner's 2,000-Year-Old Man Turns 50," *NPR*, November 28, 2009, www.npr.org/templates/story/story .php?storyId=120909130 (accessed May 12, 2012).

86 "a playing with sound" William and Sarah Schack, "On the Horizon: And Now—Yinglish on Broadway," *Commentary*, December 1951, 589.

86 "Audiences have been" Edwin Schallert, "Dieterle Will Direct 'John Paul Jones'; Terry, Blythe Returns Unique," *Los Angeles Times*, July 24, 1956, 17.

86 "struggles to correct" Mort Goode, "Liner Notes," *My Fairfax Lady* (Jubilee 2030).

86 "Britishisms into Yiddishisms" *My Fairfax Lady*, side one.

86 "When I'm through" *My Fairfax Lady*, side two.

87 "happy citizen" Arnold J. Band, "Popular Fiction and the Shaping of Jewish Identity," in *Jewish Identity in America*, ed. David M. Gordis and Yoav Ben-Horin (Los Angeles: Susan and David Wilstein Institute of Jewish Policy Studies, 1991), 221.

87 "swapping one" "'vividness, energy'" Philip Roth, *Reading Myself and Others* (New York: Penguin, 1985), 194, 197.

87 "No, this is for Jews" Beth S. Wenger, *The Jewish Americans: Three Centuries of Jewish Voices in America* (New York: Doubleday, 2007), 333.

87 "I've known Allan Sherman" Maurice Zolotow, "Spoofmaster," *Saturday Evening Post*, April 20, 1963, 26.

87 "He was just dazzling" Ray Charles, interview, April 1, 2005.

88 "*I* have a wife" Sholom Aleichem, "On Account of a Hat," in *A Treasury of Yiddish Stories*, ed. Irving Howe and Eliezer Greenberg (New York: Schocken Books, 1974), 117.

88 "Allan frequently got depressed" Zolotow, "Spoofmaster," 26.

88 "the True Sherman" Richard Gehman, "Allan Sherman: Country Club Folk Singer," *Los Angeles Herald-Examiner: American Weekly*, January 13, 1963.

89 "Summertime" Home recording by Bobby Rosengarden, provided to the author by Mark Rosengarden.

89 "What you are about" Allan Sherman, "My Fair Lady," *My Son, the Box*, disc one (Rhino Entertainment Company, RHM2 7891).

90 "Count Basie's Jewish" Sanford Pinsker, "Lenny Bruce: Shpritzing the Goyim/Shocking the Jews," in *Jewish Wry: Essays on Jewish Humor*, ed. Sarah Blacher Cohen (Bloomington: Indiana University Press, 1987), 89.

90 *The takeaway lesson* Marsha Bryan Edelman, "Continuity, Creativity, and Conflict: The Ongoing Search for 'Jewish' Music," in *You Should See Yourself: Jewish Identity in Postmodern American Culture*, ed. Vincent Brook (New Brunswick, NJ: Rutgers University Press, 2006), 121.

90 *In 1951, he wrote four* Ronald L. Smith, *Comedy on Record: The Complete Critical Discography* (New York: Garland Publishing, 1988), 587.

90 *It was especially easy* Douglas Martin, "Sylvia Froos, 89, a Versatile Former Child Star," *New York Times*, April 3, 2004, A13.

90 "Eh!" ASP.

91 "Coming Up Fast!" *Billboard*, November 4, 1950, 22; December 9, 1950, 16.

91 "The butcher said" Mickey Katz, *Geshray of DeVilde Kotchke* (Capitol Records 6595-Y).

91 *The vampy original* "Music Popularity Charts," *Billboard*, December 2, 1950, 18.

91 "I love you" Allan Sherman and Sylvia Froos, "A Satchel and a Seck," *More Folk Songs by Allan Sherman and His Friends* (Jubilee Records 5019).

91 "Sam's Song" Bing Crosby and Gary Crosby, *Gary Crosby and Friend* (Decca Records ED 2001).

91 "Isn't it a shame" Allan Sherman, "Jake's Song," *More Folk Songs*.

91 *Singer Patti Page* "The Billboard Music Popularity Charts, Honor Roll of Hits, The Nation's Top Tunes," *Billboard*, December 9, 1950, 18.

92 "Not so bad" Sylvia Froos, "Tennessee Frelich," *More Folk Songs*.

92 "Tzimished" Harry Ross, "Tzimished" (*Jubilee Records* 3521), http://faujsa.fau.edu/jsa/discography.php?jsa_num=504906-B (accessed May 12, 2012).

92 *But in 1950* "Stewart, Cher Cast Chart Spell," *Billboard*, November 8, 2003, 51.

92 "I should tell her" ASP.

92 *He had his hands full* Sherman, *Gift*, 170.

93 *But songwriter* "E.Y. Harburg," *Songwriters Hall of Fame*, www.songwritershalloffame.org/exhibits/C14 (accessed May 12, 2012).

93 "How are things" Sherman, *Gift*, 170.

93 "a transformational moment" Riv-Ellen Prell, "Community and the Discourse of Elegy: The Postwar Suburban Debate," in *Imagining the American Jewish Community*, ed. Jack Wertheimer (Waltham, MA: Brandeis University Press, 2007), 69.

93 *During the 1950s* Riv-Ellen Prell, *Fighting to Become Americans: Jews, Gender, and the Anxiety of Assimilation* (Boston: Beacon Press, 1999), 157.

93 "new, more self-assured" Band, "Popular Fiction," 220.

94 "Jewish suburban living" Prell, "Community," 69.

94 *His version was inspired* Tim J. Anderson, *Making Easy Listening: Material Culture and Postwar American Recording* (Minneapolis: University of Minnesota Press, 2006), 97; "Obituary: Sid Kuller," *The Independent*, October 13, 1993, www.independent.co.uk/news/people/obituary-sid-kuller-1510370.html (accessed May 12, 2012); *My Fairfax Lady* (Jubilee 2030). All references to *My Fairfax Lady* songs are found on this record album.

95 "All you need" Sherman, *My Son, the Box*, disc one, track 13.

95 "God and carpeting" Mark Schechner, "Dear Mr. Einstein: Jewish Comedy and the Contradictions of Culture," in Cohen, *Jewish Wry*, 151.

95 "be seen as a set" Nils Roemer and Gideon Reuveni, "Introduction," in *Longing, Belonging, and the Making of Jewish Consumer Culture*, ed. Gideon Reuveni and Nils H. Roemer (Leiden, Netherlands: Brill, 2010), 2. Also see Heinze, *Adapting to Abundance*, 4.

95 "hunger for splendor" Gay, *Unfinished*, 49, 234–35.

96 "You're a Nudnick, Sondra Goldfein" Home recording by Bobby Rosengarden, provided to the author by Mark Rosengarden.

97 "When you walk through the Bronx" Allan Sherman, *National Press Club Luncheons and Other Events*, LWO 39569, Disc 2 of 2, Library of Congress.

98 "Must you write" Home recording by Bobby Rosengarden, provided to the author by Ray Charles.

98 "Frank Cooper" Home recording by Bobby Rosengarden, provided to the author by Ray Charles.

99 *The switch in that* Robert Sherman, e-mail message to author, December 7, 2011.

99 "Sherman's new lyrics" Mimi Clar, "Sherman Folk Songs Become Gefilte Fish, *Los Angeles Times*, July 21, 1963, C5.

99 "Seventy-six Sol Cohens" ASP.

100 *My Fairfax Lady ran* "Nitery Reviews," *Daily Variety*, July 21, 1960, 6; "Variety Bills," *Variety*, September 21, 1960, 68;

"Singers Spark New Club Shows," *Los Angeles Times*, September 24, 1960, A7.

100 *Mickey Katz's popularity* Josh Kun, "The Yiddish Are Coming: Mickey Katz, Antic-Semitism, and the Sound of Jewish Difference," *American Jewish History* 87, no. 4 (December 1999): 343.

100 "They joked about father" "The Sickniks," *Time*, July 13, 1959, 42.

101 "all time best selling" *Billboard*, July 6, 1959, 31.

101 "Mother and Son" *An Evening with Mike Nichols and Elaine May* (Mercury Records, OCM 2200).

102 "A hundret dollas!" Shelly Berman, "Father and Son," *Outside Shelly Berman* (Verve LP V-15007).

102 "eyeing his own music" Bob Bernstein, "Wheeling and Dealing: Talent Tidings," *Billboard*, June 23, 1958, 6.

FIVE. OLLAWOOD!

103 "My dad just" Bill Marx, telephone interview by author, April 16, 2005.

103 *Harpo lived with* Nick Thomas, *Raised by the Stars: Interviews with 29 Children of Hollywood Actors* (Jefferson, NC: McFarland, 2011), 49.

103 *But because summer* Bill Marx, interview, April 16, 2005.

103 *That same summer* Sherman, *Gift*, 206.

104 "fairly big" Marx, interview, April 16, 2005.

104 "all the great" Marx, interview, September 26, 2011.

104 *Hillcrest Country* Neal Gabler, *An Empire of Their Own: How the Jews Invented Hollywood* (New York: Crown Publishers, 1988), 274–76.

104 "Jew-song craze" Erdman, *Staging the Jew*, 140, 145.

104 *The 1908 play* Moses Rischin, "Jews and Pluralism: Toward an American Freedom Symphony," in *Jewish Life in America: Historical Perspectives*, ed. Gladys Rosen (New York: Ktav Pub. House, 1978), 68.

104 "100 percent Americanism" John Higham, *Strangers in the Land: Patterns of American Nativism, 1860–1925* (New Brunswick, NJ: Rutgers University Press, 1994), 204.

105 "image of the Jew" Higham, *Strangers*, 281.

105 *In 1944, a poll found* John Higham, *Send These to Me: Immigrants in Urban America* (Baltimore: Johns Hopkins University Press, 1984), 171.

105 "the old suspicion" Higham, *Send*, 172.

105 "Jack Benny went" Sherman, *Gift*, 208.

106 "Jackie Gleason show" *Time*, January 20, 1961, 92.

106 "go along with" Bob Chandler, "Diary of a TV Show [Gleason's]," *Variety*, February 8, 1961, 68.

106 "The kids didn't like" Golden, interview, February 9, 2011.

106 "Allan was home a lot" Terri Leamy, telephone interview by author, February 23, 2011.

107 "Robbie would go" Debbi Whiting, telephone interview by author, May 15, 2010.

107 "My father was smart" Sherman, interview, Malibu, CA, August 24, 2011.

107 "He was very smart," Neil Rosengarden, telephone interview by author, October 23, 2009.

107 "I remember Robbie" Mark Rosengarden, telephone interview by author, December 3, 2009.

107 "I should have let" Golden, interview, October 12, 2011.

107 "I never saw anyone" Paul Lieberman, "The Boy at Camp Granada," *Los Angeles Times*, August 16, 2003, http://articles.latimes.com/2003/aug/16/entertainment/et-lieberman16 (accessed June 7, 2012).

108 "The owner called" Dee Golden, telephone interview by author, October 12, 2011.

108 "But I just hated" Lieberman, "The Boy at Camp Granada."

108 "This is Nancy, a girl" Allan Sherman, *Every 600 Years, on a Tuesday (The Journey to the Perfectly Fair)*, 1, 3. Quoted with permission of rights holder, Tom Smothers, Knave Productions, Inc.

108 "He was a lovely little guy" Bill Loeb, telephone interview by author, April 1, 2005.

109 "My friend got so pissed" Nancy

Sherman, interview by author, Park City, UT, September 25, 2011.

109 "Of all the people" Sherman, *The Rape of the APE.*, 278.

109 "One thing my father" Robert Sherman, interview by author, Malibu, CA, August 24, 2011.

109 "Mommy! Can't you keep" Allan Sherman, "Headaches," *My Son, the Nut*, Warner Bros. 1501.

109 "In his writing" Golden, interview, February 23, 2011.

109 *With a friend* Sherman, *Gift*, 189–91. Sherman flew to Los Angeles on Lincoln's birthday, per author interview with Golden, October 12, 2011.

109 "Allan was having a very" Golden, interview, February 10, 2011.

110 *Dee listened* Golden, interview, October 12, 2011.

110 *It debuted on* Vincent Terrace, *The Complete Encyclopedia of Television Programs, 1947–1979* (South Brunswick, NJ: A.S. Barnes, 1979), 2:1101.

110 "Well, Robbie will" Golden, interview, February 15, 2011.

110 "It was mad" Hal Cooper, telephone interview by author, April 6, 2005.

111 "How your husband would like" *Your Surprise Package*, Catalog ID: B:52102, The Paley Center for Media, Los Angeles.

111 "We worked till 10" Ray Charles, telephone interview by author, April 1, 2005.

111 "half a dozen saucers" "Flock of Sherman TV Projects on Tap," *Variety*, November 23, 1960, 30.

111 *His parents and* For Segal's arrival and activities in Los Angeles, see Segal, Dave, FBI file, "Teletype," March 17, 1961, 1–3.

112 *Sherman's stepbrother* Segal, Dave Daniel, Certificate of Death, Registrar-Recorder/County Clerk, County of Los Angeles.

112 "yo-yo" Sherman, *Gift*, 3, 4.

112 "After Labor Day" Earl Wilson, "It Happened Last Night," *Pittsburgh-Post Gazette*, September 1, 1961, 27.

112 *Another guest was Norman* William Grimes, "Norman Corwin, 101; Rendered Radio into Poetry," *New York Times*, October 20, 2011, B18; Todd S. Purdum,

"From That Day Forth," *Vanity Fair*, February 2011, 140.

112 "I had such a headache" Golden, interview, February 10, 2011.

113 *Besides, by the late* Edgerton, *Columbia*, 193.

113 "By the 1960s, only New" Deborah Dash Moore, *To the Golden Cities: Pursuing the American Dream in Miami and L.A.* (Cambridge, MA: Harvard University Press, 1994), 23.

113 "I would get a call" Hal Cooper, telephone interview by author, April 6, 2005.

113 "Ollavood!" Recording provided to the author by Ray Charles.

113 *It paid off with* "Two Illini Forces to Produce Tons of Tantalizing, Torrid Tunes," *Daily Illini*, February 28, 1945, 3.

114 *On September 27, 1961* Miriam Sherman vs. Allan Sherman, No. WE D-9743, "Responses to First Set of Interrogatories," filed May 8, 1967, Los Angeles Superior Court, 2.

114 *After the closing* Golden, interview, February 9, 2011.

114 *The $85,000 house* U.S. Census Bureau, www.census.gov/hhes/www/housing/census/historic/values.html (accessed December 14, 2011); Los Angeles Fire Department Historical Archive, "Film Colony Mansions Destroyed," www.lafire.com/famous_fires/MajorIncident-index.htm (accessed December 14, 2011).

114 *A loan from Dee's mother* Dee Golden, telephone interview by author, November 19, 2011. Also see Miriam Sherman vs. Allan Sherman, No. WE D-9743, "Responses to First Set of Interrogatories," 11.

114 *Sherman and Dee sold the house* "Indenture," between Allan Sherman and Dolores Sherman and Werner Mendel, Liber 6173, page 498. Deed recorded January 8, 1962, Office of the Westchester County Clerk, Westchester, New York.

114 "When we got back here" Robert Sherman, interview by author, Malibu, CA, August 24, 2011.

115 *A former publicity man* Linsey Deverich, *Wandering through La La Land with the Last Warner Brother* (Bloomington, IN: Author House, 2007), 47–48.

115 "was right out of Damon Runyon" Marx, interview, April 16, 2005.

115 *Bullets was tone-deaf* "Jim Conkling Salute Oct. 25," *Billboard*, October 16, 1961, 1.

115 *Affectionately known as the Pink* The Beverly Hills Hotel, www.beverlyhillshotel.com/history (accessed December 5, 2011).

115 *It was a stag event* Sherman, *Gift*, 212.

115 "Big Bad Jim" "Big Bad John," Box 2, Folder 13, James Conkling Papers, MSS 2020, L. Tom Perry Special Collections, Harold B. Lee Library, Brigham Young University.

116 *he did not sing it live* Sherman, *Gift*, 212.

116 "The highlight" Army Archerd, Just for Variety, *Variety*, October 27, 1961, 2.

116 "the most disastrous brush fire" Los Angeles Fire Department Historical Archive, "Official Report of the Los Angeles Fire Department," www.lafire.com/famous_fires/MajorIncident-index.htm (accessed December 14, 2011).

116 *Sherman's street* Sherman, *Gift*, 219.

116 *At night, depressed* Sherman, *Gift*, 222–23.

116 "When he was sitting" Golden, interview, February 24, 2011.

117 *He continued to promote* Allan Sherman, "Party Recording," April 10, 1962. ASP.

117 "the mainstreaming not just" Freedman, *Klezmer America*, 130, 11–12, 330–31.

118 *Ethnicity was the only* Freedman, *Klezmer America*, 11, 129.

118 "the quite anomalous" Freedman, *Klezmer America*, 136.

118 *Immigration was given* Paul Vitello, "Oscar Handlin, Historian Who Chronicled U.S. Immigration, Dies at 95," *New York Times*, September 24, 2011, D8.

118 *Jews were eager* "About John F. Kennedy's *A Nation Of Immigrants*," ADL website, www.adl.org/immigrants/ (accessed June 14, 2012).

118 *In 1959, Philip Roth's* Roth, *Reading Myself*, 205, 213–15.

118 "Unfortunately, it is not" *Billboard*, November 21, 1960, 49.

118 *Variety liked it* "Album Reviews," *Variety*, November 9, 1960, 50; "Reiner & Brooks' Comedy Click; Donegan's Sock Skiffle; Other LPs," *Variety*, September 20, 1961, 48.

119 "so damn guilty" Burton Bernstein, "Leonard Bernstein's Separate Peace with Berlin," *Esquire*, October 1961, 96.

119 "resembles an amiable" Henry Bial, *Acting Jewish: Negotiating Ethnicity on the American Stage and Screen* (Ann Arbor: University of Michigan Press, 2005), 86.

119 "Due bad facial features" Mayer to Maitland, June 29, 1962. Box 1 of 3, Folder 16738B, Warner Bros. Records, Warner Bros. Archives, School of Cinematic Arts, University of Southern California.

119 "something close to a national" Purdum, "From That Day Forth," 140.

119 "an 'Ode to the Inauguration'" Purdum, "From That Day Forth," 140.

120 "enjoys satirical comics" Arthur Gelb and Barbara Gelb, "Culture Makes a Hit at the White House," *New York Times*, January 28, 1962, L64.

120 "The food is marvelous" John F. Kennedy Presidential Library and Museum, www.jfklibrary.org/Asset-Viewer/Archives/JFKOH-LB-01.aspx (accessed December 14, 2011).

120 *The 1950s folk* William Grimes, "Irwin Silber, 84, Champion Of the Folk Music Revival, *New York Times*, September 11, 2010, A12.

120 "phenomenal success" "New Hits Take Wax Sales Out of Doldrums," *Billboard*, July 15, 1950, 10.

120 *Folk music took off* Genia Fogelson, *Harry Belafonte* (Los Angeles: Holloway House, 1991), 172; Whitfield, *In Search*, 164.

120 "tinged with a Yiddish" "Copacabana, N.Y.," *Variety*, June 7, 1961, 61.

120 "My bar mitzvah" *Ed Sullivan Show*, March 25, 1962, UCLA Film and Television Archive.

SIX. MY SON, THE FOLK SINGER

121 "A guy at the next" Joe Smith, telephone interview by author, February 1, 2005.

121 "New Yorkers, Los Angelenos" *Billboard*, October 20, 1962, 32.

121 "mostly along the Miami-Catskills" *Variety*, October 24, 1962, 64.

122   "Today's mass-communications"
      Billboard, October 27, 1962, 1.

122   "periodically a bard"   Irving Kolodin,
      "Sherman's Mighty Lyre," *Saturday
      Review*, December 8, 1962, 59.

123   *A week later*   Allan Sherman and John
      K. Maitland (signatories), "Warner
      Bros. Records, Inc., Exclusive Artist's
      Recording Agreement," June 1, 1962.
      Warner Music Group Archives.

123   "Bullets said to us"   Smith, interview,
      February 1, 2005.

123   "We had no artists"   Stan Cornyn,
      telephone interview by author, January
      28, 2005.

123   *Sherman's contract called*   "Exclusive
      Artist's Recording Agreement" June 1,
      1962. Warner Music Group Archives.

123   *Ten percent was*   Sherman, *Gift*, 247.

123   *That firm took another*   Robert
      Sherman, e-mail message to author,
      December 14, 2011.

124   "We did meetings"   Jerry Hopkins,
      e-mail message to author, May 7, 2004.

124   "He lost his money"   Golden, interview,
      February 10, 2011.

124   "He was extraordinarily"   Jerry
      Goldstein, telephone interview by author,
      September 24, 2004.

124   "He sat there"   Win Opie, telephone
      interview by author, October 19, 2004.

124   "He was sitting in the front"   Milt
      Hoffman, telephone interview by author,
      November 9, 2011.

125   "When I got to the *Steve*"   Joel
      Chaseman, telephone interview by
      author, September 1, 2011.

125   Billboard *ran*   June Bundy, "Vox Jox,"
      Billboard, July 7, 1962, 34.

125   "In his book"   Golden, interview,
      February 10, 2011.

125   "wholly original"   "Exclusive Artist's
      Recording Agreement," June 1, 1962.
      Warner Music Group Archive.

125   "Meredith loved me"   Smith, interview,
      February 1, 2005.

126   "was a lean one"   Dave Kaufman,
      "Fame? Just 'Shmame' In Allan Sherman
      Lexicon," *Daily Variety*, May 14, 1963, 8.

126   *After fame brought*   Sherman, *Gift*, 9.

126   "I knew him when"   Bill Dana,

      telephone interview by author, March 23,
      2005.

126   "The changes I have"   *Copyright Law
      Revision, Part 3, Preliminary Draft
      for Revised U.S. Copyright Law and
      Discussion and Comments on the Draft*
      (Washington, DC: U.S. Govt. Printing
      Office, 1964), 444.

127   *Warner's president, Mike Maitland*
      Sherman, *Gift*, 245.

127   *Busch, also known*   Debbi Whiting,
      telephone interview by author, May 15,
      2010.

127   "Lou would hold"   Cornyn, interview,
      January 28, 2005.

127   "Lou disciplined Allan"   Golden,
      interview, February 10, 2011.

127   "If there had been no"   Robert
      Sherman, interview by author, Malibu,
      CA, August 24, 2011.

127   "They were just having"   Whiting,
      interview, May 15, 2010.

128   *Sherman was so unfamiliar*   Robert
      Sherman, interview by author, Malibu,
      CA, August 24, 2011.

128   "There was something lovable"   Golden,
      interview, February 24, 2011.

128   "we played records"   Golden, interview,
      February 14, 2011.

128   "He was making up"   Terri Leamy,
      telephone interview by author, February
      23, 2011.

129   "most unusual new"   "'Battle Hymn'
      Sets Precedent as Pop Single," *Billboard*,
      September 14, 1959, 2.

130   *They were on their way*   Sherman, *Gift*,
      10. For studio, see Scotty Moore, the
      Official Website, www.scottymoore.net/
      studio_radiorecorders.html (accessed
      May 14, 2012).

130   *In the summer of*   Ken Vail, *Duke's
      Diary: The Life of Duke Ellington, 1950–
      1974* (Lanham, MD: Scarecrow Press,
      2002), 160.

130   "He said, 'Get the friends'"   Golden,
      interview, February 10, 2011.

130   "The organizers knew"   Theodore Bikel,
      e-mail message to author, April 13, 2011.

130   "We all laughed"   Hopkins, e-mail
      message to author, May 7, 2004.

131   "I haven't laughed"   Pat Carroll,

telephone interview by author, February 28, 2012.

131 "We all but forgot" Golden, interview, February 10, 2011.

131 *Sherman did look* Dave Kaufman, "Writers Guild Show to Flout TV's Taboos; Rush on Rogers," *Daily Variety*, November 28, 1962, 6.

131 *It was a roast* Kaufman, "Fame?" *Daily Variety*, May 14, 1963, 8.

131 "When he made" Hal Cooper, telephone interview by author, April 6, 2005.

132 "UNBELIEVABLE!!" *Call Board*, October 31, 1962. ASP.

132 "To the countless" Mike Maitland, "IN APOLOGY," *Cash Box*, October 27, 1962, 33.

132 "He was always lying down" Golden, interview, February 10, 2011.

132 "Allan was completely" Marvin Tabolsky, interview by author, Los Angeles, March 11, 2005.

133 "Things in so many" Robert Sherman, interview by author, Malibu, CA, August 24, 2011.

133 "Nancy went to camp" Golden, interview, February 14, 2011.

133 "Ole John Mercer" Bob Bach to Allan Sherman, October 17, [1962]. ASP.

133 "MY SON, THE FOLK SINGER has" Newton N. Minow to Allan Sherman, October 26, 1962. ASP.

134 *The answer was* Sherman, *Gift*, 12. The Sullivan show drew 47 million viewers in 1955, and 23 million before its cancellation in 1971. Sherman's estimate of 30 million viewers is a reasonable estimate. See Gerald Nachman, *Right Here on Our Stage Tonight! Ed Sullivan's America* (Berkeley: University of California Press, 2009), 4, 382.

134 *On October 28, he had comedy duo* "The Ed Sullivan Show," *The Classic TV Archive*, http://ctva.biz/US /MusicVariety/EdSullivan_15_(1962 –63).htm (accessed January 21, 2011).

134 "I can't say how much" Arthur Schlesinger Jr. to Allan Sherman, November 5, 1962. ASP.

134 *Kennedy singing* Sherman, *Gift*, 258.

134 "It would not surprise" Newton Minow, telephone interview by author, March 3, 2005.

134 "bug-eyed" "Millennium! Album Supersedes Singles on D.C. Hit Parade," *Daily Variety*, November 13, 1962, 7.

134 "a thin, rumpled" Edward Robb Ellis, *Diary of the Century: Tales from America's Greatest Diarist* (New York: Kodansha International, 1995), 247.

134 "Irving Berlin wants you" ASP.

135 "too many Jews" Laurence Bergreen, "Irving Berlin, This Is the Army," *Prologue Magazine* 28, no. 2 (Summer 1996), 99.

135 *The expression* David L. Gold, "On 'Jewish English in the United States,'" *Jewish Language Review* 6 (1986): 129.

136 *an approach that gives* Werner Sollors, *Beyond Ethnicity: Consent and Descent in American Culture* (New York: Oxford University Press, 1986), 251.

136 "The rhymes were" Cornyn, interview, January 28, 2005.

136 "Jewish American norms" Freedman, *Klezmer America*, 8.

136 "rule Lou Epstein" Philip Roth, *Reading Myself and Others* (New York: Farrar, Straus and Giroux, 1975), 210.

136 *That same year* Saul Bellow, introduction to *Great Jewish Short Stories*. (New York: Dell Pub. Co., 1963), 14.

137 "burden of lies" Theodor Reik, *Jewish Wit* (New York: Gamut Press, 1962), 213, 215.

137 "the distance between" Irving Howe, "The Nature of Jewish Laughter," in Cohen, *Jewish Wry*, 19.

137 *Sherman's knack for arranging* Mark Cohen, "My Fair Sadie," 57–58. Copyright © 2005 The American Jewish Historical Society. Mark Cohen's article, "My Fair Sadie: Allan Sherman and a Paradox of American Jewish Culture," was first published in *American Jewish History*, 93, no. 1 (March 2007): 51–71. Reprinted with permission from The Johns Hopkins University Press.

137 *Sherman couldn't have written* Mark Shechner, "Dear Mr. Einstein: Jewish Comedy and the Contradictions of Culture," in Cohen, *Jewish Wry*, 150–51.

138 "almost synonymous"   Stephen J.
Whitfield, *Voices of Jacob, Hands of
Esau: Jews in American Life and Thought*
(Hamden, CT: Archon Books, 1984), 133.

138 *The sentimental song*   "On the Records,"
Billboard, April 25, 1942, 75.

138 *It was at about this time*   Caroline
Evensen Lazo, *Leonard Bernstein: In Love
with Music* (Minneapolis, MN: Lerner,
2003), 63.

141 "He should live"   "My Son, the Folk
Singer," *Newsweek*, November 12, 1962,
50.

141 *Folk Singer had the*   Bob Rolontz,
"Those 2 LP's Roll On, Despite
Hitchhikers: Imitators Flood Stores
but Can't Catch Originals," *Billboard*,
December 22, 1962, 4.

141 *Comedian Morey Amsterdam*   Hank
Grant, "On the Air," *The Hollywood
Reporter*, December 4, 1962, 10.

141 *Sherman asked retailers*   "Sherman's
Bestselling Parody LPs Spin Off
'Complex' Copyright Snags," *Variety*,
December 26, 1962, 31; "Jubilee's 'Folk
Song' LP Irks Allan Sherman," *Variety*,
December 19, 1962, 55.

141 "Allan didn't make any deals"   Golden,
interview, February 10, 2011.

141 *He gave Nelson*   John K. Maitland,
president, Warner Bros. Records to Allan
Sherman c/o Durgom-Katz Associates,
September 2, 1963. Warner Music Group
Archives.

141 *"Water Boy" generated a lawsuit*
"Sherman's Bestselling Parody LPs Spin
Off 'Complex' Copyright Snags," *Variety*,
December 26, 1962, 31.

141 *It turned out*   Sherman, *Gift*, 262.

142 "the sure sign"   Hank Grant, "On the
Air," *The Hollywood Reporter*, October 18,
1962, 10.

142 "I was the first"   Gary Owens, telephone
interview by author, July 20, 2011.

142 *Another indication*   Robert Sherman,
e-mail to author, June 7, 2012.

143 "the added promotional"   Eddie Kalish,
"'Take Me to Your Meader,' Comedy
Diskings Cue Mass Demand," *Variety*,
December 5, 1962, 44.

143 *By early December*   "Demand for

Sherman Again Accents Hot Disk's
Impact on Concert Field," *Variety*,
December 12, 1962, 47; "2 Halls Full
for 'My Son at Carnegie,'" *Billboard*,
December 15, 1962, 5.

143 "All kinds of pressures"   Kaufman,
"Writers," 6.

143 "Frank Cooper"   Army Archerd, Just
for Variety, *Daily Variety*, December 10,
1962, 2.

143 "what happens when"   Kaufman,
"Writers," 6.

143 "Desilu will call you"   ASP.

143 *New project ideas*   "Rambling Reporter,"
The Hollywood Reporter, December 11,
1962, 2, and November 20, 1962, 2; "'Folk
Singer' Sherman Hits 3-Way Jackpot in
Producing, Writing, Acting," *Variety*,
November 28, 1962, 43; Dale Olson,
"Allan Sherman Turns Producer Atop
Lampoon Lacquer Click," *Daily Variety*,
November 26, 1962, 9; "New York Sound
Track," *Variety*, February 13, 1962, 7.

144 "He was a ship"   Dee Golden, telephone
interview by author, February 21, 2011.

SEVEN. MY SON, THE CELEBRITY

145 "Do you think we did"   Allan Sherman,
"Track 2," Reel #T1275. ASP.

145 *Celebrity was recorded*   "My Son, the
Book," in *Allan Sherman, My Son, the
Box*, 39; Dale Olson, "Allan Sherman
Turns Producer Atop Lampoon Lacquer
Click," *Daily Variety*, November 26,
1962, 9.

145 *It was number 28*   "Top LP's," *Billboard*,
November 10, 1962, 3; November 17, 1962,
3; November 24, 1962, 3; December 1,
1962, 3; December 8, 1962, 3.

145 *On December 15*   Bob Rolontz, "Those 2
LP's Roll On," 4.

146 "a good deal sharper"   "Sherman's
'Celebrity,' Ella's 'Swings,' Eddy's 'Guitar
Man' Top New LPs," *Variety*, December
26, 1962, 30.

146 "Who says lightning"   "The Best of the
Week's New Albums," *Billboard*, January
5, 1963, 25.

146 *Distributors agreed*   "Disk Outlook: A
Thousand Clowns," *Billboard*, December
29, 1962, 5.

146 Time *magazine kicked* "Records: My Son, the Millionaire," *Time*, January 4, 1963, 34.

146 *He wrote it in June 1959* "Television Reviews: Perry Presents," *Daily Variety*, June 15, 1959, 7.

146 "was in the avant-garde" Sollors, *Beyond Ethnicity*, 133, 137.

147 *The newsmagazine's circulation* "History of TIME," www.time.com/time/archive /collections/0,21428,c_time_history,00 .shtml (accessed May 15, 2012).

147 "I'm obsessed by Time Magazine" Allen Ginsberg, *Howl and Other Poems* (San Francisco: City Lights Books, 1983), 32.

147 *A month later* Army Archerd, Just for Variety, *Daily Variety*, March 6, 1963, 2; "Allan, Bullets Take Two," *Billboard*, May 11, 1963, 28.

148 "He was an immensely" Billy Goldenberg, telephone interview by author, February 1, 2010.

148 "He was creative" Jon Hendricks, telephone interview by author, January 12, 2012.

148 "Goldstone and Tobias" Golden, interview, April 4, 2011.

148 "Allan had a tremendous" Jerry Perenchio, telephone interview by author, March 30, 2005.

148 "He was brilliant" Bill Dana, telephone interview by author, March 23, 2005.

148 "Allan was as clever" Joe Smith, telephone interview by author, February 1, 2005.

149 Why it's good old reliable" Nancy Sherman, interview by author, Park City, UT, September 25, 2011.

150 "fathers and mothers" Bob Rolontz, "Sherman Marches on Carnegie," *Billboard*, January 12, 1963, 10.

150 "the gold standard" Nachman, *Right Here*, 7.

150 "Loyal Son" "Loyal Son: Sherman Says No to TV Till after Moore Show," *Billboard*, December 15, 1962, 5.

150 "sensational album" *The Garry Moore Show*, 1963-01-08, UCLA Film and Television Archive.

150 "I wouldn't be surprised" "Sherman 'Marches' On," *Washington Post*, February 3, 1963, A7.

151 *Mahalia Jackson had helped* "Mahalia Jackson on The Dinah Shore Show," *Jet*, June 5, 1958, 66; Bob McCann, *Encyclopedia of African American Actresses in Film and Television* (Jefferson, NC: McFarland & Co., 2010), 176; Dinah Shore & Mahalia Jackson, www.youtube .com/watch?v=4blUhPN7c34 (accessed May 15, 2012); Down by the Riverside— Mahalia Jackson; Mahalia Jackson on the Nat King Cole Show, www.youtube.com /watch?v=DVXReRfZCM8 (accessed May 15, 2012).

151 "so great that [they] must be" Pete Seeger, www.youtube.com/watch?v =LgOXqNq7fqc (accessed May 15, 2012).

151 "the standard Bronx" Gay, *Unfinished People*, 263.

151 *But Sherman's comedy* Irving Layton, *The Selected Poems of Irving Layton* (New York: New Directions, 1977), 19.

152 "Open Mouth" Horace Newcomb, *Encyclopedia of Television, Volume 1* (Chicago: Fitzroy Dearborn Publishers, 1997), 2231.

152 "it'll be interesting" "Alan [*sic*] Sherman: A Candid Conversation with America's Best-Known Philosopher/ Comedian," *Penthouse* 1, no. 6 (June 1965), n.p. ASP.

152 *The Garry Moore Show was an important* Carol Burnett, *This Time Together: Laughter and Reflection* (New York: Harmony Books, 2010), 48.

152 "her first signature song" Christopher Nickens and Karen Swenson, *The Films of Barbra Streisand* (New York: Citadel Press, 2 000), 10.

152 *On January 6, he opened* Army Archerd, Just for Variety, *Daily Variety*, January 4, 1963, 2.

153 *First, the Friday* "Allan Sherman Hottest 1-Niter Attraction in Calif. in Years," *Daily Variety*, January 17, 1963, 4.

153 *Now Christine Nelson, Jayne Meadows* Army Archerd, Just for Variety, *Daily Variety*, January 21, 1963, 2.

153 *In the summer, Rosemary Clooney* Frank Lieberman, "Allan Sherman, Minstrels Provide Delightful Evening," *Hollywood Citizen News*, July 20, 1963.

153 *An unreleased recording* Allan Sherman, recording, *Santa Monica Concert*, January 18, 1963, ASP.

153 "Sherman at this point" Dale [Olson], "Allan Sherman Revue," *Daily Variety*, January 21, 1963, 17.

153 "Sherman is a plump" "Records: My Son, the Millionaire," *Time*, January 4, 1963, 34.

153 "His parodies were brilliant" Jerry Hopkins, e-mail message to author, May 7, 2004.

154 "What else could you" Rolontz, "Sherman Marches on Carnegie," *Billboard*, January 12, 1963, 10.

154 "I think it behooves me" Sherman, in concert, Santa Monica, January 18, 1963.

154 "I'm Jewish but I don't flaunt" D.W., "Sherman Takes Rochester," *Jewish Ledger*, March 1, 1963, 12.

156 "the Jewish cultural spirit" Lederhendler, *New York Jews*, 24.

156 *In Saul Bellow's 1964 novel* Mark Cohen, "Body Language: Spoken vs. Silent Communication in Herzog," *Saul Bellow Journal* 20 (Fall 2004): 3–17.

156 *Horowitz liked the song* Army Archerd, Just for Variety, *Daily Variety*, February 7, 1963, 2.

158 "shot, stuffed and mounted" Woody Allen, "Woody Allen Routine on Moose Hunting Recalled," *NPR*, September 17, 2008, www.npr.org/templates/story /story.php?storyId=94729656 (accessed May 15, 2012).

158 "saying that the popular culture" Herbert J. Gans, "Alan [*sic*] Sherman's Sociologist Presents . . . ," *Reconstructionist*, May 3, 1963, 28.

158 "unshaven, derby-hatted" Robert E. Baker, "Anti-Semitism Is Less of a Threat," *Washington Post*, January 27, 1963, E3.

158 "will relate the experiences" "Inaugural Ball, February 2, Features Allan Sherman," *National Press Club Record* 13, no. 10 (January 1963): 1.

158 *A new club president* "Host Table" seating arrangements. ASP.

159 *The seating chart* "President Rash's Inaugural Dinner, Saturday, Feb. 2, 1963." ASP.

159 "Just the *Times*" Allan Sherman, "National Press Club Luncheons and Other Events, 2/2/63" LWO 5901 230–231, Motion Picture, Broadcasting, and Recorded Sound Division, Library of Congress.

160 "You really want to have some fun?" Gilbert Millstein, "A Negro Says It with Jokes," *New York Times Magazine*, April 30, 1961, 34, 37.

160 "Actually, our 'resemblance'" S. L. Chandler, "In a Word . . . ," [unknown origin] June 1963. ASP.

160 "Hava Nagila" Velvel Pasternak, *The Jewish Music Companion* ([United States]: Tara Publications, 2002), 93–94.

161 *He sang it as early as* Harry Belafonte, *My Song: A Memoir* (New York: Alfred A. Knopf, 2011), 99; advertisement, *Billboard*, March 30, 1957, 49; advertisement, *Billboard*, August 24, 1959, 33.

161 "to not perform it" David Kaufman, "'Here's a Foreign Song I Learned in Utah': The Anxiety of Jewish Influence in the Music of Bob Dylan," in *The Song Is Not The Same: Jews and American Popular Music*, edited by Bruce Zuckerman, Josh Kun, and Lisa Ansell (West Lafayette, IN: Purdue University Press for the USC Casden Institute for the Study of the Jewish Role in American Life, 2011), 128.

161 "has little meaning" Steven M. Cohen, "Israel in the Jewish Identity of American Jews: A Study in Dualities and Contrasts," in *Jewish Identity in America*, edited by David M. Gordis and Yoav Ben-Horin (Los Angeles: Susan and David Wilstein Institute of Jewish Policy Studies, 1991), 123.

161 "the Christian name of this song" *Steve Allen Show*, 1963-07-18, UCLA Film and Television Archive.

162 *Steve Allen helped him* Dale Olson, "Allan Sherman Turns Producer atop

Lampoon Lacquer Click," *Daily Variety*, November 26, 1962, 9.

162 *The Press Club engagement* Harold Heffernan, "Sherman's Drive to Success Takes Work," *North American Newspaper Alliance (NANA)*, February 14, 1963; Army Archerd, Just for Variety, *Daily Variety*, February 4, 1963, 2.

163 "his 'breakfast'" "Sherman 'Marches' On," *Washington Post*, February 3, 1963, A7.

163 "Show business can be a dangerous" Hendricks, interview, January 12, 2012.

163 "He loved to gamble" Marvin Tabolsky, interview by author, West Hills, CA, March 11, 2005.

164 "It kept him sane" Bill Marx, telephone interview by author, April 16, 2005.

164 "[H]e does not exactly" Zolotow, "Spoofmaster," 26.

164 *Sherman sang at the Department of Labor* David L. Perlman, "Kennedy Leads U.S. in Hailing Labor Dept. 50th Anniversary," *AFL-CIO News*, March 9, 1963, 1, 6; for seating arrangements see, "Head Table—Sheraton Hall," ASP.

164 "I have your record" Sherman, *Gift*, 282.

164 "fantastic meteoric rise" *Steve Allen Show*, 1963-03-22, UCLA Film and Television Archive.

165 *In 1963, Israel* "Out of This World: Israel's Space Program," www.mfa.gov.il /NR/rdonlyres/A7C494F2–62C2 –44BC-8FA1–148D776A67DA/0/ch76 .pdf (accessed May 15, 2012).

166 *On March 6, Daily Variety* Army Archerd, Just for Variety, *Daily Variety*, March 6, 1963, 2.

166 "Hello, star-father" Harold Banks, "Allan Shines in Fun Valley," *Boston Record American*, February 9, 1965, 21.

166 "Robbie would say" Tabolsky, interview.

166 "Friends tell me" Jean King, "My Son, the Success Story," *Topper*, June 1963, 53.

166 "You'll never amount" Heffernan, "Sherman's Drive," *NANA*, February 14, 1963.

166 "Robbie was always" Golden, interview, February 9, 2011.

166 "is still the sweet" King, "My Son, the Success Story," 53.

166 "They were not part" Billy Goldenberg, telephone interview by author, February 1, 2010.

167 *On March 27, Sherman* "Chi Chi, Palm Springs," *Variety*, April 3, 1963, 101.

167 "Bigger than Ciro's" Howard Johns, "In the Swing," *Palm Springs Life*, September 2007, www.palmspringslife.com/Palm-Springs-Life/September-2007 (accessed February 6, 2012).

167 *Owner Irwin Schuman*, "name talent policy" "Chi Chi Sets Maxine Lewis," *Billboard*, October 21, 1950, 48.

167 *The Starlite Room was* Johns, "In the Swing."

167 "Fritz Loewe delayed" Army Archerd, Just for Variety, *Daily Variety*, March 26, 1963, 2.

167 "saw fit to leave" "Chi-Chi/Are you a club" Chi Chi Tape 13—Alan [*sic*] Sherman, Side 2, Alexander Collection Recordings, Palm Springs Historical Society, Palm Springs, CA.

168 "is now an old pro" "Chi Chi, Palm Springs," *Variety*, April 3, 1963, 101.

168 "I think one of the biggest thrills" Tabolsky, interview.

168 "Sinatra, Dean Martin and Davis Jr. surprised" Army Archerd, Just for Variety, *Daily Variety*, January 24, 1963, 2.

169 *While he was there, My Son* "240 Disks in 39 Categories Vie for Industry's Upcoming Grammy Awards," *Variety*, April 17, 1963, 51.

169 "is responsible for the style" Perry Como's Kraft Music Hall, 1963-05-01, UCLA Film and Television Archive.

169 "Comedian Allan Sherman's" Gil Faggen, "A Bad Taste for 'Tonight,'" *Billboard*, May 25, 1963, 12.

169 *Steve Allen needed him* Steve Allen show, 1963-06-06, UCLA Film and Television Archive.

169 "last elegant supper club" Joel Selvin, *San Francisco: The Musical History Tour* (San Francisco: Chronicle Books, 1996), 81.

169 "Agents, press agents" Dave Kaufman, "Fame? Just 'Shmame' In Allan Sherman's Lexicon," *Daily Variety*, March 14, 1963, 8.

EIGHT. MY SON, THE NUT

170 "actually breaking down doors"
"Sherman Side Running Away for
Warner's," *Billboard*, July 27, 1963, 3.

170 "already scoring in the singles
market" "Sherman's 'Nut,' Bennett's
'Ask,' Fontaine's 'Crazy,' Ives's 'Easy,'
Cole's 'Summer' Top New LP's," *Variety*,
July 31, 1963, 92.

170 "When he was hot" Perenchio,
interview, March 30, 2005.

170 "was idolized" Smith, interview,
February 1, 2005.

170 "'Hello Muddah' is a great" Hendricks,
interview, January 12, 2012.

171 *On July 11,* Variety "Sherman 'Tonight'
Sub," *Daily Variety*, July 11, 1963, 6;
Gary R. Edgerton, *The Columbia
History of American Television* (New
York: Columbia University Press,
2007), 177.

171 *On an average night* Timberg and
Erler, *Television Talk*, 106.

171 "Sherman was always" Sheldon Schultz,
telephone interview by author, April 1,
2005.

171 *The crowd applauded* Steve Allen Show,
07–18–63, UCLA Film and Television
Archive.

171 "What impressed me most" Golden,
interview, September 22, 2011.

171 "His newest, a take-off" John G.
Houser, "Sherman (Al) Marches through
Bowl; Leaves Wake of Laughter," *Los
Angeles Herald-Examiner*, July 27,
1963, B4.

171 Billboard *reported* "Sherman Side,"
Billboard, July 27, 1963, 3.

171 Hollywood Reporter *said* "The
Notebook," *The Hollywood Reporter*, July
19, 1963.

171 *By August 4 the record* Richard F.
Shepard, "My Son, the Producer,
Performs," *New York Times*, August 4,
1963, 13.

171 *By September it was a hit* "Hits of the
World," *Billboard*, September 21, 1963, 36;
October 26, 1963, 47; November 9, 1963,
24; and December 7, 1963, 28.

171 *By then sales had reached 700,000* May
Okun, "Allan Sherman, the Success,"

Sunday News (Los Angeles), October 20,
1963, 4.

171 *New Zealand came on board* For the
Swedish version of the song, see www
.youtube.com/watch?v=vreZhL5p4V8;
for the Norwegian version, see www.
youtube.com/watch?v=e1t2qv9N_nc;
for the Israeli version, see www.enotes
.com/topic/Hello_Muddah,_Hello_
Fadduh (all accessed February 21,
2012).

172 *Its playfulness caught* Allan Sherman,
"Victor Borge sketch [no title]," ASP.

172 *Unlike most other* Lara Pellegrinelli,
"Jon Hendricks: The Father of Vocalese
at 90," *NPR*, September 16, 2011, www
.npr.org/2011/09/16/140532273/john
-hendricks (accessed May 15, 2012).

172 *On August 17* "Top LP's," *Billboard*,
August 24, 1963, 38; September 21, 1963,
34; and September 28, 1963, 28.

172 "Every Sherman Release" *Cash Box*,
September 14, 1963.

172 *At the end of September* "Top LP's,"
Billboard, September 21, 1963, 34.

172 "10 minutes of hilarity" "WB Distribs
View Label's Fall Plans," *Billboard*,
August 3, 1963, 3.

172 "He had everything" Golden,
interview, February 11, 2011.

172 "was even faster moving" "WB-Reprise
Tie Potent Hit Team," *Billboard*, August
24, 1963.

173 "eternal war" *Let's Talk About the New
Album!—Allan Sherman and You.* (RCA
Victor, SP-33-310).

174 "If you listen real close" Morris
Coplon, telephone interview by author,
April 7, 2005.

175 "What's Opera, Doc?" "What's Opera,
Doc? Opera, Pop Culture, and Mass
Media," The Paley Center for Media,
www.paleycenter.org (accessed May 15,
2012).

175 "'Hello Muddah' came to him so
fast" Golden, interview, February 24,
2011.

175 "All you'd have to do" Al Lerner,
telephone interview by author, October
3, 2011.

175 "He could do more" Bill Loeb,

telephone interview by author, April 1, 2005.

176 *That story in the book* Golden, interview, February 17, 2011; Sherman, *Gift*, 284.

176 "at the epicenter" Leslie Paris, *Children's Nature: The Rise of the American Summer Camp* (New York: New York University Press, 2008), 86–87.

177 *As a researcher in Chicago* Sollors, *Beyond Ethnicity*, 234.

177 "narrative for immigrants" Freedman, *Klezmer America*, 7–8.

178 "Oh, he had really" Saul Bellow, *Herzog* (New York: Avon, 1976), 156.

178 "Jews suburbanized" Riv-Ellen Prell, "Community," 68.

178 *Levittown, founded by* Kenneth T. Jackson, *Crabgrass Frontier: The Suburbanization of the United States* (New York: Oxford University Press, 1985), 234, 237.

178 "great American land rush" Jackson, *Crabgrass*, 282.

179 "odd-ball adaptation" Shepard, "My Son, the Producer, Performs," 13.

179 "unmistakably Jewish overtones" Nora Ephron, "The World of Allan Sherman," *New York Post*, August 4, 1963, Television 1.

179 "He wasn't just going" Hopkins, e-mail to author, May 7, 2004.

179 "let the public decide" *Tonight* show, 1963–08–05, UCLA Film and Television Library.

180 "He loved pretty girls" Tabolsky, interview.

180 "It's true" *Tonight* show, 1963–08–06, UCLA Film and Television Library.

180 "You're right, you talented man" *Tonight* show, 1963–08–08, UCLA Film and Television Library.

180 "He was great" Schultz, interview, April 1, 2005.

180 *Sherman went downtown*, Schultz, interview, April 1, 2005.

181 "Cosby did the Noah" Tabolsky, interview.

181 "We used to get" Smith, interview.

181 "a royalty of one percent" John K. Maitland to Allan Sherman, c/o Alexander Tucker, August 15, 1963.

Warner Music Group Archives.

181 "We made lots of money" Golden, interview, February 11, 2011.

181 "What is all this?" *Tonight* show, 1963–08–16, UCLA Film and Television Library.

181 "Sigmund Freud said" George Murphy, "Allan, the Folk Singer, First to Admit Singer He's Not," *Democrat and Chronicle*, February 24, 1963.

182 "The child is father" *Tonight* show, 1963–08–08, UCLA Film and Television Library.

182 *Childhood and its psychological* Sherman, *Gift*, 153–67.

182 "What psychiatrist would" Zolotow, "Spoofmaster," 26.

182 "are on the border-line" Leonard Feinberg, *The Satirist: His Temperament, Motivation, and Influence* (Ames, Iowa State University Press, 1963), 137.

182 "to debunk" Frank Stringfellow, *The Meaning of Irony: A Psychoanalytic Investigation* (Albany: State University of New York Press, 1994), 34.

183 "playing, rolling in the jungle" Sherman, *Rape of the A*P*E*, 444–45.

183 "'How can we hold'" "Allan Sherman Visits Detroit: Fired, He Finds New Fame," *Detroit Free Press*, February 18, 1963, 6-B.

183 "God help us all" Hal Cooper, telephone interview by author, April 6, 2005.

183 "He discovered girls" Perenchio, interview, March 30, 2005.

183 "Great looking chicks" Smith, interview, February 1, 2005.

183 "People go crazy" Mark Rosengarden, telephone interview by author, December 3, 2009.

183 *Sherman's college buddy* Sherman Wolf, telephone interview by author, March 1, 2005.

183 "the sort of women" Nelson W. Aldrich, *George Being George: George Plimpton's Life* (New York: Random House, 2008), 213.

183 "I think I was unique" Leonid Hambro, telephone interview by author, October 16, 2004.

183 *It was Hambro that* Douglas Martin, "James S. Moran Dies at 91; Master of the Publicity Stunt," *New York Times*, October 24, 1999, 45; Aldrich, *George*, 213.

184 "He lived a life of excess" Jerry Goldstein, telephone interview by author, September 24, 2004.

184 "I get me a bottle of champagne" Goldstein, interview, October 15, 2004.

184 *Rodgers asked Sherman* Golden, interview, February 23, 2011.

184 "is understood that" Sam Zolotow, "Allan Sherman Fathers Musical," *New York Times*, August 8, 1963, 19.

184 "Allan and I have had" Louis Calta, "News of the Rialto: Richard Rodgers Is Willing," *New York Times*, August 9, 1964, X1.

185 "Rodgers got mad" Golden, interview, February 23, 2011.

185 "He'd tell anything," Golden, interview, February 21, 2011.

185 *In October he sang* Perry Como's Kraft Music Hall, 1963–10–03, UCLA Film and Television Archive.

185 "I want to say hell" *Tonight* show, 1963–08–08, UCLA Film and Television Archive.

185 *He was at the Nugget* "Allan Sherman Set Solid into 1964," *Daily Variety*, August 30, 1963, 10; "Nitery Review: Sands," *Daily Variety*, October 15, 1963, 6.

185 "I'll always remember" Robert Lahey, "U.I. 'Unfair: Sherman,'" *Champaign-Urbana Courier*, September 28, 1963, 3.

186 "Take me back" "Hello Muddah: Illini Version," *News Gazette*, September 29, 1963, 3.

186 "Allan Sherman is a funny" *Variety*, November 20, 1963, 66.

186 *comedian Shelley Berman* Louis Sobol, "'Fair Lady' a Mine of Coincidence," *New York Journal-American*, November 18, 1963, 19.

186 "the Copa was packed" Sherman, *Gift*, 296.

186 "Comedy is a fundamentally" David S. Behrens, "It's a Tough Life, Says Sherman," *Miami Herald*, December 27, 1963, 3-BR.

186 "They have a kind" "Alan [*sic*] Sherman," *Penthouse*, June 1965, 28.

186 *The Concord was then* Myrna Katz Frommer and Harvey Frommer, *It Happened in the Catskills* (Madison: University of Wisconsin Press, 2004), 162, 152.

186 "Jump in, the water's fine" Sherman, *Gift*, 289.

187 "To be too Jewish" Sherman, *Gift*, 172.

187 "I've had an enormous" Peter J. J. Bailey, *The Reluctant Film Art of Woody Allen* (Lexington: University Press of Kentucky, 2001), 267.

187 "rather edgy about" Michael P. Kramer, "Introduction, The Vanishing Jew: On Teaching Bellow's *Seize the Day* as Ethnic Fiction," in *New Essays on "Seize the Day,"* ed. Michael P. Kramer (Cambridge: Cambridge University Press, 1998), 7.

187 "power of Jewishness" Freedman, *Klezmer America*, 330–31.

NINE. ALLAN IN WONDERLAND

188 *On February 9* Phyllis Battelle, "Assignment: America, 'It's Good to Feel Ugly,'" *New York Journal-American*, February 9, 1964.

188 My Son, the Folk Singer *sold* "His Party Pieces Have World in Tucks," *Manchester Evening News*, January 31, 1964.

188 "a fortress propped up" Lynne Olson, *Citizens of London: The Americans Who Stood with Britain in Its Darkest, Finest Hour* (New York: Random House, 2011), 72.

188 *At dinner, Sherman* For White Elephant, see Charles Foran, *Mordecai: the Life and Times* (Toronto: Knopf Canada, 2010), 283.

188 "We would go" Tabolsky, interview, March 11, 2005, West Hills, CA.

189 "He was funny" Joe Guercio, telephone interview by author, April 26, 2007.

189 "I'm pledged" Battelle, "Assignment."

189 *Between songs on their Sullivan* Gerald Nachman, *Right Here*, 355.

189 *Presley knew enough* Nachman, *Right Here*, 353.

189 *Meanwhile, the Beatles' television* Nachman, *Right Here*, 355.

189 *On August 21, 1964, he was in Seattle*
Patrick F. Diviney and Michael Allen,
"A Hard Day's Night," *Columbia, the
Magazine of Northwest History,* 10, no. 2
(Summer 1996): 6–11.

189 "I got up one day" Tabolsky, interview.

189 "Exuberance is in" Nachman, *Right
Here,* 366.

190 "may do more" "Song for Dropouts,"
Time, April 10, 1964, 76.

190 "The most fashionable concern" Fred
M. Hechinger, "The Year Ahead," *New
York Times,* September 1, 1963, E7.

190 "4 out of every 10 students" John
F. Kennedy, "Annual Message to the
Congress on the State of the Union,"
January 14, 1963, www.presidency.ucsb
.edu/ws/index.php (accessed March
27, 2011).

190 *Sherman's song took* "Sherman's 'Week'
Wail," *Daily Variety,* March 18, 1964, 15.

190 *Though he recorded it* "Liner Notes,"
Allan Sherman's *My Son, the Box,* 41.

190 *The* Time *story was a natural* "Tonight"
8 (rcf 46–4) 1840442-2-1 (April 16,
1964), 5:45–16:45. Armed Forces Radio
recording, Library of Congress.

191 *However, there were not* "Top LP's,"
Billboard, June 6, 1964, 24.

192 "If you like" Thomas Lask,
"Specializing the Comic Aim," *New York
Times,* May 3, 1964, X20.

192 "Although the humor doesn't"
"Streisand's '3rd Album,' Four Seasons,
Peter Duchin, Sherman Top New LPs,"
Variety, March 11, 1964, 44.

192 *His first idea* Army Archerd, Just for
Variety, *Daily Variety,* February 10,
1964, 2.

192 "He got very arty" Smith, interview.

193 *He told Maurice* Maurice Zolotow, "My
Friend, the Son," *Variety,* January 8, 1964,
220.

193 *A photograph taken* "Hello Mudduh,
Hello Fadduh, I've Arrived in England
on a To-ur," *Daily Herald,* February 1,
1964.

193 "I remember telling" Faith Dane,
telephone interview by author, December
6, 2004.

193 "was the most self-destructive" Steve

Allen, *More Funny People* (New York:
Stein & Day, 1982), 250.

193 "He gave away money" Golden,
interview, February 11, 2011.

194 "The startled salesman" Sidney Fields,
"My Son, the Success," *Daily News,*
November 25, 1964, 24.

194 "He was a spendthrift" Hambro,
interview, October 16, 2004.

194 "Dinner was a bacchanalian" Mickey
Sherman, telephone interview by author,
February 27, 2005.

194 "He went from" Dana, interview,
March 23, 2005.

194 *Six percent of Sherman's* Robert
Sherman, e-mail message to author,
December 14, 2011; "Jack London,
a Lawyer, Dies; Specialized in Show
Business," *New York Times,* May 12, 1987.

194 *Tucker put Sherman into exotic*
"Responses to First Set of
Interrogatories," Dolores Miriam
Sherman vs. Allan Sherman, No. WE
D-9743, Filed May 8, 1967, 7–9, Los
Angeles Superior Court.

194 "It was a completely different" Larry
E. Martindale, telephone interview by
author, March 23, 2012.

194 *When it came to capturing* Sherman
vs. Sherman, "Responses to First Set," 3.
Also see Allan Sherman to Warner Bros.
Records, March 4, 1963. Warner Music
Group Archives.

194 *In June 1964* Dorothy Kilgallen, "It
Takes One Like Brando to Orate,"
Washington Post, June 15, 1964, B8.

194 "Money was coming in" Golden,
interview, February 21, 2011.

194 *By December 1963* "Breakout Albums,"
Billboard, December 7, 1963, 24;
November 21, 1964, 28.

194 *At the same time* "Additional Terms
and Conditions," Rev. 1/30/1963,
Warner Bros. Records, Inc. to Curtain
Call Productions, Inc., 3. Warner Music
Group Archives.

195 *By the end of 1966* Sherman vs.
Sherman, "Responses to First Set," 12.

195 "copyrights owned by Allan
Sherman" Sherman vs. Sherman,
"Responses to First Set," 3, 5, 12.

195 *In 1965, Milton Bradley* Sherman vs. Sherman, "Responses," 5a.

195 *On February 20, 1964* "Chatter," *Daily Variety*, February 20, 1964, 4.

195 "Allan Sherman is about" *Variety*, May 20, 1964, 35.

195 *In the summer* "Sherman Hosts 'Tonight,'" *Daily Variety*, July 30, 1964, 10.

195 *On April 1* (Palmer House) *Where*, March 28, 1964, 1.

195 "24-karat gold" Amy Florence Fischbach, "Powering the Palmer House," *EC&M*, September 1, 2002, http://ceenews.com/mag/electric_powering_palmer_house/ (accessed May 15, 2012).

195 *During his hometown* "A Line O' Type or Two," *Chicago Tribune*, April 3, 1964, 14.

195 "Sherman Elevates" Will Leonard, "Sherman Elevates Parody to a Minor Art Form," *Chicago Tribune*, April 3, 1964, B10.

195 "Hey, that sounds Jewish!" Bob Ellison, "Who's Afraid of Show Biz?" *Chicago Sun-Times*, April 12, 1964.

195 *In May 1963, Atheneum* Sherman vs. Sherman, "Responses to First Set," 12–13.

196 *Zolotow ghostwrote* Crescent Dragonwagon, telephone interview by author, December 8, 2009.

196 *Harper & Row wanted* Sherman vs. Sherman, "Responses to First Set," 12.

196 *In June 1964, he shared* Sherman vs. Sherman, "Responses to First Set," 12.

196 "Nowadays, if you" Allan Sherman, Arnold Peyser, and Lois Peyser, *Instant Status; or, Up Your Image* (New York: G.P. Putnam's Sons, 1964), 7.

196 "Thanks, Man!" "Dear Tiger" "Among some" Sherman, *Instant Status*, 47, 63, 37.

196 "If you buy this" *Tonight*, November 20, 1964, sound recording, Archival Television Audio, Inc.

196 "devastatingly" Myrna Odell, "Allan Sherman, 'I Sing Like An Idiot,' He Says," *The Miami News*, April 16, 1963, B1.

196 *boyish, a pixie, a cherub, and elf* "Cave, Vancouver," *Variety*, June 17, 1964; May Okun, "Allan Sherman, the Success," *Sunday News* (Los Angeles), October 20,

1963, 4; Claudia Cassidy, "On the Aisle," *Chicago Daily Tribune*, February 10, 1963, 16; Bob Rolontz, "Sherman Marches on Carnegie," *Billboard*, January 12, 1963, 10.

197 "He came to our" Michael Abrahams, e-mail message to author, February 8, 2010.

197 "I read in the paper" Jay Thomas, telephone interview by author, January 10, 2012.

197 "He sat in his shorts" Loeb, interview, April 1, 2005.

197 "obscenely dressed" Cornyn, interview, January 28, 2005.

197 "I sing like" Odell, "Allan Sherman, I Sing Like," B1.

197 "I'm ugly" Battelle, "Assignment: America."

198 "His Own Little" Army Archerd, Just for Variety, *Daily Variety*, May 11, 1964, 2.

199 "I think I will review" Eric Lax, *Woody Allen* (New York: Knopf, 1991), 123, 172–73.

199 "Allen told about" Les Carpenter, "Democrats Two Big Talent Romps Net Party Over $3,000,000—and Some Gags," *Variety*, June 3, 1964, 86.

199 "Once in love with Lyndon" ASP.

200 "my body a bronzed miracle" *Tonight*, 68 (rcf 6–5) 1844482–3-1 (July 8, 1964). Armed Forces Radio recording, Library of Congress.

200 *On May 12, his* "Grammy Awards," *Daily Variety*, May 13, 1964, 11; *Tonight* 37 (rcf 52–4) 1844479–3-2 (May 27, 1964), Armed Forces Radio recording, Library of Congress.

200 *The new single* "Hot 100," *Billboard*, July 25, 1964, 24.

200 *He had to like* Lax, *Woody Allen*, 159–160.

200 "He thought of himself" Robert Sherman, interview by author, August 24, 2011, Malibu, CA.

200 "first and third situation" Woody Allen, *The Nightclub Years, 1964–1968* (EMI Comedy Classics, 1997).

202 "He entered the sexual" Hambro, interview, October 16, 2004.

202 "Sherman says, 'Leonid'" Hambro, interview, October 15, 2004.

202   "It was all done" Tabolsky, interview, March 11, 2005, West Hills, CA.

202   *In June 1964* Allan Sherman, "Liner Notes," *Peter and the Commissar* (RCA LM2773).

202   "His ambitions" Cornyn, interview, January 28, 2005.

203   *With Warner's good* "Fiedler Popping on RCA Victor as a Master of Pops and Pop," *Billboard*, October 10, 1964, 12.

203   "In all fairness" Andrew Clarke, "Sherman Pops at Tanglewood," *The Berkshire Eagle*, July 23, 1964, 8.

203   *When the album* "Album Reviews," *Billboard*, October 24, 1964, 68.

203   "an all-out campaign" "*Sherman*-Fiedler LP Gets Big RCA Push," *Billboard*, October 17, 1964, 1, 10.

203   *Red Seal targeted* Frederick Christain, "My Son, the Comedy Sensation," *Cavalier*, September 1963, 66.

203   *The album's sales peaked* "Top LP's," *Billboard*, January 16, 1965, 22; February 20, 1965, 33.

203   *Instead the Hollywood* "Allan Sherman Sings Old and New at Bowl," *Los Angeles Times*, August 16, 1964, C7.

204   "You're not IN" Sidney Skolsky, "Hollywood Is My Beat," *New York Post*, October 29, 1964, 23.

204   "This is not" "Joan Baez, 'Ben Franklin' Cast Set, 'Kennedy Wit,' 'Committee,' Doris Day, Little Anthony, Jack Jones Top LPs," *Variety*, November 11, 1964, 56.

204   *It was a* Billboard "Album Reviews," *Billboard*, November 21, 1964, 56; November 28, 1964, 28; "Top LP's," *Billboard*, January 16, 1965, 22; "Finalists for 1964 Grammy Awards," *Billboard*, March 20, 1965, 6.

205   *Critics attacked* Stephen J. Whitfield, "Fiddling with Sholem Aleichem: A History of *Fiddler on the Roof*," in *Key Texts in American Jewish Culture*, ed. Jack Kugelmass (New Brunswick, NJ: Rutgers University Press, 2003), 105.

205   "[M]iracle of miracles" Whitfield, "Fiddling," 107.

205   *Instead of being "too Jewish"* Whitfield, "Fiddling," 111.

206   "generosity of spirit" Whitfield, "Fiddling," 120.

206   "only yesterday" Norman Podhoretz, "The Rise and Fall of the American Jewish Novelist," in *Jewish Life in America: Historical Perspectives*, ed. Gladys Rosen (New York: Ktav Pub. House, 1978), 144.

206   "If only we could be like them!" Sollors, *Beyond Ethnicity*, 29.

206   "sensibility that was" Whitfield, "Fiddling," 122.

TEN. PEYTON PLACE, U.S.A.

207   "I'm not supposed" Richard F. Shepard, "My Son, the TV Star," *New York Times*, January 17, 1965, X15.

208   "Allan feels very strongly" Cecil Smith, "Sherman's Son, the Thin Man," *Los Angeles Times*, January 18, 1965, C16.

208   "ABC, NBC Pitching" "Both ABC, NBC Pitching TV Offers to Allan Sherman," *Daily Variety*, May 10, 1963, 12.

208   "people in the trade" Dave Kaufman, "On All Channels," *Daily Variety*, July 3, 1963, 12.

208   *On March 4* Roger Watkins, "BBC-2: Will It or Won't It?" *Variety*, March 4, 1964, 38.

208   *In July, NBC* Army Archerd, Just for Variety, *Daily Variety*, July 8, 1964, 2.

208   "write, produce and star" Val Adams, "Allan Sherman Plans TV Special," *New York Times*, September 25, 1964, 83.

208   *In November Sherman was* "Dicker Allan Sherman for TV Comedy Series," *Variety*, November 11, 1964, 28; "Irving Elman Dies at 96," *Variety*, November 27, 2011; "Telepix Followup," *Daily Variety*, November 12, 1964, 6.

209   *Good reviews also* "Television Reviews," *Variety*, October 14, 1964, 38.

209   "Sherman fluttered" "Tele Review," *Daily Variety*, November 30, 1964, 8.

209   *He was too weak* Army Archerd, Just for Variety, *Daily Variety*, November 3, 1964, 2.

209   "peace and quiet" Army Archerd, Just for Variety, *Daily Variety*, November 5, 1964, 2.

209   "a perfect candidate" Roberts, "How to Write a TV Show," 3.

209 *On December 1, 1964* Eleanor Roberts, "How to Write a TV Show: Check into a Hospital," *Boston Sunday Herald*, January 10, 1965, 3; Army Archerd, Just for Variety, *Daily Variety*, December 3, 1964, 2.

209 *A photograph of Sherman* Roberts, "How to Write a TV Show," 3.

209 *There was no way he could* Army Archerd, Just for Variety, *Daily Variety*, November 11, 1964, 2, and December 24, 1964, 2.

209 "He was an unshaved" Art Seidenbaum, "Allan Sherman's Loss Is Our Gain," *Los Angeles Times*, January 4, 1965, 1.

209 "It was bizarre" Sam Bobrick, telephone interview by author, July 12, 2010.

209 "the producer, the director" Roberts, "How to Write a TV Show," 3.

210 "It was an unorthodox" Reed Porter, "Sherman's 'Funny Land' A Smash Television Show," *The Hollywood Reporter*, January 20, 1965.

210 "Goodson-Todman preplanned" Robert Sherman, interview by author, August 24, 2011, Malibu, CA.

210 "as different as any show" "Television Review," *Daily Variety*, January 20, 1965, 9.

210 *"Funnyland" won the ratings* "'Funnyland' Top-Rated," *Daily Variety*, January 22, 1965, 22.

210 "The best show," "Allan Sherman's Funnyland," "about as clever" *Variety*, February 3, 1965, 37.

210 "thousands of dancers" Smith, "Sherman's Son," C16.

211 "The character of Allan Sherman" "Funnyland," 1965-01-18, UCLA Film & Television Archive.

212 *In September, the comedy* "Breakout Albums," *Billboard*, September 11, 1965, 60.

212 "To my beautiful daughter" *You Don't Have to Be Jewish*, Kapp Records, KRL-4503.

212 *The same year the parody* "'Tante' Has Uncle at WSDD," *Billboard*, November 11, 1965, 6.

212 *It was the top-selling* Stephen Battaglio, *David Susskind: A Televised Life* (New York: St. Martin's Press, 2010), 251–52; "Breakout Albums," *Billboard*, July 10, 1965, 29.

213 "Headache? Cold misery?" Maria Reidelbach, *Completely Mad: A History of the Comic Book and Magazine* (Boston: Little, Brown, 1991), 46.

213 "I don't know what" Dean Martin Presents the Rolling Stones, www .youtube.com/watch?v=qOr2a9oEzGQ (accessed April 4, 2012).

213 *By the time* "Top LP's," *Billboard*, January 16, 1965, 22.

214 "Allan Sherman's opening" "Nitery Review," *Daily Variety*, March 3, 1965, 5.

214 *In early 1965, his Aunt Edith* Allan Sherman, "A Question of Honor," *Reader's Digest*, May 1971, 78.

214 "My mother writes DeBakey" Carol Selsberg, telephone interview by author, March 9 2005.

214 "You had to know" Goldstein, interview, October 15, 2004.

214 *"Downtown" by Petula* "Hits of the World," *Billboard*, January 16, 1965, 13, 19; "Hot 100," January 30, 1965, 34.

215 Variety *spotted it* "On the Beat," *Daily Variety*, March 19, 1965, 26; "'Hullabaloo' Shot for Allan Sherman," *Daily Variety*, April 14, 1965, 14.

215 "Like so many innovations" Eddie Gallaher, "The Road to Success Is Paved by Parody," *Washington Post*, April 25, 1965, G9.

215 *He sang the parody* "Tennessee Ernie and Randall 'Palace' Emcees," *Daily Variety*, March 12, 1965, 21; "'Hullabaloo' Shot," 14.

215 *He signed a deal* Army Archerd, Just for Variety, *Daily Variety*, November 18, 1964, 2; Archerd, "Just," January 12, 1965, 2; Archerd, "Just," January 26, 1965, 2.

215 "It was Brillo" "Commercials," Inventory Number VA 13364, UCLA Film & Television Archive.

216 *He signed another* John K. Maitland, president, Warner Bros. Records, to Allan Sherman, c/o Alexander Tucker, October 21, 1965. Warner Music Group Archives.

Also see Sherman, *My Son, the Box*,
disc six.

216　*On April 25, 1965, the Friars*　"The Friars
　　　Club Charity Foundation," *The Hollywood
　　　Reporter*, April 9, 1965, 21. Jack L. Warner
　　　Collection, 1965 Scrapbook, USC
　　　Cinematic Arts Library.

216　"never-to-be-released"　Sidney Skolsky,
　　　"Jack Warner Steals 'Roast' From Friars,"
　　　Citizen-News, April 27, 1965, A-10. Jack L.
　　　Warner Collection, 1965 Scrapbook.

216　*Sherman's new manager*　"Allan
　　　Sherman, Capp Talking TV Series," *Daily
　　　Variety*, May 14, 1965, 11.

216　"Love is where you"　"Celebrity Game"
　　　07–15–1965, UCLA Film & Television
　　　Archive.

216　"Allan at the time"　Goldstein, interview,
　　　October 15, 2004.

217　"a half-hour"　Tise Vahimagi, "Serling,
　　　Rod," The Museum of Broadcast
　　　Communications, www.museum.tv
　　　/eotvsection.php (accessed May 16, 2012).

217　"They used to call"　"The Loner, " 1965–
　　　11–13, UCLA Film & Television Archive.

217　*For a moment*　Don Page, "Sherman's
　　　Talent Larger Than Life," *Los Angeles
　　　Times*, August 26, 1965, D14.

218　"Everybody in my family"　Sherman,
　　　Gift, 16, 308, 309, 318.

218　"ought to be"　"Boychick" *Newsweek*,
　　　November 1, 1965, 98.

218　"He got laughed"　Golden, interview,
　　　February 21, 2011.

218　"Allan has made"　Ben Irwin to Al
　　　Freeman, October 6, 1965, "Sands Hotel,"
　　　Special Collections, University of Nevada,
　　　Las Vegas.

218　"that somebody can"　Arthur Knight,
　　　"The Literary Life in Las Vegas," *Saturday
　　　Review*, November 6, 1965, 25.

218　"Mr. Sherman is a very"　"In Brief," *New
　　　York Times*, January 2, 1966, 200.

219　"there I was, a mere"　Sherman, *Gift*, 59.

219　*That kind of language*　Dee Golden,
　　　interview, June 14, 2012.

219　"The sex scene"　Dee Golden, interview,
　　　February 21, 2011.

219　*The Drinking Man's*　Mark E. Eberhart,
　　　*Feeding the Fire: The Lost History and
　　　Uncertain Future of Mankind's Energy*

Addiction (New York: Crown, 2007),
ch. 1.

220　"sex, in an impressive"　Elenore Lester,
　　　"The Pass-the-Hat Theater Circuit,"
　　　New York Times, December 5, 1965,
　　　100; Wendell C. Stone, *Caffe Cino:
　　　The Birthplace of Off-Off-Broadway*
　　　(Carbondale: Southern Illinois University
　　　Press, 2005), 114.

220　"Peyton Place, U.S.A."　Barbara Moore,
　　　et al., *Prime-Time Television: A Concise
　　　History* (Westport, CT: Praeger, 2006),
　　　142.

221　*In 1964, authorities*　"News from the
　　　Music Capitals of the World," *Billboard*,
　　　January 16, 1965, 18.

221　"I'll not do a Dusty"　"Sherman
　　　Won't 'Do a Dusty,'" *Sunday Express*
　　　[Johannesburg], December 5, 1965, 2.

221　*My Name Is Allan*　"Top LP's," *Billboard*,
　　　February 5, 1966, 34.

221　"sex without individuality"　"Alan [*sic*]
　　　Sherman, *Penthouse*, June 1965, 29.

ELEVEN. ODDBALL

222　"He wanted the divorce"　Golden,
　　　interview, February 14, 2011.

222　"He would call"　Billy Goldenberg,
　　　telephone interview by author, February 1,
　　　2010.

222　*A turning point*　"Nitery Notes," *Daily
　　　Variety*, December 17, 1965, 13, and "Who's
　　　Where," *Daily Variety*, January 12, 1966, 2.

223　"One thing that"　Bill Loeb, telephone
　　　interview by author, April 1, 2005.

223　*In San Francisco he met*　Golden,
　　　interview, February 14, 2011.

223　"pert, auburn-haired"　"Mills College
　　　Girls Appear in 'Pleasure of His
　　　Company,'" *Oakland Tribune*, May 11,
　　　1961, 56.

223　"Everybody knew her"　Golden,
　　　interview, February 14, 2011.

223　*In March*　Golden, interview, February
　　　24, 2011.

223　*However, she was not*　"Sherman Pops
　　　Cork," *Daily Variety*, November 24,
　　　1965, 11.

223　"We went to Houston"　Al Lerner,
　　　telephone interview by author, October 3,
　　　2011.

223 "It was very crazy" Lerner, interview, October 3, 2011.

223 *The album was recorded May 20* "Liner Notes," Sherman, *My Son, the Box*, 45.

223 "mostly more of the same" Thomas Lask, "Previewing the Comics," *New York Times*, October 30, 1966, D20.

224 "He rang the doorbell" Golden, interview, February 15, 2011.

225 "It was the saddest" Marvin Tabolsky, interview by author, March 11, 2005, West Hills, CA.

225 "the halfway house" Sam Bobrick, telephone interview by author, July 12, 2010.

225 "Sherman's delivery" "One-Man Show, Allan Sherman," *Variety*, July 13, 1966, 44.

225 *After London* Dave Feldman, "Allan Sherman Vill Sing 'Und You All Vill LISTEN,'" *The Stars and Stripes*, July 22, 1966, 2.

225 *Originally, the plan* Golden, interview, February 15, 2011.

225 "He used to say" Laurie Holloway, Skype interview by author, January 14, 2012.

225 "very bad insult" Golden, interview, February 15, 2011.

225 *According to* "Lynne Martin, aka Lynne Sanzenbacher vs. A. Sherman," No. 569195, Superior Court of the State of California for the County of San Francisco, 1–2.

226 "I became the girl" Golden, interview, February 14, 2011.

226 "I wanted to keep" Golden, interview, February 21, 2011.

226 "He was ambivalent" Golden, interview, February 15, 2011.

226 *She accompanied him* Hal Bock, "Hawaii Tradewinds," *Daily Variety*, August 9, 1966, 8; "Vaude, Café Dates," *Variety*, June 15, 1966, 60.

226 "In Australia he" Lerner, interview, October 3, 2011.

226 "Reporters called us" Golden, interview, February 15, 2011.

226 *Golden returned* Lerner, interview, October 3, 2011.

226 *The Kahala Hilton wanted* Hal Bock, "Hawaii Tradewinds," *Daily Variety*, August 30, 1966, 7.

226 *Variety reported* Army Archerd, Just for Variety, *Daily Variety*, October 25, 1966, 2.

226 *It put Sherman* "Allan Sherman's 4th Ed Sullivan Show Shot," *Daily Variety*, March 9, 1966, 8; "Sherman's Sullivan Shot," *Daily Variety*, September 9, 1966, 19. For Sherman on Sullivan August 14, 1966; October 16, 1966; and December 4, 1966, see Archival Television Audio, Inc. www.atvaudio.com/index.php.

226 "final resting place" Nachman, *Right Here*, 13.

226 *In October* "Basin St. East, N.Y. (FOLLOW UP)," *Variety*, October 26, 1966, 56.

226 *On October 16* "Television This Week," *New York Times*, October 16, 1966, 131.

226 *His hour* "Allan Sherman Set for 4 Star 'Special,'" *Daily Variety*, February 4, 1966, 6; "Four Star Preps Syndie 'Specials,'" *Variety*, March 23, 1966, 37.

227 *On his show* Allan Sherman, "Something Special" (Television program: 1965), UCLA Film & Television Archive.

230 *But Sherman could still* Mark Cohen, "My Fair Sadie: Allan Sherman and a Paradox of American Jewish Culture," *American Jewish History* 93, no. 1 (March 2007): 70–71.

232 *It did not hit* "Fox Pub Signs Sherman, Hague," *Billboard*, June 24, 1967, 4.

232 *The song was also* Sam Zolotow, "Actors, Theaters Call in Mediator," *New York Times*, May 22, 1968, 52; Leonard Feather, "Joe Williams Back at Hong Kong Bar," *Los Angeles Times*, August 9, 1968, E12; John L. Scott, "Gloria Loring in Westside Room," *Los Angeles Times*, February 1, 1969, C10.

232 "You're born, you weep" Drdemento. com, http://dmdb.org/lyrics/sherman .figleaves.html (accessed June 11, 2012).

233 "It occurred to me" William Glover, "Allan Sherman, Funnyman, Gets Back to Business," *Pacific Stars & Stripes*, November 20, 1968, 14.

233 "After our divorce" Golden, interview, February 17, 2011.

233 *In April 1967, he moved* "Dolores Miriam Sherman vs. Allan Sherman,"

Superior Court of the State of California, No. WE D-9743, filed May 8, 1967, 1.

233 "He would stand" Mark Rosengarden, interview, September 30, 2009.

233 "Linda was a real good" Goldenberg, interview, February 1, 2010.

233 "I think Linda was after" Nancy Sherman, interview by author, September 25, 2011, Park City, UT.

233 *At some point* Golden, interview, February 21, 2011.

233 "The main clear" Crescent Dragonwagon, telephone interview by author, December 8, 2009.

233 "not so funny" Hal Humphrey, "Comedy Stars in Colgate Special," *Los Angeles Times*, May 13, 1967, B3.

233 *His behavior was also unfunny* "Perry Phillips Night Sounds," *Oakland Tribune*, September 29, 1967, 35.

233 "He had his hand" David Kreitzer, telephone interview by author, October 31, 2011.

234 "He would marinate" Mark Rosengarden, telephone interview by author, September 30, 2009.

234 *On September 18, 1967* "Dolores Miriam Sherman vs. Allan Sherman," filed October 11, 1967.

234 "He was very lonely" Stoo Hample, telephone interview by author, January 19, 2010.

234 *In January he was* Chicago Tribune, January 5, 1968, A3; John L. Scott, "Vegas Opening for Pat Collins," *Los Angeles Times*, February 3, 1968, 16; Dorothy Minorca, "Stars Add Glitter to Miami Beach Season," *Chicago Tribune*, February 25, 1968, H9.

234 *In mid-June he was* "4-Day Music Fete Aids Ex-Addicts," *New York Times*, June 16, 1968; "The Straw Hat Trail," *New York Times*, June 30, 1968, 19.

234 *On June 11, 1968* Ed West, vice president, Warner Bros.–Seven Arts Records, to Allan Sherman, c/o Becker and London, June 11, 1968. Warner Music Group Archives.

235 *This time he was not* "Vacation Suggestions," *New York Times*, August 6, 1968, 41; Jay Clarke, "Miami Beach Puts Accent on Youth," *New York Times*, April 28, 1968, XX7.

235 *From August until* Los Angeles Times, August 4, 1968, B28, and August 23, 1968, F20; "Tuesday's Best," *Chicago Tribune*, September 7, 1968, C13; "TV Hour by Hour," *Chicago Tribune*, November 22, 1968, A5, and December 6, 1968, B27.

235 "He complained" Hendricks, interview, January 12, 2012.

235 "They drove up" Nancy Sherman, interview, September 25, 2011, Park City, UT.

TWELVE. HALLOWED BE THY GAME

236 "a mini-skirted" Clive Barnes, "Theatre: 'Fig Leaves Are Falling' Has Premiere," *New York Times*, January 4, 1969, 32.

237 "have been unfaithful" Alvin Klein, WNYC, 2, "Scrapbooks," Dorothy Loudon Papers.

237 "*very* low" Brendan Gill, "The Theater: In Vain," *New Yorker*, January 11, 1969, 56.

237 "Oddly enough" Martin Gottfried, "The Fig Leaves Are Falling," *Women's Wear Daily*, January 3, 1969. "Productions," Dorothy Loudon Papers.

237 "All the innuendoes" Klein, WNYC, 1.

237 "The people in Larchmont" "The New York Play: The Fig Leaves Are Falling," *The Hollywood Reporter*, January 6, 1969. "Scrapbooks," Dorothy Loudon Papers.

238 "one outstanding" "Broadway Opening: The Fig Leaves Are Falling," *Daily Variety*, January 6, 1969. "Scrapbooks," Dorothy Loudon Papers.

238 "I want to laugh" Recording of *The Fig Leaves Are Falling*, Rodgers & Hammerstein Archive, NYPL. On the recording, the character Pookie sings "All My Laughter." During previews the show's director, George Abbott, "gave it to Loudon." See Ken Mandelbaum, *Not Since Carrie: Forty Years of Broadway Musical Flops* (New York: St. Martin's Press, 1991), 81.

238 *His divorce had been* Dolores Miriam Sherman vs. Allan Sherman, Los Angeles Superior Court, Case Number WE D-9743, Application for Final Judgment of Divorce, Filed February 6, 1969; Final

Judgment of Divorce, Filed February 6, 1969.

238 "After the play" Nancy Sherman, interview by author, September 25, 2011, Park City, UT.

239 "If ever I saw" Cornyn, *Exploding*, 210–11.

239 "once Allan and Dee" Michael Hackman, telephone interview by author, April 6, 2011.

239 "My father became" Dragonwagon, interview, December 8, 2009.

239 *Instead, he seems to have* "White Plains Event for Biafra Tonight," *New York Times*, February 7, 1969, 25.

239 *He soon landed higher* "Tuesday," *Los Angeles Times*, March 9, 1969, R24; *Los Angeles Times*, March 30, 1969, S22; *Chicago Tribune*, March 17, 1969, B31; "*The Dating Game*, Allan Sherman Episode, Watermarked for Private Viewing of Mark Cohen," courtesy of Edward Zimmerman, Sony Pictures Entertainment.

239 *In a dark* Sam Lesner, "Brand new bag, beard for Sherman," *Chicago Daily News, Panorama*, December 30, 1967, 13.

239 *The show opened* Joel Whitburn, *The Billboard Book of Top 40 Hits, 9th Edition* (New York: Random House, 2010), 29.

240 *In June 1969* Marvin Fisher, "On the Music Beat," *Daily Variety*, June 12, 1969, 14.

240 "I wish I could tell you" Shel Talmy, e-mail message to author, April 30, 2012.

240 "situation comedy" Army Archerd, Just for Variety, *Daily Variety*, August 19, 1969, 2.

240 "a tedious hangover" "Television Reviews," *Daily Variety*, January 9, 1970, 24.

240 *In March he performed* Dave Kaufman, "Trumbo Wins Laurel Award" *Daily Variety*, March 16, 1970, 32.

241 *They all were invited* Bryce Nelson, "Anti-bunnies Jeer at Hefner Peace Bash," *Los Angeles Times*, April 17, 1970, 20.

241 *During the politically* "McCarthy Day Washington Rally," *Washington Post, Times Herald*, August 9, 1968, B12.

241 *Sherman ended 1970* Carillon Hotel

advertisement, *New York Times*, November 8, 1970, 432; "Writers Laurel to Poe, Davies Award to Taradash, Cox Nod to Spigelgass," *Daily Variety*, March 19, 1971, 28.

241 *On June 13, 1971* "Sherman, Norm Crosby In B'nai B'rith Show," *Daily Variety*, May 24, 1971, 10.

241 *He did a decent* "Litto 'Pepper' Rep" *Daily Variety*, September 2, 1970, 10; *Pepper and His Wacky Taxi*, www .youtube.com/watch?v=R9l-5YBgPcE (accessed April 27, 2012).

241 *By October of that year* "Where Are They Now?" *Newsweek*, October 30, 1972, 18.

241 "Not well. Pasty-faced" Goldstein, interview, September 24, 2004.

241 "collapsed face down" Dragonwagon, interview, December 8, 2009.

241 "Allan became alcoholic" Golden, interview, February 24, 2011.

241 "I was standing" Tabolsky, interview, March 11, 2005.

241 "It was sad" Tommy Smothers, telephone interview by author, January 25, 2012. For Smothers' purchase of the rights to *Every 600 Years* see, Paul Karon, "Smothers Pops Poem by Sherman," *Variety*, November 3, 1997, www.variety .com/article/VR111661009 (accessed June 12, 2012).

242 *An animated version* "Cat in the Hat," *Chicago Tribune*, March 10, 1971.

242 "an atrocious" Cecil Smith, "Travis Logan a Rare Item," *Los Angeles Times*, March 11, 1971, F16.

242 "The children felt" Allan Sherman, *Every 600 Years, on a Tuesday (The Journey to the Perfectly Fair* (unpublished manuscript, property of Tom Smothers, Knave Productions, Inc.), 6.

242 "I'm the Chief" Sherman, *Every 600 Years*, 7.

242 "rhapsody of being" Allan Sherman, "Summer's Magical Music," *Reader's Digest*, July 1971, 60.

243 "Thus the sweet" Sherman, *Every 600 Years*, 34.

243 "You climbed over" Sherman, *Every 600 Years*, 44–45.

243 "being prepped" Army Archerd, Just for
Variety, *Daily Variety*, August 9, 1971, 2.

243 *Their original agreement* Dolores
Miriam Sherman vs. Allan Sherman,
No. WE D 9743, [filing date illegible],
"Notice of Motion for Order to Clerk
to Issue Writ of Execution, Declaration
of Plaintiff Dolores Sherman, and
Memorandum of Points and Authorities
in Support Thereof," 3–6, 9.

243 *He did not have it* Dolores Miriam
Sherman vs. Allan Sherman, No. WE D
9743, filed February 20, 1973, 3–4.

244 "One night the phone rang" Golden,
interview, February 15, 2011.

244 "I said to Nancy" Golden, interview,
February 21, 2011.

244 "He met someone" Robert Sherman,
interview, August 24, 2011.

245 "'Just a minute,'" Allan Sherman, "My
Moment of Truth Happened 29 Years
Ago, but I Didn't Understand It until
Last Thursday," 10. ASP.

245 "He turns out" Lesner, "Brand new
bag," *Chicago Daily News, Panorama*,
December 30, 1967, 13.

245 "Chopin's Polonaise" Recording of
Allan Sherman at the Hungry i. ASP.

246 "hopelessly addicted" Allan Sherman,
"Griselda and the Porn-O-Phone,"
Playboy, December 1971, 262.

246 "The APE made us" Allan Sherman,
The Rape of the APE (Chicago: Playboy
Press, 1975), 8.

246 "cloaked in disappointing" John Fink,
"America Goes A*P*E*—Surviving the
sexual revolution," *Chicago Tribune*,
September 9, 1973, F7.

246 "The Magic F**k" Sherman, *Rape*,
387–90.

246 "sweet serenity" Sherman, *Rape*, 445.

247 "Sherman has a sense" Laura Green, "A
Long Way from Camp Granada," *Chicago
Sun-Times*, September 12, 1973, 77.

247 "more concerned" Sandra Pesman,
"A Funny Thing Happened to Comic
Sherman," *Chicago Daily News*,
September 8–9, 1973, 19.

247 *To prepare* Art Seidenbaum, "A
Wheeze Over Sex," *Los Angeles Times*,
October 4, 1973, A1.

247 "Haldeman, Erlichman" Jerry Hopkins,
e-mail message to author, May 7, 2004.

247 "still covered in blood" Golden,
interview, April 19, 2011.

248 *In January 1973* Army Archerd, Just for
Variety, *Daily Variety*, January 22, 1973, 2.

248 "He was a wonderful" Golden,
interview, February 14, 2011.

248 "He thought" Golden, interview,
February 15, 2011.

248 *On March 24* "TV Nostalgia Floods
Carnegie Hall as Steve Allen Stirs
Capacity Aud," *Variety*, March 28, 1973,
67.

248 *He could no longer* Golden, interview,
February 15, 2011.

248 *In October* "Dr. Seuss on the Loose,"
Daily Variety, October 17, 1973, 6.

248 *Zatt gently hinted* Sol Zatt, "A Phone
Conversation with Allan Sherman on the
Eve of His Death," *Variety*, November 28,
1973, 2, 54.

248 "Hallowed Be Thy Game" Allan
Sherman, "On Golf," Studio remote,
File T-3893-96 (5–20–73). Warner
Music Group Tape Vault, Los Angeles.
Information based on author's visit to
Tape Vault on August 24, 2011, arranged
by sound engineer Mike Johnson, and
CD recording made from this tape,
courtesy of Mike Johnson.

248 *It is a stand-up* "Allan Sherman Live
@ La Costa Country Club," File B-1755
(7–14–72). Warner Music Group Tape
Vault, Los Angeles.

249 "the downhill lie" CD recording made
from "Allan Sherman Live @ La Costa
Country Club" for author, courtesy of
Mike Johnson. All quotes are from this
recording.

249 *Joe Smith gave* Cornyn, *Exploding*, 211.

249 "I called the doctor" Cornyn,
Exploding, 211.

249 "antic wit" "Allan Sherman, Lyricist,
Dies; Noted for 'My Son' Parodies," *New
York Times*, November 22, 1973, 40.

249 *A memorial service* "Obituaries," *Daily
Variety*, November 23, 1973, 14.

249 "friends, relatives" Steve Allen, *More
Funny People* (New York: Stein and Day,
1982), 250, 253.

250   *His New York lawyer*   Golden, telephone interview by author, February 15, 2011.

250   *Golden's second husband died*   "Obituaries," *Daily Variety*, January 16, 1986, 37; "Dolores 'Dee' Sherman Golden (1925–2012)," *Park Record*, July 21, 2012, www.legacy.com/obituaries/parkrecord /obituary.aspx?pid=158649759 (accessed August 15, 2012).

250   "Allan Sherman's *geshtarben*"   Stoo Hample, telephone interview by author, January 19, 2010.

THIRTEEN. HAIL TO THEE, FAT PERSON

251   *All of his albums*   Ronald L. Smith, *Comedy on Record: The Complete Critical Discography* (New York: Garland Publishing, 1988), 587.

251   "Be home by 11!"   Richard Pryor, *That Nigger's Crazy* (Partee Records, 1974).

251   "Face it darlings"   Nachman, *Seriously Funny*, 613–14.

251   "My mother had"   Joan Rivers on the *Ed Sullivan Show*, www.youtube.com /watch?v=EpPCFoXXhF0 (accessed May 7, 2012).

252   "When someone sells"   Will Tusher, "George Carlin's Gold May Be Slow But It's Money in the Bank," *Daily Variety*, December 3, 1976, 26.

252   "Science, I don't believe in science"   Woody Allen, *Sleeper* (final scene), www.youtube.com/watch?v=I _Woa-oFy_Y (accessed May 11, 2012).

253   "Oh, sweet mystery"   *Young Frankenstein*—The Monster and Madeline Kahn hook up, www.youtube .com/watch?v=60W__Pdk5Pc (accessed May 11, 2012).

253   "Two hours each week"   *Billboard*, July 10, 1982, 19.

253   "I didn't really push"   Dr. Demento, telephone interview by author, May 10, 2012.

253   *In 1977, Warner Bros. included*   "The Joke's on Us," *Billboard*, November 12, 1977, 11; "CloseUp," 105.

253   *Another collection in 1979*   "A Deluxe Album for WB's 20th," *Billboard*, November 3, 1979, 12.

253   *For die-hard fans*   "Allan Sherman Discography," http://dmdb.org /discographies/sherman.disco.html (accessed May 11, 2012).

254   "the discovery and promotion"   Sean Elder, "Rhino on the Loose," *Mother Jones*, May 1987, 48.

254   "I Can't Stop My Leg"   http:// videosift.com/video/I-Can-t-Stop-My -Leg-Robert-Klein (accessed May 12, 2012); also see, Saturday Night Live, www.nbc.com/saturday-night-live /recaps/#cat=1&mea=5&ima=88890 (accessed May 12, 2012).

254   "The re-issued compilations"   Smith, *Comedy*, 595.

255   "often feels quite musty"   Stephen Holden, "Review/Theater; From Birth to Death, Via Allan Sherman," *New York Times*, www.nytimes.com/1992/12/09 /theater/review-theater-from-birth-to -death-via-allan-sherman.html (accessed May 6, 2012).

255   "[h]aving the ethnic"   Alvin Klein, "Theater; 'Hello Muddah, Hello Fadduh!' Opens," *New York Times*, www .nytimes.com/1993/12/19/nyregion/ theater-hello-muddah-hello-fadduh -opens.html (accessed May 6, 2012).

255   "rollicking, vodka-soaked"   Seth Rogovoy, *The Essential Klezmer: A Music Lover's Guide to Jewish Roots and Soul Music, from the Old World to the Jazz Age to the Downtown Avant-Garde* (Chapel Hill, NC: Algonquin Books of Chapel Hill, 2000), 78, 80.

255   *As the revival gathered steam*   Rogovoy, *Essential*, 88, 90–91, 96, 101–2.

256   "Every note"   Mark Slobin, *American Klezmer: Its Roots and Offshoots* (Berkeley: University of California Press, 2002), 157.

256   "aggressively unassimilated"   Josh Kun, "The Yiddish Are Coming: Mickey Katz, Antic-Semitism, and the Sound of Jewish Difference," *American Jewish History* 87 (1999): 344, 373.

256   "Jewish male who"   Lawrence J. Epstein, *The Haunted Smile: The Story of Jewish Comedians in America* (New York: Public Affairs, 2001), 239.

256 "too Jewish" How It Began 4/6, www.youtube.com/watch?v=QQ8 Ucb4nDmo&feature=relmfu (accessed May 14, 2012).

256 "it wasn't just a New York" How It Began /6, www.youtube.com/watch?v =IWq38j48dzo&feature=relmfu (accessed May 14, 2012).

256 "one of the most commercially" David Lavery and Sara Lewis Dunne, *"Seinfeld," Master of Its Domain: Revisiting Television's Greatest Sitcom* (New York: Continuum International Pub. Group, 2006), 2.

256 "the Jews in the show are not" Michelle Byers and Rosalin Krieger, "Something Old Is New Again? Postmodern Jewishness in *Curb Your Enthusiasm, Arrested Development,* and *The O.C.*" in *You Should See Yourself: Jewish Identity in Postmodern American Culture,* ed. Vincent Brook (New Brunswick, NJ: Rutgers University Press, 2006), 283.

257 "Oy vey, can you see!" Daniel Itzkovitz, "They All Are Jews," in Brook, *You Should See Yourself,* 231.

257 "Almost 40 years ago" Neil Genzlinger, "Wallflower at an Orgy of Verbal Slapstick," *New York Times,* August 3, 2001, www.nytimes.com/2001/08/03 /movies/theater-review-subtlety-plays -the-wallflower-at-an-orgy-of-verbal -slapstick.html?pagewanted=2 (accessed May 12, 2012).

257 "Has so little changed" James Schembari, "Practice Makes Perfect (and Poorer Parents)," *New York Times,* January 27, 2002, www.nytimes .com/2002/01/27/business/midstream -practice-makes-perfect-and-poorer -parents.html (accessed May 12, 2012).

259 "are key texts of American Jewish culture" Jeffrey Shandler, "Allan Sherman's 'My Son, the Folksinger'" (lecture, National Foundation for Jewish Culture lecture series on Key Texts in American Jewish Culture, Houston 2006).

259 "is depicted as a Christian" Adam Kirsch, "National Treasure," *Tablet, A New Read on Jewish Life,* April 12, 2011, www.tabletmag.com/jewish-arts-and -culture/books/64821/national-treasure (accessed May 16, 2012).

259 *When in 1977* Steve Harvey, "Last Holdouts: Phone Dial: Letters' Days Numbered," *Los Angeles Times,* July 16, 1977, A1.

260 *A New York Times story* "Seltzer: A Renaissance in Fizz," *New York Times,* September 26, 1979, C1; Joseph McLellan, "Horowitz, Wizard of the Keyboard," *Washington Post,* November 6, 1989, D1.

260 "one of the best songs ever" Stephen J. Dubner, "Summer Camp, Day 1," Freakonomics, June 30, 2008, www .freakonomics.com/2008/06/30 /summer-camp-day-1/ (accessed May 16, 2012).

260 "Not long ago" Ben Sisario, "Comedy and Conspiracy Theories," *New York Times,* September 2, 2010, www.nytimes.com/2010/09/05/arts /music/05playlist.html?_r=1 (accessed May 16, 2012).

BIBLIOGRAPHY

DISCOGRAPHY

Sherman, Allan. *My Son, the Folk Singer*. Warner Bros. 1962.

———. *My Son, the Celebrity*. Warner Bros. 1962.

———. *More Folk Songs by Allan Sherman and His Friends*. Jubilee 1962.

———. "Hello Muddah, Hello Fadduh! (A Letter from Camp)." Warner Bros. 1963.

———. *My Son, the Nut*. Warner Bros. 1963.

———. "Hello Muddah, Hello Fadduh!" Warner Bros. 1964.

———. *Allan in Wonderland*. Warner Bros. 1964.

———. *Peter and the Commissar*. RCA Victor Red Seal 1964.

———. *Let's Talk About the New Album! Allan Sherman and You. A special interview recording for radio station programming*. RCA Victor 1964.

———. *For Swingin' Livers Only*. Warner Bros. 1964.

———. "Crazy Downtown." Warner Bros. 1964.

———. *My Name Is Allan*. Warner Bros. 1965.

———. *The Best of Allan Sherman*. Valiant, 1965.

———. *Allan Sherman—Live!!! (Hoping You Are the Same)*. Warner Bros. 1966.

———. *Togetherness*. Warner Bros. 1967.

———. *The Very Best of Allan Sherman*. Warner Bros. 1976.

———. "Hello Muddah! Hello Fadduh!" In *25 Years of Recorded Comedy*. Warner Bros. 1977.

———. "Sarah Jackman" In *The Warner Bros. Records 20th Anniversary Album in Sound & Picture*. Warner Bros. 1979.

———. *Best of Allan Sherman*. Rhino, 1979.

———. *A Gift of Laughter, The Best of Allan Sherman, Volume II*. Rhino, 1986.

———. *My Son, the Greatest: The Best of Allan Sherman*. Rhino, 1988.

———. *My Son, the Box*. Rhino Entertainment Company, 2005.

ARCHIVES AND PRIVATE COLLECTIONS

Papers Held by Author

Coplon, Percy. "Certificate of Failure to Find," Percy Coplon Marriage, State of Alabama, Department of Public Health, Center for Health Statistics, Office of Vital Records, October 19, 2004.

Tonight, November 20, 1964, sound recording, Archival Television Audio, Inc.

Shandler, Jeffrey. "Allan Sherman's *My Son, the Folksinger*." Lecture, National Foundation for Jewish Culture lecture series on Key Texts in American Jewish Culture. Houston 2006. Courtesy of Prof. Shandler.

Sherman, Allan. "The Night That Leon Trotsky Died." [1944]. Courtesy of Arte Johnson.

———. Letter to Bill Pilkenton, postmarked June 24, 1945. Courtesy of Bill Pilkenton's daughter, Pamela Pilkenton Hammil.

Allan Sherman Papers, Estate of Allan Sherman

Call Board. Newsletter, Warner Bros. Records Sales Corporation. October 31, 1962.

Lester, Jerry. Letter to Allan Sherman at 340 E. 66th Street, New York, NY. n.d.

Minow, Newton N. Letter to Allan Sherman from the Federal Communications Commission. October 26, 1962.

Schlesinger, Arthur Jr. Letter to Allan Sherman from the Kennedy White House. November 5, 1962.

Sherman, Allan. Song lyrics for University of Illinois student shows, *Nothing Ventured, Mirth of a Nation*, and "Conscientious Objector of Company Z." 1943–1944.

———. Song lyrics for Rosalind Courtright, Frances Faye, Sylvia Froos, Wally Griffin, Georgie Kaye, Estelle Loring. 1945–1952.

———. Lyrics to "Around The World," "Change Partners," "Desilu," "Frank Cooper," "The

Furrier's Lament," "How Are Things with Uncle Morris," "Hymie's on the Moon," "Ollawood," " "One for My Baby (And One for Two Cents Plain)," "The Riviera," "Seventy-Six Sol Cohens," "Small World," "Summertime," "Their Doll, Sol," "There Is Nothing Like a Lox," "There's a Jaguar Leaving Soon for the Concord," "Tzimished," "When You Walk through The Bronx," "With a Little Bit of Lox," "Thunderbird," "Younger Than Springstein," "You're the Top," "You're a Nudnik, Sondra Goldfein." 1953–1961.

———. Recording of "Goldeneh Moments from Broadway" song parodies. Home recording by Bobby Rosengarden, Great Neck, New York. Provided by Mark Rosengarden. 1958–1961.

———. Recording of "Goldeneh Moments from Broadway" song parodies. Home recording by Bobby Rosengarden, Great Neck, New York. Provided by Ray Charles. 1958–1961.

———. [Untitled]. Sketch written for Victor Borge television special. [1958].

———. Recording of "Goldeneh Moments from Broadway" song parodies. Party recording. Los Angeles, California. April 10, 1962.

———. Recording of *My Son, the Celebrity* recording session. November 30, 1962.

———. Recording of Sherman in concert. Santa Monica, California. January 18, 1963.

———. Recording of Sherman at the Hungry i. San Francisco. September 1967.

———. *Every 600 Years, on a Tuesday (The Journey to the Perfectly Fair)* [1971]. Quoted with permission of rights holder, Tom Smothers, Knave Productions, Inc.

———. "My Moment of Truth Happened 29 Years Ago, but I Didn't Understand It until Last Thursday" [1971].

Brigham Young University

[Sherman, Allan.] "Big Bad John" Roast. MSS 2020, James Conkling Papers, L. Tom Perry Special Collections, Harold B. Lee Library.

Chicago Public Schools

Copelon, Allan. Registration Card. 1933, 1935–36.

Freemantle Media

I've Got a Secret. Episode of June 11, 1958.

Illinois State Archives

Register of Licensed Dentists, 1881–1886; 1903–1951, Record Group 208, Department of Registration and Education.

Roco Motor & Garage Company, Articles of Incorporation, Office of the Illinois
Secretary of State.

Library of Congress

Burtson, Bud, and Allan Sherman. *The Golden Touch, a Fable.*
The Octagonian. Sigma Alpha Mu. July 1942.
Sherman, Allan. Recording of performance at National Press Club. February 2, 1963
Tonight. 8 (rcf 46–4) 1840442-2-1 (April 16, 1964). Armed Forces Radio recording.
    Tonight. 37 (rcf 52–4) 1844479-3-2 (May 27, 1964). Armed Forces Radio recording.
    Tonight. 68 (rcf 6–5) 1844482-3-1 (July 8, 1964). Armed Forces Radio recording.

Los Angeles Unified School District

Segal, Allan. *Far and Near.* Student newspaper. September 1936–June 1938. John
    Burroughs Junior High School.
———. *Burr.* Published by the Class of S '38. John Burroughs Junior High School.
Sherman, Allan [Allan Segal]. "Scholarship Record."
———. "Witz-Krieg." *Colonial Gazette.* October 1940–June 1941. Fairfax High School.

NARA

Sherman, Allan G. Service number 16–121–278. National Personnel Records Center.

New York Public Library

Dorothy Loudon Papers. Scrapbooks and Box 13, folder 3. Billy Rose Theater Division.
The Fig Leaves Are Falling. Two CD recording. Rodgers and Hammerstein Archives of
    Recorded Sound.

Paley Center for Media, Beverly Hills, California

Your Surprise Package. Catalog ID: B:52102.

Palm Springs Historical Society

Alexander Collection Recordings, "Chi Chi" Tape 13—Alan [*sic*] Sherman, Side 2.

Tom Smothers

Sherman, Allan. *Every 600 Years, on a Tuesday (The Journey to the Perfectly Fair).* Tom
    Smothers, Knave Productions, Inc.

Sony Pictures Entertainment

The Dating Game. May 3, 1969.

UCLA Film and Television Archive

Allan Sherman's "Funnyland," 1965–01–18.
Celebrity Game, 07–15–1965.
"Commercials," Inventory Number VA 13364.
The Garry Moore Show, 1963–01–08.
I've Got a Secret [1957–06–19, 5th anniversary show].
"The Loner," 1965–11–13.
Perry Como's Kraft Music Hall, 1963–05–01.
Perry Como's Kraft Music Hall, 1963–10–03.
Something Special (Television program: 1965).
Steve Allen Show, 1963–03–22, 1963–06–06, 1963–07–18.
Tonight, 1963–08–05; 1963–08–06; 1963–08–07; 1963–08–08; 1963–08–09; 1963–08–16.

University of Illinois Archives

"Case of Allan Sherman, [deleted]," February 25, 1944, Record Series 2/9/1, Arthur C. Willard General Correspondence, 1934–46.
"Case of Allan Sherman," May 1, 1944, Record Series 2/9/1, Arthur C. Willard General Correspondence, 1934–46.
"Case of Allan Sherman," May 10, 1944, Record Series 2/9/1, Arthur C. Willard General Correspondence, 1934–46.
"Case of Allan Sherman, [deleted] and [deleted]," July 26, 1944, Record Series 2/9/1, Committee on Student Discipline, Arthur C. Willard General Correspondence, 1934–46.
"Case of Allan G. Sherman," August 31, 1944, Record Series 2/9/1, Committee on Student Discipline, Arthur C. Willard General Correspondence, 1934–46.
"Cases of Excessive Cutting in Physical Education," May 31, 1944, Record Series 2/9/1, Arthur C. Willard General Correspondence, 1934–46.
Hillel Post. Record series 41/69/806. 1941–45.
Pierson, Irene D. Letter to Dean Fred H. Turner, September 20, 1943, Record Series 41/1/1, Box 2, Dean of Students Correspondence file, 1943–66.
The Rhomer, University of Illinois Chapter of Sigma Alpha Mu, Record series 41/71/868. 1943–45.
Satyr. Record series 13/3/810. 1942.

Sherman, Allan Gerald. Transcript (with "Special Reports"). 1941–45.

Sherman, Allan. Caricature from *Satyr*, September 14, 1942. Record series 13/3/810. Courtesy of the University of Illinois at Urbana-Champaign Archives.

———. Letter to Dean Turner, September 15, 1943, Record Series 41/1/1, Box 3, Dean of Students Correspondence file, 1943–66.

———. Letter to the Assistant Dean, February 12, 1944, Record Series 15–1–16, Box 10, Liberal Arts & Sciences, Dean's Office, Student Correspondence, 1932–73.

Wallace, G.I. Letter to Dean Newcomb, June 22, 1944, Record Series 2/9/1, Box 80, Arthur C. Willard General Correspondence, 1934–46.

University of Nevada, Las Vegas.

Ben Irwin to Al Freeman, October 6, 1965. Sands Hotel Collection, Special Collections.

University of Southern California

[Advertisement] "The Friars Club Charity Foundation," *The Hollywood Reporter*, April 9, 1965. Cinematic Arts Library, Jack L. Warner Collection, 1965 Scrapbook.

Skolsky, Sidney. "Jack Warner Steals 'Roast' from Friars," *Citizen-News*, April 27, 1965. Cinematic Arts Library, Jack L. Warner Collection, 1965 Scrapbook.

Warner Bros. Archives, University of Southern California

Mayer to Mike Maitland, June 29, 1962. Warner Bros. Records, Box 1 of 3, Folder 16738B. School of Cinematic Arts.

Warner Music Group Archive

Sherman, Allan. Recording contracts and correspondence. 1962–1968.

———. "On Golf." Studio remote, File T-3893–96 (5–20–73), and "Allan Sherman Live @ La Costa Country Club," File B-1755 (7–14–72) Warner Music Group Tape Vault, Los Angeles.

Yale University, Beinecke Rare Book and Manuscript Library

Sherman, Allan, and Eugene O'Sullivan. *The Happy Medium*. 1952. Guide to the New Dramatists, Inc. Archive. Yale Collection of American Literature.

PUBLISHED SOURCES

"Balti. Op Woe: Acts Too High, No $ to Buy." *Billboard*, February 12, 1949.

Adams, Sgt. Jack. "Illini War Chant." *Daily Illini*, September 30, 1943.

Adler, Hillel, and William Fraiberg. *Memories of Ozarow*. Montreal: Ozarow Press, 1997.

Aldrich, Nelson W. *George Being George: George Plimpton's Life*. New York: Random House, 2008.

Aleichem, Sholom. "On Account of a Hat." In *A Treasury of Yiddish Stories*, edited by Irving Howe and Eliezer Greenberg, 111–17. New York: Schocken Books, 1974.

Allen, Steve. *More Funny People*. New York: Stein & Day, 1982.

Anderson, Tim J. *Making Easy Listening: Material Culture and Postwar American Recording*. Minneapolis: University of Minnesota Press, 2006.

Bacon, Gershon. "Poland from 1795 to 1939." *The YIVO Encyclopedia of Jews in Eastern Europe*. www.yivoencyclopedia.org (accessed May 15, 2012).

Bailey, Peter J. J. *The Reluctant Film Art of Woody Allen*. Lexington: University Press of Kentucky, 2001.

Band, Arnold J. "Popular Fiction and the Shaping of Jewish Identity." In *Jewish Identity in America*, edited by David M. Gordis and Yoav Ben-Horin, 215–26. Los Angeles: Susan and David Wilstein Institute of Jewish Policy Studies, 1991.

Battaglio, Stephen. *David Susskind: A Televised Life*. New York: St. Martin's Press, 2010.

Baumgarten, Jean. "Badkhonim." *The YIVO Encyclopedia of Jews in Eastern Europe*. www.yivoencyclopedia.org (accessed May 8, 2012).

Beider, Alexander. "Names and Naming." *YIVO Encyclopedia of Jews in Eastern Europe*. www.yivoencyclopedia.org (accessed May 8, 2012).

Belafonte, Harry. *My Song: A Memoir*. New York: Alfred A. Knopf, 2011.

Bellow, Saul. *Herzog*. New York: Avon, 1976.

———. "Cousins." In Saul Bellow, *Him with His Foot in His Mouth and Other Stories*. New York: Penguin, 1998.

Bergreen, Laurence. "This Is the Army." *Prologue Magazine* 28, no. 2 (Summer 1996): 95–105.

Bernstein, Bob. "Wheeling and Dealing: Talent Tidings." *Billboard*, June 23, 1958.

Bernstein, Burton. "Leonard Bernstein's Separate Peace with Berlin." *Esquire*, October 1961.

Bernstein, Leonard. "Leonard Bernstein Oral History Interview." John F. Kennedy Presidential Library and Museum (July 21, 1965): 1–19. www.jfklibrary.org /Asset-Viewer/Archives/JFKOH-LB-01.aspx (accessed December 14, 2011).

Bernstein, Lester. "London Premiere for 'Golden Touch.'" *New York Times*, July 16, 1948.

Bial, Henry. *Acting Jewish: Negotiating Ethnicity on the American Stage and Screen*. Ann Arbor: University of Michigan Press, 2005.

Birmingham Chamber of Commerce. *Birmingham City Directory 1913*. Birmingham, AL: R.L. Polk & Co., 1913.

Birmingham Chamber of Commerce. *Birmingham City Directory 1922*. Birmingham, AL: R.L. Polk & Co., 1922.

Birmingham Chamber of Commerce. *Birmingham City Directory 1937*. Birmingham, AL: R.L. Polk & Co., 1937.

Birmingham Chamber of Commerce. *Birmingham City Directory 1938*. Birmingham, AL: R.L. Polk & Co., 1938.

Bloom, Ken. *Broadway, Its History, People, and Places: An Encyclopedia*. New York: Routledge, 2004.

Brooks, Tim, and Earle Marsh. *The Complete Directory to Prime Time Network and Cable TV Shows, 1946–Present*. New York: Ballantine Books, 2007.

Brumberg, Stephen F. "Going to America, Going to School: The Immigrant—Public School Encounter in Turn-of-the-Century New York City." In *East European Jews in America, 1880–1920: Immigration and Adaptation*, part one, edited by Jeffrey S. Gurock, 397–446. New York, Routledge, 1998.

Burnett, Carol. *This Time Together: Laughter and Reflection*. New York: Harmony Books, 2010.

Calta, Louis. "'Heiress' to Bow on Rialto Sept. 29." *New York Times*, August 28, 1947.

———. "'Ballet Ballads' Due at Music Box." *New York Times*, May 18, 1948.

———. "Wiman to Offer Connelly Comedy." *New York Times*, June 17, 1948.

Clar, Mimi. "Sherman Folk Songs Become Gefilte Fish." *Los Angeles Times*, July 21, 1963.

Chandler, Bob. "Diary of a TV Show (Gleason's)." *Variety*, February 8, 1961.

Cohen, Mark. "Body Language: Spoken vs. Silent Communication in *Herzog*." *Saul Bellow Journal* 20, no. 2 (Fall 2004): 3–17

———. "My Fair Sadie: Allan Sherman and a Paradox of American Jewish Culture." *American Jewish History* 93, no. 1 (March 2007): 51–71.

Cohen, Steven M. "Israel in the Jewish Identity of American Jews: A Study in Dualities and Contrasts." In *Jewish Identity in America*, edited by David M. Gordis and Yoav Ben-Horin, 119–36. Los Angeles: Susan and David Wilstein Institute of Jewish Policy Studies, 1991.

Cole, Bill. "Annual Dance, Stunt Show Are Today." *Daily Illini*, October 10, 1942.

Coplon, Abraham George. *Man Alive! An Analysis of the Human Struggle*. Chicago: Acme, 1928.

Cornyn, Stan. *Exploding: The Highs, Hits, Hype, Heroes, and Hustlers of the Warner Music Group*. New York: Harper Collins, 2003.

Cutler, Irving. *The Jews of Chicago: From Shtetl to Suburb*. Urbana: University of Illinois Press, 1996.

Denis, Paul. *Your Career in Show Business*. New York: E.P. Dutton, 1948.

Deverich, Linsey. *Wandering through La La Land with the Last Warner Brother*. Bloomington, IN: Author House, 2007.

Diviney, Patrick F., and Michael Allen. "A Hard Day's Night." *Columbia, the Magazine of Northwest History* 10, no. 2 (Summer 1996): 6–11.

Dopson, Roland. "Birmingham Faster Asks Visitors to Skip Food Talk." *The Dothan Eagle*, September 4, 1949.

Dunning, John. *On the Air: The Encyclopedia of Old-Time Radio*. New York: Oxford University Press, 1998.

Eberhart, Mark E. *Feeding the Fire: The Lost History and Uncertain Future of Mankind's Energy Addiction*. New York: Crown, 2007.

Edelman, Marsha Bryan. "Continuity, Creativity, and Conflict: The Ongoing Search for 'Jewish' Music." In *You Should See Yourself: Jewish Identity in Postmodern American Culture*, edited by Vincent Brook, 119–33. New Brunswick, NJ: Rutgers University Press, 2006.

Edgerton, Gary R. *The Columbia History of American Television*. New York: Columbia University Press, 2007.

Ellis, Edward Robb. *Diary of the Century: Tales from America's Greatest Diarist*. New York: Kodansha International, 1995.

Elovitz, Mark H. *A Century of Jewish Life in Dixie: The Birmingham Experience*. Tuscaloosa: University of Alabama Press, 1974.

Epstein, Lawrence J. *The Haunted Smile: The Story of Jewish Comedians in America*. New York: Public Affairs, 2001.

Erdman, Harley. *Staging the Jew: The Performance of an American Ethnicity, 1860–1920*. New Brunswick, NJ: Rutgers University Press, 1997.

Fates, Gil. *What's My Line? The Inside History of TV's Most Famous Panel Show*. Englewood Cliffs, NJ: Prentice-Hall, 1978.

Feinberg, Leonard. *The Satirist: His Temperament, Motivation, and Influence*. Ames: Iowa State University Press, 1963

Fogelson, Genia. *Harry Belafonte*. Los Angeles: Holloway House, 1991.

Fogelson, Robert M. *The Fragmented Metropolis: Los Angeles, 1850–1930*. Cambridge, MA: Harvard University Press, 1967.

Foran, Charles. *Mordecai: The Life and Times*. Toronto: Knopf Canada, 2010.

Fox, Margalit. "Sheldon Keller, TV Comedy Writer, Dies at 85." *New York Times*, September 4, 2008.

Freedman, Jonathan. *Klezmer America: Jewishness, Ethnicity, Modernity*. New York: Columbia University Press, 2008.

Freeman, Florine. "Affiliate Sale Under Way; Aim 100%." *Hillel Post*, October 29, 1943.

Frommer, Myrna Katz, and Harvey Frommer. *It Happened in the Catskills*. Madison: University of Wisconsin Press, 2004.

Gabler, Neal. *An Empire of Their Own: How the Jews Invented Hollywood*. New York: Crown Publishers, 1988.

Gartner, Lloyd P. "Jewish Migrants en Route from Europe to North America: Traditions and Realities." In *East European Jews in America, 1880–1920: Immigration and Adaptation*, part one, edited by Jeffery S. Gurock, 91–105. New York: Routledge, 1998.

Gay, Ruth. *Unfinished People: Eastern European Jews Encounter America*. New York: W.W. Norton, 1996.

Gehman, Richard. "Allan Sherman: Country Club Folk Singer." *Los Angeles Herald-Examiner: American Weekly*, January 13, 1963.

———. "The Hanneler." *TV Guide*, March 16, 1963.

Glazer, Nathan. *American Judaism*. Chicago: University of Chicago Press, 1957.

Gold, David L. "On 'Jewish English in the United States.'" *Jewish Language Review* 6 (1986): 121–36.

Goode, Mort. "Liner Notes." *Billy Gray in My Fairfax Lady*. Jubilee 2030.

Goren, Arthur. *The Politics and Public Culture of American Jews*. Bloomington: Indiana University Press, 1999.

Gould, Jack. "Quiz Programs." *New York Times*, January 23, 1955.

Grimes, William. "Norman Corwin, 101; Rendered Radio into Poetry." *New York Times*, October 20, 2011.

Hall, Randal L. "Before NASCAR: The Corporate and Civic Promotion of Automobile Racing in the American South, 1903–1927." *Journal of Southern History*, 68, no. 3 (August 2002): 629–68.

Hathaway, Bob. "Acts from League Show Highlight Sing; Seniors Give Farewell Dance in Gym." *Daily Illini*, May 15, 1942.

Heinze, Andrew R. *Adapting to Abundance: Jewish Immigrants, Mass Consumption, and the Search for American Identity*. New York: Columbia University Press, 1990.

Heymann, C. David. *Liz: An Intimate Biography of Elizabeth Taylor*. New York: Carol Pub. Group, 1995.

Higham, John. *Send These to Me: Jews and Other Immigrants in Urban America*. New York: Atheneum, 1975.

———. *Strangers in the Land: Patterns of American Nativism, 1860–1925*. New Brunswick, NJ: Rutgers University Press, 1994.

Howe, Irving. "The Nature of Jewish Laughter." In *Jewish Wry: Essays on Jewish Humor*, edited by Sarah Blacher Cohen, 16–24. Detroit: Wayne State University Press.

Huber, Pat. "Sigma Alpha Mu, Tri-Delt, Evarts Win Top Honors in Stunt Show." *Daily Illini*, October 31, 1943.

Jackson, Kenneth T. *Crabgrass Frontier: The Suburbanization of the United States*. New York: Oxford University Press, 1985.

Jauch, Fritz. "Gallant Illini Suffer First Loss." *Daily Illini*, October 25, 1942.

Joselit, Jenna Weissman. "'Harness My Zebras': American Jews and the Pursuit of Pleasure." In *American Judaism in Popular Culture*, edited by Leonard J. Greenspoon and Ronald Simkins, 1–16. Omaha, NE, Creighton University Press, 2006.

Kaufman, David. "'Here's a Foreign Song I Learned in Utah': The Anxiety of Jewish Influence in the Music of Bob Dylan." In *The Song Is Not the Same: Jews and American Popular Music*, edited by Bruce Zuckerman, Josh Kun, and Lisa Ansell, 115–36. West Lafayette, IN: Purdue University Press for the USC Casden Institute for the Study of the Jewish Role in American Life, 2011.

Kazin, Alfred. *Contemporaries*. Boston: Little, Brown, 1962.

Kennedy, President John F. "Annual Message to the Congress on the State of the Union, January 14, 1963." www.presidency.ucsb.edu/ws/index.php (accessed March 27, 2011).

Knight, Arthur. "The Literary Life in Las Vegas." *Saturday Review*, November 6, 1965.

Kolodin, Irving. "Sherman's Mighty Lyre." *Saturday Review*, December 8, 1962.

Korelitz, Seth. "The Menorah Idea: From Religion to Culture, from Race to Ethnicity." *American Jewish History* 85, no. 1 (March 1997): 75–100.

Kramer, Michael P. "The Vanishing Jew: On Teaching Bellow's *Seize the Day* as Ethnic Fiction." In *New Essays on "Seize the Day,"* edited by Michael P. Kramer, 1–24. Cambridge: Cambridge University Press, 1998.

Kuller, Sid. *Billy Gray in My Fairfax Lady*. Jubilee Records 2030.

Kun, Josh. "The Yiddish Are Coming: Mickey Katz, Antic-Semitism, and the Sound of Jewish Difference." *American Jewish History* 87, no. 4 (December 1999): 343–74.

Kuznets, Simon. "Immigration of Russian Jews to the United States: Background and Structure." In *East European Jews in America, 1880–1920: Immigration and Adaptation*, part one, edited by Jeffery S. Gurock, 1–90. New York: Routledge, 1998.

Lahlein, Bob. "Campus Scout." *Daily Illini*, October 31, 1942.

Lavery, David, and Sara Lewis Dunne. *"Seinfeld," Master of Its Domain: Revisiting Television's Greatest Sitcom*. New York: Continuum International Pub. Group, 2006.

Lax, Eric. *Woody Allen: A Biography*. New York: Knopf, 1991.

Lederhendler, Eli. "Guides for the Perplexed: Sex, Manners, and Mores for the Yiddish Reader in America." In *East European Jews in America, 1880–1920: Immigration and Adaptation*, part two, edited by Jeffery S. Gurock, 537–57. New York: Routledge, 1998.

———. *New York Jews and the Decline of Urban Ethnicity, 1950–1970*. Syracuse, NY: Syracuse University Press, 2001.

———. "Rereading the Americanization Narratives of Antin, Zangwill, and Cahan." In *Imagining the American Jewish Community*, edited by Jack Wertheimer, 253–70. Waltham, MA: Brandeis University Press, 2007.

Levenson, Sam. *Everything but Money*. New York: Simon and Schuster, 1966.

Levine, David O. *The American College and the Culture of Aspiration, 1915–1940*. Ithaca, NY: Cornell University Press, 1986.

Lieberman, Paul. "The Boy at Camp Granada." *Los Angeles Times*, August 16, 2003.

Lydon, Michael. *Ray Charles: Man and Music*. New York: Riverhead, 1998.

Lyman, Michael D., and Gary W. Potter. *Organized Crime*. Upper Saddle River, NJ: Prentice Hall, 1997.

Mandelbaum, Ken. *Not Since Carrie: Forty Years of Broadway Musical Flops*. New York: St. Martin's Press, 1991.

Martin, Douglas. "Sylvia Froos, 89, a Versatile Former Child Star." *New York Times*, April 3, 2004.

Matthews, Fred. "Louis Wirth and American Ethnic Studies." In *The Jews of North America*, edited by Moses Rischin, 123–43. Detroit: Wayne State University Press, 1987.

McCann, Bob. *Encyclopedia of African American Actresses in Film and Television*. Jefferson, NC: McFarland & Co., 2010.

Millstein, Gilbert. "A Negro Says It with Jokes." *New York Times Magazine*, April 30, 1961.

Moore, Barbara, et al. *Prime-Time Television: A Concise History*. Westport, CT: Praeger, 2006.

Moore, Deborah Dash. *To the Golden Cities: Pursuing the American Dream in Miami and L.A.* Cambridge, MA: Harvard University Press, 1994.

Nachman, Gerald. *Right Here on Our Stage Tonight!* Berkeley: University of California Press, 2009.

Newcomb, Horace. *Encyclopedia of Television, Volume 1*. Chicago: Fitzroy Dearborn Publishers, 1997.

Nickens, Christopher, and Karen Swenson. *The Films of Barbra Streisand*. New York: Citadel Press, 2000.

Olson, Lynne. *Citizens of London: The Americans Who Stood with Britain in Its Darkest, Finest Hour*. New York: Random House, 2011.

Ostwald, Arnold. "Campus Night Club Returns with New, Entertaining Show." *Daily Illini*, November 28, 1942.

Paris, Leslie. *Children's Nature: The Rise of the American Summer Camp*. New York: New York University Press, 2008.

Pasternak, Velvel. *The Jewish Music Companion*. [United States]: Tara Publications, 2002.

Pinsker, Sanford. "Lenny Bruce: Shpritzing the Goyim/Shocking the Jews." In *Jewish Wry: Essays on Jewish Humor*, edited by Sarah Blacher Cohen, 89–104. Bloomington: Indiana University Press, 1987.

Podhoretz, Norman. "The Rise and Fall of the American Jewish Novelist." In *Jewish Life in America: Historical Perspectives*, edited by Gladys Rosen, 141–50. New York: Ktav Pub. House, 1978.

Pomerenze, Seymour Jacob. "Aspects of Chicago Russian Jewish Life, 1893–1915." In *The Chicago Pinkas*, edited by Simon Rawidowicz, 113–36. Chicago: College of Jewish Studies, 1952.

Prell, Riv-Ellen. *Fighting to Become Americans: Jews, Gender, and the Anxiety of Assimilation*. Boston: Beacon Press, 1999.

———. "Community and the Discourse of Elegy: The Postwar Suburban Debate." In *Imagining the American Jewish Community*, edited by Jack Wertheimer, 67–90. Waltham, MA: Brandeis University Press, 2007.

Prichard, Merrill. "P.E. Department Erects Display." *Daily Illini*, September 24, 1942.

Pryor, Richard. *That Nigger's Crazy*. Partee Records, 1974.

Purdum, Todd S. "From That Day Forth." *Vanity Fair*, February 2011.

Rabinowitz, Howard N. "Nativism, Bigotry and Anti-Semitism in the South." In *Anti-Semitism in America*, edited by Jeffrey S. Gurock, 647–61. New York: Routledge, 1998.

Reidelbach, Maria. *Completely Mad: A History of the Comic Book and Magazine*. Boston: Little, Brown, 1991.

Reik, Theodor. *Jewish Wit*. New York: Gamut Press, 1962.

Rischin, Moses. "Jews and Pluralism: Toward an American Freedom Symphony." In *Jewish Life in America: Historical Perspectives*, edited by Gladys Rosen, 61–91. New York: Ktav Pub. House, 1978.

———. Foreword to *The Jews of Los Angeles, 1849–1945: An Annotated Bibliography*, compiled by Sara G. Cogan, vii–xi. Berkeley, CA: Western Jewish History Center, Judah L. Magnes Memorial Museum, 1980.

Roemer, Nils, and Gideon Reuveni. Introduction to *Longing, Belonging, and the Making of Jewish Consumer Culture*, edited by Gideon Reuveni and Nils H. Roemer, 1–22. Leiden, Netherlands: Brill, 2010.

Rogovoy, Seth. *The Essential Klezmer: A Music Lover's Guide to Jewish Roots and Soul Music, from the Old World to the Jazz Age to the Downtown Avant-Garde*. Chapel Hill, NC: Algonquin Books of Chapel Hill, 2000.

Roth, Philip. *Reading Myself and Others*. New York: Penguin, 1985.

Sanua, Marianne. "'We Hate New York': Negative Images of the Promised City as a

Source for Jewish Fraternity and Sorority Members, 1920–1940." In *An Inventory of Promises: Essays on American Jewish History in Honor of Moses Rischin*, edited by Jeffrey S. Gurock and Mark Lee Raphael, 235–63. Brooklyn, NY: Carlson Publishing, Inc., 1995.

———. *Going Greek: Jewish College Fraternities in the United States, 1895–1945.* Detroit: Wayne State University Press, 2003.

Schack, William, and Sarah Schack. "On the Horizon: And Now—Yinglish on Broadway." *Commentary*, December 1951.

Schallert, Edwin. "Dieterle Will Direct 'John Paul Jones'; Terry, Blythe Returns Unique." *Los Angeles Times*, July 24, 1956.

Schechner, Mark. "Dear Mr. Einstein: Jewish Comedy and the Contradictions of Culture." In *Jewish Wry: Essays on Jewish Humor*, edited by Sarah Blacher Cohen, 141–57. Detroit: Wayne State University Press.

Seller, Maxine S. "World of our Mothers: The Women's Page of the Jewish Daily Forward." In *East European Jews in America, 1880–1920: Immigration and Adaptation*, part two, edited by Jeffery S. Gurock, 513–36. New York: Routledge, 1998.

Selvin, Joel. *San Francisco: The Musical History Tour*. San Francisco: Chronicle Books, 1996.

Sewelovitz, Sara S. "The Call to the Open." In *The Mirror*, edited by Mary E. Forbes and Anita Waldhorst, 12. Birmingham, AL: Birmingham High School, 1911. http://bplonline.cdmhost.com (accessed May 7, 2012).

Sharp, Rosalie Wise. *Rifke, an Improbable Life*. Toronto: ECW Press, 2007.

Sherman, Allan. "A Football for Grandma." *Kiwanis Magazine*, May 1959.

———. "A Football for Grandma." *Readers Digest*, February 1960.

———. Liner notes. Bill Cosby, *Bill Cosby Is a Very Funny Fellow, Right!* Warner Bros. 1963.

———. Liner notes. Bill Cosby, *I Started Out as a Child*. Warner Bros. 1964.

———. "Sex and the Single Sherman." *Playboy*, July 1965.

———. *A Gift of Laughter*. New York: Atheneum, 1965.

———. "A Question of Honor." *Reader's Digest*, May 1971.

———. "Summer's Magical Music." *Reader's Digest*, July 1971.

———. "Griselda and the Porn-O-Phone." *Playboy*, December 1971.

———. *The Rape of the A.P.E.* Chicago, Playboy Press, 1973.

Sherman, Allan, Arnold Peyser, and Lois Peyser. *Instant Status; or, Up Your Image*. New York: G.P. Putnam's Sons, 1964.

Shuman, Nick. "Humor, Melodious Score Highlight 'Nothing Ventured' Production." *Daily Illini*, February 20, 1943.

Sicher, Efraim. *Jews in Russian Literature after the October Revolution: Writers and Artists between Hope and Apostasy.* Cambridge: Cambridge University Press, 1995.

Slobin, Mark. *American Klezmer: Its Roots and Offshoots.* Berkeley: University of California Press, 2002.

Smith, Ronald L. *Comedy on Record: The Complete Critical Discography.* New York: Garland Publishing, 1988.

Sollors, Werner. *Beyond Ethnicity: Consent and Descent in American Culture.* New York: Oxford University Press, 1986.

Sorkin, Sidney. *Bridges to an American City: A Guide to Chicago's Landsmanshaften, 1870 to 1990.* New York: Peter Lang, 1993.

Squire, Larry R. *The History of Neuroscience in Autobiography.* Vol. 5. Amsterdam: Elsevier Academic Press, 2006.

Stone, Wendell C. *Caffe Cino: The Birthplace of Off-Off-Broadway.* Carbondale: Southern Illinois University Press, 2005.

Strauss, Lauren B. "Staying Afloat in the Melting Pot: Constructing an American Jewish Identity in the *Menorah Journal* of the 1920s." *American Jewish History* 84, no. 4 (December 1996): 315–31.

Strickland, Edwin. "Tarrant 'Fatty' to Try 100-Day Fast on Pole." *Birmingham News*, August 25, 1949.

Stringfellow, Frank. *The Meaning of Irony: A Psychoanalytic Investigation.* Albany: State University of New York Press, 1994.

Tannen, Deborah. "New York Jewish Conversational Style." *International Journal of the Sociology of Language* 30 (1981): 133–49.

Terrace, Vincent. *The Complete Encyclopedia of Television Programs, 1947–1979.* South Brunswick, NJ: A.S. Barnes, 1979.

Thomas, Nick. *Raised by the Stars: Interviews with 29 Children of Hollywood Actors.* Jefferson, NC: McFarland, 2011.

Timberg, Bernard, and Bob Erler, *Television Talk: A History of the TV Talk Show.* Austin: University of Texas Press, 2002.

Toll, William. "Horace M. Kallen: Pluralism and American Jewish Identity." *American Jewish History* 85, no. 1 (1997): 57–74.

Tygiel, Jules. Introduction to *Metropolis in the Making*, edited by Tom Sitton and William Francis Deverell, 1–10. Berkeley: University of California Press, 2001.

United Press International (UPI). "Admitted Land Swindler Offers to Aid Arizona." *The Hour*, March 25, 1977.

United States Government. *Copyright Law Revision, Part 3, Preliminary Draft for Revised U.S. Copyright Law and Discussion and Comments on the Draft.* Washington, DC: U.S. Government Printing Office, 1964.

Vail, Ken. *Duke's Diary: The Life of Duke Ellington, 1950–1974*. Lanham, MD: Scarecrow Press, 2002.

Vance, H. C. "Sensational Crashes at Big Race Meet, Auto Races Most Exciting Ever; Three Injured." *Birmingham News*, October 30, 1913.

Vitello, Paul. "Oscar Handlin, Historian Who Chronicled U.S. Immigration, Dies at 95." *New York Times*, September 24, 2011.

Wakefield, Dan. *New York in the 50s*. Boston: Houghton Mifflin, 1992.

Wakin, Daniel J. "Leonid Hambro, 86, Pianist with an Astounding Memory, Dies." *New York Times*, October 26, 2006.

Warnke, Nina. "Immigrant Popular Culture as Contested Sphere: Yiddish Music Halls, the Yiddish Press, and the Processes of Americanization, 1900–1910." *Theater Journal* 48, no. 3 (1996): 321–35.

Wenger, Beth S. *The Jewish Americans: Three Centuries of Jewish Voices in America*. New York: Doubleday, 2007.

Whitburn, Joel. *The Billboard Book of Top 40 Hits, 9th Edition*. New York: Random House, 2010.

Whitfield, Stephen J. *Voices of Jacob, Hands of Esau: Jews in American Life and Thought*. Hamden, CT: Archon Books, 1984.

——— . *American Space, Jewish Time*. Hamden, CT: Archon Books, 1988.

——— . "Movies in America as Paradigms of Accommodation." In *The Americanization of the Jews*, edited by Robert M. Seltzer and Norman J. Cohen, 79–94. New York: New York University, 1995.

——— . "The Braided Identity of Southern Jewry." In *Anti-Semitism in America*, edited by Jeffrey S. Gurock, 686–710. New York: Routledge, 1998.

——— . *In Search of American Jewish Culture*. Waltham, MA: Brandeis University Press, 1999.

——— . "Is It True What They Say about Dixie?" *Southern Cultures* 8, no. 2 (2002): 8–37.

——— . "Fiddling with Sholem Aleichem: A History of *Fiddler on the Roof*." In *Key Texts in American Jewish Culture*, edited by Jack Kugelmass, 105–25. New Brunswick, NJ: Rutgers University Press, 2003.

Wirth, Louis. *Culture Conflicts in the Immigrant Family*. Chicago: University of Chicago, 1925.

——— . *The Ghetto*. Chicago: University of Chicago Press, 1956.

Wirth-Nesher, Hana. "The Accented Imagination: Speaking and Writing Jewish America." In *Imagining the American Jewish Community*, edited by Jack Werthheimer, 286–303. Waltham, MA: Brandeis University Press, 2007.

Zolotow, Maurice. "Spoofmaster." *Saturday Evening Post*, April 20, 1963.

*Note: All titles of works without an author are assumed
to be Sherman's and are designated by type of work.*

Adams, Jack, 49
African Americans, 151–52, 160
"Aha!—A Drama in Sex Acts (Printer's
  Error)" (playlet), 45
albums. *See individual album titles*
Allan in Wonderland (album), 190–93
Allan Sherman Enterprises, 195
Allan Sherman Live!!! (album), 223–24
Allen, Steve, 40, 77, 122–23, 124–25, 153,
  162, 250
Allen, Woody, 95, 187, 199–200, 201–2,
  252–53
"All My Laughter" (lyrics), 238
"Al 'n Yetta" (parody), 173

America (Stewart), 256–57
Americanism. *See* assimilation vs. ethnic
  identity
anger, comedy as expression of, 6, 43
Anshe Emet synagogue, 37, 61–62
Anti-Defamation League of the B'nai
  B'rith, 13, 104, 158
anti-Semitism, 17, 35, 105, 119, 158
Army enlistment, Sherman's short, 49
assimilation vs. ethnic identity: balance
  for Jewish entertainers (1960s), 186–87;
  Christianized musicals created by Jews,
  90, 92–93; early 20th-century push for
  assimilation, 104–5; and immigrant

experience, xiii, 12–14, 105; Jewish struggle with, xiii, 12–14, 82, 156; and Jewish suburbanization, 93–94, 178; in Los Angeles, 22; and New York Jewishness, 60; and Percy Coplon, 17; Rose's assimilation, 15–16, 19, 20, 29; Sherman's last essay on, 245; Sherman's ridiculing of assimilation, 99–100; Sherman's tightrope walk between, 3–4

"Ballad of Harry Lewis, The" (parody), xii, 129, 140, 157

Bass, Ben/Sam. *See* Segal, Dave

Beatles phenomenon, 189–90

Belafonte, Harry, 128–29, 161

Bell, Daniel, 118

Bellow, Saul, xiii, 11–12, 13, 136–37, 156–57, 178, 187

Benny, Jack, 105, 154

Bergler, Edmund, 182

Berlin, Irving, 41, 51, 134–35

Berman, Shelly, 101–2

Bernstein, Leonard, 119, 120, 138

Best of Allan Sherman, The (album), 253–54

"Bewitched" (parody), 84, 91

"Big Bad Jim" (parody), 115–16

Bikel, Theodore, 129, 130

Billboard, 145–46, 170

Birmingham, Alabama, 16–17, 24, 38–39

blacks, 151–52, 160

Bobrick, Sam, 209

Borge, Victor, 75, 80

Boston Pops concert, 200, 201, 202–3

Broadway musical, Sherman's, 48, 66, 226, 232–33, 234, 236–37

"Bronx Birdwatcher, The" (parody), 173

Brooks, Mel, 77, 85–86, 165, 212, 252, 253

Brougham, John, 146–47

Bruce, Lenny, 89–90, 101

Burtson, Bud, 59

Busch, Lou, 107, 116, 127–28, 148, 223, 238–39

"Bye Bye Blumberg" (parody), 204–5

Caesar, Sid, 70, 85–86

Cahn, Sammy, 148

"Call Me" (parody), 227

Camp Granada Game, 195

Camp Ojibwa, Wisconsin, 54

"Campus Scout" column, 35–36, 40–41, 42, 45, 50

Capp, Al, 216

Carlin, George, 252

Carnegie Hall, 153, 154

Carp, Jacob, 15

Carr, Joe "Fingers." *See* Busch, Lou

Carroll, Pat, 131

Carson, Johnny, 171, 181, 182, 183

"Catastrophe" (poem), 4

Catskill Mountain resorts, 186–87

Chackes, Alexander (brother-in-law), 56

Chackes, Dolores "Dee" (wife), 54, 55–57, 60–62. *See also* Golden, Dee; Sherman, Dolores

Chackes, Emanuel (father-in-law), 56

Chackes, Theresa (née Silberstein) (mother-in-law), 56

"Change Partners" (Sherman parody), 98

Charles, Ray, 78, 87, 97

Charley Weaver Show (TV show), 106

Chaseman, Joel, 125

Chicago, Illinois, 2–3, 10–13, 19, 24–26, 30, 37–38, 195

"Chi Chi" (parody), 167–68

Chi Chi club, 167–68

childhood: damage to Sherman from, 7, 22–32, 182–85; Sherman's comic contrasts with adulthood, 137, 173–74, 177; Sherman's idealization of, 23, 80, 109, 180, 182–83, 192–93, 218–19, 228, 243

"Chim Chim Cheree" (Sherman's parody), 220

"Chopped Liver" (parody), 117, 133

"Civilians of 1943, The" (poem), 51–52

civil rights movement, 219

classical music, Sherman's inventive use of, 175

Clorfene, Bruce, 34, 35, 38, 40, 44–45, 46, 49, 52, 54

Cohen, Elliot, 63

Cole, Louise Goldstein, 38

Colgate Comedy Hour (TV show), 233

college years: academic and behavior problems, 50, 53–54; choosing a school, 34–35; Dee Chackes, 54, 55–57; deflating pretension, 42; Jewish caricature issue in Satyr, 46–47; Mirth of a Nation, 53; name change and father, 38–39; Nothing Ventured, 48–49; sexual proclivities, 41–42, 44–46; and short Army enlistment, 49; Sigma Alpha Mu, 43–44; song parodies, 41, 42–43, 47–48, 50–52, 54–55; writing for Daily Illini, 33–34, 35–36, 39, 40–41, 42, 45, 50, 53

comedy: as expression of anger, 6, 43; hard-driving shift after Sherman, 251–52; and Jewish identity dilemma, 245; and psychosis, 182; psycho-social

benefits of Sherman's humor, 137; rise of albums of recordings, 101; and seduction, 5–6, 45; as Sherman's savior, 112; sick comics era, 100–101; trauma and despair as origin of, 6–7. See also song parodies

"Comin' Thro' the Rye" (Sherman's parody), 146

Commentary (magazine), 63

Como, Perry, 81, 169

concert tours. See live performances

Conkling, Jim, 115–16

"Conscientious Objector of Company Z, The" (parody), 48

consumption as social practice, 95

Cooper, Frank, 98–99

Cooper, Hal, 110–11, 113, 131, 183

Cooper, Lee, 3

Copacabana, New York City, 186

Copelon, Allan, 39. See also Sherman, Allan

Copelon, Hilda (half-sister), 38

Copelon, Rose (mother). See Sherman, Rose

Coplon, Abraham (uncle), 3, 19, 38, 66–67

Coplon, Morris (cousin), 3, 14, 17, 38, 174

Coplon (Copelon), Allan. See Sherman, Allan

Coplon (Copelon), Percy (father), 16–20, 21–22, 23, 24, 38–39, 66–68

Coplon (Kaplan), Keile (grandmother), 16–17, 18, 38

Coplon (Kaplan), Moses (grandfather), 16–17, 18, 38

copyright law, 125–26, 141–42

Cornyn, Stan, 123, 127, 136, 202–3

Corwin, Norman, 112
Cosby, Bill, 180–81, 194
Crane, Bob, 142, 148–49
"Crazy Downtown" (parody), 214–15
Curb Your Enthusiasm (TV show), 256
Curtain Call Productions, 195
Curtis, Tony, 80–81
"Customers" (parody), 258–59

Daily Illini, Sherman's writing for, 33–34, 35–36, 39, 40–41, 42, 45, 50, 53
Dana, Bill, 119, 126, 148, 194
Dane, Faith, 193
Dating Game, 239–40
David, Larry, 256
Department of Labor dinner, 164
"Desilu" (parody), 143
Dessen, Ed, 45
Dickinson, Angie, 211, 216
"Did I Ever Really Live?" (original song), 232
Diplomat Hotel, Miami, 168–69, 186
"Don't Burn Down Bidwell's" (parody), 42–43
"Don't Buy the Liverwurst" (parody), 151
"Don't Take my Pin" (parody), 55, 57
Dragonwagon, Crescent, 76, 77, 233, 239
Dr. Demento radio program, 253
"Drop-Outs March, The" (parody), 190
Dubner, Stephen J., 260
Durgom, George "Bullets," 77, 115–16, 123, 132–33, 194
Dylan, Bob, 161, 219

Ed Sullivan Show (TV show), 150, 226
"Eh!" (parody), 90
"Eleanor, Eleanor" (original song), 53

Emerson, Faye, 71, 72, 77, 78
Entratter, Jack, 153
Epstein, Yehuda Arie Leib ha-Levi, 9, 10
ethnicity: acceptance of in America, 122, 206; blacks, 151–52, 160; freedom of expression in 1960s, 117–18; Jewish expression of, xiii; triumph of in Sherman's parodies, 259. *See also* Jewish ethnic identity
European appearances, 188–89
Evening with Nichols and May, An (album), 101
Every 600 Years, on a Tuesday (unpublished manuscript), 108, 109, 242–43
"Everything's Up to Date in Berchtesgaden" (parody), 52

Farrell, Skip, 113–14
Fates, Gil, 80
"Father and Son" (Berman), 101–2
fatness: and comic personality, 2; genetic component, 40; and gluttony, 6, 26, 40, 65, 112, 189, 193, 194; overcoming social handicap in college, 36; psychological basis for Sherman's, 49, 197–98; in song parodies, 40, 162, 197–98
Faye, Frances, 69
Fiddler on the Roof, 205–6, 231
Fiedler, Arthur, 202
Fig Leaves Are Falling, The (musical play), 48, 66, 232–33, 234, 236–37
folk music movement, 120, 127, 136, 140–41
food, love as, 25–26, 88, 194. *See also* fatness

"Football for Grandma, A" (story), 82, 109

For Swingin' Livers Only! (album), 204–5

"Frank Cooper" (parody), 98–99

Freud, Sigmund, 181–82

Froos, Silvia, 90, 91, 92

"Funnyland" (TV pilot), 207–12, 213, 217

Gans, Herbert J., 158

Garry Moore Show (TV show), 150, 152

Gehman, Betsey, 77

Gehman, Dick, 76–77, 88, 166

Gershwin, George, 89

Gershwin, Ira, 89

Gift of Laughter, A (book), 23, 218

Gift of Laughter, A (The Best of Allan Sherman, Volume II) (album), 254

Gilbert, Syril, 9, 11, 12, 14–15, 24, 61, 73, 74–75

Ginsberg, Allen, 147

"Girl with the Golden Arm, The" (stunt show), 45

Glazer, Nathan, 118

Gleason, Jackie, 106

Golden, Bill, 248

Golden, Dee (wife): on audience for recording session, 130; on Busch's influence, 127; on Dave Vern, 76; death of, 250; on the divorce, 222, 224–25, 233; on family disruptions, 106; on *I've Got a Secret* experience, 73, 77–78; on Lynne Martin, 223; on marriage to Sherman, 60–61; on popularity of Sherman's live shows, 171; on Rose Segal, 37, 67, 68, 74; on Sherman's absenteeism, 106; on Sherman's childhood penchant for entertaining, 21; on Sherman's extended family, 11, 12, 26, 27; on Sherman's financial irresponsibility, 81; on Sherman's golf obsession, 78; on Sherman's move to LA alone, 109–10; on Sherman's psychological problems, 49, 124, 193; on Sherman's weight problem, 40; on Sherman's work habits, 64; on Sherman's writing vs. behavior, 109; on traveling with Sherman after separation, 226; on Westinghouse vs. Sherman, 125; on writing of "Hello Muddah . . .", 175. *See also* Sherman, Dolores

Goldenberg, Billy, 148, 166, 222

"Golden Earrings," instant parody of, 149

"Goldeneh Moments from Broadway" (parody), 88–100, 102, 104, 117, 125, 147, 155

Golden Touch, The (musical play), 58–60, 62–64, 65–66

Goldman, Olive, 52

Goldstein, Jerry, 124, 184, 214, 241

"Good Advice" (Sherman), 192

Goodbye, Columbus (Roth), 94, 118, 136, 178

Goodson, Mark, 244

Goodson-Todman Productions, 71, 78–79, 80, 81–82, 195

Grammy Awards and nominations, 200, 204

Grant, Cary, 179–80

Green, Eddie, 132

Green, Lorne, 212, 217

"Green Stamps" (parody), 190–91

Gregory, Dick, 160

Griffin, Wally, 65

"Griselda and the Porn-o-Phone" (short story), 245–46

Guercio, Joe, 188, 189

Hackman, Michael, 239

Hague, Albert, 232

"Hail to Thee, Fat Person" (parody), 176–77

"Hallowed Be Thy Game" (comedy routine), 248–49

Hambro, Leonid, 21, 43, 75, 76, 183–84, 194, 202

Hamer, Bill, 40, 46, 51

Hample, Stoo, 234

"Handicaps of 1957" (variety show), 83

Happy Medium, The (play), 79

"Harvey and Sheila" (parody), 161–62, 260

"Have Yourself a Wonderful Time" (original song), 68

"Headaches" (parody), 109

Healy, Eunice, 66

Hefner, Hugh, 241

"Hello Muddah, Hello Fadduh! (A Letter from Camp)" (parody), xii–xiii, 23, 54, 170–72, 173–76, 253

Hello Muddah, Hello Fadduh! (book), 196

Hello Muddah, Hello Fadduh! (musical revue), 255, 257

Henderson, Skitch, 77

Hendricks, Jon, 148, 163, 170, 172, 235

"Here's to the Crabgrass" (parody), 177–78

Hill, Rudy, 249

Hillel Post (newspaper), 36, 39, 44, 45

"His Own Little Island" (original song), 198

Hoffman, Irving, 134

Hoffman, Milt, 124–25

Holloway, Laurie, 225

Hollywood Bowl, 171, 203–4

Hopkins, Jerry, 124, 130–31, 153, 179, 247

"Horowitz" (parody), 156

Horowitz, Vladimir, 156

"How Are Things with Uncle Morris" (parody), 92–94

Howe, Irving, 137

"Humpty Dumpty" (parody), 2

"Hungarian Goulash" (parody), 175

"Hymie's on the Moon" (parody), 165

I Can't Dance (book), 196

Idelsohn, Abraham Zvi, 161

"If I Were a Tishman" (Sherman), 231–32

immigrant experience, xiii, 10–14, 105, 141

Instant Status; or, Up Your Image (book with Peyser and Peyser), 196

Irwin, Ben, 218

Isenberg, Daniel, 18

Israel and American Jews, 161

Israeli music, 120

"It's a Most Unusual Play" (parody), 220

I've Got a Secret (TV show), 70–72, 77–79, 80–81, 88, 106, 195

Jackson, Kenneth T., 178

"Jake's Song" (parody), 91

Jewish caricature issue in *Satyr*, 46–47

Jewish ethnic identity: America's embrace of, 205–6; and creative community of 1940s–50s, 76; as essentially parodic, 138, 259; grandparents' preservation of, 16–17, 25–26; Rose's temporary adoption of, 24; and Sherman as

milestone of social change, 158–59, 160–61, 176; Sherman's embrace of, 8, 32, 34–35, 60, 63–64, 82, 93, 135–36, 154–55, 156–57, 160; Sherman's last piece on, 244–45; Sherman's move away from, 212; Sherman's parodic use of, 58–59, 62–63, 136–37, 204–5; sick comedy's watering-down of, 101; societal momentum for renewal of, 85–87, 116–20; and Vernon Hills Country Club, 83–84. *See also* assimilation vs. ethnic identity
"Jew song" tradition, 104–5
Johnson, Arte, 34, 55
Johnson, Lyndon B., 199, 209
"Just the *Times*" (parody), 159

Kallen, Horace, 63, 64
Kaplan, Mordechai, 63
Kaplan, Peretz (father). *See* Coplon (Copelon), Percy
Katz, Mickey, 86, 91, 100, 255, 256
Kazin, Alfred, 14
Keller, Sheldon, 36, 43–44, 52, 193
Kennedy, John F., xi–xii, 117–18, 119–20, 134, 164, 186
King, Alan, 177
Klein, Robert, 254
klezmer music tradition, 255–56
Kline, Dorothy, 78
Kreitzer, David, 233–34
Kuller, Sid, 94

language, Sherman's comic talent with, 4. *See also* song parodies
"Last Laugh at the Sixties, A" (TV show), 240

Las Vegas, engagements in, 152–53, 185, 218
Leamy, Terri, 106–7, 128
Leave It to Mike (radio show), 65
Lerner, Al, 223
Lester, Jerry, 65, 70
Levenson, Sam, 76
Liber, Ben Zion, 13
Lichtenstein, Ben, 61
Lieberman, Paul, 107
Lipset, Seymour Martin, 118
"Little Butterball" (parody), 197–98
"Little David Susskind" (parody), 151–52
"Live! Be Happy! Enjoy!" (original song), 69
live performances: 1962, 133, 143; 1963, 149–50, 152–57, 158–63, 164–65, 167–69, 171, 185–87; 1964, 190, 195, 200, 201, 202–4; 1965, 218, 221; 1966, 116, 222–23, 225, 226; 1968, 234; 1969, 239; 1970–1971, 241; 1972, 248
Loeb, Bill, 108, 175, 197, 216, 223, 225
Loner, The (TV show), 217–18
Los Angeles, California, 1–2, 22–23, 24, 27–31, 103, 109–11, 113–14
Loudon, Dorothy, 151, 237
"Lovely as a Lullaby" (original song), 49, 113–14
Lustig, Abraham (great uncle), 10, 22
Lustig, Esther (Mrs. L. Sherman) (grandmother). *See* Sherman, Esther
Lustig, Leib (great-grandfather), 8–9

Macarus, Dorothy (cousin), 19, 66
Mailand, Vivian, 12, 27
Maitland, Mike, 116, 132, 148, 172
Martin, Lynne, 223, 225

Martindale, Larry E., 194

Marx, Bill, 103, 115, 164

Marx, Harpo, xii, 103–4, 105, 153, 218

Mason, Jackie, 120, 135–36

Masquerade Party (TV show), 81

Matchmakers (TV show project), 107

Meader, Vaughn, 141, 143, 147

Meadows, Jayne, 71, 72, 77

media's response to Sherman, 121, 122,
171, 179, 186, 195

Merrill, Howard, 65, 70, 71

Minkus, Seena, 45, 46

Minow, Newton N., xi, 133–34, 213

Mirth of a Nation (musical play), 53

Moore, Garry, 71–72

Moran, Jim, 184

Morgan, Henry, 81

Mulkin, Flora Mae, 38

musical background for Sherman, 9–10,
41. *See also* song parodies

Music to Dispense With (commercial
parody), 216

My Fairfax Lady (Kuller) (play), 86,
94–95, 100, 258–59

My Fair Lady (Sherman's parody), 95–96,
204, 258–59

My Name is Allan (album), 219–20, 221,
227

My Son, the Box (boxed set), 257–58

My Son, the Celebrity (album), xii, 145–
49, 172–73, 179

My Son, the Folk Singer (album): "The
Ballad of Harry Lewis," xii, 129, 140,
157; broad popularity of, xii, 121–22,
142–43, 188; commercial success of,
132, 145–46, 169, 172; cultural critique
power of parody, 121, 138–41; Grammy

award nomination, 169; legacy of,
205–6, 259; legal complications,
125–27, 141–42; mental fragmentation
over new ideas after, 142–44; "My
Zelda," 129, 140; and preliminary move
to parody, 92; recording contract,
123–24; recording session for, 129–31;
rush of fame from, 132, 133–35; "Sarah
Jackman," 2, 20, 121–22, 129, 130,
135–37, 151, 227–28; "Shake Hands with
Your Uncle Max," 21, 129, 138–39; and
Sherman's self-destructiveness, 126;
"Sir Greenbaum's Madrigal," 140; "The
Streets of Miami," xii, 129, 139, 198;
thematic coherence of, 173; writing of,
40, 126–29

*My Son, the Greatest: The Best of Allan
Sherman* (album), 254

My Son, the Nut (album), xii, 166, 170,
172–78

"My Zelda" (parody), 129, 140

National Press Club Inaugural Ball,
158–62

NBC television, 207–8, 213

Nelson, Barry, 237

Nelson, Christine, 131, 141, 155, 228

New York City, 13, 24, 34, 59, 60, 64–65,
68–69, 106, 186, 226

New York Times (newspaper), 179

Nightlife (TV show), 184

"Night That Leon Trotsky Died, The"
(parody), 54

Nothing Ventured (musical play),
48–49

"Oddball" (parody), 228–29

"Off-tackle Murder, The" (play), 42

"Oh Boy" (parody), 129

"Oldest Established, The," instant parody of, 149

"Ollavood" (parody), 113

"Once in Love with Lyndon" (parody), 199

"Once Upon a Serenade" (original song), 49

"One Hippopotami" (parody), 175

"On the Streets Where We Live" (parody), 95–96

Opie, Win, 124

Oppenheimer, Jess, 131

O'Sullivan, Eugene, 79

Outside Shelly Berman (album), 101–2

"Over the Rainbow," 162

overweight condition. See fatness

"Overweight People" (parody), 162

Owens, Gary, 142

Page, Patti, 91

"Painless Dentist Song, The" (parody), 227

parent-child relationships, and Sherman's parodies, 171, 173–77. See also childhood

parody: and Jewish humor, 138, 259; power of cultural critique, 121, 138–41; Sherman's junior high beginnings, 2; Sherman's preliminary move to, 92; and Yiddish vs. English, 96. See also song parodies

pathos, Sherman's use of, 139–40

Penthouse interview, 221

Pepper and His Wacky Taxi (film), 241

Perenchio, Jerry, 132, 148, 170, 183

Perry Como Show (TV show), 169, 185

Perry Presents (TV show), 81, 106

Peter and the Commissar (album), 128, 202–3

Peyser, Arnold and Lois, 196

"Peyton Place, U.S.A." (parody), 220–21

Phil Silvers on Broadway (TV show), 80

Physics Student's Valentine, The (poem), 31

Pierson, Irene, 50

Pilkenton, Bill, 48, 60

pin hanging at college, 36, 41–42, 45

Poland, 8–10

Poller, Lou, 27

Pryor, Richard, 251

Raden, Evelyn, 2–3

radio, writing for, 65

Radio Recorders, 130

Rape of the A*P*E, The (book), 109, 182–83, 246–47, 248

RCA Victor Red Seal, 203

Reiner, Carl, 85–86, 87, 216

religion, Sherman's family, 9

Resnick, Joe, 17

"Ringo" (Sherman's parody), 217

Rivers, Joan, 251–52

"Road to Urbana, The" (original song), 48–49

Rodgers, Richard, xii, 52, 84, 87–88, 184–85

Rolling Stones, 213

Roosevelt, Eleanor, 51

Roosevelt, Franklin D., 51

Rosengarden, Bobby, 77–78

Rosengarden, Mark, 107, 183, 233

Rosengarden, Neil, 78, 107

Rosten, Leo, 32

Roth, Philip, 94, 118, 136, 178

Sahl, Mort, 101

Salinger, Pierre, 162

Sam Fox Publishing Co., 232

Sandlin, Dwight M., 38

"Sarah Jackman" (parody), 2, 20, 121–22, 129, 130, 135–37, 151, 227–28

"Satchel and a Seck, A" (parody), 91

Satyr (college weekly), 39, 41, 46–47

Schultz, Sheldon, 171, 180

Schuman, Irwin, 167

"Second Hand Nose" (parody), 224

Segal, Allan. *See* Sherman, Allan

Segal, Dave (stepfather), 3, 27–29, 30, 37–38, 62, 68, 74, 111–12

Segal, Helen, 37

Segal, Rose (née Sherman) (mother): adoption of third child and other eccentricities, 68; as agent of Sherman's self-destructiveness, 40; Chicago adventures, 37–38; and Dave Segal, 27, 29; death and legacy of, 73–74; on Percy's death, 67–68; at Sherman's breaking-and-entering sorority hearing, 54; and Sherman's marriage, 60–61. *See also* Sherman, Rose

Segal, Sharon "Sherry" (half-sister), 27, 68, 74

Segal, Sheldon Harvey (half-brother), 29, 37, 68, 74, 112

Seinfeld, Jerry, 176

Seinfeld (TV show), 256

Selsberg, Carol (cousin), 11, 12, 214

"Seltzer Boy" (parody), 141–42

Serling, Rod, 216, 217

"Seventy-Six Sol Cohens" (parody), 99–100, 125, 155

sexuality: and childishness for Sherman, 183; comedy as currency for satisfying, 5–6; excesses of fame and, 183–84; family promiscuities, 3, 11; and "Funnyland," 212; International Beauty Pageant on *Tonight,* 180; pin hanging at college, 36, 41–42, 45; Sherman's early adolescent awareness, 4–5, 31; Sherman's hypocritical puritanism, 220–21; Sherman's obsession with, 41–42, 44–46, 183, 189, 202, 215, 233, 245–47; Woody Allen vs. Sherman, 201–2, 252–53; as writing subject, 1, 68–69, 71–72, 136–37, 245–46

"Shake Hands with Your Uncle Max" (parody), 21, 129, 138–39

Shandler, Jeffrey, 259, 260

Shannon, Hugh, 56–57

Sheinberg, Jackie, 20, 39

"Sheriff of Fetterman's Crossing, The" (TV episode), 217

Sherman, Allan: acting talent, 217–18; aftermath of Goodson-Todman firing, 81–82; alcohol consumption, 40, 116, 225, 234, 241; ancestral legacy, 8–14; asthma, 40, 49, 163; birth, 20; buddies, 75–78; chaos of childhood, 1–7, 22–32, 182–85; comedic genius, 4, 26, 33–34, 36, 43, 52, 143–44, 148–49; on comedy, 186; death of, 249–50; and Dee, 55–56, 57, 65; divorce, 222, 224–25, 232–33, 234, 238; downward slide in later years, 222–35; drug use, 234; early comedy writer work, 65, 68–69; early life in large Jewish family, 20–21; education, 26, 29–30, 36, 41, 49–50, 53–54; fame and its consequences, xi–xiii, 132,

133–35, 142–44, 150–51, 166, 214; family dysfunction as adult, 105–10, 166; family of origin's dysfunctions, 16–20, 26–27, 30–31, 61; and father, 16–20, 39; financial gains and losses, 65, 75, 81, 106, 114–15, 124, 126, 193–96, 234, 243–44; gambling, 110, 124, 163, 244; generosity, 214; gluttony, 6, 26, 40, 65, 112, 189, 193, 194; golf obsession, 78; grandparents as model for, 14, 82; gullibility, 123, 141–42, 150, 169, 193–94; and Harpo Marx, 103–4; health issues, 40, 49, 124, 163, 193, 209, 241, 247; hedonism, 68–69, 183–84, 188–89, 193–94, 233–34, 238; humor as savior of mood, 112–13; idealization of childhood, 23, 80, 109, 180, 182–83, 192–93, 218–19, 228, 243; lack of discretion, 185; last name permutations, 30–31; legacy, 251–60; loneliness, 222; marriage, 37, 60–62; and mother, 4, 7, 14–16, 23–24, 36, 40, 54, 60–61, 73–74; and new Jewish comedy, 212–13; overbearing and mean facet of personality, 34, 105–11, 182, 190–91, 192; physical appearance, 46–47, 197; post-Goodson-Todman adventures, 81; psychiatric care, 182, 226; relating to audience, 200–201; self-destructiveness, 40, 75, 124, 126, 163–64, 193–94, 207–8, 222, 225, 235, 239, 241, 247–48; self-hatred, 49, 179, 181–82, 197–98, 226–29; smoking, 40, 65, 163; sociability, 21, 34, 75, 112–13, 153–55, 156; societal momentum for breakthrough, 116–20; struggling in NYC, 64–65; vestiges of ethnic discomfort, 186–87; weight problem, 40, 49, 197–98; will, 250; wit and charm, 1–2, 3, 34, 36, 45, 75; and Woody Allen, 199–200, 201–2; work habits, 64–65, 80, 128; writing talent, 5, 26, 109, 126, 201. *See also* college years; Jewish ethnic identity; live performances; sexuality; song parodies; television appearances; *individual albums by name*

Sherman, Dolores "Dee" (née Chackes) (wife): and Allan, 65; clothes model job, 64–65; contribution to song parody writing, 128; courtship of, 54, 55–57; marriage of, 60–62; origins of, 56–57; remarriage of, 248; as rudder for Sherman, 144. *See also* Golden, Dee

Sherman, Edith (aunt), 214

Sherman, Esther (née Lustig) (grandmother), xiii, 2–3, 8–9, 10, 11–12, 14, 24–26, 73, 82

Sherman, Kate (aunt), 8, 15

Sherman, Leon (grandfather), xiii, 2–3, 8, 10–11, 12, 24–26, 73, 82

Sherman, Mickey (cousin), 3, 12, 194

Sherman, Morris "Maury" (uncle), 11, 12, 25, 110

Sherman, Nancy (daughter), 73, 108, 109, 133, 233, 235, 238, 244

Sherman, Robert (son): anger toward father, 109; assimilation vs. ethnic identity, 15–16, 19, 20, 29; birth, 70; on Busch's contribution, 127; camp fiasco for, 107–8; on chaos of fame for family, 133; childhood isolation, 106–7; current activities of, 250; in

Europe with Dad, 225; on "Funnyland," 210; health problem, 247; move to LA (1961), 110, 114; orientation to show-biz and young adult brashness, 166; on parody-writing process, 99, 128, 130, 131, 200–201; on Sherman's song knowledge, 41; work in television production, 244

Sherman, Rose (mother): immigration to U.S., 8; neglect of Allan, 24; and Percy Coplon (Copelon), 19–20, 22, 23, 67–68; personality of, 3, 14–15; relationship to "Dave," 24; and Sherman's multiple fathers, 7; and Sherman's psychological problems, 4, 14, 24. *See also* Segal, Rose

Shriner, Herb, 80

"Shticks and Stones" (parody), 137, 151

sick comics, 100–101

Sigma Alpha Mu (SAM), 43–44

"Signs" (poem), 230–31

Silberstein, Theresa (Mrs. E. Chackes) (mother-in-law), 56

Silver, Roy, 180

Silverman, Moses J., 62

Silvers, Phil, 80

Sinatra, Frank, 168

Singer, Allie, 109

Siren (student magazine), 33

"Sir Greenbaum's Madrigal" (parody), 140

"Skin" (parody), 191

"Small World" (Sherman's parody), 155–56

Smith, Joe, 123, 125, 128, 148, 170, 183, 192, 249

Smothers, Tommy, 241–42

societal impacts and influences:

American Jewish experience, 256–57; consumption as social practice, 95; Sherman's role, 85–87, 116–20, 137, 147, 157–60, 259–60; youth culture of 1960s, 189–90, 213, 224, 237. *See also* ethnicity

Something Special (TV show), 226–29

song parodies: college years, 41, 42–43, 51–52, 54–55; continued success of (1965), 214–16; copyright challenges, 125–26, 141–42; as cultural critique, 138–41; Dee's contribution to writing, 128; on fatness, 40, 162, 197–98; increased popularity (early 1960s), 119–20; for Los Angeles social events, 113–14; media's response to, 121, 122, 171, 179, 186, 195; recording plans for, 91, 101–2; Sherman's comedic genius, 4, 26, 33–34, 36, 43, 52, 143–44, 148–49; sociological significance of, 259; successful elements of, 147; writing and recording prior to fame, 85, 87–102, 91; writing process, 175–76. *See also individual albums and song titles*

South Africa, performance in, 221

South Passaic (parody), 87–88

"Spanish Flea" (Sherman's parody), 239

spirituals, Negro, parodies of, 151

Stack, Robert, 180

Steuer, W. B., 64, 66

Steve Allen Show (TV show), 122–23, 124–25, 164–65, 171

Stewart, Jon, 256–57

Stewart, Larry, 40

"Streets of Miami, The" (parody), xii, 129, 139, 198

Streisand, Barbra, 119

Stricker, Helen, 12

Sturner, John, 84

suburban life, and Jewish identity, 93–94, 177–78

Sullivan, Ed, 134

"Summer's Magical Music" (article), 242

"Summertime" (Sherman's parody), 89

Swain, Henry, 35

Tabolsky, Marvin, 133, 163, 164, 166, 168, 180, 188–89, 225, 241

"Taking Lessons" (parody), 223–24, 257

Talmy, Shel, 240

"Tau Lamba Tau (The Lover Type)" society, 44

television appearances: 1963, 149–52, 164–65, 169, 171, 179–81, 182, 185; 1964, 190, 200; 1965, 184, 207–12, 213, 215–16, 217–18; 1966, 226–29; 1967, 233; 1968, 235; 1969, 239; 1970, 240; 1973, 248

television writer/producer career: Borge special, 80; drawing down of New York-era, 106; *I've Got a Secret,* 70–72, 77–79, 80–81, 88, 106, 195; *Matchmakers,* 107; *Perry Presents,* 81, 106; *Phil Silvers on Broadway,* 80; *Steve Allen Show,* 122–23, 124–25; *What's Going On?,* 80; Writers Guild awards show, 131, 143, 241; *You're in the Picture,* 106; *Your Surprise Package,* 109, 110–11, 114, 116

"Tennessee Frelich" (parody), 91–92

That Was the Week That Was (TV show), 190

"There Is Nothin' Like a Dame" (Sherman's parody), 87–88

"There's No Place Like Home—On Wheels!" (article), 7

"This Is Where I Came In" (original song), 53

Thomas, Jay, 197, 223

Time (magazine), 101, 146–47

"Time of Your Life, The" (original song), 68

Todd, Mike, 60

Togetherness (album), 229–32, 239

Tonight (TV show), 149, 169, 171, 179–81, 182, 200

Toppel, Helen, 28–29

tours. *See* live performances

Trillin, Calvin, 72

Truman, Harry, 105

Tucker, Alexander, 194

Turner, Fred H., 50

Twain, Mark, 45

"2000 Year Old Man" routine (Reiner and Brooks), 87

2000 Years with Carl Reiner and Mel Brooks (album), 118–19, 136

"Tzimished" (parody), 92

University of Illinois, 33–34, 35, 185–86. *See also* college years

Variety (magazine), 170, 171

Vern, Dave, 75–76, 111

Vernon Hills Country Club, 83–84

Very Best of Allan Sherman, The (album), 254

Warner, Jack, 116, 216

Warner Bros. Records, 116, 123–24, 132, 148, 172, 181, 195, 202–3, 234–35, 249

Warren, Earl, 159

Warren, Ned, 64, 66

Wattenberg, Philip B., 126

weight problem. *See* fatness

Weinstein, Howard, 40

"Westchester Hadassah" (parody), 229–30

Westinghouse and *Steve Allen Show* debacle, 125

What's Going On? (TV show), 80

What's My Line? (TV show), 70–71

"When I Was a Lad" (Sherman's parody), 146

"When You Walk through the Bronx" (parody), 97–98

White House dinner, 162–63

Whiting, Debbi, 107, 127–28

Wildberg, Jack, 64, 66

Wilson, Earl, 69

Wilson, Meredith, 99, 125, 155

Wirth, Louis, 12, 14, 85

"Witz-Krieg" (newspaper column), 31–32

Wolf, Sherman, 35, 183

"Won't You Come Home Disraeli?" (parody), 43, 146–47

World War II, 105

"Wouldn't It Be Lovely" (Sherman's parody), 95

Writers Guild awards show, 131, 143, 241

Yankovic, Weird Al, 215

Yiddish language and culture, xiii, 11, 13, 25–26, 86, 91, 96

Youngman, Henny, 88

"You're a Nudnick, Sondra Goldfein" (parody), 96–97

You're in the Picture (TV show), 106

Your Show of Shows (TV show), 70, 85–86

Your Surprise Package (TV show), 109, 110–11, 114, 116

youth culture and Sherman, 189–90, 213, 224, 237

Zangwill, Israel, 104

Zatt, Sol, 248

"Zeta House Murder, The" (playlet), 46

Zolotow, Maurice, 76–77, 87, 88, 164, 196, 218, 239